World Economic and Financial Surveys

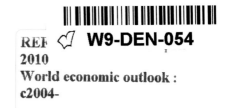
WORLD ECONOMIC OUTLOOK
April 2010

Rebalancing Growth

International Monetary Fund

Production: IMF Multimedia Services Division
Cover and Design: Luisa Menjivar and Jorge Salazar
Composition: Maryland Composition

Cataloging-in-Publication Data

World economic outlook (International Monetary Fund)
 World economic outlook : a survey by the staff of the International Monetary Fund. —
Washington, DC : International Monetary Fund, 1980–
 v. ; 28 cm. — (1981–1984: Occasional paper / International Monetary Fund, 0251-6365).
— (1986– : World economic and financial surveys, 0256-6877)

Semiannual.
Has occasional updates, 1984–

 1. Economic history, 1971–1990 — Periodicals. 2. Economic history, 1990– —
Periodicals.   I. International Monetary Fund.   II. Series: Occasional paper (International
Monetary Fund).   III. Series: World economic and financial surveys.

HC10.W7979   84-640155   338.5'443'09048—dc19
                                                    AACR2 MARC-S
ISBN 978-1-58906-915-2

Please send orders to:
International Monetary Fund, Publication Services
700 19th Street, N.W., Washington, D.C. 20431, U.S.A.
Tel.: (202) 623-7430   Fax: (202) 623-7201
E-mail: publications@imf.org
www.imfbookstore.org

CONTENTS

Figures

ASSUMPTIONS AND CONVENTIONS

A number of assumptions have been adopted for the projections presented in the *World Economic Outlook*. It has been assumed that real effective exchange rates remained constant at their average levels during February 23–March 23, 2010, except for the currencies participating in the European exchange rate mechanism II (ERM II), which are assumed to have remained constant in nominal terms relative to the euro; that established policies of national authorities will be maintained (for specific assumptions about fiscal and monetary policies for selected economies, see Box A1); that the average price of oil will be $80.00 a barrel in 2010 and $83.00 a barrel in 2011 and will remain unchanged in real terms over the medium term; that the six-month London interbank offered rate (LIBOR) on U.S. dollar deposits will average 0.5 percent in 2010 and 1.7 percent in 2011; that the three-month euro deposit rate will average 0.9 percent in 2010 and 1.6 percent in 2011; and that the six-month Japanese yen deposit rate will yield on average 0.6 percent in 2010 and 0.7 percent in 2011. These are, of course, working hypotheses rather than forecasts, and the uncertainties surrounding them add to the margin of error that would in any event be involved in the projections. The estimates and projections are based on statistical information available through mid-April 2010.

The following conventions are used throughout the *World Economic Outlook:*

. . .   to indicate that data are not available or not applicable;

—   between years or months (for example, 2008–09 or January–June) to indicate the years or months covered, including the beginning and ending years or months;

/   between years or months (for example, 2008/09) to indicate a fiscal or financial year.

"Billion" means a thousand million; "trillion" means a thousand billion.

"Basis points" refer to hundredths of 1 percentage point (for example, 25 basis points are equivalent to ¼ of 1 percentage point).

In figures and tables, shaded areas indicate IMF staff projections.

If no source is listed on tables and figures, data are drawn from the World Economic Outlook (WEO) database.

When countries are not listed alphabetically, they are ordered on the basis of economic size.

Minor discrepancies between sums of constituent figures and totals shown reflect rounding.

As used in this report, the terms "country" and "economy" do not in all cases refer to a territorial entity that is a state as understood by international law and practice. As used here, the term also covers some territorial entities that are not states but for which statistical data are maintained on a separate and independent basis.

The boundaries, colors, denominations, and any other information shown on the maps do not imply, on the part of the International Monetary Fund, any judgment on the legal status of any territory or any endorsement or acceptance of such boundaries.

This version of the *World Economic Outlook* is available in full on the IMF's website, www.imf.org. Accompanying it on the website is a larger compilation of data from the WEO database than is included in the report itself, including files containing the series most frequently requested by readers. These files may be downloaded for use in a variety of software packages.

Inquiries about the content of the *World Economic Outlook* and the WEO database should be sent by mail, forum, or fax (telephone inquiries cannot be accepted) to

World Economic Studies Division
Research Department
International Monetary Fund
700 19th Street, N.W.
Washington, D.C. 20431, U.S.A.
Forum address: www.imf.org/weoforum   Fax: (202) 623-6343

PREFACE

The analysis and projections contained in the *World Economic Outlook* are integral elements of the IMF's surveillance of economic developments and policies in its member countries, of developments in international financial markets, and of the global economic system. The survey of prospects and policies is the product of a comprehensive interdepartmental review of world economic developments, which draws primarily on information the IMF staff gathers through its consultations with member countries. These consultations are carried out in particular by the IMF's area departments—namely, the African Department, Asia and Pacific Department, European Department, Middle East and Central Asia Department, and Western Hemisphere Department—together with the Strategy, Policy, and Review Department; the Monetary and Capital Markets Department; and the Fiscal Affairs Department.

The analysis in this report was coordinated in the Research Department under the general direction of Olivier Blanchard, Economic Counsellor and Director of Research. The project was directed by Jörg Decressin, Assistant Director, Research Department, and Petya Koeva Brooks, Division Chief, Research Department.

The primary contributors to this report are Abdul Abiad, Ravi Balakrishnan, Mitali Das, Prakash Kannan, Daniel Leigh, and Marco Terrones. Toh Kuan, Gavin Asdorian, Stephanie Denis, Angela Espiritu, Murad Omoev, Andy Salazar, Min Kyu Song, Ercument Tulun, and Jessie Yang provided research assistance. Saurabh Gupta, Mahnaz Hemmati, Laurent Meister, Emory Oakes, Liessel Ampie, Vladimir Bougay, Anastasia Francis, Wendy Mak, Shamiso Mapondera, Nhu Nguyen, and Steve Zhang managed the database and the computer systems. Jemille Colon, Tita Gunio, Patricia Medina, and Sheila Tomilloso Igcasenza were responsible for word processing. Other contributors include Nese Erbil, Roberto Garcia-Saltos, Thomas Helbling, Doug Laxton, Petar Manchev, Troy Matheson, Dirk Muir, Susanna Mursula, Shaun Roache, Petia Topalova, Charalambos Tsangarides, and Marina Rousset. David Romer of the Research Department provided advice and encouragement. Tito Boeri and Christopher Meissner were external consultants. Kevin Clinton provided comments and suggestions. Linda Griffin Kean of the External Relations Department edited the manuscript and coordinated the production of the publication.

The analysis has benefited from comments and suggestions by staff from other IMF departments, as well as by Executive Directors following their discussion of the report on April 7, 2010. However, both projections and policy considerations are those of the IMF staff and should not be attributed to Executive Directors or to their national authorities.

The global recovery is proceeding better than expected but at varying speeds—tepidly in many advanced economies and solidly in most emerging and developing economies. World growth is now expected to be 4¼ percent. Among the advanced economies, the United States is off to a better start than Europe and Japan. Among emerging and developing economies, emerging Asia is leading the recovery, while many emerging European and some Commonwealth of Independent States economies are lagging behind. This multispeed recovery is expected to continue.

As the recovery has gained traction, risks to global financial stability have eased, but stability is not yet assured. Our estimates of banking system write-downs in the economies hit hardest from the onset of the crisis through 2010 have been reduced to $2.3 trillion from $2.8 trillion in the October 2009 *Global Financial Stability Report*. However, the aggregate picture masks considerable differentiation within segments of banking systems, and there remain pockets that are characterized by shortages of capital, high risks of further asset deterioration, and chronically weak profitability. Deleveraging has so far been driven mainly by deteriorating assets that have hit both earnings and capital. Going forward, however, pressures on the funding or liability side of bank balance sheets are likely to play a greater role, as banks reduce leverage and raise capital and liquidity buffers. Hence, the recovery of private sector credit is likely to be subdued, especially in advanced economies.

At the same time, better growth prospects in many emerging economies and low interest rates in major economies have triggered a welcome resurgence of capital flows to some emerging economies. These capital flows however come with the attendant risk of inflation pressure and asset bubbles. So far, there is no systemwide evidence of bubbles, although there are a few hot spots, and risks could build up over a longer-term horizon. The recovery of cross-border financial flows has brought some

real effective exchange rate changes—depreciation of the U.S. dollar and appreciation of other floating currencies of advanced and emerging economies. But these changes have been limited, and global current account imbalances are forecast to widen once again.

The outlook for activity remains unusually uncertain, and downside risks stemming from fiscal fragilities have come to the fore. A key concern is that room for policy maneuvers in many advanced economies has either been exhausted or become much more limited. Moreover, sovereign risks in advanced economies could undermine financial stability gains and extend the crisis. The rapid increase in public debt and deterioration of fiscal balance sheets could be transmitted back to banking systems or across borders.

This underscores the need for policy action to sustain the recovery of the global economy and financial system. The policy agenda should include several important elements.

The key task ahead is to reduce sovereign vulnerabilities. In many advanced economies, there is a pressing need to design and communicate credible medium-term fiscal consolidation strategies. These should include clear time frames to bring down gross debt-to-GDP ratios over the medium term as well as contingency measures if the deterioration in public finances is greater than expected. If macroeconomic developments proceed as expected, most advanced economies should embark on fiscal consolidation in 2011. Meanwhile, given the still-fragile recovery, the fiscal stimulus planned for 2010 should be fully implemented, except in economies that face large increases in risk premiums, where the urgency is greater and consolidation needs to begin now. Entitlement reforms that do not detract from demand in the short term—for example, raising the statutory retirement age or lowering the cost of health care—should be implemented without delay.

Other policy challenges relate to unwinding monetary accommodation across the globe and managing capital flows to emerging economies. In major advanced economies, insofar as inflation expectations remain well anchored, monetary policy can continue being accommodative as fiscal consolidation progresses, even as central banks begin to withdraw the emergency support provided to financial sectors. Major emerging and some advanced economies will continue to lead the tightening cycle, since they are experiencing faster recoveries and renewed capital flows. Although there is only limited evidence of inflation pressures and asset price bubbles, current conditions warrant close scrutiny and early action. In emerging economies with relatively balanced external positions, the defense against excessive currency appreciation should include a combination of macroeconomic and prudential policies, which are discussed in detail in the *World Economic Outlook* and *Global Financial Stability Report*.

Combating unemployment is yet another policy challenge. As high unemployment persists in advanced economies, a major concern is that temporary joblessness will turn into long-term unemployment. Beyond pursuing macroeconomic policies that support recovery in the near term and financial sector policies that restore banking sector health (and credit supply to employment-intensive sectors), specific labor market policies could also help limit damage to the labor market. In particular, adequate unemployment benefits are essential to support confidence among households and to avoid large increases in poverty, and education and training can help reintegrate the unemployed into the labor force.

Policies also need to buttress lasting financial stability, so that the next stage of the deleveraging process unfolds smoothly and results in a safer, competitive, and vital financial system. Swift resolution of nonviable institutions and restructuring of those with a commercial future is key. Care will be needed to ensure that too-important-to-fail institutions in all jurisdictions do not use the funding advantages their systemic importance gives them to consolidate their positions even further. Starting securitization on a safer basis is also essential to support credit, particularly for households and small and medium-size enterprises.

Looking further ahead, there must be agreement on the regulatory reform agenda. The direction of reform is clear—higher quantity and quality of capital and better liquidity risk management—but the magnitude is not. In addition, uncertainty surrounding reforms to address too-important-to-fail institutions and systemic risks make it difficult for financial institutions to plan. Policymakers must strike the right balance between promoting the safety of the financial system and keeping it innovative and efficient. Specific proposals for making the financial system safer and for strengthening its infrastructure—for example, in the over-the-counter derivatives market—are discussed in the *Global Financial Stability Report*.

Finally, the world's ability to sustain high growth over the medium term depends on rebalancing global demand. This means that economies that had excessive external deficits before the crisis need to consolidate their public finances in ways that limit damage to growth and demand. Concurrently, economies that ran excessive current account surpluses will need to further increase domestic demand to sustain growth, as excessive deficit economies scale back their demand. As the currencies of economies with excessive deficits depreciate, those of surplus economies must logically appreciate. Rebalancing also needs to be supported with financial sector reform and growth-enhancing structural policies in both surplus and deficit economies.

Olivier Blanchard
Economic Counsellor

José Viñals
Financial Counsellor

In 2010, world output is expected to rise by about 4¼ percent, following a ½ percent contraction in 2009. Economies that are off to a strong start are likely to remain in the lead, as growth in others is held back by lasting damage to financial sectors and household balance sheets. Activity remains dependent on highly accommodative macroeconomic policies and is subject to downside risks, as fiscal fragilities have come to the fore. In most advanced economies, fiscal and monetary policies should maintain a supportive thrust in 2010 to sustain growth and employment. But many of these economies also need to urgently adopt credible medium-term strategies to contain public debt and later bring it down to more prudent levels. Financial sector repair and reform are additional high-priority requirements. Many emerging economies are again growing rapidly and a number have begun to moderate their accommodative macroeconomic policies in the face of high capital inflows. Given prospects for relatively weak growth in the advanced economies, the challenge for emerging economies is to absorb rising inflows and nurture domestic demand without triggering a new boom-bust cycle.

Recovery Has Proceeded Better than Expected

The global recovery has evolved better than expected, with activity recovering at varying speeds—tepidly in many advanced economies but solidly in most emerging and developing economies. Policy support was essential to jump-start the recovery. Monetary policy has been highly expansionary and supported by unconventional liquidity provision. Fiscal policy provided a major stimulus in response to the deep downturn. Among advanced economies, the United States is off to a better start than Europe and Japan. Among emerging and developing economies, emerging Asia is in the lead. Growth is also solidifying in key Latin American and other emerging and developing economies but continues to lag in many emerging European and various Commonwealth of Independent States (CIS) countries. Sub-Saharan Africa is weathering the global crisis well, and its recovery is expected to be stronger than following past global downturns.

The recoveries in real and financial activity are mutually supportive, but access to credit remains difficult for some sectors. Money markets have stabilized. Corporate bond and equity markets have rebounded. In advanced economies, the tightening of bank lending standards is ending, and the credit crisis appears to be bottoming out. In many emerging and developing economies, credit growth is reaccelerating. Nevertheless, financial conditions remain more difficult than before the crisis. Especially in advanced economies, bank capital is likely to remain a constraint on growth as banks continue to retrench their balance sheets. Sectors that have only limited access to capital markets—consumers and small and medium-size enterprises—are likely to continue to face tight limits on their borrowing. In a few advanced economies, rising public deficits and debt have contributed to a sharp increase in sovereign risk premiums, posing new risks to the recovery.

Together with real and financial activity, cross-border financial flows from advanced to many emerging economies have also rebounded strongly. Key drivers include rapid growth in emerging economies, large yield differentials in their favor, and a returning appetite for risk. The recovery of cross-border flows has come with some real effective exchange rate changes—depreciation of the U.S. dollar and appreciation of some other floating currencies of advanced and emerging economies. But relative to precrisis levels, changes have been generally limited, and global current account imbalances are forecast to widen again over the medium term.

Multispeed Recovery Will Continue

The world economy is poised for further recovery but at varying speeds across and within regions. Global growth is projected to reach 4¼ percent in 2010 and 2011. Advanced economies are now expected to expand by 2¼ percent in 2010, and by 2½ percent in 2011, following a decline in output of more than 3 percent in 2009. Growth in emerging and developing economies is projected to be over 6¼ percent during 2010–11, following a modest 2½ percent in 2009. As Chapters 1 and 2 explain, economies that are off to a strong start are likely to continue to lead the recovery, as growth in others is held back by lasting damage to financial sectors and household balance sheets. The recovery under way in the major advanced economies will be relatively sluggish compared with recoveries from previous recessions. Likewise, the recoveries in many economies of emerging Europe and the CIS are likely to be sluggish compared with those expected for many other emerging economies.

The outlook for activity remains unusually uncertain, even though a variety of risks have receded. Risks are generally to the downside, with those related to public debt growth in advanced economies having become sharply more evident. In the near term, a risk is that, if unchecked, market concerns about sovereign liquidity and solvency in Greece could turn into a full-blown and contagious sovereign debt crisis, as explained in the April 2010 *Global Financial Stability Report* (GFSR). More generally, the main concern is that room for policy maneuver in many advanced economies has either been largely exhausted or is much more limited, leaving the fragile recoveries exposed to new shocks. In addition, bank exposures to real estate continue to pose downside risks, mainly in the United States and parts of Europe.

Policies Need to Sustain and Strengthen Recovery

Given the large amount of public debt that has been accumulated during this recession, in many advanced economies exit policies need to emphasize fiscal consolidation and financial sector repair. This will allow monetary policy to remain accommodative without leading to inflation pressure or financial market instabilities. In emerging and developing economies, priorities depend on room available for fiscal policy maneuvers and on current account positions. Spillovers related to fiscal policies are particularly relevant for the major advanced economies, as

large deficits and the lack of well-specified medium-term fiscal consolidation strategies in these economies could adversely affect funding costs of other advanced or emerging economies.

Medium-Term Fiscal Consolidation Strategies Are Urgently Needed

Fiscal policy provided major support in response to the deep downturn. At the same time, the slump in activity and, to a much lesser extent, stimulus measures pushed fiscal deficits in advanced economies to about 9 percent of GDP. Debt-to-GDP ratios in these economies are expected to exceed 100 percent of GDP in 2014 based on current policies, some 35 percentage points of GDP higher than before the crisis.

Regarding the near term, given the fragile recovery, fiscal stimulus planned for 2010 should be fully implemented, except in countries that are suffering large increases in risk premiums—these countries need to begin fiscal consolidation now. Looking further ahead, if macroeconomic developments proceed as expected, most advanced economies should embark on significant fiscal consolidation in 2011. Countries urgently need to design and implement credible fiscal adjustment strategies, emphasizing measures that support potential growth. These should include clear timelines to bring down gross debt-to-GDP ratios over the medium term. Also needed are reforms to entitlement spending that lower spending in the future but do not depress demand today.

The fiscal challenges are different in a number of emerging economies, with some important exceptions. The public debt problem in these economies is more localized—as a group, these economies' public debt ratios are at about 30 to 40 percent of GDP and, given their high growth, are expected to soon be back on a declining path. Many emerging Asian economies entered the crisis with relatively low public debt levels and can afford to maintain an expansionary fiscal stance. This will help rebalance the mix between externally and domestically driven growth. But these economies will need to be alert to growing price pressures and emerging financial instability and to allow their currencies to appreciate to combat overheating. Other major emerging economies, however, have less fiscal room to maneuver and should withdraw support as the recovery gains more traction. Fiscal policy in low-income economies will also need to be redirected toward medium-term considerations as private and external demand recovers.

Monetary Accommodation Needs to Be Unwound Cautiously and Capital Inflows Managed

Still-low levels of capacity utilization and well-anchored inflation expectations are expected to keep inflation in check in most economies. Significant upside risks to inflation are confined to emerging economies that have a history of unstable price levels or have limited economic slack. In major advanced economies, monetary policy can remain accommodative as fiscal consolidation progresses, provided inflation pressure remains subdued. This can be achieved even as central banks begin to withdraw the emergency support provided to financial sectors. In major emerging and some advanced economies that are experiencing faster recoveries, central banks have already begun to reduce the degree of monetary accommodation or are expected by the markets to do so over the coming year. These economies will probably continue to lead the tightening cycle, as they are expected to recover faster than major advanced economies. In some emerging economies, overcapacity in some sectors and deteriorating credit quality also point to the need to tighten credit.

In emerging economies with excessive surpluses, monetary tightening should be supported with nominal effective exchange rate appreciation as excess demand pressures build, including in response to continued fiscal support to facilitate demand rebalancing or capital inflows. In others, monetary tightening may be complicated: it could attract more capital inflows, lead to exchange rate appreciation, and thereby undermine competitiveness. If exchange rate overshooting becomes a concern, countries should consider fiscal tightening to ease pressure on interest rates; some buildup of reserves; and possibly stricter controls on capital inflows—mindful of the potential to create new distortions—or looser controls on outflows.

Financial Sectors Must Be Repaired and Reformed

Together with fiscal adjustment, more progress with financial sector repair and reform is the top priority for a number of advanced economies to sustain recovery. Moreover, financial market inefficiencies and regulatory and supervisory failures played a major role in the crisis and need to be remedied to build a stronger financial system. For advanced economies, the April 2010 GFSR has lowered its estimate of actual and prospective bank write-downs and loan loss provisions during 2007–10 from $2.8 trillion to $2.3 trillion, two-thirds of which had been recognized by the end of 2009. Progress in remedying financial inefficiencies and reforming prudential policies and frameworks will increase the effectiveness of monetary policy and reduce the risk of the ample supply of liquidity finding an outlet in renewed speculative distortions. At the same time, emerging economies will need to continue to strengthen their prudential policies and frameworks in anticipation of growing capital inflows.

Policies to Support the Unemployed and Foster Employment Are Essential

High unemployment poses major social problems. In advanced economies, unemployment is projected to stay close to 9 percent through 2011 and then to decline only slowly. Chapter 3 explains that unemployment responses have been markedly different across advanced economies because of differences in output declines, labor market institutions, and factors such as financial stress and house price busts. Moreover, in many countries problems are larger than the headline unemployment rate statistics suggest because many individuals are underemployed or have dropped out of the labor force. In this setting, a major concern is the potential for temporary joblessness to turn into long-term unemployment and to lower potential output growth. To limit damage to the labor market, macroeconomic policies need to be appropriately supportive of the recovery where possible. At the same time, policies need to foster wage flexibility and provide adequate support for the jobless.

Rebalancing Global Demand Is Key to Buoy and Sustain Growth

For the world economy to sustain a high-growth trajectory, the economies that had excessive external deficits before the crisis need to consolidate their public finances in ways that limit damage to potential growth and demand. Concurrently, economies that ran excessive current account surpluses will need to further increase domestic demand to sustain growth, as excessive-deficit economies scale back their demand (and imports) in response to lower expectations about future income. As the currencies of economies with excessive deficits depreciate, then logically those of surplus economies must appreciate. Rebalancing needs to be supported with financial sector reform and structural policies in both surplus and deficit economies. Policymakers will need to exploit policy synergies, especially between fiscal policy and structural reform.

Global demand rebalancing is not a new issue. Chapter 4 reviews the historical experience of economies with large current account surpluses. It finds that reversing current account surpluses has typically not been associated with losses in economic growth, with a variety of macroeconomic and structural policies playing an important role in countering output losses from real exchange rate appreciation.

GLOBAL PROSPECTS AND POLICIES

The global recovery has evolved better than expected, but in many economies the strength of the rebound has been moderate given the severity of the recession. In 2010, world output is expected to rise by about 4¼ percent, which represents an upward revision of 1 percentage point from the October 2009 World Economic Outlook (WEO) and is similar to the January 2010 WEO Update. Economies that are off to a strong start are likely to remain in the lead, as growth in others is held back by lasting damage to financial sectors and household balance sheets. Activity remains dependent on highly accommodative macroeconomic policies and is subject to downside risks, as room for countercyclical policy maneuvers has sharply diminished and fiscal fragilities have come to the fore. Monetary, fiscal, and financial policymakers will need to ensure a smooth transition of demand from the government to the private sector and from economies with excessive external deficits to those with excessive surpluses. In most advanced economies, fiscal and monetary policies should maintain a supportive thrust this year to further sustain growth and employment. But many of these economies also need to urgently adopt credible strategies to contain public debt and later bring it down to more prudent levels. Financial sector repair and reform are also high-priority requirements. Many emerging economies have resumed a high rate of growth and a number have begun to moderate their accommodative macroeconomic policies in the face of high capital inflows. Given prospects for relatively weak growth in the advanced economies, the challenge for emerging economies is to absorb these inflows and nurture domestic demand without triggering a new boom-bust cycle.

Recovery Is Stronger than Expected, but Speed Varies

The recovery has been stronger than expected thus far, as confidence has picked up among consumers and businesses as well as in financial markets (Figure 1.1; Table 1.1). World real GDP growth reached about 3¼ percent on an annualized basis during the second quarter of 2009 and rose to over 4½ percent during the second half of the year. In advanced economies, a nascent turn in the inventory cycle and slowing deterioration (followed recently by improvements) in U.S. labor markets contributed to the positive developments, and strong orders and a recovering corporate bond market helped foster investment. In the key emerging and developing economies, final domestic demand was very strong, helped by the turn in the inventory cycle, and external demand was lifted by the normalization of global trade.

Global activity is recovering at varying speeds, tepidly in many of the advanced economies but solidly in most emerging and developing economies. The United States is off to a somewhat later but better start than Europe or Japan. This may be surprising, considering that the United States was the epicenter of the crisis and had an unusually large need to rebuild private savings. The stronger U.S. recovery may reflect a variety of differences between the United States and the euro area and Japan: fiscal stimulus was larger; the nonfinancial corporate sector is less reliant on bank credit, which remains constrained, whereas bond markets have staged a comeback;[1] nonfinancial corporate balance sheets are stronger and rapid restructuring has boosted productivity; and the Federal Reserve reacted earlier and with larger policy rate cuts to lower levels in real terms. In contrast, the large appreciation of the yen may have weighed on the recovery of Japan's exports, which fell sharply during the global trade slump, and the reemergence of deflation has pushed up real borrowing rates and wages. The euro area's trade links with troubled emerging European and Commonwealth of Independent States (CIS) economies and the euro's intermittent appreciation have curbed the euro area's exports. In addition, several euro area economies were hit particularly hard by the financial and real estate crises.

---

[1] Bank loans to nonfinancial corporations in the euro area are four to five times larger than bonds issued by these corporations; in the United States, bonds are a more important source of corporate funding.

Table 1.1. Overview of the *World Economic Outlook* Projections
(Percent change, unless otherwise noted)

			Year over Year				Q4 over Q4		
			Projections		Difference from January 2010 WEO Projections		Estimates	Projections	
	2008	2009	2010	2011	2010	2011	2009	2010	2011
World Output[1]	**3.0**	**−0.6**	**4.2**	**4.3**	**0.3**	**0.0**	**1.7**	**3.9**	**4.5**
Advanced Economies	**0.5**	**−3.2**	**2.3**	**2.4**	**0.2**	**0.0**	**−0.5**	**2.2**	**2.5**
United States	0.4	−2.4	3.1	2.6	0.4	0.2	0.1	2.8	2.4
Euro Area	0.6	−4.1	1.0	1.5	0.0	−0.1	−2.2	1.2	1.8
Germany	1.2	−5.0	1.2	1.7	−0.3	−0.2	−2.4	1.2	2.1
France	0.3	−2.2	1.5	1.8	0.1	0.1	−0.3	1.5	1.9
Italy	−1.3	−5.0	0.8	1.2	−0.2	−0.1	−3.0	1.4	1.3
Spain	0.9	−3.6	−0.4	0.9	0.2	0.0	−3.1	−0.1	1.8
Japan	−1.2	−5.2	1.9	2.0	0.2	−0.2	−1.4	1.6	2.3
United Kingdom	0.5	−4.9	1.3	2.5	0.0	−0.2	−3.1	2.3	2.6
Canada	0.4	−2.6	3.1	3.2	0.5	−0.4	−1.2	3.4	3.3
Other Advanced Economies	1.7	−1.1	3.7	3.9	0.4	0.3	3.2	2.8	4.4
Newly Industrialized Asian Economies	1.8	−0.9	5.2	4.9	0.4	0.2	6.1	3.4	5.9
Emerging and Developing Economies[2]	**6.1**	**2.4**	**6.3**	**6.5**	**0.3**	**0.2**	**5.2**	**6.3**	**7.3**
Central and Eastern Europe	3.0	−3.7	2.8	3.4	0.8	−0.3	1.9	1.3	4.1
Commonwealth of Independent States	5.5	−6.6	4.0	3.6	0.2	−0.4	…	…	…
Russia	5.6	−7.9	4.0	3.3	0.4	−0.1	−3.8	1.7	4.2
Excluding Russia	5.3	−3.5	3.9	4.5	−0.4	−0.6	…	…	…
Developing Asia	7.9	6.6	8.7	8.7	0.3	0.3	8.6	8.9	9.1
China	9.6	8.7	10.0	9.9	0.0	0.2	10.7	9.4	10.1
India	7.3	5.7	8.8	8.4	1.1	0.6	6.0	10.9	8.2
ASEAN-5[3]	4.7	1.7	5.4	5.6	0.7	0.3	5.0	4.2	6.2
Middle East and North Africa	5.1	2.4	4.5	4.8	0.0	0.1	…	…	…
Sub-Saharan Africa	5.5	2.1	4.7	5.9	0.4	0.4	…	…	…
Western Hemisphere	4.3	−1.8	4.0	4.0	0.3	0.2	…	…	…
Brazil	5.1	−0.2	5.5	4.1	0.8	0.4	4.3	4.2	4.2
Mexico	1.5	−6.5	4.2	4.5	0.2	−0.2	−2.4	2.3	5.5
Memorandum									
European Union	0.9	−4.1	1.0	1.8	0.0	−0.1	−2.2	1.3	2.0
World Growth Based on Market Exchange Rates	1.8	−2.0	3.2	3.4	0.2	0.0	…	…	…
World Trade Volume (goods and services)	**2.8**	**−10.7**	**7.0**	**6.1**	**1.2**	**−0.2**	**…**	**…**	**…**
Imports									
Advanced Economies	0.6	−12.0	5.4	4.6	−0.1	−0.9	…	…	…
Emerging and Developing Economies	8.5	−8.4	9.7	8.2	3.2	0.5	…	…	…
Exports									
Advanced Economies	1.9	−11.7	6.6	5.0	0.7	−0.6	…	…	…
Emerging and Developing Economies	4.0	−8.2	8.3	8.4	2.9	0.6	…	…	…
Commodity Prices (U.S. dollars)									
Oil[4]	36.4	−36.3	29.5	3.8	6.9	−4.1	…	…	…
Nonfuel (average based on world commodity export weights)	7.5	−18.7	13.9	−0.5	8.1	2.1	…	…	…
Consumer Prices									
Advanced Economies	3.4	0.1	1.5	1.4	0.2	−0.1	0.8	1.3	1.6
Emerging and Developing Economies[2]	9.2	5.2	6.2	4.7	0.0	0.1	4.9	5.8	4.0
London Interbank Offered Rate (percent)[5]									
On U.S. Dollar Deposits	3.0	1.1	0.5	1.7	−0.2	−0.1	…	…	…
On Euro Deposits	4.6	1.2	0.9	1.6	−0.4	−0.7	…	…	…
On Japanese Yen Deposits	1.0	0.7	0.6	0.7	0.0	0.0	…	…	…

Note: Real effective exchange rates are assumed to remain constant at the levels prevailing during February 23–March 23, 2010. Country weights used to construct aggregate growth rates for groups of economies were revised. When economies are not listed alphabetically, they are ordered on the basis of economic size.

[1]The quarterly estimates and projections account for 90 percent of the world purchasing-power-parity weights.

[2]The quarterly estimates and projections account for approximately 77 percent of the emerging and developing economies.

[3]Indonesia, Malaysia, Philippines, Thailand, and Vietnam.

[4]Simple average of prices of U.K. Brent, Dubai, and West Texas Intermediate crude oil. The average price of oil in U.S. dollars a barrel was $61.78 in 2009; the assumed price based on future markets is $80.00 in 2010 and $83.00 in 2011.

[5]Six-month rate for the United States and Japan. Three-month rate for the Euro Area.

Activity in emerging and developing economies is leading the way (Figure 1.2). In key emerging Asian economies output already exceeds precrisis levels by a wide margin, and output growth, averaging about 10 percent during 2009:Q2–Q4, is outpacing estimates of full-capacity (potential) output growth. By the third quarter of 2009, growth began to exceed estimates of potential output in a number of Latin American economies too. However, production levels in this region have barely reached precrisis levels, and there is still economic slack in many countries. Recovery is lagging in a number of economies in emerging Europe and the CIS, although some are beginning to rebound strongly from deep troughs. Middle Eastern economies are benefiting from rising demand for oil and rising oil prices. Experience in sub-Saharan Africa is diverse. Most middle-income economies and oil exporters, which experienced sharp decelerations or contractions in output in 2009, are now recovering, supported by the rebound in global trade and commodity prices. In most low-income economies, output growth, after slowing in 2009, is now again close to trend rates.

Financial Conditions Are Easing, but Not for All Sectors

Policy intervention on an unprecedented scale helped improve financial conditions and real activity (Figure 1.3). Money markets have stabilized, equity markets have rebounded, and the credit cycle may be turning up. In advanced economies, the tightening of bank lending standards is ending and credit appears to be bottoming out. For these economies, the April 2010 *Global Financial Stability Report* (GFSR) has also lowered its estimate of actual and prospective bank write-downs and loan loss provisions over 2007–10 from $2.8 trillion to $2.3 trillion, two-thirds of which had been recognized at the end of 2009. In China, credit and some asset markets are booming, to such an extent that the People's Bank of China has taken various measures to moderate the pace of lending, including raising the renminbi reserve requirement ratio for depository financial institutions (Figure 1.4). Credit is accelerating elsewhere in emerging Asia but is stabilizing in Latin America. In emerg-

Figure 1.1. Current and Forward-Looking Indicators[1]
(Annualized percent change of three-month moving average over previous three-month moving average unless noted otherwise)

Global activity has rebounded, as evidenced by accelerating world trade, industrial production, and retail sales. Employment continues to contract in advanced economies but is expanding again in emerging economies, helped by strong potential growth. Industrial confidence has returned to precrisis levels, but household confidence in advanced economies continues to lag, reflecting subdued employment.

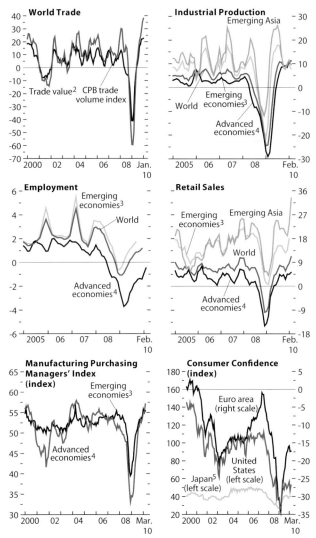

Sources: Netherlands Bureau for Economic Policy Analysis for CPB trade volume index; for all others, Haver Analytics and NTC Economics; and IMF staff calculations.
[1] Not all economies are included in the regional aggregations. For some economies, monthly data are interpolated from quarterly series.
[2] In SDR terms.
[3] Argentina, Brazil, Bulgaria, Chile, China, Colombia, Estonia, Hungary, India, Indonesia, Latvia, Lithuania, Malaysia, Mexico, Pakistan, Peru, Philippines, Poland, Romania, Russia, South Africa, Thailand, Turkey, Ukraine, and Venezuela.
[4] Australia, Canada, Czech Republic, Denmark, euro area, Hong Kong SAR, Israel, Japan, Korea, New Zealand, Norway, Singapore, Sweden, Switzerland, Taiwan Province of China, United Kingdom, and United States.
[5] Japan's consumer confidence data are based on a diffusion index, where values greater than 50 indicate improving confidence.

Figure 1.2. Global Indicators[1]
(Annual percent change unless noted otherwise)

Real GDP growth picked up starting in 2009:Q2. However, output in most regions of the world remains below or around precrisis levels. The exception is emerging Asia, which accounts for a growing share of world activity. Commodity prices have rebounded in response to expanding activity.

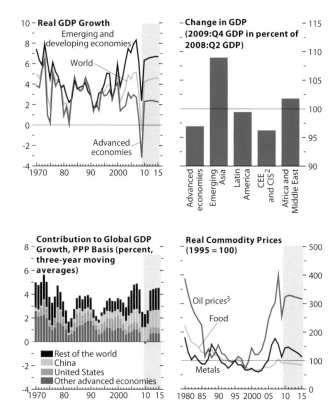

Source: IMF staff estimates.
[1]Shaded areas indicate IMF staff projections. Aggregates are computed on the basis of purchasing-power-parity (PPP) weights unless noted otherwise.
[2]CEE: central and eastern Europe; CIS: Commonwealth of Independent States.
[3]Simple average of spot prices of U.K. Brent, Dubai Fateh, and West Texas Intermediate crude oil.

ing Europe, credit continues to contract but at a decelerating pace.

Nevertheless, financial conditions remain more difficult than before the crisis, especially in advanced economies. In a few advanced economies, rising public deficits and debt have contributed to a sharp increase in sovereign risk premiums, creating spillovers into other economies and markets. At the same time, constraints on bank capital and sluggish nonfinancial credit growth continue to impair the supply of credit, and buoyant corporate bond issues have not taken up the slack. Bank capital is likely to remain a constraint, especially in Europe, as banks seek to lower their leverage multiples. Deleveraging needs in the U.S. banking sector are lower but still significant for regional banks. In general, sectors that have only limited access to capital markets—consumers and small and medium-size enterprises—are likely to continue to face tight limits on their borrowing. So far, public lending programs and guarantees have been vital in channeling credit to these sectors.

Capital Is Again Flowing to Emerging Economies

Together with real and financial activity, cross-border financial flows from advanced to emerging economies have picked up, primarily reflecting a recovery from deep retrenchment in 2008 (Figure 1.4). Both equity and bond flows have accelerated since the end of 2008, although syndicated loan issuance remains below precrisis levels. The growth in cross-border flows has come mostly from outside the banking sector, as banks continue to retrench their balance sheets. Key drivers behind the renewed capital flows include rapid growth in emerging economies, large yield differentials in their favor, and returning appetite for risk. The renewed flows have eased financial conditions in many emerging economies and prompted some authorities to be watchful of increasing property prices, in some cases taking measures to rein in domestic credit growth. Thus far, evidence for broader asset price overvaluation is limited, according to the April 2010 GFSR.

The recovery of cross-border flows has come with some real effective exchange rate changes—

depreciation of the U.S. dollar and appreciation of floating currencies of some other advanced and emerging economies—but compared with pre-crisis levels, changes have generally been limited (Figures 1.5 and 1.6). There are exceptions. The economies in the Middle East saw some significant appreciation, those in emerging Europe some significant depreciation, and the Japanese yen appreciated significantly. These changes were generally in line with the medium-term fundamentals for these economies. However, currencies of a number of emerging Asian economies remain undervalued, substantially in the case of the renminbi, and the U.S. dollar and euro remain on the strong side relative to medium-term fundamentals.

The concomitant narrowing of global current account imbalances has a significant temporary component. Among the major economies, the current account surplus of China fell from about 9½ percent of GDP in 2008 to 5¾ percent of GDP in 2009, reflecting the slump in global manufacturing and trade but also a steep rise in public spending. Over the same period, the deficit of the United States fell from about 5 percent of GDP to about 3 percent, as household savings rose and investment slumped. Both economies benefited from lower oil prices, which in turn reduced the large surpluses of Middle Eastern economies. However, IMF staff estimates suggest that current account imbalances will rise noticeably as global trade continues to recover, financing improves, and commodity prices stabilize at higher levels (Figure 1.6).

Policy Support Has Been Essential in Fostering Recovery

Extraordinary policy intervention since the crisis has all but eliminated the risk of a second Great Depression, laying the foundation for recovery. The interventions were essential to prevent a downward debt-deflation spiral, in which increasingly severe difficulties would have fed back and forth between the financial system and the rest of the economy.

- Fiscal policy provided major support in response to the deep downturn, especially in advanced economies. At the same time, the slump in activity and, to a much lesser extent, stimulus measures

Figure 1.3. Developments in Mature Credit Markets

Financial conditions in advanced economies have improved noticeably, as evidenced by declining interbank, credit default swap (CDS), and corporate spreads and recoveries in equity markets. The tightening of bank lending conditions is coming to an end, suggesting a nascent turn in the credit cycle. The decline in bank credit has been large relative to most recessions.

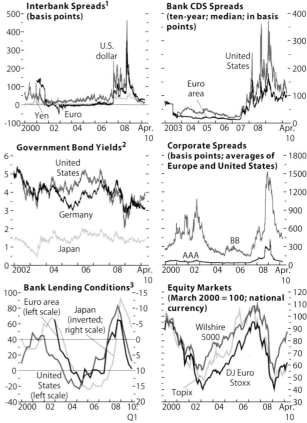

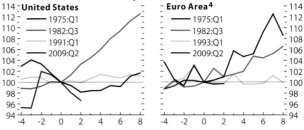

Sources: Bank of Japan; Bloomberg Financial Markets; European Central Bank; Federal Reserve Board of Governors; Merrill Lynch; and IMF staff calculations.

[1] Three-month London interbank offered rate minus three-month government bill rate.

[2] Ten-year government bonds.

[3] Percent of respondents describing lending standards as tightening "considerably" or "somewhat" minus those indicating standards as easing "considerably" or "somewhat" over the previous three months. Survey of changes to credit standards for loans or lines of credit to enterprises for the euro area; average of surveys on changes in credit standards for commercial/industrial and commercial real estate lending for the United States; diffusion index of "accommodative" minus "severe," Tankan survey of lending attitude of financial institutions for Japan.

[4] Euro area consists of France, Germany, and Italy.

Figure 1.4. Emerging Market Conditions

Financial conditions have improved markedly in many emerging markets. Equity markets have staged a strong rebound, interest rate spreads have come down, and new issues are up. Private credit growth, however, continues to contract or move sideways in Latin America and emerging Europe.

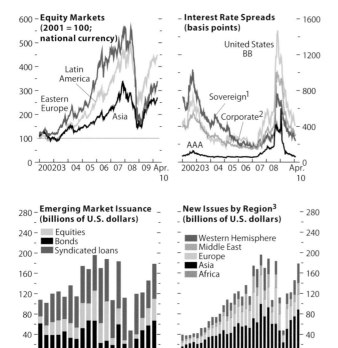

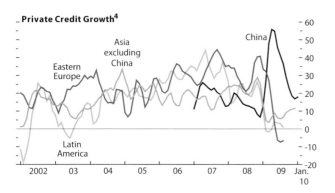

Sources: Bloomberg Financial Markets; Capital Data; IMF, *International Financial Statistics;* and IMF staff calculations.
[1]JPMorgan EMBI Global Index spread.
[2]JPMorgan CEMBI Broad Index spread.
[3]Total of equity, syndicated loans, and international bond issues.
[4]Annualized percent change of three-month moving average over previous three-month moving average.

pushed fiscal deficits in advanced economies up to about 9 percent of GDP (Figure 1.7). Debt-to-GDP ratios in these economies are expected to exceed 100 percent of GDP in 2014 based on current policies, some 35 percentage points of GDP higher than before the crisis. The expected increases are mostly a result of declines in output and reduced tax payments as a result of lower asset prices and diminished financial sector activity; discretionary fiscal stimulus and direct support to the financial sector stemming from the crisis account for less than one-fifth of the debt increases.

- Monetary policy has been highly expansionary and has been supported by unconventional liquidity provision. Policy rates were brought down to record lows, close to zero in many advanced economies (Figure 1.8). Other exceptional measures include public commitments to keep interest rates low for an extended time, outright purchases of long-term government bonds to reduce longer-term yields, and support for dysfunctional markets (including for asset-backed securities). As a result, central bank balance sheets in some of the largest economies expanded rapidly until recently. Many central banks in emerging economies also introduced special liquidity or credit facilities, including to alleviate the acute global shortage of dollar funding.

- Government guarantees and capital injections for financial institutions have provided indispensable backing to the system.

Multispeed Recovery to Continue during 2010–11

Two factors underlying the stronger-than-expected start to the global recovery will continue to sustain growth during much of 2010, while the effect of fiscal stimulus gradually diminishes. The first is the better-than-expected state of financial markets, where public support is already being phased out. In particular, there are signs that credit is close to stabilizing, and the recovery of household wealth should provide continued support to consumption. The second is the inventory cycle: the large fall in global inventories, which resulted from the plunge in production during 2008:Q4–2009:Q1, is now slowing or reversing. The fear of a new depression had triggered rapid destocking, with production quickly scaled back in anticipation of a major decline in consumption. With this decline averted, firms are now running down inventories at a much reduced pace or are rebuilding them. Under plausible scenarios, this process may continue through much of 2010.

The next question is whether the stronger rebound in the inventory cycle is a harbinger of healthy recovery. For the major advanced economies, this is not expected to be true (Figure 1.9). In the United States, where destocking has been pronounced, inventory investment may add about 1 percentage point to GDP growth during 2010. In the euro area and Japan, the contribution from inventories is likely to be more limited, because the previous drawdown was less drastic than in the United States. Moreover, there are few other indications that private spending in these three economies will lead a strong recovery, given that credit will remain hard to come by for many agents, investment will be held back by low capacity utilization, and unemployment will weigh on consumption (see Chapter 3). In the meantime, public deficits will have to be scaled back. This is likely to dampen growth by cutting into incomes and thereby further reducing spending by liquidity-constrained consumers. It might also prompt households to scale back their expectations for future disposable income (including expected long-term returns on their assets) and to increase their precautionary saving. The extent to which this will diminish growth is hard to gauge; much will depend on the credibility and quality of fiscal adjustment.

For emerging economies the picture is more positive. Inventory investment is likely to make a significant contribution to growth in the short term, on account of prospects for improved demand in both advanced and emerging economies. With global trade rebounding, stocks must be rebuilt after the drawdown of 2008–09, just as in the advanced economies. Furthermore, countries such as Brazil, China, India, and Indonesia are already sustaining a strong rebound, even in the face of weak recovery in the advanced economies, quickly reattracting capital flows. This is because most emerging and developing economies did not suffer long-lasting shocks to their

Figure 1.5. External Developments
(Index, 2000 = 100; three-month moving average unless noted otherwise)

Although currencies have gyrated during the crisis, they have not moved much relative to precrisis levels, except in emerging Europe and the Middle East. Also, the Japanese yen appreciated significantly. Many emerging economies began to build up reserves, after financial stress started to ease in mid-2009.

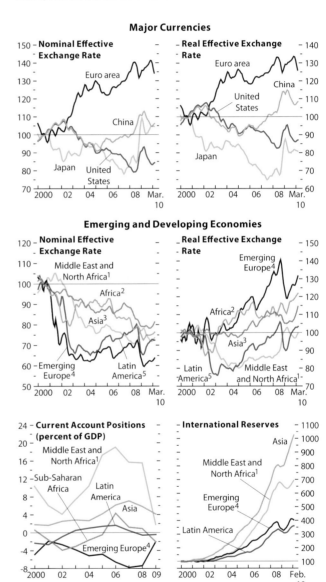

Sources: IMF, *International Financial Statistics;* and IMF staff calculations.
[1]Bahrain, Djibouti, Egypt, Islamic Republic of Iran, Jordan, Kuwait, Lebanon, Libya, Oman, Qatar, Saudi Arabia, Sudan, Syrian Arab Republic, United Arab Emirates, and Republic of Yemen.
[2]Botswana, Burkina Faso, Cameroon, Chad, Republic of Congo, Côte d'Ivoire, Equatorial Guinea, Ethiopia, Gabon, Ghana, Guinea, Kenya, Madagascar, Mali, Mauritius, Mozambique, Namibia, Niger, Nigeria, Rwanda, Senegal, South Africa, Tanzania, Uganda, and Zambia.
[3]Asia excluding China.
[4]Bulgaria, Croatia, Estonia, Hungary, Latvia, Lithuania, Poland, Romania, and Turkey.
[5]Argentina, Brazil, Chile, Colombia, Mexico, Peru, and Venezuela.

Figure 1.6. Global Imbalances

Current account surpluses and deficits narrowed as global trade declined and commodity prices fell. However, as the global economy recovers, imbalances are projected to grow again, but to remain lower than before the crisis. This is consistent with a drop in expected income growth in economies that ran excessive current account deficits before the crisis.

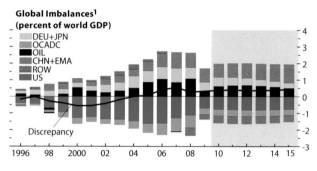

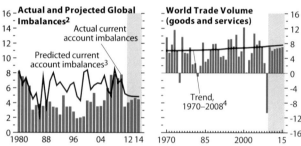

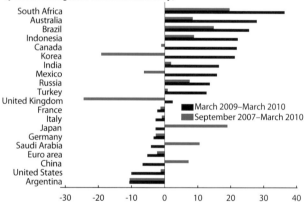

Source: IMF staff estimates.

[1]CHN+EMA: China, Hong Kong SAR, Indonesia, Korea, Malaysia, Philippines, Singapore, Taiwan Province of China, and Thailand; DEU+JPN: Germany and Japan; OCADC: Bulgaria, Croatia, Czech Republic, Estonia, Greece, Hungary, Ireland, Latvia, Lithuania, Poland, Portugal, Romania, Slovak Republic, Slovenia, Spain, Turkey, and United Kingdom; OIL: Oil exporters; ROW: rest of the world; US: United States.

[2]Measured as standard deviation of country-specific current accounts in G20 economies.

[3]Based on a 10-year rolling regression of global current account imbalance on world GDP growth and oil prices.

[4]Average growth rates for individual countries, aggregated using purchasing-power-parity weights; the aggregates shift over time in favor of faster-growing economies, giving the line an upward trend.

financial systems or large increases in unemployment rates, and many have been able to deploy sizable fiscal and monetary stimulus. This reflects a widespread strengthening of policy frameworks and institutions in response to earlier crises as well as accelerating potential growth, driven by market-oriented reforms.

Historically, sound domestic policies and strong underlying potential have provided a number of emerging and developing economies with some insulation against recessions in advanced economies (Figure 1.10). For example, Asian economies pulled through the deep recession of the early 1980s relatively well, helped by policy frameworks that improved their resilience to external shocks. The same was true for a broader range of emerging and developing economies following the 2001 recession in advanced economies. A positive feature for the present recovery is that most emerging economies did not have externally funded booms—exceptions being various emerging European and some CIS economies. Thus, the prospects for emerging and developing economies may be less dependent on those for advanced economies during the current recovery than in the wake of some past global recessions.

Overall, the world looks poised for further recovery at varying speeds across and within various regions (Figure 1.11; Table 1.1). Global growth is projected at about 4¼ percent in 2010 and 2011. For both advanced and emerging economies, the new forecast for 2010 has an upward revision to output of about 1 percentage point relative to the October 2009 WEO, but it is broadly similar to the January 2010 WEO Update; for 2011, the forecast is broadly unchanged relative to the two previous issues of the WEO. Advanced economies are now expected to expand by 2¼ percent in 2010, following a more than 3 percent decline in output in 2009, and by 2½ percent in 2011. Growth in emerging and developing economies is expected to be over 6¼ percent during 2010–11, following a modest 2½ percent in 2009.

The recovery under way in the major advanced economies will be relatively sluggish, both compared with recoveries following the major (but less deep) recessions of the mid-1970s, early 1980s, and early 1990s and compared with the recoveries forecast for many emerging economies. Several euro area economies that were hit particularly hard or have run out of macroeconomic policy room are likely to lag behind their major peers. By contrast, Australia and the newly industrialized Asian economies are off to a strong start and will likely stay in the lead. The pace of recovery will also diverge significantly among emerging and developing economies: the Asian economies, which suffered less during the downturn, are leading the recovery—in terms of both smaller output gaps and higher growth rates—and are forecast to continue to do so. In sub-Saharan Africa, most economies are expected to stay close to their potential output growth rates. Recovery in the economies of emerging Europe and the CIS will continue to lag behind, with some exceptions.

In general, economies that are in the lead of recovery are likely to remain there. Conversely, those that experienced larger drops in output during the crisis will not necessarily experience stronger recoveries (Figure 1.9).[2] As Chapter 2 discusses in more depth, output developments are determined by many factors, a number of which have lasting consequences. These include the extent of damage to financial sectors, household balance sheets, and cross-border funding and the room available for policy maneuvers to combat recession.[3] Contrary to some perceptions, the type of exchange rate regime does not appear to have had a major impact on growth in this crisis (Box 1.1).

Inflation Pressures Are Generally Subdued but Diverge

The still-low levels of capacity utilization and well-anchored inflation expectations are expected to keep inflation low (Figure 1.12). The limited decline in inflation in many advanced economies is puzzling given the exceptionally large falls in output. Core inflation in the euro area has lately fallen under 1 percent, down from under 2 percent at the

[2] The "Zarnowitz rule"—whereby deep recessions are followed by rapid recoveries—will generally not apply. For details on this rule, see Zarnowitz (1992).

[3] However, looking behind these regional groupings at country specifics, much is still not understood about what drove economic activity during this recession. For further discussion, see Berkmen and others (2009); Claessens and others (2010); and Blanchard, Faruqee, and Das (2010). On the lasting impact of financial shocks, see Cardarelli, Elekdag, and Lall (2009) and Chapter 3 of the April 2009 *World Economic Outlook*.

Figure 1.7. General Government Fiscal Balances and Public Debt
(Percent of GDP unless noted otherwise)

Fiscal balances have deteriorated, mainly because of falling revenue resulting from decreased real and financial activity. Fiscal stimulus has played a major role in stabilizing output but has contributed little to increases in public debt, which are especially large in advanced economies. Most advanced economies need to lower their deficits substantially to stabilize their debt-to-GDP ratios; some are experiencing growing financial market pressure to do so soon. However, all countries need to make significant progress over the coming decade: spending on aging populations will only make matters worse.

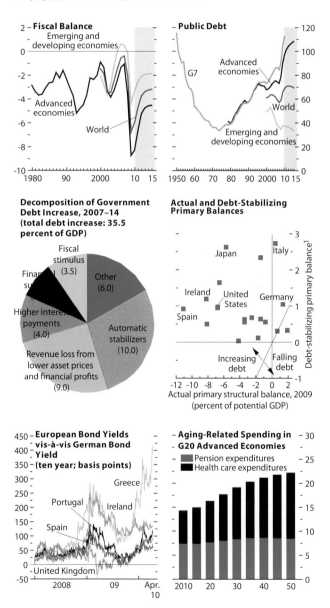

Sources: Country authorities; Datastream; European Commission (2009); Fiscal Monitor Database; Organization for Economic Cooperation and Development; and IMF staff estimates.
[1] Based on real GDP growth projected for 2008–14.

Figure 1.8. Measures of Monetary Policy and Liquidity in Selected Advanced Economies

(Interest rates in percent unless noted otherwise)

Policy rates were cut to near zero in major advanced economies and were brought down significantly in many emerging economies. Markets expect a prolonged period of very low rates for the advanced economies and some significant rate hikes in various emerging economies, which are seen to be closer to full capacity and subject to higher inflation risks.

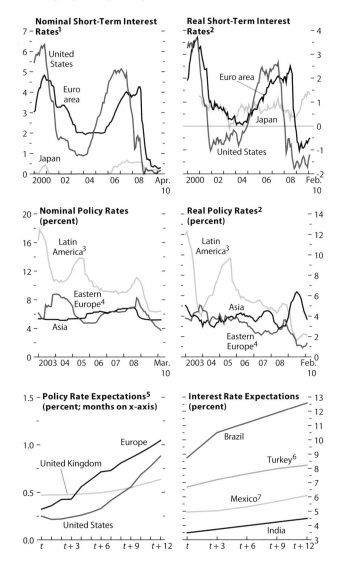

Sources: Bloomberg Financial Markets; Eurostat; Haver Analytics; and IMF staff calculations.
[1] Three-month treasury bill.
[2] Relative to core inflation.
[3] Argentina, Brazil, Chile, Colombia, Mexico, and Peru.
[4] Bulgaria, Estonia, Hungary, Latvia, Lithuania, and Poland.
[5] Expectations are based on the federal funds rate for the United States, the sterling overnight interbank average rate for the United Kingdom, and the euro interbank offered forward rates for Europe; updated April 12, 2010.
[6] Average ask/bid spread of the Turkish Lira Reference Interest Rate (TRLIBOR) as of April 12, 2010.
[7] Based on futures of 28-day interbank rates.

peak in 2008; in the United States it has been running about 1½ percent, down from somewhat over 2 percent; and in the United Kingdom it appears to have moved sideways (excluding the likely impact of one-time effects). In Japan, price dynamics turned appreciably from very low core inflation to negative inflation, which slightly exceeded 1 percent in February 2010. In general, the correlation between the drop in core inflation from its 2008 peaks and the increase in unemployment rates is weaker than during the 2001 recession (Figure 1.13). Beyond the fact that the financial crisis affected economies' potential output to differing degrees, various factors may explain this:

- Inflation expectations have generally remained well anchored, testifying to the credibility of accommodative monetary and fiscal policies as well as public support for financial repair.
- Nominal downward rigidities become more binding at very low inflation rates, slowing or inhibiting further falls.
- Labor hoarding—a reluctance to lay off existing employees even during the slowdown—may have raised unit labor costs.
- In the face of weak revenues and tight financial conditions, firms may resist lowering prices and margins in an effort to rebuild working capital.

Moreover, the strong cyclical position of key emerging economies—before and after the crisis—has limited the decline in inflation pressure at the global level. In particular, recovering demand (especially in Asia) provided a strong boost to commodity prices, which explains why excess capacity in commodity production and excess inventories for many commodities markets are both lower than usual for this stage of the global cycle (Figure 1.2; Appendix 1.1). In many emerging economies, inflation has been quite variable from year to year and has been higher than in the advanced economies. This pattern persists. In various Latin American, Middle Eastern, and CIS economies, inflation slowed but remained relatively high throughout the cycle, and in India it rose strongly. Inflation fell appreciably in Russia and moderately in Brazil; prices in China actually declined for a while but are now rising.

Looking ahead, in most advanced economies headline inflation rates should broadly converge to present levels of core inflation as high unemployment discourages high wage settlements and energy prices remain stable or increase only modestly (Table 1.1)—March 2010 futures markets foresee only modest oil price increases, from $78.25 in 2010 to $82.50 in 2011, although prices have lately been somewhat higher. Risks for deflation remain pertinent in light of the weak outlook for GDP growth and persistent wide gaps between actual and potential output (Figure 1.13).

For emerging and developing economies, sustained increases in inflation are not projected during the recovery, although inflation is likely to remain quite variable wherever consumer prices are more sensitive to commodity prices.[4] Otherwise, significant upside inflation risks are confined to economies with a history of unstable price levels and to those that are growing strongly but have little excess productive capacity—including a number of emerging Asian economies and others for which markets are pricing in appreciable policy rate hikes during 2010 (Figure 1.8).

Important Risks Remain amid Sharply Diminished Room for Policy Maneuvers

The outlook for activity remains unusually uncertain. Risks are generally to the downside, and although a variety of risks have receded, downside risks related to the growth of public debt in advanced economies have become sharply more evident. The main concern is that room for policy maneuvers in many advanced economies has either been largely exhausted or has become much more limited, leaving these fragile recoveries exposed to new shocks. In addition, bank exposure to real estate continues to pose downside risks, mainly in the United States and parts of Europe. One upside risk that has diminished is that the potential for positive financial surprises is now lower, given the extent of the financial recovery that has already taken place. Even so, reduction in uncertainty may continue to foster a stronger-than-expected improvement in financial market sentiment and prompt a larger-than-expected rebound in capital flows, trade, and private demand. One downside risk that has diminished is that the systemic risks

[4] See Chapter 3 of the October 2008 *World Economic Outlook*.

Figure 1.9. Prospects for Near-Term Activity

Based on the historical relationship between global industrial production and retail sales, the global slowdown during 2008:Q4–2009:Q1 was significantly driven by inventory drawdowns. This process has now reversed and will help support growth during 2010. However, high unemployment in the advanced economies will limit demand, as will impaired financial systems. Output recovery will be sluggish by past standards. More generally, countries that suffered large slowdowns or contractions in activity during the crisis will not necessarily rebound quickly, because they are dealing with long-lasting shocks.

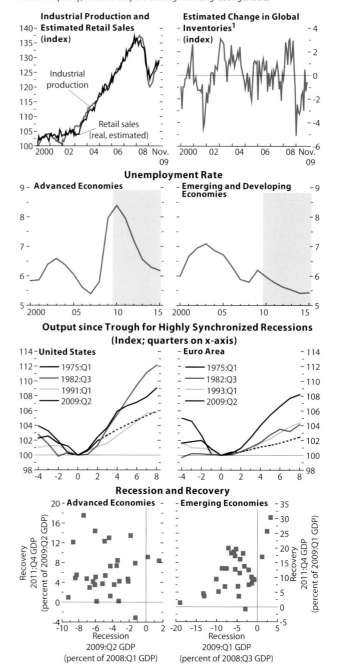

Source: IMF staff calculations.
[1]Based on deviations from an estimated (cointegration) relationship between global industrial production and retail sales.

Figure 1.10. Emerging Economies: GDP Growth by Recession Episode

(Percent change from one year earlier)

During recessions in advanced economies, output in emerging economies has varied, slowing down sharply during the early 1980s but holding up well during the 1990s and in 2001. Furthermore, developments have varied across countries. Following the recession of the early 1980s, output growth moved onto a higher trajectory in emerging Asia but dropped in Latin America. Following the 2001 recession, output growth remained strong in all emerging economies.

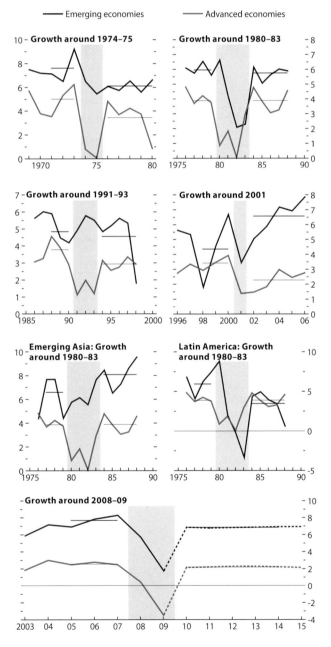

Source: World Economic Outlook database.

originating in the financial sector have fallen further as the recovery has become more robust.

The IMF staff's quantitative indicators broadly confirm these qualitative insights (Figure 1.14).[5] Specifically, risks as measured by falling dispersion in analysts' forecasts for real GDP growth have diminished but remain to the downside. Options prices on the S&P 500 indicate some upside risks from financial surprises, although these are now smaller than in October 2009. Concerns about upside surprises on inflation that may require earlier-than-expected monetary policy action have remained unchanged, judging by analysts' expectations. Term spread data point to broadly balanced risks to growth, as yield curves have steepened modestly since October 2009. Options prices for futures on petroleum and other commodities suggest small downside risks to growth from another commodity price spike in the near term—risks for sharp price increases are higher in the medium term, as spare capacity and inventory buffers diminish.

Sovereign risk premiums for some of the more fiscally vulnerable economies have again seen a steep increase, amid significant volatility (Figure 1.7). In the near term, the main risk is that, if unchecked, market concerns about sovereign liquidity and solvency in Greece could turn into a full-blown and contagious sovereign debt crisis, as explained in the April 2010 GFSR. A widespread public debt scare across major advanced economies appears unlikely, because together these economies have broad tax and investor bases. However, even here, risk assessments by investors are likely to increasingly differentiate among economies, showing greater sensitivity to deteriorating budgetary outlooks.

Risks related to sovereign debt could depress output for a variety of reasons. They could prompt premature withdrawal of fiscal stimulus that undermines recovery or limit the scope of new stimulus in response to new adverse shocks. As activity weakens, households and investors could lose confidence in governments' ability to design and implement sound consolidation plans and in response could sharply reduce their spending because of con-

---

[5] For a detailed discussion of the methodology used to construct the fan chart, see Elekdag and Kannan (2009).

cerns that taxes will increase or that prospects for growth, wages, and investment returns will diminish. Abrupt changes in exchange rates that distort production present further concerns.

The simulation in Figure 1.15 helps illustrate the potential role of confidence, limited room for policy maneuver, and relevant interactions. It shows the baseline projections (red line) and adds one shock: a confidence-induced drop in aggregate demand in advanced economies.[6] The resulting downside scenario (blue line) assumes that fiscal policy cannot offset this shock and that monetary policy is constrained at present levels. Households would experience continued weak labor market conditions and housing prices would drop further, following the expiration of key policy support measures. Firms would postpone hiring and investment and bank lending conditions would tighten with mounting loan delinquencies. Given weak recovery prospects in advanced economies, including for the growth of imports, emerging economies as a group would experience difficulties in sustaining exports and growth—monetary policy would be unable to offset the effects on output of the sequence of negative shocks, given its gradual impact. The result would be a delay in the recovery of several years, with unemployment declining at a slower pace and with persistent deflation in Japan.

Policies Need to Sustain and Strengthen Recovery

Policymakers are faced with major challenges. In many advanced and a number of emerging economies, they need to rebalance demand away from the public and toward the private sector, while consolidating public finances and repairing the financial sector. In a number of emerging and developing economies, policymakers need to increasingly tap domestic sources for growth, as demand from other economies will likely remain weaker than before the crisis. These rebalancing acts are proceeding but not without problems. Many advanced economies continue to struggle to repair and reform their financial

[6]The simulations are based on a six-region version of the IMF's Global Projection Model. See Garcia-Saltos and others (forthcoming).

Figure 1.11. Global Outlook

(Real GDP; quarterly percent change from one year earlier, unless noted otherwise)

Global growth is forecast to recover in all regions but remain below precrisis levels over the medium term. Accordingly, relative to precrisis trends, some activity has been permanently lost. Losses are particularly large in emerging Europe and the Commonwealth of Independent States (CIS), where recovery in many countries will be slow and medium-term growth rates appreciably lower than before the crisis. Recovery is also expected to be sluggish in a number of advanced economies, although less so in the United States than in the euro area and Japan.

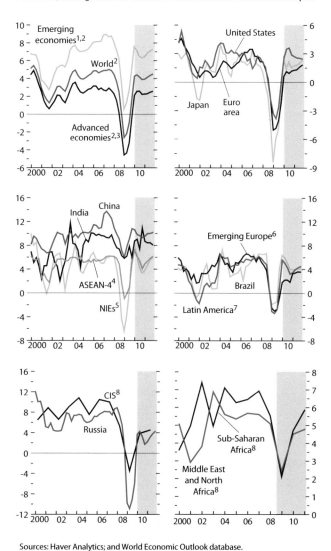

Sources: Haver Analytics; and World Economic Outlook database.
[1]Comprises China, India, Russia, South Africa, Turkey, and economies listed in footnotes 4, 6, and 7.
[2]Includes only economies that report quarterly data.
[3]Australia, Canada, Czech Republic, Denmark, euro area, Hong Kong SAR, Israel, Japan, Korea, New Zealand, Norway, Singapore, Sweden, Switzerland, Taiwan Province of China, United Kingdom, and United States.
[4]Indonesia, Malaysia, Philippines, and Thailand.
[5]Newly industrialized Asian economies (NIEs) comprise Hong Kong SAR, Korea, Singapore, and Taiwan Province of China.
[6]Bulgaria, Estonia, Hungary, Latvia, Lithuania, and Poland.
[7]Argentina, Brazil, Chile, Colombia, Mexico, Peru, and Venezuela.
[8]Annual percent change from one year earlier.

Box 1.1. Lessons from the Crisis: On the Choice of Exchange Rate Regime

Although emerging market economies were not at the epicenter of the global financial crisis, the experience of the past couple years may nevertheless hold important lessons for them. One such lesson concerns the choice of exchange rate regime—an obvious question being whether the regime can help explain how emerging market economies fared during this crisis, particularly in terms of output losses and growth resilience.[1] Theory suggests that exchange rate flexibility, by easing adjustment, should be associated with smaller output losses in the face of external shocks. This is also a popular perception of the current crisis—that economies with more flexible exchange rate regimes weathered the crisis better. What we find, however, is that economies with pegged regimes fared neither better nor worse than those with floats. Tentative work suggests that good performers, whether operating in the context of pegs or floats, allowed their real exchange rates to move in a direction that reduced initial misalignments.

A first look at the raw data on growth performance during the crisis yields the surprising result that both in absolute terms and in relation to previous performance, economies with floats—broadly construed to include the range from free floating to crawl-like arrangements—averaged larger output declines than pegs (first figure).[2] At the beginning of the crisis,

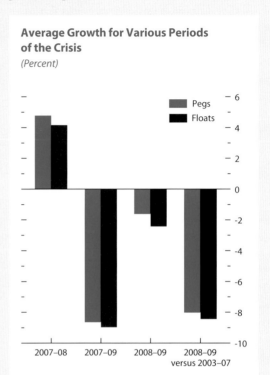

Average Growth for Various Periods of the Crisis
(Percent)

Source: IMF staff calculations.

average growth was more than half a percentage point higher for economies with pegged exchange rate regimes compared with those with floating regimes. As the crisis intensified, average growth declines for economies with pegs were smaller than for those with floats (8.6 and 1.6 percentage point declines for pegs in the periods 2007–09 and 2008–09, respectively, compared with 9.0 and 2.5 percentage point declines for floats). This same discrepancy holds for output declines as measured in relation to the economy's previous growth performance (first figure, righthand bar).

What accounts for this? In part, perceptions that economies with pegs fared worse may simply be

---

The author of this box is Charalambos Tsangarides.

[1] A recent IMF study found that intermediate (neither rigidly fixed nor freely floating) exchange rate regimes are associated with the highest average growth performance by capturing some of the benefits of pegs (low nominal and real exchange rate volatility, trade integration) while avoiding the main drawbacks (exchange rate overvaluation). The study also found, however, that economies with pegged and intermediate regimes are more likely to experience currency and financial crises, although not growth crises (see Ghosh, Ostry, and Tsangarides, 2010). Another IMF study uses revised projections for GDP growth in 2009 (comparing forecasts prior to and after the intensification of the crisis in September 2008) and finds that exchange rate flexibility helped buffer the impact of the crisis (see Berkmen and others, 2009).

[2] The sample consists of 50 emerging market economies. Based on the IMF's de facto exchange rate classification at the end of each period of the analysis, the following are categorized as pegs: hard pegs (with no separate legal tender or a currency board), conventional pegged arrangements, pegs within horizontal bands, and crawling pegs. Others are cat-

---

egorized as floats. Of the four growth episodes, the first three calculate real GDP growth rates between 2007–08, 2007–09, and 2008–09, and the fourth compares growth in 2008–09 with growth in 2003–07. It is also possible that the choice of exchange rate regime may have affected growth performance prior to the crisis as well. This is why we examine both the absolute and the relative growth performance.

mistaken, driven by a few exceptional cases (such as the output declines in the Baltic economies) rather than based on a representative sample. But this misperception may be also, in part, an artifact of classification, because some economies with pegs responded to the crisis by moving to a more flexible regime (in order to use the exchange rate as an adjustment tool). Indeed, there was a distinct dip in the number of economies with pegs—particularly soft pegs and/or intermediate regimes—following the onset of the crisis, and this mostly reversed by 2010 (second figure). A similar, temporary shift toward de facto flexibility was observed after the Asian crisis. Although it remains true that economies that maintained their less flexible regimes may have fared better, it may be misleading to include economies that switched the category of their new regime if the reason they switched was related to their ability to respond to the crisis under their original regime. For example, if pegs are associated with asset bubbles that turn to busts, triggering both the economic downturn and the exit from the pegged regime, then it would be unfair to attribute the poor growth performance to

the subsequent float. In addition to regime switching, another potential effect that casts doubt on the results of the first figure is that simple averages do not control for other factors that are likely to affect growth resilience in the crisis, including the impact of demand from trading partners.

To address these two issues, we remove economies that switched regime classification during 2008–09 and keep the economy categorized under the regime in place at the beginning of the period. Using regression analysis to control for partner country growth and commodity terms of trade, short-term external debt, reserve levels, and other determinants, as well as regime switching, we then estimate growth performance using the growth during 2008–09 relative to growth during 2003–07 as the dependent variable (table). The third figure presents predicted growth rates for pegs and floats based on regression analysis on the current regime, classifying economies throughout the period by the regime prevailing in December 2007 (second column) and eliminating all economies that switched regimes during the period of analysis (third column). The regression analysis controlling for

Growth during 2008–09 relative to 2003–07 and Exchange Rate Regime Classification

	Current Regime Classification		Excluding Switchers	
	(1)	(2)	(3)	(4)
Regime (1= fixed)	0.00535	0.01746	0.00395	0.01990
	(0.0151)	(0.0119)	(0.0168)	(0.0144)
Partner Growth 2008–09	2.35200***	1.39511**	2.4490***	1.11200
	(0.4250)	(0.6222)	(0.4240)	(0.7210)
Terms of Trade 2008–09	0.00065**	0.00083***	0.00056*	0.00086***
	(0.0003)	(0.0003)	(0.0003)	(0.0003)
Short-Term Debt to GDP, 2006		0.00275***		−0.00268***
		(0.0008)		(0.0009)
Reserves to GDP, 2006	0.00050	0.00136*	0.00051	0.00059
	(0.0006)	(0.0008)	(0.0006)	(0.0007)
Current Account Balance to GDP	0.00083	0.00010	0.00032	0.00004
	(0.0019)	(0.0013)	(0.0021)	(0.0013)
Net Portfolio Investment to GDP	0.00276	0.01159	0.00268	0.00227
	(0.0041)	(0.0073)	(0.0039)	(0.0066)
Constant	0.01140	0.04369	0.00915	0.03790***
	(0.0151)	(0.0141)	(0.0146)	(0.0144)
Observations	45	39	38	32
R^2	0.58	0.60	0.59	0.63

Note: Robust standard errors are in parentheses . *, **, and *** denote significance at the 10 percent, 5 percent, and 1 percent level, respectively.

Box 1.1 *(continued)*

Exchange Rate Regime Classifications, 2001–09
(Percent)

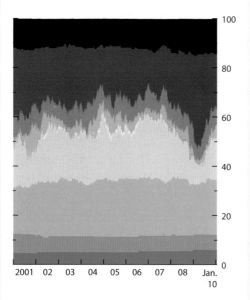

Source: IMF, *Annual Report on Exchange Arrangements and Exchange Restrictions.*

Predicted Average Growth, 2008–09 versus 2003–07 Using Regression Analysis
(Percent)

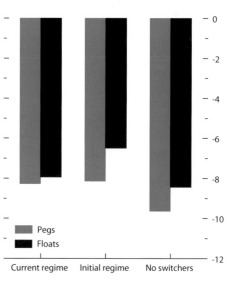

Source: IMF staff calculations.

regime switching and other potential factors affecting performance alters considerably the picture presented in the first figure: economies with pegged regimes fared no better than those with floats, and there is no residual difference in growth performance between pegs and floats (third figure).[3]

In sum, popular perceptions that emerging market economies with floating exchange rate regimes necessarily fared better during the global

[3] Estimated regression coefficients on the regime classification are not statistically significant, which suggests that fixed exchange rates are not associated with better growth performance than floats.

financial crisis do not appear to be supported by our investigation. After controlling for regime switches and taking account of other likely determinants of growth performance such as the magnitude of the external demand shock, growth performance for floats is no different from that for pegs. Although this result is not as surprising as the initial snapshot (that economies with floats did not perform better in the crisis), it nevertheless presents a puzzle. Given that economies with pegs have a natural disadvantage in dealing with shocks because they have forgone the use of the exchange rate as an adjustment tool, why did they fare no worse than economies with floats? More work is needed to formulate a concrete answer to this question, but some preliminary work suggests that during the crisis the good performers' real exchange rates tended to move in the "right" direction—that is, in the direction of reducing initial misalignments—and that before the crisis they had better reserve coverage of short-term debt.

sectors, which is essential for sustained growth of private demand. Moreover, pressures remain for trade and financial protectionism. Concurrently, a concern in various emerging economies is that surging capital inflows may cause new boom-bust cycles. Some economies are resisting exchange rate appreciation that could support stronger domestic demand and reduce excessive current account surpluses, out of concern that appreciation could destabilize their economies.

International Coordination Is Essential for Strong, Sustained Recovery

Multispeed recoveries imply that policies will necessarily be tied to individual country circumstances, with the exit from supportive measures dependent on a self-sustaining recovery taking hold. But there are spillovers when the timing of policy actions varies, and economies should take these into account in setting policies. Spillovers related to fiscal policies are particularly relevant in the major advanced economies: domestic tightening has a negative impact on exports of other economies, and large deficits and the lack of well-specified medium-term fiscal consolidation strategies have a negative impact on the interest rates and risk premiums of fiscally challenged economies. In addition, resistance to capital inflows or exchange rate appreciations in some large emerging economies could undermine trade patterns or financial conditions for other emerging or advanced economies. Furthermore, some observers caution that exceptionally low interest rates in advanced economies could spur capital outflows, with potentially destabilizing effects for the recipient emerging economies.

Exit policies should help address the structural and macroeconomic policy shortcomings that gave rise to unbalanced growth and large global imbalances over the past decade.[7] Shortcomings in the financial systems of advanced economies encouraged excessive borrowing and depressed

---

[7] Recall that current account imbalances raise concerns only to the extent that they are rooted in domestic or systemic distortions or if they create risks of disruptive internal adjustment (Dutch disease) or global dislocation (disorderly depreciation of an international reserve currency). For a more detailed discussion, see Blanchard and Milesi-Ferretti (2009).

Figure 1.12. Global Inflation
(Twelve-month change in the consumer price index unless noted otherwise)

Inflation pressures are projected to remain low, held down by high unemployment rates and excess capacity. Inflation has been higher and more volatile in emerging economies, and inflation pressures could resurface more easily there than in advanced economies.

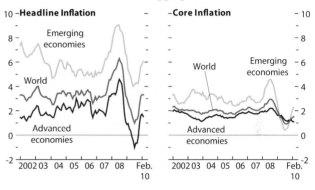

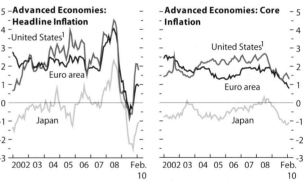

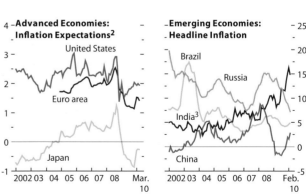

Source: IMF staff calculations.
[1] Personal consumption expenditure deflator.
[2] One-year-ahead *Consensus Forecasts*. The December values are the average of the surrounding November and January values.
[3] Consumer price index for industrial workers.

Figure 1.13. Inflation, Deflation Risk, and Unemployment

In advanced economies, the increase in unemployment and decrease in inflation are less correlated than during a similar period following the 2001 recession. In emerging economies, changes in unemployment and changes in inflation are generally poorly correlated. Deflation risks have receded at the global level, according to various indicators, but they remain pertinent in a number of advanced economies.

Rate Differences from Peaks

■ 2000–01 peak   ■ 2008 peak

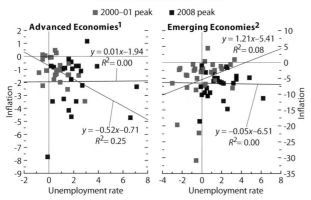

Deflation Vulnerability Indicator: Key Economies[3]

■ High risk   ■ Moderate risk   ■ Low risk

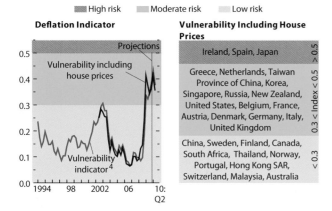

Sources: Bloomberg Financial Markets; Haver Analytics; and IMF staff calculations.
[1]Excludes Australia (2000–01 peak).
[2]Excludes three countries: Argentina (2000–01 peak), Estonia, and Latvia (both 2008 peak).
[3]For details on the construction of this indicator, see Decressin and Laxton (2009). The figure also features an expanded indicator, which includes house prices. Vulnerability is as of 2009:Q4.
[4]Major advanced and emerging economies.

private saving. At the same time, gaps in markets and government programs in a number of emerging economies boosted private saving to very high levels. Insufficient fiscal consolidation during good times in many advanced economies compounded these effects, as did the vast accumulation of official reserves by emerging Asian economies.

• In economies that need to rebuild savings and face relatively greater fiscal challenges, there is both a domestic and an international case for putting fiscal exit first. Furthermore, these economies need to accelerate financial sector repair and reform to build a stronger financial system and foster a more rapid return to robust growth. This would permit monetary policy to remain accommodative without causing inflation pressure or new financial market instabilities at home or abroad. Progress on both fronts is particularly important for the United States, given its systemic role in international financial markets, but also for other advanced economies that can affect the sovereign risk premiums of other economies.

• In economies with excessive current account surpluses and solid public finances, fiscal exit can wait while excess demand pressures are being addressed by reining in credit growth and allowing exchange rate appreciation. This is essential for China, given its large role in the global market. Greater currency adjustment in Asia would facilitate adjustment in other emerging economies that may fear losing market share if their currencies were to appreciate alone. Many emerging and developing economies also need to continue strengthening their financial stability frameworks to protect against speculative booms as they continue to attract capital.

The G20 Framework for Strong, Sustainable and Balanced Growth offers a forum to discuss and help achieve the required coordination of national policies. The next subsections of this chapter consider the fiscal, monetary, and financial policy challenges in more detail, and the final section presents simulations illustrating the benefits of policy coordination.

Credible Medium-Term Fiscal Policy Strategies Are Urgently Needed

In many advanced and a number of emerging economies, fiscal consolidation is a top priority and should precede the normalization of monetary policy. Economies need to make more progress in developing and communicating credible medium-term fiscal adjustment strategies. The goal should be to stabilize and eventually reverse the rise in public debt. This is mainly a challenge for many advanced economies, whose debt ratios have reached postwar highs in the context of subdued growth prospects (Figure 1.7). By contrast, the public debt problem in emerging economies is more localized—as a group, these economies' public debt ratios are about 30 to 40 percent of GDP and, given their high growth, can soon be on a declining path again.

Given the still-fragile nature of the recovery, the fiscal stimulus planned for 2010 should be fully implemented, except in some economies that already need to begin to consolidate. These include economies that are facing large public deficits and debt and related pressures on sovereign risk premiums.

Looking further ahead, if macroeconomic developments proceed as expected, most advanced economies should embark on significant fiscal consolidation in 2011. However, the appropriate timing for tightening can differ among economies, depending on the strength of the recovery, external imbalances, levels of public debt and primary balances, and other fiscal variables that affect market perceptions.

Economies urgently need to design and implement credible fiscal policy strategies with clear time frames to bring down gross debt-to-GDP ratios over the medium term (see IMF, 2010a). In the short term, absent such plans, room for policy maneuver in response to new shocks could be heavily constrained. Looking further ahead, high debt ratios could impede fiscal flexibility, raise economy-wide interest rates, increase the vulnerability of fiscally challenged economies, and constrain growth. Furthermore, without reassurances that consolidation will occur in a way that supports labor supply and investment, expectations about future growth

Figure 1.14. Risks to the Global Outlook

Risks to the global outlook are lower now than in October 2009, despite some recent widening, judging by the dispersion of analysts' forecasts for GDP growth. Option prices on the S&P 500 suggest that upside risks from financial markets have diminished, possibly reflecting both the strong recovery in these markets and new volatility in some public debt markets. Options prices for oil suggest that downside risks to growth from high prices have also diminished.

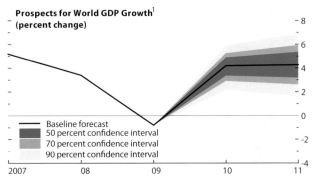

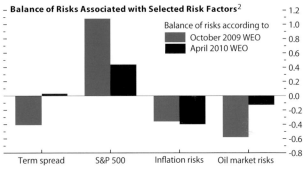

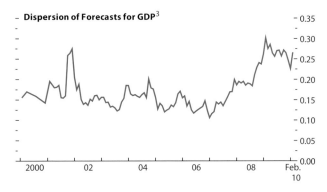

Sources: Bloomberg Financial Markets; Chicago Board Options Exchange; Consensus Economics; and IMF staff estimates.

[1]The fan chart shows the uncertainty around the World Economic Outlook (WEO) central forecast with 50, 70, and 90 percent probability intervals. As shown, the 70 percent confidence interval includes the 50 percent interval, and the 90 percent confidence interval includes the 50 and 70 percent intervals. See Appendix 1.2 in the April 2009 WEO for details.

[2]Bars depict the coefficient of skewness expressed in units of the underlying variables. The values for inflation risks and oil market risks are entered with the opposite sign since they represent downside risks to growth.

[3]The series measures the dispersion of GDP forecasts for the G7 economies (Canada, France, Germany, Italy, Japan, United Kingdom, United States), Brazil, China, India, and Mexico.

Figure 1.15. Downside Scenario: A Loss of Momentum

(All variables in levels unless noted otherwise; quarters on x-axis)

Significant downside risks to the growth outlook remain. The biggest risk is that confidence in the recovery will falter in advanced economies, resulting in lower demand, tighter credit conditions, and continued weakness in the labor market. A more protracted recovery in advanced economies will produce significant spillover effects in emerging economies through trade and financial channels.

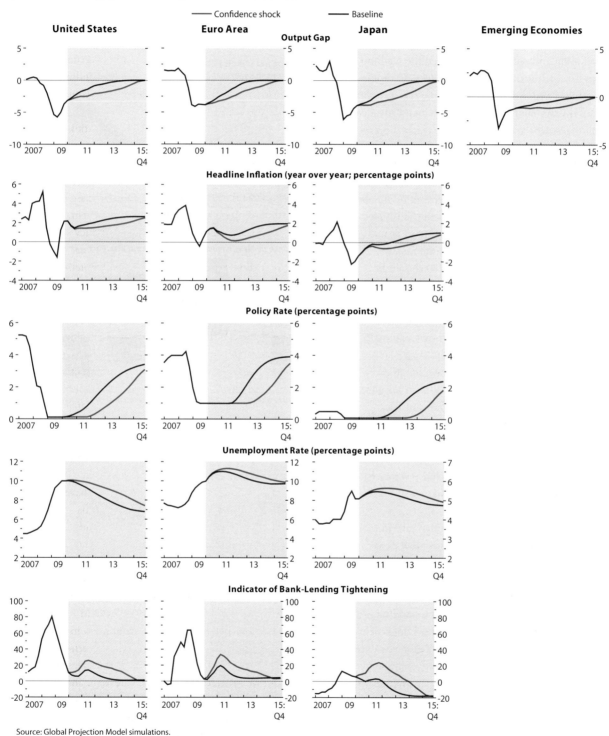

Source: Global Projection Model simulations.

may be lowered, savings raised, and investment postponed in advanced economies. As the downside scenario above suggests, the consequences of such an outcome could be severe, including for emerging economies that currently do not face high public deficits or debt. In the meantime, fiscal authorities in many economies should be actively managing their debt profiles to lengthen maturities and diversify investor bases.

Appropriate debt targets will depend on economy-specific characteristics. These include mobility of the tax base, composition of debt, depth of domestic financial markets, diversification of the investor base, vulnerability to shocks, and aging-related pressures on future public spending. Stabilizing the debt-to-GDP ratio at postcrisis levels will require significant adjustment in primary structural balances (by 4 to 5 percentage points of GDP or more if higher debt leads to higher interest rates and lower growth). To create room for fiscal support in the event of future crises and room for rising aging-related spending, debt-to-GDP ratios will have to be brought down. For example, in order for many advanced economies to reduce debt-to-GDP ratios below 60 percent (the median ratio among advanced economies prior to the crisis) by 2030, on average, the structural primary balance would have to improve by 8 percentage points of GDP by 2020 and would have to be maintained at that level for the following decade.

Such sizable adjustment in debt-to-GDP ratios will require substantial expenditure and revenue measures, above and beyond those already announced. The withdrawal of the 2009–10 stimulus measures will not reduce government spending by more than about 1½ percent of GDP. In advanced economies, entitlement spending, which constitutes a large and growing part of the budget, can be changed only gradually, and the extent to which discretionary spending can bear the burden of adjustment in the short term varies as a function of the size of government. However, for many economies revenue increases seem likely to be an inevitable part of medium-term budgetary strategies. These could usefully focus on broadening tax bases, especially by eliminating distortionary exemptions, such as those favoring owner-occupied housing, debt-financed consumption, or use of particular fuels.

Desirable reforms to entitlement spending should be implemented without delay. The longer-term expenditure implications of these programs are huge when aging populations are taken into account (Figure 1.7). As they stand, typical current entitlement programs imply off-balance-sheet liabilities well in excess of actual public debt. Measures such as linking statutory retirement age to life expectancy or improving the efficiency of health care spending would not impede the current recovery and would deal with the longer-term problems.

Strong fiscal policy frameworks and institutions that comprehensively cover the public sector would help support adjustment. Adopting or strengthening fiscal rules with explicit fiscal targets and monitoring by independent fiscal agencies could help shore up the necessary broad consensus for adjustment, anchoring expectations and guiding fiscal policy implementation over the medium term. Related credibility gains, in turn, can help mitigate potential short-term output losses from consolidation. Accordingly, steps in this direction should also be taken without delay.

The fiscal challenges are different for emerging economies, with some important exceptions. Many of the emerging Asian economies entered the crisis with relatively low public debt levels. China, in particular, can afford to maintain an expansionary fiscal stance as it seeks to rebalance externally generated and domestically driven growth, including by expanding subsidized health insurance for rural workers and strengthening its pension system. Other major emerging economies, however, have less fiscal room for maneuver: Brazil and India already have relatively large public sectors and debt, as do a number of Middle Eastern economies. In these and other economies in similar circumstances, new public sector efforts to promote long-term growth and foster social development will have to be funded by making cutbacks in less productive spending or closing loopholes in the revenue base. In sub-Saharan Africa, government spending plans were maintained or increased in the face of lower-than-anticipated revenue in 2009. As recovery is established, the focus of fiscal policy will need to return to medium-term considerations, including debt sustainability.

Monetary and Financial Accommodation Needs to Be Unwound Cautiously, while Managing Capital Inflows

In the major advanced economies, monetary policy can remain accommodative as fiscal consolidation progresses, provided inflation pressure remains subdued. This can be achieved even while central banks begin to withdraw the emergency support provided to banks and financial markets.[8] Some of the support facilities are already winding down as private market activity revives. But the persistence of vulnerabilities may require others to remain in place for some time, including for example, wider eligible collateral assets for central bank credit and programs for purchasing private sector securities and securitized loans, in particular mortgage-backed paper. Central banks that have purchased significant amounts of securities can neutralize the impact of these facilities on monetary conditions by using standard liquidity-absorption techniques—reverse repurchase agreements, open-market sales of treasury bills or central bank paper, and interest-bearing term deposit facilities at central banks.

In major emerging and some advanced economies that are experiencing faster recoveries, central banks have already begun to reduce the degree of monetary accommodation (for example, Australia, China, India, Israel, Malaysia, Norway) or are expected by markets to do so over the coming year (Figure 1.8). Because recovery in these economies is likely to be faster than in major advanced economies, they will probably continue to lead the tightening cycle. In some economies, overcapacity in some sectors and credit-quality deterioration point to the need for further tightening.

In emerging economies with excessive surpluses, monetary tightening should be supported with nominal effective exchange rate appreciation as excess demand pressures build, including in response to continued fiscal support to facilitate demand rebalancing or in response to capital inflows. In others, monetary tightening may be complicated, because it could undermine competi-

tiveness and amplify foreign-currency borrowing. Calls for advanced economies to tighten monetary policy in order to alleviate pressures for appreciation of emerging economy currencies are misguided. First, it is necessary for some major emerging economies to rebalance external and domestic demand, and capital flows help achieve this. Second, differentials in short-term yields are only one among several drivers of capital flows—growth-prospect differentials are important as well, especially for equity flows. And third, fiscal spillovers are likely to be more important than monetary spillovers. The priority in major advanced economies is to put in place sound medium-term fiscal programs; as fiscal support is phased out, tightening monetary policies prematurely could undercut global recovery.

The first-best response would be for both advanced and emerging economies to improve their macroprudential, regulatory, and supervisory frameworks to stem speculative flows. Although this is not a short-term solution, some specific macroprudential measures could be considered (such as limits on foreign-currency loans by banks). If the potential for exchange rate overshooting to undermine competitiveness becomes a concern, economies should consider fiscal tightening to ease pressure on interest rates, some buildup of reserves, and possibly imposing some controls on capital inflows or removing controls on outflows. Any controls on inflows should be designed to accommodate implementation costs, the scope for circumvention in today's financial markets, and the potential for creating new distortions, notably diversion of flows to other economies.[9]

Repairing and Reforming the Financial Sector Is Essential for Sustained Recovery

Alongside fiscal consolidation, more progress with financial sector repair and reform is a top priority for a number of advanced economies. Financial market inefficiencies and regulatory and supervisory failures played a major role in the crisis and need to be remedied to build a stronger financial system. Progress in remedying financial inefficiencies and reforming prudential policies and frameworks will also increase

---

[8] For a discussion of these measures and related policy challenges, see Klyuev, De Imus, and Srinivasan (2009) and IMF (2010b).

[9] For further discussion, see Ostry and others (2010).

the effectiveness of monetary policy and reduce the risk that the ample supply of liquidity accompanying an accommodative monetary policy might find an outlet in renewed speculative distortions.

Reforms of prudential frameworks should ensure that the financial sector plays a greater stabilizing role over the business cycle. Given the increasingly integrated nature of financial markets and institutions, effective repair, reform, and deployment of macroprudential tools will require coordination across countries. These and other challenges are discussed in depth in the April 2010 GFSR.

In the short term, major work is still needed to repair damage wrought by the crisis:

- Bank recapitalization: More capital is required to absorb deterioration in credit quality and to support healthy credit growth in the future in the face of tighter regulatory standards.
- Bank resolution and restructuring: This will facilitate the return to health of the banking system and help avoid further turbulence from weaker institutions as extraordinary policy support is withdrawn.
- Reviving markets for securitized assets: These remain impaired and dependent on official support, yet they have become a normal part of the bank lending process in many advanced economies.

Looking further ahead, much work remains to reestablish market discipline. This can be achieved only through action on a number of fronts: better and more adaptable prudential policies and frameworks, including bank resolution regimes that provide authorities with broad powers to intervene in financial institutions; higher capital requirements; new funding instruments (such as contingent convertible bonds); incentives to keep financial institutions smaller and more manageable; requirements for institution-specific resolution plans; fees to cover bailout costs (ex ante and ex post);[10] and, as needed, direct restrictions on the size and scope of financial activities. Proposals exist to cover all these issues, and the challenge is to meld them together in a way that

enhances the role of the financial system as one of the drivers of growth, including its integration across borders. At the international level, despite improvements made over the years, the crisis has revealed important gaps in supervision, in the process of burden sharing, and in procedures for resolution of failing institutions. These need to be remedied.

There Is a Need to Support Job Creation and the Unemployed

High unemployment poses major social problems. In advanced economies, unemployment is projected to stay close to 8½ percent through 2011 and then to decline only slowly (Figure 1.9). Moreover, the problem is even larger than the statistics suggest. Many of the employed are working shortened hours or in temporary jobs with few benefits. Others would like to find work but have given up searching and are thus no longer recorded as unemployed in the statistics. There is no single measure for broader unemployment or underemployment, but available data suggest that it can often be higher by 25 to 50 percent than headline unemployment rates (see Chapter 3).

The response of unemployment to the sharp declines in output during the crisis has been markedly different across advanced economies. For example, in the United States, the headline unemployment rate increased by about 4 percentage points, but in Germany, the unemployment rate increased only to a limited extent. Chapter 3 finds that these cross-country differences can be explained largely by variations in output declines, institutional differences, and factors such as financial stress and house price busts. Short-time work programs have also been important in dampening the unemployment response in some economies, notably Germany.

Given the expected sluggish recovery in output and the lingering effects of financial stress, the unemployment rate is forecast to remain high through 2011, although employment growth is expected to turn positive in many economies during 2010. Accordingly, a major concern is the potential for temporary joblessness to turn into long-term unemployment and to lower potential output growth. Appropriately stimulative macroeconomic policies are the first line

---

[10] In particular, proposals for a broad-based financial sector tax should aim to charge for the commitment of possible public sector support and align incentives so as to reduce systemic risks.

of defense against such an outcome. The second line is sound restructuring of the banking system: Chapter 3 demonstrates that recoveries from recessions associated with financial crises tend to generate little job growth, largely because of the dependence on bank financing of some employment-intensive sectors (such as construction and small and medium-size enterprises). It follows that restoring the health of the banking system would make an important contribution to employment growth. In addition, policymakers could consider innovative programs that facilitate access to capital markets for small and medium-size enterprises.[11]

Labor market policies are the third line of defense. Adequate unemployment benefits are essential to support confidence among households and to avoid large increases in poverty. Education and training can help reintegrate the unemployed into the labor force. Wage flexibility is important for facilitating a reallocation of labor in economies that have suffered major sectoral shocks. Earned income tax credits and similar programs can facilitate wage adjustment and help mitigate the effects of wage losses on living standards. Insuring individuals against wage losses they might incur when accepting jobs in other sectors or industries could also help in this regard, as Chapter 3 explains.[12]

Other measures, such as temporary subsidies for hiring, can be useful in advancing job creation in this environment of high macroeconomic uncertainty. However, the design of such programs is critical as experience has been mixed: for example, in some cases, a large portion of such subsidies was spent on jobs that would have been created anyway. Some

economies have resorted to subsidizing short-time positions (see Chapter 3); again, these programs may be useful, particularly to the extent that activity is depressed by temporary, confidence-related forces. But their effectiveness and efficiency are likely to diminish over time.

Direct regulatory protection of existing positions may save some jobs in the short term but does little to create jobs over time. Economies that have suffered large losses of temporary employment should consider wholesale reform of employment protection legislation, with a view to breaking down the two-tiered, temporary-versus-permanent nature of some labor markets, which can stand in the way of on-the-job training and productivity growth and can undermine social cohesion. This might involve tightening temporary employment laws but relaxing restrictive permanent employment laws. In so doing, care would have to be taken not to undermine incentives to create jobs early during this recovery.

In most emerging and developing economies, increases in unemployment have generally been more contained than in the advanced economies.[13] However, in a number of these economies a larger portion of unemployment is likely to go unrecorded, and conditions in labor markets are generally worse than headline numbers suggest. In these economies, too, it is important to reduce unemployment and mitigate its harmful consequences. Education and vocational training programs, better job intermediation services, and a well-targeted social safety net can help.

The World's Poorest Economies Coped Better than in the Past

The world's low-income economies have suffered from the crisis, but their economic growth has held up much better than during previous advanced economy recessions. This testifies to their improved policy frameworks, which had boosted precrisis growth rates well above those recorded during the 1990s. Growth in these economies declined from about 7 percent in 2007 to about 4¾ percent in 2009 and is projected to return to about 5½

[11] Policymakers could consider developing new, standardized products to bundle loans or equity for such enterprises and implementing temporary measures to support their placement in markets. However, such products must have strong incentives for careful monitoring of these enterprises' operations.

[12] Individuals are often reluctant to accept wage cuts, and this may be especially relevant for economies that have traditionally seen relatively large nominal wage increases or experienced a long period of strong labor market conditions; or, at the microeconomic level, for long-tenured workers in declining industries (for example, in the automobile and steel sectors). Currently, insurance is offered only for (no-fault) unemployment—that is, a total rather than partial wage loss. This can undermine the incentive to accept lower-paying jobs. For further discussion, see Babcock and others (2009).

[13] Important exceptions are many countries in emerging Europe and the CIS.

percent in 2010.[14] Nonetheless, the fallout from the slowdown in terms of increased poverty has been significant. Estimates suggest that by the end of 2010, 64 million more people will have slipped into extreme poverty than without the crisis.[15] Many of these economies may find it harder to gain or regain access to foreign financing for development purposes. This puts a premium on developing their domestic financial systems. At the same time, advanced economies must maintain their development aid, even as they embark on major fiscal consolidation programs.

Global Demand Rebalancing: The Role of Credibility and Policy Coordination

For the world economy to sustain a high growth trajectory, the economies that had excessive external deficits before the crisis need to consolidate their public finances in ways that limit damage to potential growth and demand while restructuring their financial sectors to avoid renewed speculative excesses. Economies with excessive surpluses need to develop new sources of demand, as economies with excessive deficits scale back their imports in response to lower expectations about future income. IMF staff projections show that relative to precrisis trends, output losses by 2015 in economies with excessive external deficits before the crisis—which together account for roughly 27 percent of world GDP—will amount to about 15 percent of 2007 GDP (Figure 1.16).

Global demand rebalancing is not a new issue. Chapter 4 reviews the historical experience of economies with large surpluses. Germany, for example, ran globally significant current account surpluses in the late 1960s and early 1970s, which, as a share of global current account balances, were similar to those of China today (roughly 20 percent).[16] Germany too faced pressures to rebalance and did so successfully

---

[14] The economies comprise those that are eligible for access to the IMF's Poverty Reduction and Growth Trust (PRGT). During the major advanced economy recessions of the early 1980s, growth in PRGT economies fell below 2 percent; during the recessions of the early 1990s, output stagnated.

[15] See World Bank (2010).

[16] However, the total size of current account imbalances was smaller than today because capital markets were much less developed.

Figure 1.16. Medium-Term Growth Prospects and Precrisis Currency Valuations[1]

(Index, 2006 = 100)

All countries are facing lower growth prospects than before the crisis. However, countries that were judged to have overvalued currencies before the crisis and thus excessive external deficits have seen a larger downgrade of medium-term growth prospects than countries whose currencies were judged to be aligned or undervalued. Large increases in private savings in countries with currencies that were overvalued before the crisis are playing a major role in lowering potential growth.

Spring 2007 WEO (right scale)   April 2010 WEO (right scale)
Output loss (percent of 2007 GDP; left scale)

Source: IMF staff calculations.
[1]Based on the IMF staff's Consultative Group on Exchange Rate Issues (CGER). CGER countries include Argentina, Australia, Brazil, Canada, Chile, China, Colombia, Czech Republic, euro area, Hungary, India, Indonesia, Israel, Japan, Korea, Malaysia, Mexico, Pakistan, Poland, Russia, South Africa, Sweden, Switzerland, Thailand, Turkey, United Kingdom, and United States. Hungary is not included in the current WEO private national savings calculation. For a detailed discussion of the methodology for the calculation of exchange rates' over- or undervaluation, see Lee and others (2008).
[2]These countries account for 25.5 percent of global GDP.
[3]These countries account for 32.7 percent of global GDP.
[4]These countries account for 27.0 percent of global GDP.

during the 1970s. Studying a broad range of experiences in advanced and emerging economies, Chapter 4 finds that reversing current account surpluses has typically not been associated with losses in economic growth: policy-driven surplus reversals (and related exchange rate appreciations) are only one among many determinants of economic growth and are generally not decisive.[17] In some cases, expansionary macroeconomic policies helped boost domestic demand as foreign demand fell in response to exchange rate appreciations;[18] in other cases, exchange rate appreciation helped stem overheating; in still others, economies adopted broader structural reforms or their exports climbed the product quality ladder.

Compared with earlier periods, imbalances are now much larger, and successful global demand rebalancing will require more significant actions in both deficit and surplus economies. Policymakers will need to exploit macroeconomic and structural policy synergies, especially for fiscal consolidation in economies with external deficits.

Regarding macroeconomic policies, exit from accommodative fiscal positions is more of a concern for economies with excessive external deficits than for those with external surpluses. This exit should be achieved with measures that do not undermine potential growth—for example, through reforms to entitlement spending, increases in consumption and fuel taxes, and elimination of distortions that lower private saving, foster leverage, and boost investment in real estate. In economies with excessive external surpluses and room for policy maneuvers, fiscal policy can remain accommodative. In major emerging economies with large surpluses, fiscal measures could usefully be targeted toward improved programs for health care, pensions, and education. As the currencies of economies with excessive deficits depreciate, then logically those of surplus economies must appreciate. It would be preferable to achieve this by adjustments to nominal exchange rates than by adjustments to prices, as the latter typically takes much longer.

Regarding structural policies, financial sector reforms are the key to preventing new boom-bust cycles in both advanced and emerging economies, especially in those with excessive external deficits. A number of these economies also need to reform labor and product markets, rebuild competitiveness, and accelerate job growth, notably those with limited room for monetary or fiscal policy maneuvers (for example, some euro area and emerging European economies). In advanced and emerging economies with excessive external surpluses and high domestic saving rates, structural policies need to support domestic demand and the development of nontradables sectors. Particularly in emerging economies, regulatory frameworks for services and financial markets, including corporate governance, need further development to improve the efficiency of investment.

The benefits of a comprehensive and consistent set of macroeconomic and structural policies in terms of world growth can be illustrated with two sets of scenarios (Figures 1.17a and 1.17b).[19]

- In one set of scenarios (Figure 1.17a), fiscal-deficit-to-GDP ratios are eventually reduced relative to the baseline by about 3 percentage points in the United States and Japan and by 2 percentage points in the euro area. The measures comprise cutbacks in transfers and government consumption, significant hikes in consumption taxes, and reductions in labor and capital income taxes that are designed to raise potential output. The fiscal measures are implemented as one package gradually over five years. Crucially, in one scenario they are assumed to be fully credible immediately; in others, credibility grows as implementation proceeds. As the figure shows, with full credibility, real GDP in the United States and euro area is actually higher than in the absence of fiscal adjustment, because lower labor and capital taxes stimulate investment and employment. With limited but growing credibility, investment is postponed, employment and consumption weaken, and real GDP stays below the baseline for some time.

---

[17] By contrast, a large literature emphasizes that trade openness is key for growth.

[18] During a second rebalancing episode in Japan in the mid-1980s, overly expansionary demand policies may have contributed to the asset price bubble.

[19] These scenarios have been developed using the IMF staff's Globally Integrated Monetary and Fiscal (GIMF) Model. See Kumhof and others (2010).

- The second set of scenarios (Figure 1.17b) illustrates the benefits of additional policies designed to raise potential output and rebalance global demand, relative to a fiscal-adjustment scenario where full credibility is achieved gradually. China adopts structural reforms to raise productivity in the nontradables sector, lower household and corporate saving, and allow its nominal effective exchange rate to appreciate. In addition, the euro area, Japan, and other economies adopt a variety of reforms to raise potential growth, leading agents to save somewhat less in anticipation of higher incomes in the future. These reforms noticeably raise GDP relative to the fiscal-adjustment scenario, and—significantly—they lead to higher output relative to the baseline in all economies.

The key point to take away from these simulations is that the major challenges facing policymakers can be addressed in ways that enhance medium-term growth prospects and thereby limit damage to output in the short term. Much depends on the specific policy measures and their credibility. In this regard, the benefits of strong fiscal policy frameworks and institutions that support credibility could be substantial in economies that need to consolidate and reform their public finances, even if credibility gains in the short term will probably not be large enough to forestall some output loss from fiscal adjustment.

Appendix 1.1. Commodity Market Developments and Prospects

The authors of this appendix are Kevin Cheng, Nese Erbil, Thomas Helbling, Shaun Roache, and Marina Rousset.

Following their collapse in the wake of the financial crisis, commodity prices bottomed out in February 2009 and staged a sharp rebound thereafter. By the end of 2009, the IMF commodity index had risen more than 40 percent from its trough, largely on account of large increases in petroleum prices (over 70 percent) and metal prices (about 60 percent) (Figure 1.18, top panel). Despite these gains, however, at the end of 2009 the IMF commodity index in real terms was still 25 percent below its peak level of July 2008 (Table 1.2). With global economic and financial conditions improving

Figure 1.17a. Fiscal Consolidation Packages Designed to Raise Potential Output under Different Assumptions about Credibility
(Percent deviation from control)

The medium-term effects of fiscal consolidation in the advanced economies will depend on the expenditure and tax instruments that are used. Some illustrative simulations with the Global Integrated Monetary Fiscal (GIMF) Model show that fiscal policies designed to raise potential output (lower taxes on capital and labor and higher taxes on consumption goods) could be successful in raising world output in the short term if they result in large downward revisions in expectations for future levels of debt and taxes on capital and labor. The simulations have been constructed under different assumptions about credibility to show the implications if agents are initially skeptical that the policies will be followed.

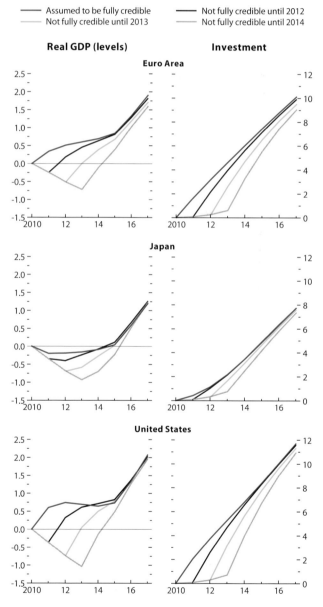

Source: Global Integrated Monetary Fiscal Model simulations.

Figure 1.17b. Scenarios Designed to Raise Potential Output and Reduce Government Deficits

Based on the IMF's multicountry GIMF Model, some scenarios have been developed to illustrate the benefits of supporting fiscal consolidation with structural policies designed to increase investment and potential output.

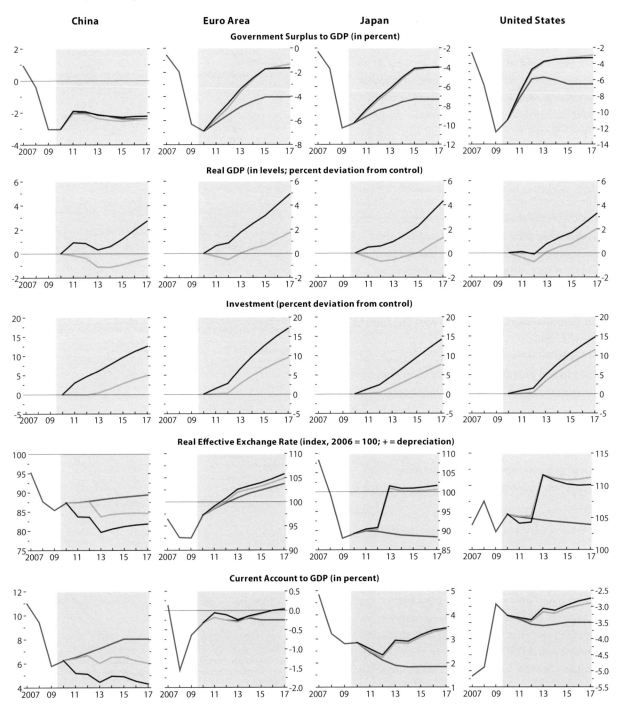

Source: Global Integrated Monetary Fiscal Model.

through 2009, commodity price volatility normalized after rising sharply during the Great Recession.

The sharp decline and subsequent rebound in commodity prices over the past year and a half is in notable contrast to previous global downturns and recoveries. Box 1.2 presents detailed IMF staff analysis comparing this cycle with earlier episodes. The conclusion is that a number of factors help explain why commodities have recovered more quickly and more extensively during this recovery. Most notable are the stronger-than-expected global recovery and the increasingly important role of emerging and developing economies in global commodity markets. In particular, the pace of recovery has been far quicker than anticipated in emerging Asian economies, where consumption of commodities has grown fastest in recent years. Another factor is smaller increases in excess inventories relative to average stock-use ratios (the commodity market equivalent of inventory-to-sales ratios) for many commodities. In addition, the U.S. dollar depreciation during this recovery and steady, low real U.S. interest rates stand in contrast to previous cycles, when real interest rates steadily increased and the U.S. dollar appreciated.

Despite the rapid price rebounds during this global recovery, a number of key commodity markets remain in contango, with spot prices below futures prices, suggesting the absorption of excess inventories after the global recession—the inventory adjustment process—is ongoing. As discussed in Box 1.3, the slow adjustment is not unusual. Following previous recessions, it often took futures curves some time—ranging from about three months to well over a year—to revert to their typical shape during "normal" market conditions. The typical slope of a futures curve varies by commodity, reflecting a range of factors, including the relative proportion of hedging by producers and consumers, the costs of storage, and the speed with which new supply can be brought to the market during periods when inventories are low. Despite these differences, when the physical market moves into a period of unexpectedly abundant supply, as it did during the Great Recession, commodity futures curves all tend to steepen markedly, with the spot and

Figure 1.18. Commodity and Petroleum Prices

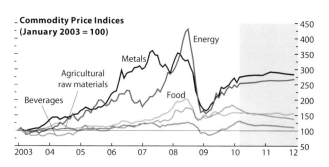

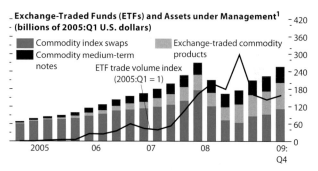

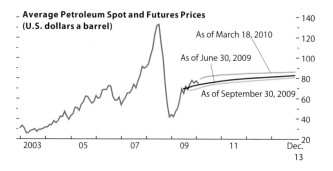

Sources: Barclays Capital; Bloomberg Financial Markets; and IMF staff estimates.
[1]The current dollar figures provided by Barclays Capital were deflated by the IMF commodity price index to take out the effect of valuation changes due to commodity price movements.
[2]The Continuous Commodity Index is a futures contract on a composite of 17 commodity futures prices (equally weighted), which is traded at the New York Board of Trade. Price prospects are based on prices of futures options as of March 10, 2010.

Table 1.2. Commodity Real Price Developments

(Real commodity price indices, monthly; average 1990–99=100)

	December 2009	Peak March 2008	Trough February 2009	Average 2000–09
Commodity Price Index	172.1	230.6	123.2	133.6
Nonfuel	106.2	131.4	85.2	89.0
Food	97.4	122.7	88.9	82.6
Beverages	120.1	110.7	99.6	77.6
Industrial Inputs	114.2	143.7	79.4	97.6
Agricultural Raw Materials	73.8	77.7	58.9	75.2
Metal	162.3	222.3	103.9	124.3
Fuel	271.9	380.9	180.7	201.1
Crude Oil	283.5	392.6	161.5	203.3

Commodity Real Price Volatility (percent)[1]

	2009	2008	2000–09	1991–99
Commodity Price Index	5.2	10.0	5.2	4.0
Nonfuel	2.7	6.0	2.8	1.7
Food	3.8	6.2	3.2	2.2
Beverages	3.0	7.0	4.6	6.0
Industrial Inputs	4.1	6.4	3.7	2.2
Agricultural Raw Materials	4.1	4.4	3.1	2.7
Metal	5.2	8.1	4.9	3.7
Fuel	7.2	12.5	7.5	5.5
Crude Oil	8.5	13.9	8.8	9.2

Sources: IMF commodity price database; and IMF staff calculations.

[1]Volatility is calculated using the standard deviation of monthly changes in real commodity price indices (deflated by the U.S. consumer price index).

near-term futures prices falling by more than longer-dated futures prices.

On the financial front, investment inflows into commodity-related assets rose sharply during 2009, reflecting the continued relative attractiveness of this asset class (Figure 1.18, second panel). According to estimates by market participants, commodity-related assets under management reached $257 billion at the end of 2009—only slightly below their all-time peak in 2008. However, despite these inflows, there remains little evidence that financial investment has a significant sustained impact on commodity prices above and beyond current and expected supply-demand fundamentals. If anything, inflows tend to follow changes in fundamentals and prices, rather than the other way around. Recent disaggregated data from the U.S. Commodities Futures Trading Commission, which allow for a more comprehensive analysis of the impact of financial investors, support this view.

Near-term commodity price prospects depend importantly on the timing and strength of the global recovery. Upward price pressures from a further strengthening of demand will continue as global growth accelerates. Such pressures, however, will likely be moderated by high spare capacity and supply responses to the price rebound, albeit to varying degrees depending on the commodity. Furthermore, normalization of policy interest rates will likely raise the cost of inventory holdings, thereby reducing the incentive to hold inventories. For commodity markets, the policy normalization in emerging economies—where output gaps have been closing faster than in advanced economies—will be particularly relevant. As noted, these economies have been the main contributors to incremental demand, including, in many instances, for stock-holding purposes.

Information from commodity option and futures prices suggests that investors and hedgers anticipate future price increases to be gradual and that they still see little probability of another commodity price spike, notwithstanding the recent uptick in prices (Figure 1.18, third panel). Nevertheless, some upside price risks remain, particularly if the global recovery continues to be more buoyant than expected. Other risk factors include heightened geopolitical tensions, major supply disruptions, abrupt increases in desired inventory stocks, and an unexpected depreciation of the U.S. dollar.

Over the medium term, commodity prices are projected to remain high by historical standards. Commodity demand is expected to grow again rapidly as the global recovery takes hold, whereas spare capacity and inventory buffers will likely decline over time. The tension between rapid demand and sluggish capacity growth is therefore likely to reemerge once the global recovery matures into a sustained expansion, thereby keeping prices at elevated levels by historical standards, as discussed in previous issues of the *World Economic Outlook*.

Oil and Other Energy Markets

After recovering rapidly from their crisis lows in the second quarter of 2009, oil prices have largely remained range-bound since mid-2009, fluctuating

Box 1.2. How Unusual Is the Current Commodity Price Recovery?

The sharp rebound in commodity prices in the wake of the most severe global recession in the period since World War II has taken many observers by surprise. How unusual was this rebound, given the experience with previous global downturns and recoveries? If it was unusual, what factors could explain the differences in recent commodity price behavior? This box addresses these questions. Specifically, it compares real commodity price and inventory behavior during this downturn-and-recovery cycle with previous cycles, including their relationship with other economic and financial indicators.

Relevant historical episodes were identified using turning points in advanced economy industrial production, for which monthly data were available for the sample period 1950–2009.[1] This measure of the business cycle excludes emerging economies, which are increasingly important commodity consumers. However, given that advanced economies accounted for a large share of world output during much of the sample period, this measure should accurately identify the turning points in global business cycles.

Examining previous downturns and recoveries in commodity prices suggests the following stylized facts about real commodity price and inventory behavior during such episodes.

- Commodity prices and industrial production, on average, tend to peak at about the same time before the trough in the cycle (at 13 and 15 months, respectively), but commodity prices experience larger declines, falling by more than 20 percent compared with about 8 percent for industrial production (first figure).[2]

The main authors of this box are Shaun Roache and Marina Rousset.

[1]The Bry-Boschan cycle-dating routine was used to identify turning points. Industrial production data were used for the United States from 1950 through 1959. See Cashin, McDermott, and Scott (2002) for a similar approach.

[2]Commodity prices are measured using an equally weighted index of beverages, energy, food, metals, and raw materials. The most important commodities in each group (three beverages, three energy commodities, six food crops, six metals, and three raw materials) were also equally weighted within each group. Before the IMF index start date of January 1957, the equally weighted Commodity Research Bureau index was used.

Commodity Price Cycles: Past and Present (1950–2010)

(U.S. dollar index = 100 at trough in advanced economy industrial production (IP) on y-axis, months from trough in advanced economy IP on x-axis)

Commodity prices: ——Current - - - Six-cycle average

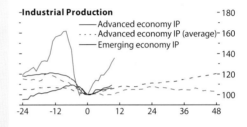

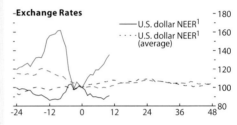

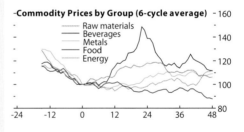

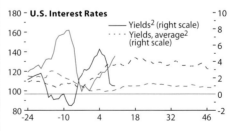

Sources: Bloomberg Financial Markets; Global Financial Data; IMF commodity price database; and IMF staff calculations.
[1]Nominal effective exchange rate.
[2]Real three-month Treasury bill yields.

Box 1.2 *(continued)*

Inventory and Spare Capacity Cycles
(Percentage point difference from trend)

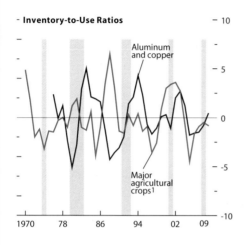

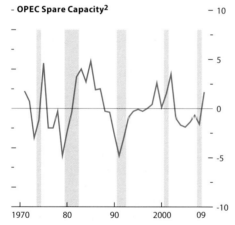

Sources: Energy Information Administration; International Energy Agency; United States Department of Agriculture; World Bureau of Metal Statistics; and IMF staff estimates.
[1]Includes corn (maize), rice, soybeans, and wheat.
[2]As percent of global consumption. OPEC = Organization of Petroleum Exporting Countries.

- During the recovery phase, which is measured from the trough in industrial production, commodity prices have tended to rise at a relatively gradual rate; after 12 and 18 months, they increase by about 2 percent and 5 percent, whereas industrial

production increases by 8 percent over both horizons (second figure).
- Exchange rates and real U.S. interest rates may explain part of the weak commodity price response to recovery during earlier episodes. Over the previous six cycles, the U.S. dollar appreciated and real interest rates rose, on average, one to two years after the start of the recovery, both of which would tend to lower commodity prices, other things being equal.
- In terms of types of commodities, industrial production recovers faster than prices for the majority of the individual commodity groups one to three years after the start of the recovery. The exceptions are beverages and raw materials, for which prices rise by more than industrial production one to two years after recovery.
- In terms of the supply-demand balance, inventory-to-consumption ratios typically increase during downturns in industrial production, peak sometime after the trough, and then typically fall. Based on year-end annual data starting in 1976, the inventory-to-use ratio for base metals (aluminum and copper) rose by about 7½ percentage points compared with its trend level, on average, for the three downturns corresponding most closely to the cycles in 1980–82, 1991–92, and 2001 (second figure).[3] For major agricultural crops (corn, rice, soybeans, wheat), this same ratio increased by about 2 percentage points to reach about 1½ percentage points above trend during four cycles since 1970. For crude oil, OPEC spare capacity increased by 4¾ percentage points relative to trend during the downturns, although the size of these changes has fallen significantly since the 1980s.

Set against these historical precedents, it becomes clear that for commodity prices, the current cycle is different.

- Prices fell much further and faster during the Great Recession and have subsequently recovered far more quickly. Compared with an

---

[3]The trend was derived using a Hodrick-Prescott filter. The ratios were extrapolated beyond 2009 using forecasts of the first differences from an ARIMA (*p*,*q*) model selected by information criteria to reduce end-point bias.

average cycle, commodity prices dropped by three times the usual amount in a quarter of the usual time.

- During the current recovery, commodity prices have rebounded more quickly, rising by 33 percent since the trough (as of February 2010) compared with the near 7 percent and 9 percent increases in advanced economy and emerging economy industrial production, respectively (as of December 2009).
- The behavior of supply-demand balances during this cycle has been similar to previous episodes in terms of direction, with inventories and spare capacity both rising. However, the increases in stock-use ratios have tended to be smaller, except in oil markets, and most commodity markets appear not to have moved into a state of extreme oversupply, as in previous recessions. The ratio for major crops, for example, has increased by 3¼ percentage points from its low point in 2005, but since the onset of the recession it has remained largely unchanged.

A number of factors may help explain why commodity prices have recovered faster and by more during this recovery. One may be that the initial decline was so abrupt and steep that prices overshot on the downside, so that the subsequent rebound simply reflects an adjustment from oversold conditions. However, this does not explain the underlying fundamental forces that could have caused the V-shaped recovery in prices. One explanation for this is the stronger-than-expected recovery in global demand, which was driven largely by extraordinary macroeconomic policy support. A second is the changing structure of commodity demand, with emerging economies accounting for an increasing share of global consumption across a range of commodities, and the lead role of emerging economies, in the recovery. In particular, the pace of recovery in emerging Asia, where consumption of commodities has grown fastest in recent years, has been far quicker than anticipated.

The decline and recovery of commodity prices have been more synchronized with equity markets in the current cycle than in the past, which may lead some observers to identify financial investment as a possible explanation. Increased comovement, however, likely reflects the sensitivity of both markets to broader economic developments. Although the scale of the price changes during this cycle has been large, other market developments, including changes in the slopes of futures curves and the buildup of inventories, have been within the range of historical experience. This indicates that demand- and supply-related fundamentals, rather than financial investment, continue to play the dominant role in commodity price formation.

The rapid rebound of growth in emerging economies and the relatively weaker pickup in advanced economy demand have also affected other commodity price fundamentals. Specifically, the U.S. dollar has depreciated since the trough in industrial production, particularly against some emerging economy currencies, while U.S. real interest rates have remained low (the rise just before and after the trough in industrial production largely reflects the effects of rising and falling oil prices on headline inflation). This is in sharp contrast to previous cycles—particularly in the 1980s—in which real interest rates steadily increased and the U.S. dollar appreciated.

between $70 and $80 a barrel (Figure 1.18, lower panel), although they have traded above that range since early April 2010. The bounded fluctuations have reflected opposing effects from the adjustment of oil demand and supply to the normalization of global economic and financial conditions, respectively.

Price support at the lower end of the band stemmed from the rebound in global oil consump-

tion as the recovery in global activity progressed (Figure 1.19, top left panel). On an annual basis, the International Energy Agency estimates that global oil demand fell by 1.3 million barrels a day (mbd) in 2009, a 1½ percent decline (Table 1.3). This reduction is somewhat larger than expected, given the usual relationship between global oil demand and global GDP—the elasticity is slightly below ½

Box 1.3. Commodity Futures Price Curves and Cyclical Market Adjustment

Inventory cycles for commodities reflect shifting supply-demand balances, and in many cases, the global business cycle explains much of their variation. During recessions, inventories typically increase as demand unexpectedly weakens, and the Great Recession was no exception, with stockpiles climbing across a broad range of commodities. These fluctuations in inventories influence the shape of futures price curves, because spot prices tend to be more sensitive to current physical market conditions than futures prices, which are more strongly influenced by expectations about the future. In particular, as inventories build through economic downturns, spot prices fall by more than futures prices, leading the curve to steepen and move into "contango." In contrast, during periods when demand is unexpectedly strong and inventories fall to relatively low levels, as they did for many commodities during 2007–08, spot prices rise above futures prices, resulting in an inverted price curve referred to as "backwardation" (the first figure shows for aluminum the difference between the spot price and price on a futures contract for delivery in six months discounted by interest rates). This box explores the behavior of these futures price curves in more detail, focusing on how they adjust following a shock. It also provides evidence that inventory levels play a key role in the adjustment process. The analysis focuses on six base metals (aluminum, copper, lead, nickel, tin, zinc) for which inventory data are available at a daily frequency for 1997–2009.

Unlike financial assets, for which interest rate arbitrage determines the relationship between spot and futures prices, the slope of commodity price curves incorporates storage costs and a convenience yield in addition to interest rates. The convenience yield is often defined as the marginal benefit that accrues to the inventory holder from holding an additional unit of the physical good—for example, for a manufacturer that uses commodities as an input, the ability to avoid input shortages and production shutdowns. This results in spot prices being higher relative to the futures price than in the absence of such a benefit. These marginal ben-

The authors of this box are Shaun Roache and Nese Erbil.

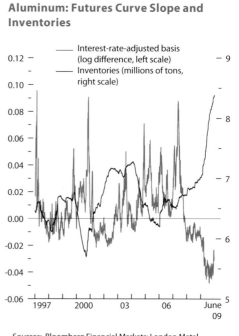

Aluminum: Futures Curve Slope and Inventories

Sources: Bloomberg Financial Markets; London Metal Exchange; and IMF staff calculations.

efits are often assumed to be decreasing in the level of inventories; in other words, an extra unit of the commodity is much more valuable when stocks are low than when stocks are high. This implies that the effect of changes in current or expected future inventory levels will affect the convenience yield and the shape of the futures price curve differently depending on the initial inventory level.

It is possible to consider a market that is "normal" in terms of the average relationships between spot prices, futures prices, interest rates, and inventories given that cointegration tests for base metals indicate that these variables share a stable long-term relationship. Taking interest rates as exogenous, this means that when the relationship between these market variables deviates from normal, often due to a shock in the supply-demand balance that causes the difference between spot and futures prices to change, prices and inventories will adjust over time back toward their long-term equilibrium.

Empirical evidence suggests that the adjustment toward long-term equilibrium varies with the market conditions prevailing when markets are hit by a shock. In other words, there are nonlinearities in the adjustment process. Specifically, tests for so-called threshold behavior suggest that the speed of adjustment toward long-term equilibrium varies depending on the initial slope of the futures curve.[1] The tests suggest that there are three different adjustment regimes present in major metals markets. When the futures curve is backwardated (typically because inventory levels are relatively low), the adjustment tends to be more rapid than when the curve is in steep contango (which often signals that supply is abundant and inventories are relatively high).[2] For a 1 percentage point shock to the futures curve (imposed as simultaneous and opposing shocks to spot and six-month futures prices), the time taken for half the initial shock to dissipate is approximately twice as long compared with a situation when the market is initially in contango (referred to as regime 1 in the second figure) than when the market is in backwardation (regime 3).

The diminishing marginal utility of inventories—and its effects on the convenience yield—is likely to be the mechanism driving these results. In particular, when backwardated, the market is providing strong incentives for market participants without an immediate business need for the physical commodity to sell at prevailing spot prices. For producers, this could be interpreted as an incentive to increase production and deliver supply immediately to the spot market, whereas for consumers it may weaken demand, all of which would serve to raise usable inventories back to "normal" levels. The change in expectations for inventory levels would then have a relatively large effect on convenience yields and cause spot prices to fall rapidly lower toward futures prices. In contrast,

[1] Two tests for nonlinearity of the adjustment process were used: the ordered autoregression approach of Tsay (1989) and the Andrews-Quandt breakpoint procedure.

[2] Results are from a vector error-correction model in which spot prices, futures prices, and inventories are endogenous variables. The adjustments were calculated using impulse responses from simultaneous and opposing shocks applied to the reduced-form residuals of the spot price and futures price equations. Confidence intervals for the half-life adjustment duration were calculated using 500 bootstrapped replications.

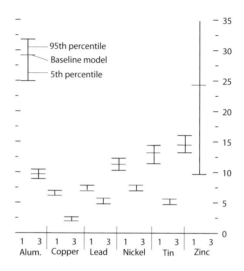

Half-life of 1 Percentage Point Futures Curve Shock[1]
(Six-month maturity; commodity and regime (1 or 3) on the x-axis, days on the y-axis)

Source: IMF staff estimates.
[1] The y-axis has been truncated at 35 days, and zinc is the outlier, with a 95th percentile value close to 50.

when in steep contango there are strong incentives for producers to curtail production and for other market participants to buy in the spot market, hold inventory, and hedge their position using futures contracts. These responses would serve to reduce usable inventories, but if the effect of these changes on convenience yields is smaller than in backwardation, then the slope of the futures curve would be relatively insensitive.[3] In other words, consistent with the results from the analysis of base metals, the market would remain in steep contango for longer—in some cases significantly longer—than in the case of backwardation.

Futures price curves have been in steep contango across a broad range of commodities since the third quarter of 2008. Compared with previous recessions, the duration of this contango

[3] Inventories tied up in financing deals for arbitrage trades are often not available for immediate use, and this serves to reduce usable inventory levels.

Box 1.3 *(continued)*

has not been especially long, underscoring the extent to which these conditions can persist. However, contango has been particularly steep across a number of commodities, including base metals and crude oil, reflecting the size of the initial demand shock. Curves have begun to flatten in recent months in many cases, in part due to the recovery in demand and evidence that the inventory cycle has decisively turned lower (for example, crude oil) or has started to flatten (for example, base metals). Further gradual adjustment toward "normal" market conditions is likely over coming quarters, conditional on continued global economic recovery. However, as inventory levels for many commodities are still relatively low for this point in the cycle from a long-term perspective, there are upside risks for prices and for renewed backwardation looking further ahead.

based on data for 1985–2008—considering the 36½ percent decline in oil prices over the same period. The sharper-than-expected decline was the result of a strong demand contraction in Organization for Economic Cooperation and Development economies. In contrast, consumption in emerging and developing economies rose by 1.8 percent, somewhat more than expected based on GDP elasticities and actual growth outcomes in these economies.

Price pressure at the upper end of the band was capped by the recovery in global oil production from the lows recorded in the second quarter of 2009. Higher production by both Organization of Petroleum Exporting Countries (OPEC) and non-OPEC suppliers contributed to the improvement. Production by the economies in OPEC, which are subject to production quotas, increased by some 0.6 mbd from the lows reached in January 2009 (Figure 1.19, top right panel). Quota discipline has thus fallen below 60 percent, but the quotas have not yet been revised in light of firming oil market conditions.

Non-OPEC supply also increased in 2009 rather than falling, as had been expected early in the year after the persistent weakness in recent years (Figure 1.19, second row, left panel). Higher U.S. production, mainly from new offshore capacity coming onstream in the Gulf of Mexico, and a recovery in production in Russia were the main sources of improved non-OPEC supply. The latter seems to have reflected, in part, expectations of tax cuts on exports from eastern Siberian fields, one of the new frontiers in Russian oil production.

Turning to market balances, the supply rebound has lagged the demand recovery, and the global oil market has gradually moved from excess supply with inventory accumulation in early 2009 toward more balanced demand supply, with a decrease in excess inventories. OPEC spare capacity, however, has not yet decreased from the high reached during the recession despite some production increases through 2009, as new capacity has come onstream (Figure 1.19, second row, right panel). On the price side, this adjustment was reflected in a decline in the spread between futures and spot prices, whereas on the physical market, it was reflected in a decline in excess inventories (inventories above five-year average levels). Even so, the adjustment is not yet complete. The oil futures curve has not yet returned to the usual state of "backwardation" (a downward-sloping futures curve).

The near-term outlook for oil prices depends importantly on the interaction between upward pressure from demand increases as global growth accelerates in 2010 and the supply response. Indeed, the recent rise in prices above the $70 to $80 range has largely reflected expectations of accelerating global economic growth and stronger-than-expected oil demand increases. With both OPEC spare capacity and OECD inventories still above recent historical averages, upward price pressure should remain moderate for some time, barring any significant change to the medium-term outlook. Even so, the call on OPEC (difference between global demand and non-OPEC supply) is expected to increase markedly in 2010, and the price dynamics will depend on producers' readiness to tap their spare capacity.

Looking to the medium term, the oil price outlook depends on prospects for maintaining sustainable demand-supply balances. On the supply side, oil discovery developments have been promising. In the first half of 2009, reported findings of new oil deposits were about 10 billion barrels, the highest rate (annualized) since the late 1990s. The rise in the rate of new discoveries is not surprising, given recent increases in the net value of oil reserves and the corresponding incentives for exploration (Figure 1.19, third row, left panel). In this respect, the price collapse in late 2008 turned out to be mostly a temporary setback, as oil prices recovered much of the losses, while investment costs decreased. Indeed, the Baker-Hughes international oil rig count has already recovered some of the losses of late 2008 and early 2009.

Although discovery developments have been encouraging, they do not address all supply concerns. The main bottlenecks in recent years have been the slow development of new fields and the maintenance of existing fields. The main reasons are long time-to-build lags, especially at the technological frontier, but also unfavorable investment regimes in many economies. There is some hope, however, that the higher oil prices and the increased value of oil reserves will boost oil sector investment. The substantial rise in capital expenditure by oil companies in recent years suggests that higher prices have already had some effect.

On the consumption side, oil consumption is projected to expand at a robust pace in emerging and developing economies, notwithstanding efficiency gains from declining energy intensity (Figure 1.19, third row, right panel). Another factor that will affect the longer-term demand for all fuels is the recent changes in the structure of relative energy prices (Figure 1.19, bottom panel). In contrast with oil prices, natural gas prices in the United States and Canada have recovered only a small share of the losses sustained during 2008–09, given rapid production growth resulting from technological advances in extracting natural gas from shale deposits. On the other hand, international coal prices have rebounded strongly with the emergence of China as a net importer.

Metals

Metals posted the second largest price rebound (after petroleum) among all commodity groups in

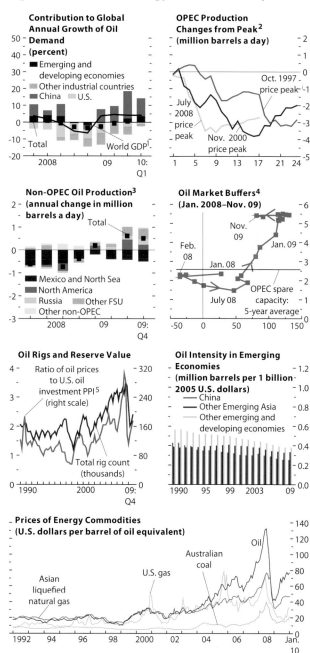

Figure 1.19. World Energy Market Developments

Sources: Baker Hughes; Bloomberg Financial Markets; IMF Primary Commodity Price System; International Energy Agency; and IMF staff calculations.
[1]Annual change in percent.
[2]Organization of Petroleum Exporting Countries (OPEC) membership as of the first month of each episode. Months from oil price peak on x-axis.
[3]North Sea: Norway and United Kingdom. North America: United States and Canada. Other FSU: other former Soviet Union.
[4]Organization for Economic Cooperation and Development stocks—deviations from five-year average (million barrels) on x-axis, OPEC spare capacity (million barrels a day) on y-axis.
[5]Averages of U.S. Producer Price Index (PPI) is for oil and gas well drilling services, oil and gas support services, and oil and gas machinery and equipment.

Table 1.3. Global Oil Demand and Production by Region

(Millions of barrels a day)

	2008	2009	2010 Proj.	2009 H1	2009 H2	Year-over-Year Percent Change 2003–05 Avg.	2006	2007	2008	2009	2010 Proj.	2009 H1	2009 H2
Demand													
OECD[1]	47.6	45.5	45.4	45.5	45.4	1.3	−0.6	−0.7	−3.3	−4.4	−0.2	−5.5	−3.3
North America	24.2	23.3	23.4	23.2	23.4	2.0	−0.8	0.4	−5.1	−3.6	0.5	−5.6	−1.6
Of Which:													
United States	19.8	19.1	19.1	19.0	19.1	1.7	−0.5	−0.1	−5.9	−3.7	0.1	−5.7	−1.6
Europe	15.3	14.5	14.4	14.6	14.4	0.7	0.1	−2.1	0.0	−5.4	−0.7	−4.0	−6.8
Pacific	8.1	7.7	7.6	7.7	7.6	0.4	−1.6	−1.0	−3.6	−4.8	−1.5	−7.9	−1.5
Non-OECD	38.6	39.5	41.2	38.7	40.2	4.4	4.0	4.4	3.5	2.1	4.5	0.3	3.9
Of Which:													
China	7.9	8.5	9.1	8.1	8.9	10.1	8.3	4.4	4.3	7.8	7.2	2.5	13.0
Other Asia	9.7	10.0	10.3	10.0	9.9	3.2	2.7	5.7	1.2	3.0	3.0	1.2	4.9
Former Soviet Union	4.2	3.9	4.1	3.8	4.0	1.2	2.9	2.7	0.1	−5.9	5.0	−7.4	−4.4
Middle East	7.1	7.2	7.6	7.0	7.5	4.8	4.4	3.2	8.6	2.0	4.9	1.2	2.6
Africa	3.2	3.2	3.3	3.2	3.1	4.0	0.5	4.0	3.8	−0.3	3.1	0.9	−1.4
Latin America	5.9	6.0	6.2	5.8	6.1	2.4	3.4	5.5	3.8	0.9	3.5	0.1	1.7
World	86.2	84.9	86.6	84.3	85.6	2.5	1.2	1.5	−0.3	−1.5	2.0	−2.9	0.0
Production													
OPEC (current composition)[2,3]	35.6	33.3	34.6	33.1	33.6	6.2	0.8	−1.0	2.9	−6.4	…	−7.6	−5.2
Of Which:													
Saudi Arabia	10.4	9.3	…	9.3	9.3	7.5	−1.2	−4.7	4.2	−10.5	…	−10.5	−10.5
Nigeria	2.1	2.1	…	2.0	2.2	6.0	−4.4	−4.7	−8.2	−0.4	…	−4.1	3.0
Venezuela	2.6	2.4	…	2.3	2.4	1.6	−5.8	−7.8	−2.0	−7.4	…	−9.7	−4.9
Iraq	2.4	2.5	…	2.4	2.5	2.5	4.9	9.9	14.0	2.3	…	−1.1	5.8
Non-OPEC	50.7	51.5	52.0	51.2	51.7	1.0	1.1	0.9	−0.3	1.5	1.1	0.4	2.5
Of Which:													
North America	13.9	14.3	14.2	14.1	14.4	2.0	−0.8	0.4	−5.1	−3.6	0.5	−5.6	−1.6
North Sea	4.3	4.1	3.9	4.3	4.0	−5.7	−7.6	−5.0	−5.1	−4.6	−6.6	−3.0	−6.2
Russia	10.0	10.2	10.4	10.1	10.3	7.7	2.2	2.4	−0.7	2.0	2.0	1.2	2.8
Other Former Soviet Union[4]	2.8	3.1	3.2	3.0	3.1	7.9	3.9	12.1	2.9	9.2	3.3	3.7	15.1
Other Non-OPEC	19.6	19.8	20.4	19.7	19.9	1.0	18.6	0.6	2.2	0.8	2.9	0.8	0.9
World	86.4	84.8	…	84.3	85.4	3.1	0.9	0.1	1.0	−1.8	…	−2.9	−0.7
Net Demand[5]	−0.2	0.1	…	0.0	0.2	−0.5	−0.5	1.2	−0.2	0.1	…	0.0	0.3

Sources: International Energy Agency, *Oil Market Report,* April 2010; and IMF staff calculations.

[1]OECD = Organization for Economic Cooperation and Development.

[2]OPEC = Organization of Petroleum Exporting Countries. Includes Angola (which joined OPEC in January 2007) and Ecuador (which rejoined OPEC in November 2007, after suspending its membership from December 1992 to October 2007).

[3]Totals refer to a total of crude oil, condensates, and natural gas liquids. Figure for 2010 is the call on OPEC implied by the demand and non-OPEC supply projections.

[4]Other Former Soviet Union includes Azerbaijan, Belarus, Georgia, Kazakhstan, Kyrgyz Republic, Tajikistan, Turkmenistan, Ukraine, and Uzbekistan.

[5]Difference between demand and production. In the percent change columns, the figures are in percent of world demand.

2009. After losing more than half its precrisis peak value, the IMF daily metal index bottomed out around February 2009, doubling its value from the trough by the end of 2009, with the largest price gains posted by copper, lead, and zinc.

The sharp price rebound was largely driven by the stronger-than-expected recovery in emerging economies (Figure 1.20, top right panel), with supply factors also playing a supportive role. On the demand side, although metal consumption declined in most economies in 2009, Chinese demand grew about 24 percent, reflecting the effect of China's stimulus package and public investment (Figure 1.20, second metal panel). On the supply side, the price rebound impetus was also supported by sustained production cuts. Labor disputes (such as strikes) and stricter environmental standards (such as those pertaining to lead production and China's energy surcharge on aluminum production) have also aided the price rebound. With strong demand and limited domestic supply, China's metal imports rebounded sharply in 2009, with imports of nickel, tin, and lead growing more than fivefold between their postcrisis lows and the subsequent peaks (Figure 1.20, middle left panel).

A key factor underpinning the direction of metal prices is the growth path of metal demand in China—the largest metal consumer. During 2003–08, China's metal consumption grew at an average annual rate of about 16 percent, accounting for more than 80 percent of world demand growth. China's metal demand increased at a faster rate than output, and so its metal intensity—metal consumption per unit of GDP—increased during this period. In contrast, cross-country evidence suggests that metal intensity tends to decrease when per capita income rises (Figure 1.20, middle right panel). With the recent increases, China's metal intensity appears to be significantly above the value predicted by a cross-country regression, given its per capita income. If China's metal intensity were to normalize to cross-country norms, this would imply a slowing of its own metal consumption growth as well as slower growth in total global consumption. For example, if Chinese metal demand grew at 5 percent a year—half the projected GDP growth

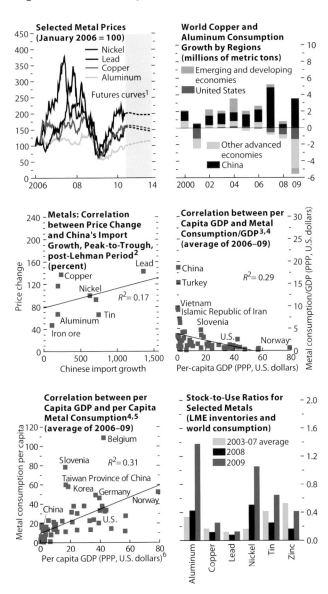

Figure 1.20. Developments in Metal Markets

Sources: Bloomberg Financial Markets; World Bureau of Metal Statistics; and IMF staff calculations.
[1]Prices as of March 18, 2010.
[2]Peaks and troughs in price and import volume vary by metal. Import peaks: April 09 (tin and lead), June 09 (copper), July 09 (nickel and zinc), September 09 (aluminum). Import troughs: September 08 (copper), November 08 (nickel and zinc), December 08 (tin and lead), March 09 (aluminum). Price peaks: August 09 (nickel), January 10 (aluminum, copper, tin, lead, zinc). Price troughs: December 08 (copper, lead, zinc), February 09 (aluminum), March 09 (nickel, tin).
[3]Metal consumption/GDP is measured in tons per million U.S. dollars.
[4]Sample includes 59 economies.
[5]Metal consumption per capita is measured in tons per thousand people.
PPP = Purchasing Power Parity.

Figure 1.21. Recent Developments in Markets for Major Food Crops

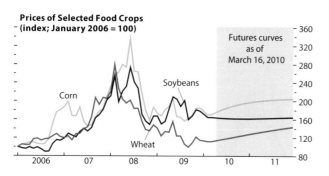

Prices of Selected Food Crops
(index; January 2006 = 100)

Futures curves as of March 16, 2010

Corn
Soybeans
Wheat

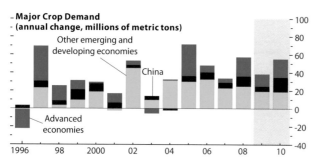

Major Crop Demand
(annual change, millions of metric tons)

Other emerging and developing economies
China
Advanced economies

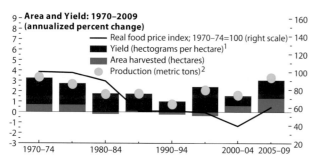

Area and Yield: 1970–2009
(annualized percent change)

— Real food price index; 1970–74=100 (right scale)
■ Yield (hectograms per hectare)[1]
■ Area harvested (hectares)
○ Production (metric tons)[2]

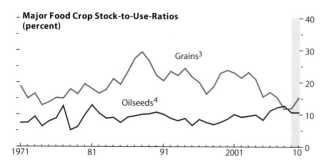

Major Food Crop Stock-to-Use-Ratios
(percent)

Grains[3]
Oilseeds[4]

Sources: Bloomberg Financial Markets; UN Food and Agriculture Organization; U.S. Department of Agriculture estimates; and IMF staff estimates.
[1] Area-weighted yield for nine grains, three oilseeds, cocoa, coffee, and sugar.
[2] Actual production index growth may differ slightly from the summation of yield and area growth, which provides only an approximation of production.
[3] Includes barley, corn, millet, rice, sorghum, rye, and wheat.
[4] Includes palm kernel, rapeseed, and soybean oilseeds.

rate—global metal demand would increase by only about 2½ percent annually, compared with 4½ percent in recent years (other things being equal). That said, it remains uncertain whether and when a normalization of metal intensity in China will occur. Given that China's per capita metal consumption is still low relative to other emerging economies (Figure 1.20, bottom left panel) and given forecasts of continued robust growth, including in construction, a sharp slowdown in the growth of global metal demand does not seem an imminent risk at this point.

Metal prices are expected to rise only gradually, in line with the general outlook for commodities as reflected in futures prices, given above-average stock-to-use ratios for major metals (Figure 1.20, bottom right panel).

Food

Unlike many other commodities, food prices have recovered only modestly from the trough in December 2008, although they have generally fallen by less than prices of other commodities during the Great Recession. They have started this year by broadly declining. The IMF food price index has fallen by 5 percent since the end of 2009 (Figure 1.21, top panel). Supply has been the common determinant of price developments across most food and beverage commodities since prices reached their trough. For many major crops—including corn, rice, soybeans, and wheat—expectations for supply over the current and next harvest years have been steadily outpacing those for demand. There have been some notable exceptions, such as sugar and cocoa, for which negative supply shocks in key producers have driven prices significantly higher.

Recent increases in supply for many major crops continue a trend of rising production, which began around 2005 and which appears, in part, to be a response to structurally higher demand and higher real prices. Higher food consumption in emerging economies (Figure 1.21, upper middle panel), increasing demand for crops as biofuels, and the possible impact of increasing financialization on the demand for inventories have all been identified

as contributing factors to a potentially permanent increase in demand. In response, during the five years through 2009, supply has expanded rapidly compared with historical growth rates. Rising yields have contributed to this growth, but in recent years farmers have also increased harvested acreage after a long period of decline (Figure 1.21, lower middle panel). This supply response has eased some of the market tightness, which emerged from the supply-demand deficits during 2000–07, but stock-to-use ratios for major grains—particularly corn, rice, and wheat—remain significantly
below their long-term averages, reflecting the particularly rapid growth of demand in recent years and a sluggish supply response (Figure 1.21, bottom panel).

Food supply prospects over the medium term will largely depend on yield improvements rather than on increases in harvested area. Although the potential to increase harvested area exists in some regions, net additions of productive land will be partially offset by constraints on water resources, soil degradation, and increasing urbanization. Yields will be influenced by
changes in climate, pests and diseases, land quality, the cost of inputs such as fertilizers, and research and development (R&D) spending. Recent decades have seen a slowdown in the growth rate of agricultural R&D spending, and—given a wide body of evidence indicating that investments in agricultural R&D have yielded high returns, albeit with long and variable lags—this suggests that food supply growth may fall short of the levels seen during much of the period since World War II (Alston, Beddow, and Pardey, 2009). With global demand growth likely to remain high, this suggests that food commodity markets may remain relatively tight and that, in the absence of continued unanticipated increases in supply, the risk to real food prices remains tilted toward the upside.

References

Alston, Julian M., Jason M. Beddow, and Philip G. Pardey, 2009, "Agricultural Research, Productivity, and Food Prices in the Long Run," *Science*, Vol. 325, No. 5945, pp. 1209–10.

Babcock, Linda, William Congdon, Lawrence Katz, and Sendhil Mullainathan, 2009, "Notes on Behavioral Economics and Labor Market Policy," December (unpublished).

Berkmen, Pelin, Gaston Gelos, Robert Rennhack, and James Walsh, 2009, "The Global Financial Crisis: Explaining Cross-Country Differences in the Output Impact," IMF Working Paper 09/280 (Washington: International Monetary Fund).

Blanchard, Olivier, and Gian Maria Milesi-Ferretti, 2009, "Global Imbalances: In Midstream?" IMF Staff Position Note 09/29 (Washington: International Monetary Fund).

Blanchard, Olivier, Hamid Faruqee, and Mitali Das, 2010, "The Impact Effect of the Crisis on Emerging Market Countries," paper presented at Brookings Panel on Economic Activity, March 18–19 (Washington: International Monetary Fund).

Cardarelli, Roberto, Selim Elekdag, and Subir Lall, 2009, "Financial Stress, Downturns, and Recoveries," IMF Working Paper 09/100 (Washington: International Monetary Fund).

Cashin, Paul, C. John McDermott, and Alasdair Scott, 2002, "Booms and Slumps in World Commodity Prices," *Journal of Development Economics*, Vol. 69 (October 1), pp. 277–96.

Claessens, Stijn, Giovanni Dell'Ariccia, Deniz Igan, and Luc Laeven, 2010, "Lessons and Policy Implications from the Global Financial Crisis," IMF Working Paper 10/44 (Washington: International Monetary Fund).

Decressin, Jörg, and Douglas Laxton, 2009, "Gauging Risks for Deflation," IMF Staff Position Note 09/01 (Washington: International Monetary Fund).

Elekdag, Selim, and Prakash Kannan, 2009, "Incorporating Market Information into the Construction of the Fan Chart," IMF Working Paper 09/178 (Washington: International Monetary Fund).

Garcia-Saltos, Roberto, Charles Freedman, Douglas Laxton, Petar Manchev, and Troy Matheson, forthcoming, "The Global Projection Model: Mark I," IMF Working Paper (Washington: International Monetary Fund).

Ghosh, Atish R., Jonathan D. Ostry, and Charalambos Tsangarides, 2010, *Exchange Rate Regimes and the Stability of the International Monetary System,* IMF Occasional Paper No. 270 (Washington: International Monetary Fund).

International Monetary Fund (IMF), 2010a, "Strategies for Fiscal Consolidation in the Post-Crisis World" (Washington, February). www.imf.org/external/np/pp/eng/2010/020410a.pdf.

———, 2010b, "Exiting from Monetary Crisis Intervention Measures—Background Paper" (Washington, February). www.imf.org/external/np/pp/eng/2010/012510.pdf.

Klyuev, Vladimir, Phil De Imus, and Krishna Srinivasan, 2009, "Unconventional Choices for Unconventional Times: Credit and Quantitative Easing in Advanced Economies," IMF Staff Position Note 09/27 (Washington: International Monetary Fund).

Kumhof, Michael, Douglas Laxton, Dirk Muir, and Susanna Mursula, 2010, "The Global Integrated Monetary and Fiscal Model (GIMF)—Theoretical Structure," IMF Working Paper 10/34 (Washington: International Monetary Fund).

Lee, Jaewoo, Gian Maria Milesi-Ferretti, Jonathan Ostry, Alessandro Prati, and Luca Antonio Ricci, 2008, *Exchange Rate Assessments: CGER Methodologies,* IMF Occasional Paper No. 261 (Washington: International Monetary Fund).

Ostry, Jonathan D., Atish R. Ghosh, Karl Habermeier, Marcos Chamon, Mahvash S. Qureshi, and Dennis B.S. Reinhardt, 2010, "Capital Inflows: The Role of Controls," IMF Staff Position Note 10/04 (Washington: International Monetary Fund).

Tsay, Ruey S., 1989, "Testing and Modeling Threshold Autoregressive Processes," *Journal of the American Statistical Association*, Vol. 84, No. 405, pp. 231–40.

World Bank, 2010, *Global Economic Prospects 2010: Crisis, Finance, and Growth* (Washington).

Zarnowitz, Victor, 1992, *Business Cycles: Theory, History, Indicators, and Forecasting,* NBER Studies in Business Cycles, Vol. 27 (Chicago: University of Chicago Press).

CHAPTER 2

COUNTRY AND REGIONAL PERSPECTIVES

As the global economy comes out of its deepest downturn since World War II, the prospects for growth vary substantially across and within regions (Figure 2.1). In some economies average growth during 2010–11 is projected to exceed 10 percent, whereas in others it is expected to be negative. Apart from the differences in trend growth rates, the pattern observed in the world growth map reflects the varying speeds of recovery toward full-capacity output across economies and regions.

As discussed in Chapter 1, supporting the recovery are easing financial conditions, normalizing trade, rebounding capital flows, a turn in the inventory cycle, and, importantly, growth-stimulating policies. In some cases, however, holding back the recovery are unhealed financial systems and weak public or household balance sheets. The relative importance of these factors differs greatly across economies and regions.

What helps explain the different speeds of recovery across economies? Although there is no simple answer to this question, the analysis of current (near-term) growth projections reveals several striking patterns (Figure 2.2). In particular, economies with larger output losses during the Great Recession are expected to recover more

slowly than those that fared better. Moreover, those that entered the crisis with preexisting domestic imbalances (as evidenced by large current account deficits, credit booms, and the like) are typically projected to experience more sluggish recoveries. More limited room for policy maneuvers, as measured by high public debt levels, is also associated with more muted projected recoveries. Of course, there are exceptions to these patterns, and many other country-specific factors remain important.

Two additional features of the projections stand out. First, many advanced economies are expected to undergo more subdued recoveries than most emerging and developing economies. Second, the recovery is projected to be strongest in Asia and weakest in emerging Europe.

Against this backdrop, Chapter 2 presents the economic outlook and discusses key policy challenges across economies and regions, starting with North America (Canada, United States), followed by Asia and other advanced economies (Australia, New Zealand), Europe, the Commonwealth of Independent States (CIS), Latin America and the Caribbean (LAC), the Middle East and North Africa (MENA), and sub-Saharan Africa.

Figure 2.1. Average Real GDP Growth during 2010–11
(Percent)

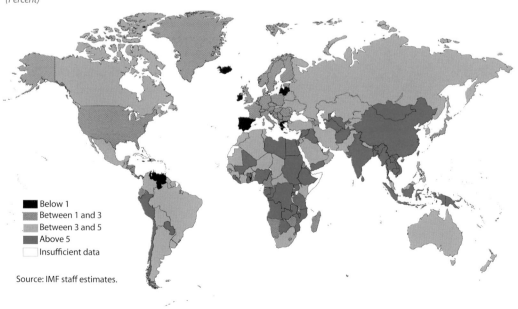

■ Below 1
▨ Between 1 and 3
▨ Between 3 and 5
■ Above 5
□ Insufficient data

Source: IMF staff estimates.

Figure 2.2. Decomposing the Variation in 2010–11 Growth Projections

The large variation in the 2010–11 growth outlook, both across and within regions, reflects differences in underlying (trend) growth, the severity of the downturn during the crisis, precrisis current account positions, and the level of public debt, among other factors.

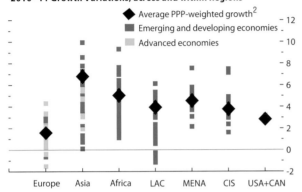

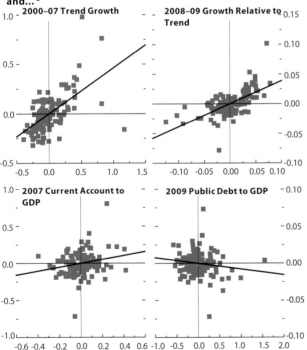

Source: IMF staff estimates.

[1]CIS: Commonwealth of Independent States, Georgia, and Mongolia; LAC: Latin American and the Caribbean; MENA: Middle East and North Africa; USA+CAN: United States and Canada.

[2]PPP = purchasing power parity.

[3]Based on a regression of projected 2010–11 average GDP growth on these variables, as well as the projected 2010–11 partner GDP growth and the 2008–09 change in the real effective exchange rate. Each partial regression scatterplot shows the relationship between projected 2010–11 growth and one variable, after controlling for the effect of all the other variables.

A Stimulus-Driven U.S. Recovery Is under Way

A stimulus-led recovery is under way in the United States, but private demand remains soft. Substantial monetary and fiscal easing, alongside other policies aimed directly at the financial and housing sectors, has provided a broad-based fillip to growth—the IMF staff estimates that the fiscal stimulus boosted real GDP growth by about 1 percentage point in 2009. In response to the stimulus and a robust inventory cycle, real GDP grew at a seasonally adjusted annualized rate of 2.2 percent in the third quarter of 2009 and by 5.6 percent in the fourth quarter (Figure 2.3). But private final demand is still subdued and remains well below precrisis levels. In the fourth quarter, consumption rose by only 1.6 percent as households continued to rebuild wealth; reduced inventory drawdowns contributed more than half of growth. During the same period, net exports also made a modest positive contribution to growth, as the rebound in global trade and recovery in partner economies boosted exports.

The labor market remains unusually weak. Since the start of the crisis, more than 7 million jobs have been lost, and 8.8 million people are involuntarily working part-time. The rate at which jobs are being lost has slowed substantially, but employment growth remains negative, and the unemployment rate had reached 10 percent by the end of 2009, although it decreased marginally during the first quarter of 2010. The increase in the unemployment rate is somewhat greater than expected given the behavior of GDP. As discussed in more detail in Chapter 3, the house price bust and an extraordinary degree of financial stress help explain this more adverse unemployment response.

Financial market strains have continued to ease, but credit conditions remain on the tight side. Liquidity spreads such as the LIBOR-OIS (the difference between the three-month London interbank offered rate and the three-month overnight index swap rate) and investment-grade spreads have mostly returned to precrisis levels. Equity markets have recovered from lows reached in early 2009, and corporate bond issuance is now running above precrisis levels. However, as discussed in Chapter 1 of the April 2010 *Global Financial Stability Report* (GFSR), lending surveys indicate weak loan demand, as many sectors continue to deleverage. Moreover, with banks' balance sheets still not fully repaired from the crisis, and with losses mounting in certain sectors such as commercial real estate, financial conditions may remain a drag on growth, particularly for small and medium-size enterprises that cannot access capital markets. In addition, private securitization remains largely moribund; given the importance of this funding channel for lending in the precrisis period, a continued lack of securitization will pose an increasing constraint to finance and growth.

Reflecting these conditions, the recovery ahead is expected to be gradual, particularly when the effects of the stimulus subside. Real GDP is projected to grow by 3 percent in 2010 (Table 2.1), an upward revision of ½ percentage point relative to the January 2010 *WEO Update* and 1½ percentage points relative to the October 2009 *World Economic Outlook* (WEO). The recovery will be tempered by households' continued need to rebuild wealth, the expected slow but necessary process of financial sector repair and deleveraging, and continued weakness in the labor market. The removal of policy stimulus will subtract from growth, which will moderate to 2.6 percent in 2011. Unemployment is projected to remain high in 2010, at 9½ percent (year-average basis; Table 2.2), before declining to 8¼ percent in 2011 as employment growth picks up. And inflation is expected to remain subdued, at 2 percent in 2010 and 1¾ percent in 2011, given continued economic slack.

Uncertainty around the outlook remains elevated but is lower than in the October 2009 WEO, and the risks to the 2010 growth projection appear roughly balanced. Continued weakness in real estate (including the commercial sector) or fresh turbulence in financial markets could weigh negatively on activity. However, these risks could be offset by more-resilient-than-expected private demand if confidence improves, by additional stimulus, or by a more-buoyant-than-expected inventory cycle. The balance of risks for 2011 and beyond remains on the downside; any further stimulus would likely

Figure 2.3. United States: A Stimulus-Supported Recovery

Substantial stimulus has supported the U.S. recovery, but private demand remains muted and the labor market is unusually weak. Financial market conditions have normalized and the housing market has tentatively stabilized. But credit conditions, although no longer tightening, remain tight.

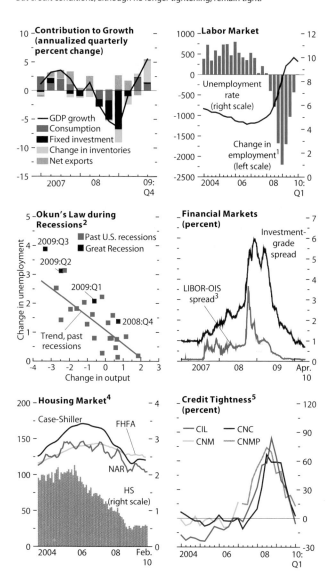

Sources: Bloomberg Financial Markets; Haver Analytics; and IMF staff calculations.
[1]Quarterly change in total nonfarm payrolls, thousands.
[2]Change in output is percent change from one year earlier. Change in unemployment is percentage point difference from one year earlier.
[3]LIBOR-OIS spread is the difference between the three-month London interbank offered rate (LIBOR) and the three-month overnight index swap (OIS) rate.
[4]Index: January 2002 = 100; Case-Shiller Composite 20; FHFA: Federal Housing Finance Agency; HS: housing starts in millions; NAR: National Association of Realtors.
[5]All series come from the Senior Loan Officer Survey. CIL: banks tightening commercial and industrial loans to large firms; CNC: banks tightening standards for consumer credit cards; CNM: banks tightening standards for mortgages to individuals; CNMP: banks tightening standards for prime mortgages to individuals.

Table 2.1. Selected Advanced Economies: Real GDP, Consumer Prices, and Current Account Balance
(Annual percent change unless noted otherwise)

	Real GDP				Consumer Prices[1]				Current Account Balance[2]			
			Projections				Projections				Projections	
	2008	2009	2010	2011	2008	2009	2010	2011	2008	2009	2010	2011
Advanced Economies	**0.5**	**−3.2**	**2.3**	**2.4**	**3.4**	**0.1**	**1.5**	**1.4**	**−1.3**	**−0.4**	**−0.4**	**−0.5**
United States	0.4	−2.4	3.1	2.6	3.8	−0.3	2.1	1.7	−4.9	−2.9	−3.3	−3.4
Euro Area[3,4]	0.6	−4.1	1.0	1.5	3.3	0.3	1.1	1.3	−1.5	−0.6	−0.3	−0.2
Japan	−1.2	−5.2	1.9	2.0	1.4	−1.4	−1.4	−0.5	3.2	2.8	2.8	2.4
United Kingdom[3]	0.5	−4.9	1.3	2.5	3.6	2.2	2.7	1.6	−1.5	−1.3	−1.7	−1.6
Canada	0.4	−2.6	3.1	3.2	2.4	0.3	1.8	2.0	0.5	−2.7	−2.6	−2.5
Other Advanced Economies	1.7	−1.1	3.7	3.9	4.3	1.5	2.2	2.2	3.1	5.1	4.4	4.3
Memorandum												
Newly Industrialized Asian Economies	1.8	−0.9	5.2	4.9	4.5	1.3	2.3	2.3	4.9	8.9	6.6	6.6

[1]Movements in consumer prices are shown as annual averages. December–December changes can be found in Table A6 in the Statistical Appendix.
[2]Percent of GDP.
[3]Based on Eurostat's harmonized index of consumer prices.
[4]Current account position corrected for reporting discrepancies in intra-area transactions.

boost growth mainly this year, and a negative near-term shock to the housing or financial markets would likely have its largest impact next year.

This outlook frames the balancing act facing fiscal policy—the need to support growth now and to secure fiscal stability over the medium term. Given the present weaknesses and risks in the labor and housing markets, a case can be made for additional, targeted support to those sectors. However, given the size of U.S. fiscal imbalances, a credible plan for fiscal sustainability will need to accompany any such measures to limit the risk of rising long-term interest rates, which would dampen growth. Such a plan would also allow fiscal room to maneuver in 2011 if downside risks materialize.

When the recovery is solidly under way, fiscal consolidation should be a top priority. The medium-term fiscal outlook is daunting—under conservative assumptions about growth and interest rates and absent action, the deficit would rise to 8 percent of GDP in 2020, with the federal debt exceeding 100 percent of GDP—and significant additional adjustment would be needed to put public debt on a sustainable path. Furthermore, health care reform will be essential to bring medical costs under control. The recent progress toward reform is welcome, including signs that it may contribute modestly to medium-term deficit reduction, although the yield in terms of cost control remains uncertain. Accompanying headway in social security

reform could help address entitlement spending (yielding smaller, but more predictable, gains compared with health care reform).

Meanwhile, the ongoing, extraordinarily accommodative stance of monetary policy should continue to support recovery. Although the Federal Reserve has communicated its exit strategy and continued to develop tools to implement the exit, it has also stressed its intention to maintain accommodation as needed. It has also signaled that it is committed to withdrawing excess liquidity and normalizing monetary policy gradually—an appropriate strategy in light of uncertainties about both the economic outlook and the strength of the monetary transmission mechanism, particularly given high excess liquidity and remaining weaknesses in financial sector balance sheets.

Looking beyond the recovery, restoring the financial sector to full health and addressing the gaps in regulation highlighted by the crisis will be essential for stable medium-term growth. A consensus is building around reforms that would strengthen supervision and regulation, including through an expanded perimeter; improving the resolution mechanism for systemically important nonbank financial institutions to provide options other than bankruptcy and bailout; and shoring up the infrastructure for financial markets. Reforms would also provide an opportunity to address the "too-big-to-fail" problem by creating incentives to reduce

Table 2.2. Advanced Economies: Unemployment

(Percent)

	2008	2009	Projections 2010	Projections 2011
Advanced Economies	**5.8**	**8.0**	**8.4**	**8.0**
United States	5.8	9.3	9.4	8.3
Euro Area	7.6	9.4	10.5	10.5
Germany	7.2	7.4	8.6	9.3
France	7.9	9.4	10.0	9.9
Italy	6.8	7.8	8.7	8.6
Spain	11.3	18.0	19.4	18.7
Netherlands	2.8	3.5	4.9	4.7
Belgium	7.0	8.0	9.3	9.4
Greece	7.6	9.4	12.0	13.0
Austria	3.9	5.0	5.4	5.5
Portugal	7.6	9.5	11.0	10.3
Finland	6.4	8.3	9.8	9.6
Ireland	6.1	11.8	13.5	13.0
Slovak Republic	9.6	12.1	11.6	10.7
Slovenia	4.4	6.2	7.4	6.8
Luxembourg	4.4	7.0	6.2	5.7
Cyprus	3.6	5.3	6.1	6.4
Malta	5.8	7.1	7.3	7.2
Japan	4.0	5.1	5.1	4.9
United Kingdom	5.6	7.5	8.3	7.9
Canada	6.2	8.3	7.9	7.5
Korea	3.2	3.7	3.5	3.4
Australia	4.3	5.6	5.3	5.1
Taiwan Province of China	4.1	5.9	5.4	4.9
Sweden	6.2	8.5	8.2	7.7
Switzerland	2.7	4.1	5.0	4.1
Hong Kong SAR	3.5	5.1	4.8	4.5
Czech Republic	4.4	6.7	8.8	8.5
Norway	2.6	3.2	3.5	3.5
Singapore	2.2	3.0	2.8	2.6
Denmark	1.7	3.3	4.2	4.7
Israel	6.1	7.7	7.4	7.1
New Zealand	4.2	6.2	7.2	6.6
Iceland	1.6	8.0	9.7	8.6
Memorandum				
Newly Industrialized Asian Economies	3.4	4.3	4.1	3.8

size and complexity. This would help streamline the U.S. regulatory structure, avoid gaps and inconsistencies, and support renewed (but safer) securitization activity.

In turn, a more sustainable foundation for U.S. growth will facilitate the rebalancing of global demand. The key to putting growth on a more sustainable footing is repairing both private and public balance sheets—and, in particular, savings. Households have stepped up their saving to rebuild their wealth, but the outlook for

private saving remains uncertain. This reinforces the need for the government to shift its focus toward medium-term fiscal consolidation to provide the boost in national saving necessary to reduce the external imbalance. Accordingly, it is less likely that current account deficits—which shrank substantially in the past year—will return to the unusually large levels that prevailed before the crisis.

Turning to Canada, the recovery there is also expected to be protracted, reflecting more moderate demand growth than in the United States as well as the substantial strengthening of the Canadian dollar. Output growth is projected at 3 percent in 2010 and 3¼ percent in 2011 (see Table 2.1). Canada entered the global crisis in good shape, and thus the exit strategy appears less challenging than elsewhere. The main priorities are returning Canada's debt to a downward trajectory, ensuring that financial stability remains intact—amid rising house prices—and raising Canada's labor productivity and potential growth.

Asia Is Staging a Vigorous and Balanced Recovery

Although the downturn in many Asian economies in late 2008 was steeper than expected, the recovery came quickly and was just as sharp. Output growth in 2009 in almost all Asian economies was stronger than projected in the October 2009 WEO, with Japan a notable exception. The V-shaped recovery points to an overall slowdown that was more moderate than in other regions. The recovery has also been more balanced in Asia than elsewhere, with output growth in most economies supported by both external and domestic demand. And even though macroeconomic stimulus was substantial, private demand also gained traction in many economies. Ample policy room and strong sectoral balance sheets suggest that for many economies in the region, the recovery will be relatively robust.

Four factors have supported Asia's recovery. First, the rapid normalization of trade following the financial dislocation in late 2008 greatly benefited

Figure 2.4. Asia: Average Real GDP Growth during 2010–11
(Percent)

- Below 1
- Between 1 and 3
- Between 3 and 5
- Above 5
- Insufficient data

Source: IMF staff estimates.

the export-oriented economies in the region. Second, the bottoming out of the inventory cycle, both domestically and in major trading partners such as the United States, is boosting industrial production and exports. Third, a resumption of capital inflows into the region—in response to widening growth differentials and a renewed appetite for risk—has created abundant liquidity in many economies. Finally, domestic demand has been resilient, with strong public and private components in many of the region's economies. This resilience is in part attributable to the fact that stronger balance sheets were in place at the onset of this crisis, in both the private sector and the public sector. Low public debt levels allowed many Asian economies to implement strong and timely countercyclical policy responses to the crisis—IMF staff estimates indicate that fiscal stimulus added 1¾ percentage points to Asia's growth in 2009. Monetary loosening also eased financial conditions across the region—through aggressive cuts in policy interest rates and, in some economies, measures to increase liquidity.

Against this backdrop, Asia's GDP is projected to grow by 7 percent in both 2010 and 2011 (Figure 2.4; Table 2.3). Significant differences remain within the region, however:

- In both China and India, strong domestic demand will support the recovery. In China, GDP growth exceeded the government's 8 percent target in 2009 and is expected to be close to 10 percent in both 2010 and 2011. What has been so far mainly a publicly driven growth path, built on infrastructure investment, is expected to turn toward stronger private consumption and investment. In India, growth is projected to be 8¾ percent in 2010 and 8½ percent in 2011, supported by rising private demand. Consumption will strengthen as the labor market improves, and investment is expected to be boosted by strong profitability, rising business confidence, and favorable financing conditions.

- The strength in final domestic demand in India and especially China is expected to have positive spillovers for other Asian economies, particularly exporters of commodities and capital goods. In Korea, economic activity is expected to expand by 4½ percent in 2010 and 5 percent in 2011, strongly accelerating from ¼ percent in 2009. This reflects not just strong export growth—with capital exports to China an important element—but also a continued boost from the inventory

Table 2.3. Selected Asian Economies: Real GDP, Consumer Prices, and Current Account Balance
(Annual percent change unless noted otherwise)

	Real GDP				Consumer Prices[1]				Current Account Balance[2]			
			Projections				Projections				Projections	
	2008	2009	2010	2011	2008	2009	2010	2011	2008	2009	2010	2011
Asia	**5.2**	**3.5**	**6.9**	**7.0**	**5.8**	**2.0**	**4.1**	**2.8**	**4.0**	**3.6**	**3.4**	**3.3**
Advanced Asia	**0.2**	**−3.0**	**3.1**	**3.2**	**2.8**	**−0.1**	**0.3**	**0.8**	**2.4**	**3.1**	**2.6**	**2.4**
Japan	−1.2	−5.2	1.9	2.0	1.4	−1.4	−1.4	−0.5	3.2	2.8	2.8	2.4
Australia	2.4	1.3	3.0	3.5	4.4	1.8	2.4	2.4	−4.4	−4.1	−3.5	−3.7
New Zealand	−0.1	−1.6	2.9	3.2	4.0	2.1	2.1	2.5	−8.6	−3.0	−4.6	−5.7
Newly Industrialized Asian Economies	**1.8**	**−0.9**	**5.2**	**4.9**	**4.5**	**1.3**	**2.3**	**2.3**	**4.9**	**8.9**	**6.6**	**6.6**
Korea	2.3	0.2	4.5	5.0	4.7	2.8	2.9	3.0	−0.6	5.1	1.6	2.2
Taiwan Province of China	0.7	−1.9	6.5	4.8	3.5	−0.9	1.5	1.5	6.2	11.2	8.5	7.7
Hong Kong SAR	2.1	−2.7	5.0	4.4	4.3	0.5	2.0	1.7	13.6	11.1	12.1	10.1
Singapore	1.4	−2.0	5.7	5.3	6.5	0.2	2.1	1.9	19.2	19.1	22.0	22.4
Developing Asia	**7.9**	**6.6**	**8.7**	**8.7**	**7.4**	**3.1**	**5.9**	**3.7**	**5.7**	**4.1**	**4.1**	**4.1**
China	9.6	8.7	10.0	9.9	5.9	−0.7	3.1	2.4	9.4	5.8	6.2	6.5
India	7.3	5.7	8.8	8.4	8.3	10.9	13.2	5.5	−2.2	−2.1	−2.2	−2.0
ASEAN-5	**4.7**	**1.7**	**5.4**	**5.6**	**9.3**	**2.9**	**4.8**	**4.6**	**2.7**	**5.1**	**3.3**	**2.2**
Indonesia	6.0	4.5	6.0	6.2	9.8	4.8	4.7	5.8	0.0	2.0	1.4	0.4
Thailand	2.5	−2.3	5.5	5.5	5.5	−0.8	3.2	1.9	0.6	7.7	2.5	0.3
Philippines	3.8	0.9	3.6	4.0	9.3	3.2	5.0	4.0	2.2	5.3	3.5	2.3
Malaysia	4.6	−1.7	4.7	5.0	5.4	0.6	2.0	2.1	17.5	16.7	15.4	14.7
Vietnam	6.2	5.3	6.0	6.5	23.1	6.7	12.0	10.3	−11.9	−7.8	−6.9	−6.0
Other Developing Asia[3]	**3.9**	**3.7**	**4.3**	**5.0**	**12.9**	**11.5**	**9.1**	**7.4**	**−2.3**	**−0.8**	**−1.0**	**−1.3**
Memorandum												
Emerging Asia[4]	7.0	5.6	8.2	8.2	7.0	2.9	5.4	3.5	5.6	4.9	4.5	4.5

[1]Movements in consumer prices are shown as annual averages. December–December changes can be found in Tables A6 and A7 in the Statistical Appendix.

[2]Percent of GDP.

[3]Other Developing Asia comprises Islamic Republic of Afghanistan, Bangladesh, Bhutan, Brunei Darussalam, Cambodia, Fiji, Kiribati, Lao People's Democratic Republic, Maldives, Myanmar, Nepal, Pakistan, Papua New Guinea, Samoa, Solomon Islands, Sri Lanka, Timor-Leste, Tonga, and Vanuatu.

[4]Emerging Asia comprises all economies in Developing Asia and the Newly Industrialized Asian Economies.

cycle and a boost in business investment in response to high capacity utilization and strong business confidence. All these factors should help offset the impact of the expected withdrawal of fiscal stimulus in 2010.

- The ASEAN-5 economies[1] are projected to grow by 5½ percent in 2010. Private domestic demand is expected to be the main driver of growth, with net exports playing a lesser role than in the past, reflecting stronger imports relative to historical standards. Among the ASEAN-5, the Indonesian economy has proved to be remarkably resilient, with output growing at 4½ percent in 2009 compared with 1¾ percent for the ASEAN-5 as a whole, thanks to strong domestic demand and

---

[1] Association of Southeast Asian Nations comprising Indonesia, Malaysia, Philippines, Thailand, and Vietnam.

less dependence on trade. Indonesia's growth is expected to accelerate to 6 percent in 2010 and to 6¼ percent in 2011, reflecting a pickup in private investment.

- Australia's GDP growth is projected to be 3 percent in 2010 and 3½ percent in 2011, helped by strong demand for commodities, particularly from China. Growth in 2010 will be led by domestic demand, both private and public, with the pickup in commodity prices expected to boost investment in the resource sector. New Zealand's output growth—projected at 3 percent in 2010 and 3¼ percent in 2011—will be supported by higher commodity export prices, especially for dairy products, and by stronger domestic demand on the back of higher farm incomes, permanent income tax cuts, and recovering house prices.

Figure 2.5. Asia: A Vigorous and Balanced Rebound

The normalization of global trade, a turn in the inventory cycle, and stimulus-supported demand have underpinned Asia's quick recovery. Renewed capital inflows have put pressure on exchange rates, which has been absorbed mainly by further reserve accumulation.

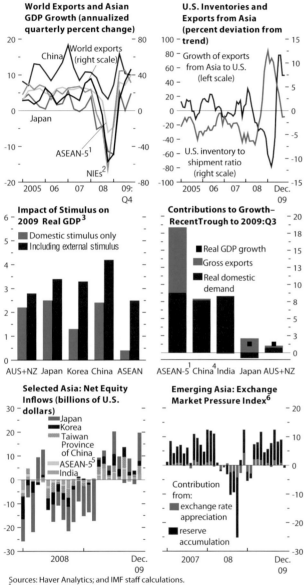

Sources: Haver Analytics; and IMF staff calculations.
[1] Excluding Vietnam.
[2] Newly industrialized Asian economies (NIEs) comprise Hong Kong SAR, Korea, Singapore, and Taiwan Province of China.
[3] "Domestic stimulus only" refers to the impact of fiscal stimulus in the country or country group; "Including external stimulus" adds the impact of regional and global fiscal stimulus measures. Estimates are based on multipliers from the IMF's Global Integrated Monetary and Fiscal Model. AUS+NZ= Australia and New Zealand.
[4] For China, quarter of slowest growth (2009:Q1) to 2009:Q3.
[5] Excluding Malaysia.
[6] The exchange market pressure index is defined as the change in nominal exchange rate vis-à-vis U.S. dollar plus the ratio of change in international reserves to the monetary base. The index is the average of China, Hong Kong SAR, India, Indonesia, Korea, Malaysia, Philippines, Singapore, and Thailand.

- In Japan, exports have helped support a tentative recovery, but spillovers to autonomous domestic demand have so far been limited; domestic demand is likely to remain weak as a result of several factors, including the reemergence of deflation, continued excess capacity, and a weak labor market. Continued yen appreciation in 2010 could dampen the contribution of net exports to growth, particularly in comparison with the rest of Asia. As a result, the outlook depends crucially on planned fiscal policy support and the global upturn. GDP is projected to grow by 2 percent in 2010, supported by fiscal stimulus and rising exports. A more broad-based recovery is expected for 2011, following a moderate pickup in business investment.

Varied policy challenges face the region's economies. For those that have depended on exports to drive growth, the primary challenge will be to deal with slowing demand from major trading partners such as the United States. For economies such as India, which are relatively more closed and which have relied on stimulus to support growth, the main challenge will be to ensure durable fiscal consolidation, including by implementing fiscal and other structural reforms. And Japan faces significant challenges in strengthening domestic demand and fighting off deflation, given the need to bring down the high level of public debt and with the policy rate near the zero bound.

For policymakers in Asia's export-driven economies, who now face the prospect of weaker external demand conditions, a key challenge is to effect a durable rebalancing toward domestic sources of growth. Stimulus measures have played a major role in the recent strength of domestic demand in many of the region's economies (Figure 2.5), and for domestic demand to remain robust, autonomous private demand will have to strengthen further. Rebalancing away from external demand, however, is likely to entail different measures for different economies in the region. For example, boosting domestic consumption will be a priority in China, through improved access to finance for small enterprises and households and stronger corporate governance and social safety nets to reduce precautionary saving. On the other hand, Korea's and Japan's growth prospects will benefit mainly from raising productivity in the service sector. For many ASEAN economies, notably the Philippines, Thailand, and Malaysia, improving the environment for private investment can play an important role in boosting private domestic demand. Greater exchange rate flexibility in many economies would also facilitate rebalancing by raising households' purchasing power and helping shift productive resources from the tradables to the nontradables sector.

Given the region's strong recovery, planning the speed and sequencing of the exit from stimulative macroeconomic policies must become a policy priority. Withdrawing accommodative policy stances is becoming an option in several economies, but the fragility of the recovery in major advanced economies suggests that there are risks from moving too swiftly in that direction. Persistent differences in domestic cyclical conditions within Asia also warrant different timing and sequencing in the exit from policy support.

On the fiscal front, despite the relatively stronger fiscal response in 2009, only a few Asian economies appear to face debt-sustainability challenges on a scale similar to those in many advanced economies. If the strength of autonomous private domestic demand is uncertain, continued fiscal support would be appropriate, especially in economies that face weaker demand from abroad and demand-rebalancing challenges. For regional economies with high public debt levels and the need to maintain fiscal support—such as Japan—developing and communicating credible medium-term consolidation plans would be advisable, for several reasons. First, it would make the remaining fiscal support even more effective. Second, it would help restore the fiscal room necessary to deal with future shocks and help address aging-related spending pressures. And finally, it would help reduce the likelihood of negative spillovers from fiscal concerns in other advanced economies.

With regard to monetary policy, it may not be too early to start unwinding the stimulus if output gaps are closing and inflation pressures are beginning to emerge. This appears to be the case already for a few economies in the region, including

Australia, India, and Malaysia, where authorities have already started tightening monetary policy. In China, the withdrawal of the exceptional monetary stimulus introduced in 2009 will also minimize the risks from excessively easy credit conditions. For other economies in the region where the recovery of private demand is more uncertain and where output gaps are likely to close more slowly, policymakers should avoid premature tightening of monetary conditions. And for Japan, with the reemergence of deflation, the current accommodative monetary policy stance remains appropriate, but additional easing measures may be necessary if deflation persists.

Although domestic cyclical considerations may argue for early monetary tightening in some economies, these should be weighed against the risk of attracting further capital inflows. Large capital inflows can complicate macroeconomic management with their potential to generate inflation pressures, feed credit and asset price boom-and-bust cycles, and create pressure for steep and sudden real exchange rate appreciation. Although asset price increases to date appear to be mostly in line with those in previous recoveries, as discussed in the April 2010 GFSR, conditions of high external and domestic liquidity and rising credit growth could give rise to bubbles in the medium term.

An appropriate response to the risks from large capital inflows may well involve a variety of measures, depending on circumstances—an issue discussed in greater detail in Chapter 4 of the April 2010 GFSR. For economies where excessively large surpluses contribute to global imbalances, slowing the effects of inflows on credit growth by allowing more exchange rate flexibility would help address both problems. Other potential policy responses include strengthening macroprudential measures, tightening fiscal policy, and, if still needed, some form of capital controls.

Europe Is Facing an Uneven Recovery and Complex Policy Challenges

Among the hardest hit during the global crisis, Europe is coming out of recession at a slower pace

Figure 2.6. Europe: Average Real GDP Growth during 2010–11
(Percent)

Source: IMF staff estimates.

than other regions. Within both advanced and emerging Europe, country experiences and recovery prospects vary considerably. A substantial macroeconomic stimulus has supported the recovery in core advanced European economies, although private demand has yet to take a firm hold. At the same time, large current account and fiscal imbalances threaten the recovery in some smaller European countries, with potentially damaging effects on the rest of the region.

Having entered the crisis with substantial imbalances, Europe suffered greatly. Among the worst performers were advanced and emerging European economies that had experienced large current account deficits and domestic imbalances. External financing constraints forced a sharp decline in output in some emerging European economies, particularly those with large current account deficits and heavy dependence on foreign financing (for example, Baltics, Bulgaria, Romania). The reversal of construction and credit booms, accompanied by banking sector problems, led to an output collapse in some euro area countries. Substantial output losses, costly crisis-related measures, and one-time factors led to very large fiscal deficits in a number of countries (for example, Greece, Ireland, Lithuania, Portugal, Spain, United Kingdom). And although current account imbalances have adjusted in many emerging European countries, they remain substantial (and difficult to unwind) in a number of euro area countries that cannot use currency depreciation as a mechanism to improve competitiveness.

There are several powerful forces holding back the recovery in Europe. Sizable fiscal and current account imbalances are constraining recovery in several euro area countries, with potentially negative spillover effects to the rest of Europe. Indeed, concerns about sovereign solvency and liquidity in Greece (and possible contagion effects on other vulnerable euro area countries) have threatened the normalization in financial market conditions. Separately, unresolved problems in the banking sector, which plays a key role in financial intermediation in Europe, have hampered the return to normality. In addition, remaining external financing constraints, vulnerable household and corporate balance sheets, and financial sector deleveraging have limited the speed of the recovery in the hardest-hit economies in emerging Europe.

Nevertheless, the ongoing recovery in Europe has been supported by several factors. First, the turn in the inventory cycle boosted activity in the euro area during the second half of 2009. Second, the normalization of global trade has contributed significantly to growth in the euro area and in emerging Europe. Third, forceful policies have also fostered recovery, including supportive macroeconomic and financial sector measures for many European economies and coordinated assistance from multilateral institutions for the hardest-hit economies in the region.

Against this backdrop, Europe's growth performance is expected to be modest. In particular, advanced Europe's GDP is projected to grow at 1 percent in 2010, edging up to 1¾ percent in 2011. Emerging Europe's growth in real activity is expected to be 3 percent in 2010, picking up to 3½ percent in 2011. These aggregate projections, however, do not capture the pronounced differences in outlook across the region (Figures 2.6 and 2.7; Table 2.4):

Figure 2.7. Europe: A Moderate Recovery Held Back by Fiscal and External Imbalances
(Percent)

Many economies in advanced and emerging Europe faced the global crisis with substantial current account imbalances and weak fiscal positions. Current account deficits narrowed during the crisis in many cases, especially in emerging Europe. But fiscal balances deteriorated sharply across the board, as a result of large output losses and costly crisis-related measures. Consequently, some countries in the region emerged from the crisis with weak external and public sector balance sheets. These imbalances are dimming the prospects for growth in these countries.

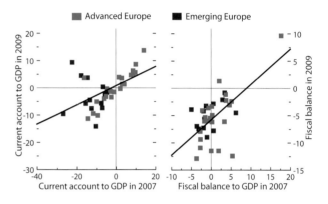

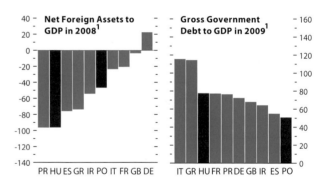

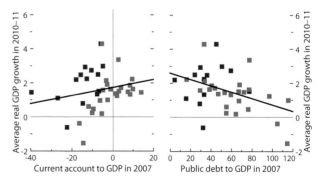

Source: IMF staff estimates.
[1]DE: Germany; ES: Spain; FR: France; GB: United Kingdom; GR: Greece; HU: Hungary; IR: Ireland; IT: Italy; PO: Poland; PR: Portugal.

Table 2.4. Selected European Economies: Real GDP, Consumer Prices, and Current Account Balance
(Annual percent change unless noted otherwise)

	Real GDP				Consumer Prices[1]				Current Account Balance[2]			
			Projections				Projections				Projections	
	2008	2009	2010	2011	2008	2009	2010	2011	2008	2009	2010	2011
Europe	**1.0**	**−4.0**	**1.3**	**1.9**	**4.0**	**1.2**	**2.0**	**1.7**	**−0.7**	**0.2**	**0.3**	**0.4**
Advanced Europe	**0.7**	**−4.1**	**1.0**	**1.7**	**3.4**	**0.6**	**1.4**	**1.4**	**−0.1**	**0.4**	**0.7**	**0.8**
Euro Area[3]	0.6	−4.1	1.0	1.5	3.3	0.3	1.1	1.3	−1.5	−0.6	−0.3	−0.2
Germany	1.2	−5.0	1.2	1.7	2.8	0.1	0.9	1.0	6.7	4.8	5.5	5.6
France	0.3	−2.2	1.5	1.8	3.2	0.1	1.2	1.5	−2.3	−1.5	−1.9	−1.8
Italy	−1.3	−5.0	0.8	1.2	3.5	0.8	1.4	1.7	−3.4	−3.4	−2.8	−2.7
Spain	0.9	−3.6	−0.4	0.9	4.1	−0.3	1.2	1.0	−9.6	−5.1	−5.3	−5.1
Netherlands	2.0	−4.0	1.3	1.3	2.2	1.0	1.1	1.3	4.8	5.2	5.0	5.3
Belgium	0.8	−3.0	1.2	1.3	4.5	−0.2	1.6	1.5	−2.5	−0.3	−0.5	−0.1
Greece	2.0	−2.0	−2.0	−1.1	4.2	1.4	1.9	1.0	−14.6	−11.2	−9.7	−8.1
Austria	2.0	−3.6	1.3	1.7	3.2	0.4	1.3	1.5	3.5	1.4	1.8	1.7
Portugal	0.0	−2.7	0.3	0.7	2.7	−0.9	0.8	1.1	−12.1	−10.1	−9.0	−10.2
Finland	1.2	−7.8	1.2	2.2	3.9	1.6	1.1	1.4	3.0	1.4	2.0	1.8
Ireland	−3.0	−7.1	−1.5	1.9	3.1	−1.7	−2.0	−0.6	−5.2	−2.9	0.4	−0.1
Slovak Republic	6.2	−4.7	4.1	4.5	3.9	0.9	0.8	2.0	−6.5	−3.2	−1.8	−1.9
Slovenia	3.5	−7.3	1.1	2.0	5.7	0.8	1.5	2.3	−6.2	−0.3	−1.5	−1.2
Luxembourg	0.0	−4.2	2.1	2.4	3.4	0.8	1.0	1.3	5.3	5.7	11.2	11.6
Cyprus	3.6	−1.7	−0.7	1.9	4.4	0.2	2.7	2.3	−17.7	−9.3	−11.4	−10.9
Malta	2.1	−1.9	0.5	1.5	4.7	1.8	2.0	2.1	−5.4	−3.9	−5.1	−5.1
United Kingdom	0.5	−4.9	1.3	2.5	3.6	2.2	2.7	1.6	−1.5	−1.3	−1.7	−1.6
Sweden	−0.2	−4.4	1.2	2.5	3.3	2.2	2.4	2.1	7.8	6.4	5.4	5.8
Switzerland	1.8	−1.5	1.5	1.8	2.4	−0.4	0.7	1.0	2.4	8.7	9.5	9.6
Czech Republic	2.5	−4.3	1.7	2.6	6.3	1.0	1.6	2.0	−3.1	−1.0	−1.7	−2.4
Norway	1.8	−1.5	1.1	1.8	3.8	2.2	2.5	1.8	18.6	13.8	16.8	16.7
Denmark	−0.9	−5.1	1.2	1.6	3.4	1.3	2.0	2.0	2.2	4.0	3.1	2.6
Iceland	1.0	−6.5	−3.0	2.3	12.4	12.0	6.2	3.8	−15.8	3.8	5.4	1.8
Emerging Europe	**2.9**	**−3.8**	**2.9**	**3.4**	**8.0**	**4.7**	**5.3**	**3.6**	**−7.3**	**−2.0**	**−3.3**	**−3.6**
Turkey	0.7	−4.7	5.2	3.4	10.4	6.3	9.7	5.7	−5.7	−2.3	−4.0	−4.4
Poland	5.0	1.7	2.7	3.2	4.2	3.5	2.3	2.4	−5.1	−1.6	−2.8	−3.2
Romania	7.3	−7.1	0.8	5.1	7.8	5.6	4.0	3.1	−12.2	−4.4	−5.5	−5.5
Hungary	0.6	−6.3	−0.2	3.2	6.1	4.2	4.3	2.5	−7.2	0.4	−0.4	−1.0
Bulgaria	6.0	−5.0	0.2	2.0	12.0	2.5	2.2	2.9	−24.2	−9.5	−6.3	−5.8
Croatia	2.4	−5.8	0.2	2.5	6.1	2.4	2.3	2.8	−9.2	−5.6	−6.3	−6.8
Lithuania	2.8	−15.0	−1.6	3.2	11.1	4.2	−1.2	−1.0	−11.9	3.8	2.7	2.6
Latvia	−4.6	−18.0	−4.0	2.7	15.3	3.3	−3.7	−2.5	−13.0	9.4	7.0	6.3
Estonia	−3.6	−14.1	0.8	3.6	10.4	−0.1	0.8	1.1	−9.4	4.6	4.7	3.9

[1]Movements in consumer prices are shown as annual averages. December–December changes can be found in Tables A6 and A7 in the Statistical Appendix.
[2]Percent of GDP.
[3]Current account position corrected for reporting discrepancies in intra-area transactions.

- In advanced Europe, recovery is projected to be gradual and uneven among euro area countries. Specifically, euro-area-wide GDP is expected to grow at 1 percent in 2010 and 1½ percent in 2011. The recovery is expected to be moderate in Germany and France, where export growth is limited by external demand, investment is held back by excess capacity and credit constraints, and consumption is tempered by higher unem-

ployment. Coming out even more slowly from the recession will be smaller euro area economies, where growth is constrained by large fiscal or current account imbalances (Greece, Ireland, Portugal, Spain). Outside the euro area, the prospects for recovery in advanced Europe are similarly diverse. In the United Kingdom, the recovery is projected to continue at a moderate pace, with previous sterling depreciation bolstering net exports even as domestic demand likely remains subdued.

- In emerging Europe, growth prospects also vary widely. Economies that weathered the global crisis relatively well (Poland) and others where domestic confidence has already recovered from the initial external shock (Turkey) are projected to rebound more strongly, helped by the return of capital flows and the normalization of global trade. At the same time, economies that faced the crisis with unsustainable domestic booms that had fueled excessively large current account deficits (Bulgaria, Latvia, Lithuania) and those with vulnerable private or public sector balance sheets (Hungary, Romania, Baltics) are expected to recover more slowly, partly as a result of limited room for policy maneuvers.

The uncertainty around the outlook in Europe has increased since the October 2009 WEO, with two downside risks becoming more pronounced. In the near term, the main risk is that, if unchecked, market concerns about sovereign liquidity and solvency in Greece could turn into a full-blown sovereign debt crisis, leading to some contagion (see Chapter 1 of the April 2010 GFSR). This reinforces the importance of efforts by the Greek authorities to reestablish the credibility of their fiscal policy. The financial support package agreed upon by euro area countries, the European Commission, and the European Central Bank to be provided if necessary is a welcome and important step to ensure that jitters about Greece do not lead to financial instability or create significant adverse effects on balance sheets and banking systems in Europe. A second downside risk lies in the need to adjust fiscal and current account imbalances in peripheral economies. Although resolving these imbalances is expected to dampen growth, delays in taking decisive policy action could lead to a protracted process punctuated with occasional crises.

Regarding fiscal policy, the priority is to make credible commitments to debt sustainability while proceeding with planned stimulus measures in 2010 where this is feasible. In some cases, large deficits need to be reversed promptly to address concerns about debt sustainability (Greece, Ireland, Portugal, Spain). However, in core euro area economies where

fiscal sustainability is not in question (Germany), the current plans to execute stimulus measures in full remain appropriate. Outside the euro area, several economies have already undertaken early consolidation (Hungary, Iceland, Latvia, Turkey). Across most European economies, however, the key fiscal challenge will be to commit, prepare, and communicate credible plans for fiscal consolidation. These should involve moving to sufficiently high primary surpluses in order to place public debt on a stabilizing and, eventually, declining path.

Monetary policy should remain highly accommodative in most cases. Recovery prospects are still sluggish, and so inflation pressures remain subdued. Indeed, in advanced Europe, core inflation is projected to remain low and stable (about 1 percent in the euro area), as inflation expectations are well anchored. Hence, in the euro area, it is appropriate to keep interest rates exceptionally low and to withdraw quantitative measures and unwind collateral requirement changes very gradually. This will help support the recovery in core economies while facilitating fiscal and real-economy adjustments in peripheral economies. In emerging Europe, inflation prospects are generally contained but more differentiated, owing to the variation in exchange rate regimes and output-recovery prospects across these economies (see Table 2.4). In most of these countries (with flexible exchange rate regimes and independent monetary policy), central banks could also afford to keep interest rates relatively low in the near term in order to support activity.

Another key policy challenge relates to Europe's financial sector. To the extent that they remain unresolved, banking sector issues will likely hamper the credit supply (see Chapter 1 of the April 2010 GFSR). These include the need for continued deleveraging to rebuild liquidity and capital buffers, the uncertainty about future bank restructuring, and the need to absorb additional write-downs. Moreover, growing sovereign risk poses another challenge for financial systems in Europe. These issues call for completion of the restructuring and recapitalization of vulnerable financial institutions, stabilizing funding, and reevaluating bank models.

In many ways, the most important task ahead is to strengthen EU policy frameworks to promote better adjustment mechanisms in good times and bad. The global crisis and its ripple effects have exposed weaknesses in existing policy arrangements on various fronts that need to be corrected to ensure Europe's future financial stability and growth.

- A reformed fiscal framework should incorporate a better mechanism for preventing and resolving fiscal imbalances. It could move in the direction of common fiscal rules and should include close monitoring of fiscal policies and public balance sheets.

- A stronger structural policy framework would help economies raise productivity, improve competitiveness, and reduce imbalances. Major amendments to the EU 2020 Agenda will be necessary to ensure its credible and effective delivery. A workable strategy rather than a focus on rigid targets should be at its core, which will require moving beyond the open method of coordination.

- Finally, given the cross-border nature of many European financial institutions and the potential for large spillovers across countries within the region, there is a strong case for an improved financial framework. The proposed new supervisory and regulatory structure should be put in place as planned and complemented with further work on an integrated crisis-prevention, -management, and -resolution mechanism.

The CIS Economies Are Recovering at a Moderate Pace

Having suffered a large output collapse during the crisis, the CIS region is emerging from the recession at a moderate pace. As in Europe, economic prospects across the region differ considerably.

Underpinning recovery in the CIS are several factors. First, higher commodity prices (oil, gas, metals) are once again supporting production and employment in commodity-exporting economies in the region. Second, the normalization of global trade and capital flows is helping CIS economies recover. Third, the turnaround in real activity in Russia is benefiting the rest of the region by boosting external demand for employment, capital, and goods from these economies. Fourth, IMF programs are supporting several economies in the region, and, whenever possible, expansionary domestic policies are fostering domestic demand. In addition to these positive forces, there are also negative factors that are holding back growth in several economies in the region, including lingering financial sector vulnerability and heavy dependence on external financing.

In this context, real activity in the CIS region is projected to expand by 4 percent in 2010, before moderating slightly to 3½ percent in 2011. But within the region, growth prospects are diverse (Figure 2.8; Table 2.5):

- In Russia, growth is expected to stage a modest recovery, reaching 4 percent in 2010. However, this largely reflects base effects and a turn in the inventory cycle. Despite relatively high oil prices and substantial government stimulus, underlying private domestic demand is likely to be subdued, with bad loans in the banking system expected to stifle credit and consumption growth.

- Benefiting from high commodity prices, energy exporter Uzbekistan is expected to remain among the top performers in the region in 2010, growing at 8 percent. Higher volumes of gas exports and large-scale investments are expected to raise growth in Turkmenistan, which is projected at 12 percent in 2010. More generally, economies with less externally linked financial sectors are expected to continue to do best.

Risks to the outlook in the CIS region are broadly balanced. For most CIS economies, growth prospects remain highly dependent on the speed of recovery in Russia, which could surprise in either direction.

Faced with different economic circumstances, the policy challenges in the region are also diverse.

- On the financial front, the main policy tasks vary widely across economies. For instance, in Russia, these include completing the exit from crisis-related liquidity and other measures by restoring more stringent regulatory requirements, developing plans for unwinding the forbearance already

Figure 2.8. Commonwealth of Independent States: Average Real GDP Growth during 2010–11[1]
(Percent)

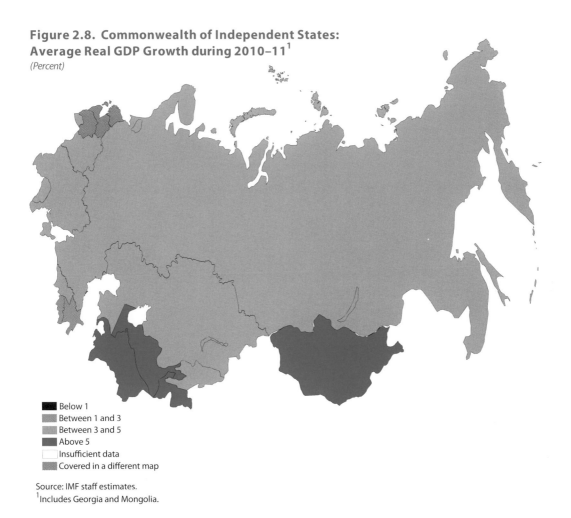

Below 1
Between 1 and 3
Between 3 and 5
Above 5
Insufficient data
Covered in a different map

Source: IMF staff estimates.
[1]Includes Georgia and Mongolia.

granted, and dealing with undercapitalized or insolvent banks. In Kazakhstan, the top priority is to implement a comprehensive solution to the problems in the banking sector, including by means of detailed independent assessment of the balance sheets of large banks.

- For monetary policy, because most economies in the region operate under pegged or heavily managed exchange rate regimes, the main challenge will be to calibrate the policy response to both domestic and external considerations. In many CIS economies, inflation is projected to decline, although it will remain at relatively high levels (Figure 2.9). Amid a more favorable external environment, and in some instances due to IMF programs supporting confidence, many regional currencies have reversed previous depreciations, leaving greater room than

during the crisis for monetary accommodation in response to sluggish domestic demand.

- On the fiscal front, some policymakers have rightly undertaken countercyclical fiscal expansion (for example, Russia), although concerns remain about the size and reversibility of expenditures. In some of the hardest-hit economies, however, policy room has been more limited despite the presence of multilateral and donor support, which helped prevent even deeper adjustments in fiscal balances.

Latin America and the Caribbean Are Recovering at a Robust Pace

Having weathered the global downturn comparatively well, the LAC region is posting a strong

Table 2.5. Commonwealth of Independent States: Real GDP, Consumer Prices, and Current Account Balance
(Annual percent change unless noted otherwise)

	Real GDP				Consumer Prices[1]				Current Account Balance[2]			
			Projections				Projections				Projections	
	2008	2009	2010	2011	2008	2009	2010	2011	2008	2009	2010	2011
Commonwealth of Independent States (CIS)[3]	**5.5**	**−6.6**	**4.0**	**3.6**	**15.6**	**11.2**	**7.2**	**6.1**	**4.9**	**2.6**	**4.0**	**3.6**
Russia	5.6	−7.9	4.0	3.3	14.1	11.7	7.0	5.7	6.2	3.9	5.1	4.6
Ukraine	2.1	−15.1	3.7	4.1	25.2	15.9	9.2	8.9	−7.1	−1.7	−2.3	−2.3
Kazakhstan	3.2	1.2	2.4	4.2	17.1	7.3	7.3	6.6	4.6	−3.1	0.7	−0.2
Belarus	10.0	0.2	2.4	4.6	14.8	13.0	7.3	6.2	−8.6	−12.9	−10.4	−9.2
Azerbaijan	10.8	9.3	2.7	0.6	20.8	1.5	4.7	3.5	35.5	23.6	25.3	24.2
Turkmenistan	10.5	4.1	12.0	12.2	14.5	−2.7	5.0	5.4	18.7	−9.7	−8.7	1.3
Mongolia	8.9	−1.6	7.2	7.1	26.8	6.3	7.3	5.3	−14.0	−5.6	−6.6	−16.5
Low-Income CIS	**8.6**	**4.7**	**4.5**	**3.9**	**15.8**	**6.2**	**6.8**	**6.3**	**12.0**	**7.9**	**8.6**	**8.1**
Uzbekistan	9.0	8.1	8.0	7.0	12.7	14.1	9.2	9.4	12.5	5.1	5.1	5.0
Georgia	2.3	−4.0	2.0	4.0	10.0	1.7	4.9	5.0	−22.7	−12.2	−14.2	−13.8
Armenia	6.8	−14.4	1.8	3.0	9.0	3.4	6.8	5.2	−11.5	−13.8	−13.0	−12.6
Tajikistan	7.9	3.4	4.0	5.0	20.4	6.5	7.0	8.3	−7.7	−7.3	−8.0	−8.3
Kyrgyz Republic	8.4	2.3	4.6	5.3	24.5	6.8	8.4	7.6	−8.1	3.5	−15.4	−12.5
Moldova	7.8	−6.5	2.5	3.6	12.7	0.0	7.7	5.7	−16.3	−7.9	−9.7	−9.7
Memorandum												
Net Energy Exporters[4]	5.7	−6.0	4.1	3.5	14.5	10.9	7.0	5.8	7.0	3.8	5.3	4.8
Net Energy Importers[5]	4.5	−9.6	3.3	4.3	21.3	13.1	8.4	7.8	−8.6	−5.7	−5.9	−5.9

[1]Movements in consumer prices are shown as annual averages. December–December changes can be found in Table A7 in the Statistical Appendix.

[2]Percent of GDP.

[3]Georgia and Mongolia, which are not members of the Commonwealth of Independent States, are included in this group for reasons of geography and similarities in economic structure.

[4]Net Energy Exporters comprise Azerbaijan, Kazakhstan, Russia, Turkmenistan, and Uzbekistan.

[5]Net Energy Importers comprise Armenia, Belarus, Georgia, Kyrgyz Republic, Moldova, Mongolia, Tajikistan, and Ukraine.

recovery. More balanced than in most other areas, output growth in the region is supported by both external and domestic demand.

Recovery in the LAC region has been shaped by a number of factors. First, accommodative policies are helping underpin domestic demand. Second, good fundamentals (sound financial systems, solid balance sheets) are helping the region recover and reattract capital flows in an improved global financial environment. Third, higher commodity prices and external demand are supporting growth in many economies, given their dependence on commodity-related earnings. However, weak external demand for tourism from North America and Europe is impeding growth in a number of economies in the region, especially in the Caribbean, whereas lower remittances are affecting many LAC economies.

Against this backdrop, GDP in the LAC region is projected to grow at 4 percent in 2010 and 2011, although prospects vary considerably across the region (Figure 2.10; Table 2.6).

- The recovery is projected to be especially strong in many commodity-exporting, financially integrated economies, which account for about two-thirds of the LAC region's GDP. In Brazil, growth in 2010 is expected to rebound to 5½ percent, led by strong private consumption and investment. Despite a devastating earthquake, Chile's GDP is projected to grow at about 4¾ percent in 2010 and 6 percent in 2011, supported by highly accommodative policies, a recovery in commodity prices, and reconstruction efforts. In Mexico, growth is expected to rebound to 4¼ percent in 2010, helped in part by the U.S. recovery. In Peru, the top growth performer of the region, GDP is projected to expand by 6¼ percent in 2010, mostly thanks to favorable internal dynamics and high commodity prices.

- Growth prospects are more subdued in other commodity-exporting economies in the region, although there is still considerable variation within this group. For instance, the rebound is projected to be relatively strong in Bolivia and Paraguay, whereas the recovery is expected to be delayed and weak in Venezuela, given ongoing power shortages.

- The recovery is also expected to be less strong in many commodity-importing economies in the region that have large tourism sectors (Antigua and Barbuda, The Bahamas, Barbados, St. Lucia). Weaker prospects for tourism, coupled with limited policy room to support the recovery, are expected to weigh on near-term growth.

The risks to LAC growth are substantial but broadly in balance. The main downside risks are external to the region. They relate to the fragility of the recovery in advanced economies and a potential weakness in commodity prices. There are also significant upside risks, however. These include even stronger internal dynamics, which could attract higher capital flows.

Given the region's diverse growth outlook, policy challenges vary widely across LAC economies. For many of the strong performers in the region, the central issue is related to when and how to exit from accommodative macroeconomic policies. For most tourism-intensive economies, the key challenge is to manage the recovery and maintain macroeconomic stability with limited policy choices, given high levels of public debt. Across the region, the issue of how to respond to large capital inflows will require deft policy management.

On the fiscal front, the sluggish recovery in advanced economies calls for keeping existing stimulus in place until domestic recoveries are firmly entrenched, especially where the economy is below potential. Nevertheless, the reversal of policy stimulus will need to proceed as soon as risks of domestic overheating (Brazil) or adverse debt dynamics become a concern. In economies with more limited fiscal room, the focus should be on maintaining targeted measures that ease hardship on the poor (for example, in the Caribbean). Once the recovery has gathered momentum, the stance of monetary policy should start moving from highly accommodative to more neutral. As output gaps are narrowing and inflation pressures are building at varying speeds, some of the economies with inflation-targeting regimes (Brazil) seem closer to that turning point than others (Colombia, Mex-

Figure 2.9. Commonwealth of Independent States (CIS): A Modest Recovery Ahead

The CIS region is coming out of the recession at a moderate pace, with considerable differentiation in economic prospects across the region. The turnaround in Russia is helping other economies in the region. Higher commodity prices are supporting the recovery in net energy exporters. Amid a more favorable external environment, capital flows are expected to return, but only gradually. Some regional currency depreciations have reversed, helping slow inflation.

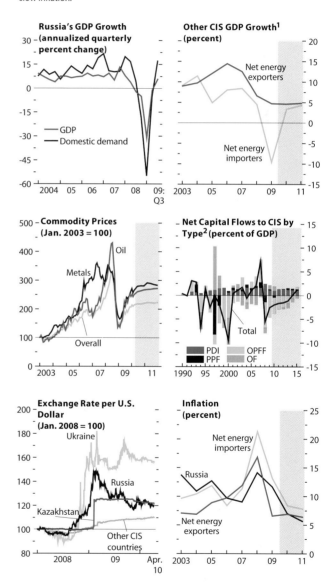

Sources: Haver Analytics; IHS Global Insight; IMF Primary Commodity Price System; and IMF staff estimates.
[1]Net energy exporters include Azerbaijan, Kazakhstan, Turkmenistan, and Uzbekistan. Net energy importers include Armenia, Belarus, Georgia, Kyrgyz Republic, Moldova, Mongolia, Tajikistan, and Ukraine.
[2]OF: official flows; OPFF: other private financial flows; PDI: private direct investment; PPF: private portfolio investment.

Figure 2.10. Latin America and the Caribbean: Average Real GDP Growth in 2010 –11
(Percent)

Below 1
Between 1 and 3
Between 3 and 5
Above 5
Insufficient data

Source: IMF staff estimates.

Table 2.6. Selected Western Hemisphere Economies: Real GDP, Consumer Prices, and Current Account Balance
(Annual percent change unless noted otherwise)

	Real GDP				Consumer Prices[1]				Current Account Balance[2]			
			Projections				Projections				Projections	
	2008	2009	2010	2011	2008	2009	2010	2011	2008	2009	2010	2011
Western Hemisphere	**4.3**	**−1.8**	**4.0**	**4.0**	**7.9**	**6.0**	**6.2**	**5.9**	**−0.6**	**−0.5**	**−1.0**	**−1.2**
South America and Mexico	**4.3**	**−1.9**	**4.1**	**4.0**	**7.6**	**6.1**	**6.3**	**6.0**	**−0.3**	**−0.3**	**−0.9**	**−1.1**
Brazil	5.1	−0.2	5.5	4.1	5.7	4.9	5.1	4.6	−1.7	−1.5	−2.9	−2.9
Mexico	1.5	−6.5	4.2	4.5	5.1	5.3	4.6	3.7	−1.5	−0.6	−1.1	−1.4
Argentina[3]	6.8	0.9	3.5	3.0	8.6	6.3	10.1	9.1	1.5	2.8	2.0	2.0
Colombia	2.4	0.1	2.2	4.0	7.0	4.2	3.5	3.7	−2.8	−1.8	−3.1	−2.9
Venezuela	4.8	−3.3	−2.6	0.4	30.4	27.1	29.7	33.1	12.3	2.5	10.5	10.8
Peru	9.8	0.9	6.3	6.0	5.8	2.9	1.5	1.8	−3.7	0.2	−0.7	−1.8
Chile	3.7	−1.5	4.7	6.0	8.7	1.7	2.0	3.0	−1.5	2.2	−0.8	−2.1
Ecuador	7.2	0.4	2.5	2.3	8.4	5.1	4.0	3.5	2.2	−1.1	−0.6	−1.6
Bolivia	6.1	3.3	4.0	4.0	14.0	3.5	3.3	3.7	12.1	3.5	2.6	2.0
Uruguay	8.5	2.9	5.7	3.9	7.9	7.1	6.2	6.0	−4.8	0.8	−1.0	−0.9
Paraguay	5.8	−4.5	5.3	5.0	10.2	2.6	3.9	3.6	−2.4	−0.2	−1.5	−1.2
Central America[4]	**4.3**	**−0.6**	**2.7**	**3.7**	**11.2**	**3.5**	**3.5**	**4.1**	**−9.1**	**−2.0**	**−5.4**	**−5.7**
Caribbean[5]	**2.9**	**0.4**	**1.5**	**4.3**	**12.0**	**3.6**	**6.4**	**4.8**	**−1.6**	**−3.1**	**−2.0**	**−1.2**

[1]Movements in consumer prices are shown as annual averages. December–December changes can be found in Table A7 in the Statistical Appendix.

[2]Percent of GDP.

[3]Private analysts estimate that consumer price index inflation has been considerably higher. The authorities have created a board of academic advisors to assess these issues. Private analysts are also of the view that real GDP growth has been significantly lower than the official reports since the last quarter of 2008.

[4]Central America comprises Costa Rica, El Salvador, Guatemala, Honduras, Nicaragua, and Panama.

[5]The Caribbean comprises Antigua and Barbuda, The Bahamas, Barbados, Belize, Dominica, Dominican Republic, Grenada, Guyana, Haiti, Jamaica, St. Kitts and Nevis, St. Lucia, St. Vincent and the Grenadines, Suriname, and Trinidad and Tobago.

ico). In the event that risks to growth materialize, monetary policy in these economies should stay nimble in both directions. Nevertheless, there is also an argument for keeping interest rates low for a longer period than justified by domestic cyclical considerations, because higher interest rates may attract speculative capital inflows.

Given its comparatively strong rebound, the LAC region may draw further inflows of foreign capital, which would pose an additional policy challenge. Although the current account position of the region is projected to remain in a small deficit, key economies have already attracted sizable flows into domestic equities and government bonds (Figure 2.11). Recent policy responses in the region have included allowing currency appreciation, accumulating foreign exchange reserves, and reintroducing capital controls. The appropriate response to potential further pressures in the region will continue to depend on economy-spe-

cific circumstances. In addition to the above-mentioned policies, it may also include adjusting the macroeconomic policy mix, specifically tightening fiscal policy and strengthening macroprudential measures.

The Middle East and North Africa Region Is Recovering at a Good Pace

The MENA region is growing out of its downturn at a good speed. Economic prospects across the region are quite diverse (Figure 2.12), shaped by different constellations of underlying forces.

There are several factors molding the shape of the MENA region's recovery. Pushing it forward are at least two forces. First, higher commodity prices and external demand are boosting production and exports in many economies in the region. Second, government spending programs are playing a key

Figure 2.11. Latin America and the Caribbean: A Robust Recovery[1]

Growth in Latin America and the Caribbean has rebounded, led by strong domestic consumption. Production levels have increased sharply, especially in Brazil. The ongoing recovery has been supported by improving financial conditions. Equity prices have reversed their declines and even exceeded precrisis levels in some economies. Despite accommodative monetary policies, good fundamentals are helping the region reattract capital flows, leading to currency appreciation in some cases.

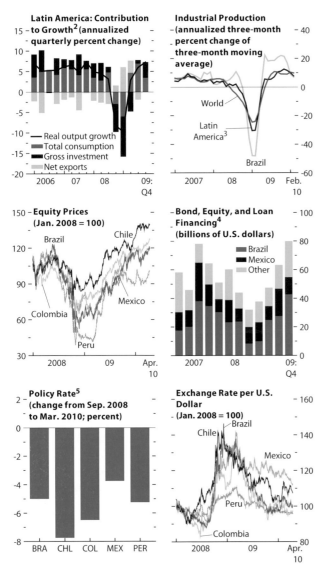

Sources: Bloomberg Financial Markets; Dealogic; Haver Analytics; IHS Global Insight; and IMF staff calculations.
[1]Latin America includes Argentina, Brazil, Chile, Colombia, Ecuador, Mexico, Peru, Uruguay, and Venezuela.
[2]Latin America excluding Uruguay.
[3]Latin America excluding Ecuador and Uruguay.
[4]Total issuance.
[5]BRA: Brazil; CHL: Chile; COL: Colombia; MEX: Mexico; PER: Peru.

role in fostering the recovery. In some economies, vulnerable financial sectors and weak property markets are holding it back (Kuwait, United Arab Emirates). The sluggish recovery in Europe is putting a damper on export growth, workers' remittances, and tourism revenues in other parts of the MENA region (Morocco, Tunisia), although the latest data suggest that these flows are gradually improving.

Considering these and other factors, GDP in the Middle East and North Africa is projected to grow at 4½ percent in 2010, edging up to 4¾ percent in 2011. As in other regions, recovery prospects vary substantially across MENA economies (Figure 2.13; Table 2.7).

- In the group of oil exporters, the strongest performer is Qatar, where real activity is projected to expand by 18½ percent in 2010, underpinned by continued expansion in natural gas production and large investment expenditures. In Saudi Arabia and Kuwait, GDP is expected to grow at about 3¾ percent and 3 percent, respectively, this year supported in both cases by sizable government infrastructure investment. In the United Arab Emirates, growth in 2010 is projected to be subdued at 1¼ percent, with property-related sectors expected to contract further.
- In the group of oil importers, Egypt's GDP is projected to grow 5 percent in 2010 and 5½ percent in 2011, helped by stimulative fiscal and monetary policies. Morocco and Tunisia will continue to grow at rates of 3¼ to 4 percent in 2010 and 4½ to 5 percent in 2011, assuming exports, tourism, remittances, and foreign direct investment continue to improve.

There is substantial uncertainty about this outlook, with two key risks on the downside. The first risk is that a slower-than-expected recovery in advanced economies could dampen commodity prices and tourism. This would adversely affect the region's export earnings, fiscal and external balances, and growth. The second risk relates to the aftermath of the Dubai World debt crisis, whose economic impact has so far been relatively limited but whose full impact may

Figure 2.12. Middle East and North Africa: Average Real GDP Growth in 2010–11
(Percent)

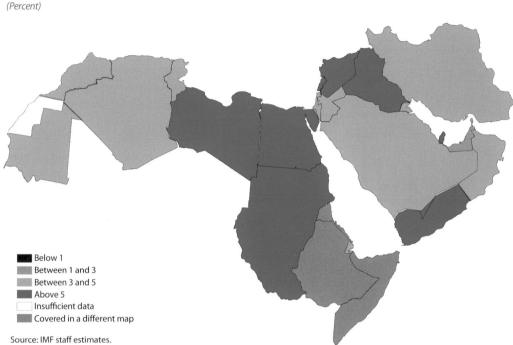

Below 1
Between 1 and 3
Between 3 and 5
Above 5
Insufficient data
Covered in a different map

Source: IMF staff estimates.

not be felt for some time. In particular, a possible repricing of quasi sovereign debt could have a lasting effect on financial systems, corporate sectors, and, more generally, economic activity in the area.

Fiscal policy has played a critical role in cushioning the impact of the global crisis on the region and in supporting its recovery. Government investment programs, especially in infrastructure, will continue to boost domestic demand in the near term in many MENA economies. These measures should remain in place to help cement the recovery. High debt levels, however, constrain the scope for fiscal stimulus in some oil-importing economies.

Given subdued inflation pressures, monetary policy should continue to be used as a countercyclical tool, if feasible. This pertains to MENA economies with nonpegged exchange rate regimes (Egypt). For other economies in the region that have hard pegs to the dollar (Saudi Arabia, United Arab Emirates), monetary policy mirrors U.S. policy and is appropriately stimulative.

With regard to financial sector policy, assistance to financial systems has helped contain vulnerabilities and spillovers, especially from the Gulf Cooperation Council region. In spite of such support, banks in the region have become more cautious, following recent episodes of financial sector distress that occurred amid sharp corrections in property

Figure 2.13. Middle East and North Africa (MENA): Growing out of Its Downturn[1]

Higher commodity prices and external demand are boosting production and exports in many economies in the region. Government spending programs are playing a key role in fostering the recovery, especially in oil-exporting countries with stronger public debt positions. Nevertheless, real credit is expected to be sluggish as credit demand remains weak in many economies and credit supply is held back by declining property markets and vulnerable financial sectors in some economies.

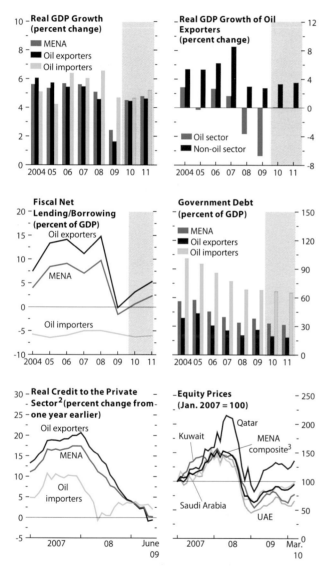

Sources: Haver Analytics; IMF, *International Financial Statistics*; and IMF staff estimates.

[1]Oil exporters include Algeria, Bahrain, Iraq, Islamic Republic of Iran, Kuwait, Libya, Oman, Qatar, Saudi Arabia, Sudan, United Arab Emirates (UAE), and Republic of Yemen. Oil importers include Djibouti, Egypt, Jordan, Lebanon, Mauritania, Morocco, Syrian Arab Republic, and Tunisia.
[2]Deflated by consumer price index.
[3]Includes Bahrain, Egypt, Jordan, Kuwait, Lebanon, Morocco, Oman, Qatar, Saudi Arabia, Tunisia, and UAE.

markets. This will likely curb the availability of bank loans and, ultimately, credit growth.

Turning to the external sector, current account surpluses in the MENA region are expected to widen again as the recovery proceeds. Specifically, the current account surplus of the region, which declined from 15½ percent of GDP in 2008 to 1¾ percent of GDP in 2009, is now projected to rise to 5¼ percent of GDP in 2010. But the recent increases in public spending on non-energy-related sectors should be helpful in diversifying activity toward these sectors, rebalancing regional growth, and reducing the region's current account surplus. Nonetheless, further efforts are needed to achieve such diversification, which will benefit not only the MENA region but the global economy as well.

Africa Is Coming through the Crisis Well

Sub-Saharan Africa has weathered the global crisis well, and its recovery from the slowdown in 2009 is expected to be stronger than following past global downturns. Although some middle-income and oil-exporting economies were hit hard by the collapse in export and commodity markets, the region managed to avoid a contraction in 2009, growing by 2 percent last year. Its growth is projected to accelerate to 4¾ percent this year and to 6 percent in 2011 (Figure 2.14; Table 2.8). The region's quick recovery reflects the relatively limited integration of most low-income economies into the global economy and the limited impact on their terms of trade, the rapid normalization in global trade and commodity prices, and the use of countercyclical fiscal policies. Remittances and official aid flows have also been less affected than anticipated by the recessions in advanced economies (Figure 2.15). Banking sectors have so far proved generally resilient, and private capital inflows have resumed into the region's more integrated economies.

Shocks from the global crisis hit sub-Saharan Africa mainly through the trade channel. Reflecting their greater openness to trade, the region's middle-income economies were among the hardest hit. Output in South Africa declined by 1¾ percent

Table 2.7. Selected Middle East and North African Economies: Real GDP, Consumer Prices, and Current Account Balance

(Annual percent change unless noted otherwise)

	Real GDP				Consumer Prices[1]				Current Account Balance[2]			
			Projections				Projections				Projections	
	2008	2009	2010	2011	2008	2009	2010	2011	2008	2009	2010	2011
Middle East and North Africa	**5.1**	**2.4**	**4.5**	**4.8**	**13.5**	**6.6**	**6.5**	**6.4**	**15.5**	**1.8**	**5.2**	**7.0**
Oil Exporters[3]	**4.6**	**1.6**	**4.5**	**4.6**	**14.6**	**5.7**	**6.0**	**6.3**	**19.6**	**3.4**	**7.8**	**10.0**
Islamic Republic of Iran	2.3	1.8	3.0	3.2	25.4	10.3	8.5	10.0	7.2	2.4	2.3	1.7
Saudi Arabia	4.3	0.1	3.7	4.0	9.9	5.1	5.2	5.0	27.9	5.5	9.1	10.8
Algeria	2.4	2.0	4.6	4.1	4.9	5.7	5.5	5.2	20.2	0.3	2.5	3.4
United Arab Emirates	5.1	−0.7	1.3	3.1	11.5	1.0	2.2	3.0	8.5	−3.1	7.8	7.7
Kuwait	6.4	−2.7	3.1	4.8	10.5	4.7	4.5	4.0	40.8	25.8	31.6	32.6
Iraq	9.5	4.2	7.3	7.9	2.7	−2.8	5.1	5.0	15.1	−19.4	−21.0	−5.5
Qatar	15.8	9.0	18.5	14.3	15.0	−4.9	1.0	3.0	33.0	16.4	25.1	39.4
Sudan	6.8	4.5	5.5	6.0	14.3	11.3	10.0	9.0	−9.0	−12.9	−8.4	−8.5
Oil Importers[4]	**6.5**	**4.7**	**4.6**	**5.2**	**10.1**	**9.1**	**8.0**	**6.7**	**−3.4**	**−4.2**	**−4.4**	**−4.1**
Egypt	7.2	4.7	5.0	5.5	11.7	16.2	12.0	9.5	0.5	−2.4	−2.6	−2.1
Morocco	5.6	5.2	3.2	4.5	3.9	1.0	2.0	2.6	−5.2	−5.0	−5.0	−4.4
Syrian Arab Republic	5.2	4.0	5.0	5.5	15.2	2.5	5.0	5.0	−3.6	−4.5	−4.0	−3.5
Tunisia	4.6	3.0	4.0	5.0	5.0	3.7	4.2	3.5	−4.2	−3.4	−2.7	−3.0
Lebanon	9.0	9.0	6.0	4.5	10.8	1.2	5.0	3.4	−11.5	−11.1	−12.8	−12.8
Jordan	7.8	2.8	4.1	4.5	14.9	−0.7	5.3	4.6	−10.3	−5.6	−8.9	−9.7
Memorandum												
Israel	4.0	0.7	3.2	3.5	4.6	3.3	2.3	2.6	0.7	3.7	3.9	3.7
Maghreb[5]	3.7	2.9	4.2	4.7	5.5	3.7	4.2	4.0	16.3	1.3	4.5	5.3
Mashreq[6]	7.0	4.8	5.0	5.4	12.3	11.9	10.0	8.1	−2.5	−4.0	−4.4	−4.0

[1]Movements in consumer prices are shown as annual averages. December–December changes can be found in Tables A6 and A7 in the Statistical Appendix.

[2]Percent of GDP.

[3]Includes Bahrain, Libya, Oman, and Republic of Yemen.

[4]Includes Djibouti and Mauritania.

[5]The Maghreb comprises Algeria, Libya, Mauritania, Morocco, and Tunisia.

[6]The Mashreq comprises Egypt, Jordan, Lebanon, and Syrian Arab Republic.

in 2009. Although the rebound in world trade is supporting recovery, South Africa's growth—projected at 2½ percent in 2010 and 3½ percent in 2011—will be tempered by high unemployment, tight credit conditions, and the recent strength of the rand.

Declining global demand and the collapse in oil prices also dealt a blow to the region's major oil exporters. Fiscal surpluses, some of which had been substantial, were cut markedly, and some economies swung into fiscal deficit. As a result, output growth in these economies slowed by 3½ percentage points to 4 percent in 2009, although strong performance in the non-oil economy allowed Nigeria, the region's largest oil producer,

to avoid a substantial slowdown. The recovery of oil prices and stronger global demand will raise growth for these economies to 6¾ percent in 2010 and 7 percent in 2011.

In the region's low-income economies the slowdown in economic activity was more modest, owing to their more limited trade and financial integration. Growth in a number of the more fragile economies even accelerated last year, reflecting mainly stronger policies and reconstruction assistance following periods of civil conflict, economic instability, and previous external shocks. For the low-income economies as a whole, output is projected to grow by 4¾ percent in 2010 and 6¾ percent in 2011.

**Figure 2.14. Sub-Saharan Africa:
Average Real GDP Growth in 2010 –11**
(Percent)

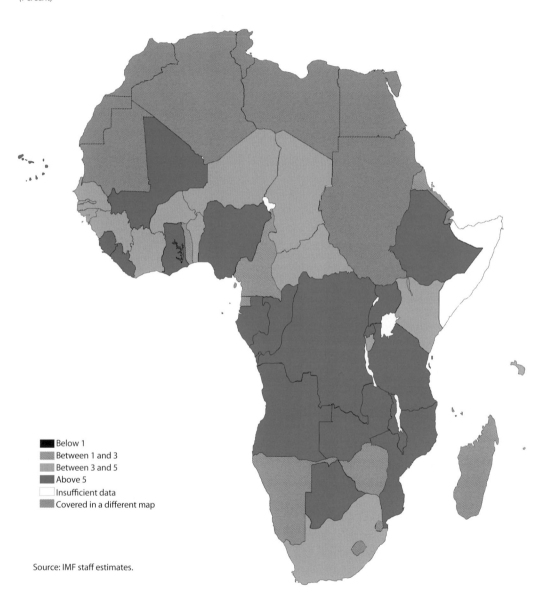

Below 1
Between 1 and 3
Between 3 and 5
Above 5
Insufficient data
Covered in a different map

Source: IMF staff estimates.

Table 2.8. Selected Sub-Saharan African Economies: Real GDP, Consumer Prices, and Current Account Balance

(Annual percent change unless noted otherwise)

	Real GDP				Consumer Prices[1]				Current Account Balance[2]			
			Projections				Projections				Projections	
	2008	2009	2010	2011	2008	2009	2010	2011	2008	2009	2010	2011
Sub-Saharan Africa	**5.5**	**2.1**	**4.7**	**5.9**	**11.6**	**10.6**	**8.0**	**6.9**	**0.9**	**−2.1**	**−1.7**	**−2.0**
Oil Exporters	**7.4**	**3.9**	**6.8**	**7.1**	**10.9**	**11.7**	**11.5**	**9.0**	**15.1**	**5.0**	**7.7**	**7.3**
Nigeria	6.0	5.6	7.0	7.3	11.6	12.4	11.5	9.5	20.4	11.6	12.4	12.0
Angola	13.2	−0.4	7.1	8.3	12.5	14.0	15.0	9.8	7.5	−3.3	3.6	3.1
Equatorial Guinea	10.7	5.3	0.9	2.1	4.3	7.1	7.1	6.6	9.9	−13.8	−5.0	−10.8
Gabon	2.7	−1.4	5.4	4.9	5.3	2.1	7.5	9.0	21.3	11.6	2.1	2.3
Chad	−0.4	−1.6	4.4	3.9	8.3	10.1	6.0	3.0	−13.7	−32.5	−29.7	−26.3
Congo, Republic of	5.6	7.6	12.1	6.6	6.0	4.3	4.0	3.0	−1.2	−12.4	−0.5	2.9
Middle-Income	**3.6**	**−1.8**	**2.8**	**3.7**	**11.5**	**7.1**	**5.7**	**5.7**	**−6.5**	**−4.2**	**−5.4**	**−6.9**
South Africa	3.7	−1.8	2.6	3.6	11.5	7.1	5.8	5.8	−7.1	−4.0	−5.0	−6.7
Botswana	3.1	−6.0	6.3	5.1	12.6	8.1	6.1	6.2	4.9	−5.1	−7.6	−7.7
Mauritius	4.2	1.5	4.1	4.7	9.7	2.5	2.1	2.4	−10.4	−8.2	−8.6	−8.3
Namibia	3.3	−0.7	1.7	2.2	10.0	9.1	6.5	5.9	2.7	−2.2	−6.6	−5.0
Swaziland	2.4	0.4	1.1	2.5	13.1	7.6	6.2	5.6	−4.1	−6.3	−12.8	−12.4
Cape Verde	5.9	4.1	5.0	5.5	6.8	1.2	1.4	2.0	−12.4	−19.4	−25.1	−24.3
Seychelles	−0.9	−7.6	4.0	5.0	37.0	31.8	3.2	2.5	−44.7	−23.1	−32.5	−28.8
Low-Income[3]	**5.8**	**4.3**	**4.7**	**6.7**	**12.4**	**12.9**	**7.0**	**6.1**	**−8.5**	**−6.6**	**−8.0**	**−7.5**
Ethiopia	11.2	9.9	7.0	7.7	25.3	36.4	3.8	9.3	−5.6	−5.0	−7.8	−9.3
Kenya	1.5	2.1	4.1	5.8	13.1	11.8	8.0	5.0	−6.9	−6.2	−6.7	−6.4
Tanzania	7.4	5.5	6.2	6.7	10.3	12.1	7.8	5.0	−9.8	−9.4	−8.0	−8.2
Cameroon	2.9	2.0	2.6	2.9	5.3	3.0	3.0	2.7	−1.8	−2.7	−4.3	−4.9
Uganda	8.7	7.1	5.6	6.4	7.3	14.2	10.5	7.5	−3.2	−4.8	−5.3	−6.1
Côte d'Ivoire	2.3	3.8	3.0	4.0	6.3	1.0	1.4	2.5	2.4	7.3	4.4	3.2

[1]Movements in consumer prices are shown as annual averages. December–December changes can be found in Table A7 in the Statistical Appendix.

[2]Percent of GDP.

[3]Includes Benin, Burkina Faso, Burundi, Central African Republic, Comoros, Democratic Republic of the Congo, Eritrea, The Gambia, Ghana, Guinea, Guinea-Bissau, Lesotho, Liberia, Madagascar, Malawi, Mali, Mozambique, Niger, Rwanda, São Tomé and Príncipe, Senegal, Sierra Leone, Togo, Zambia, and Zimbabwe.

The risks to the outlook in the region are varied, but three are worth highlighting. First, in addition to the direct impact of a more hesitant recovery in advanced economies, a recovery pattern that gave rise to large swings in commodity prices would have varied effects on the region. For example, higher-than-expected energy prices would benefit oil exporters but dampen growth and raise inflation in the region's oil importers. Second, although bilateral aid held up relatively well during the global downturn, the outlook for official aid flows to the region as a whole is subject to downside risks, given the large output declines in major donor economies, their possibly protracted recoveries, and heightened fiscal pressures. Finally, political uncertainty in several economies, particularly in West Africa, has

the potential to dampen their economic growth and spill over to their neighbors.

The use of countercyclical fiscal policy during the global downturn, in contrast to previous downturns, was a welcome development in the region. In most cases, the sustainability of public debt trajectories has not been adversely affected, a testament to improved fiscal positions in a number of sub-Saharan African economies in the run-up to the downturn. As private and external demand begins to recover, countries will need to rebuild fiscal room, turning from the near-term objective of stabilizing output to medium-term considerations, such as increasing spending on growth-enhancing priorities, including infrastructure, health, and education.

Finally, attracting private capital flows—and ensuring that macroeconomic policy successfully accommodates them—will continue to be a major policy challenge. More than a third of economies in sub-Saharan Africa remain on the margins of international capital markets and dependent on official forms of external financing. For these economies, the same reforms that are needed to raise productive potential—including promoting trade and financial sector development, encouraging domestic saving and investment, raising standards of governance, and strengthening institutions—are also likely to help attract private inflows on a sustained basis. For the region's more advanced economies, macroeconomic policy will need to take into account the renewed inflows of foreign capital to avoid overheating, unwarranted appreciation, and asset price booms.

Figure 2.15. Sub-Saharan Africa (SSA): Rebounding Strongly

Declining trade and commodity prices hurt sub-Saharan Africa during the crisis, but the recovery of both is supporting the rebound. Countercyclical fiscal balances and the stability of nonportfolio flows have also helped cushion the impact of the crisis in the region.

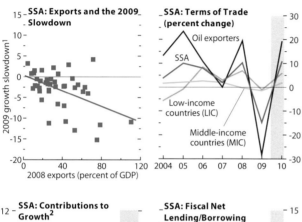
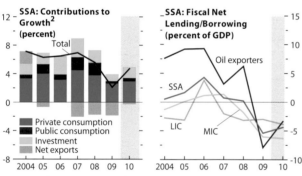
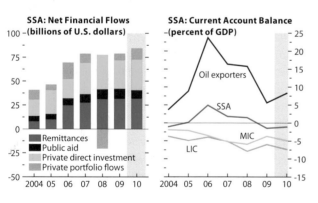

Source: IMF staff estimates.
[1] 2009 real GDP growth relative to average real GDP growth in 2003–07.
[2] Excluding Liberia, São Tomé and Príncipe, and Zimbabwe.

UNEMPLOYMENT DYNAMICS DURING RECESSIONS AND RECOVERIES: OKUN'S LAW AND BEYOND

The global economy is recovering from its deepest downturn since World War II, but the speed of recovery differs greatly across regions. For many advanced economies—where the financial crisis was centered—recovery is expected to be slow. In this context, persistently high unemployment may be the key policy challenge facing these economies as recovery gains traction.

During the Great Recession, output and unemployment responses differed markedly across advanced economies (Figure 3.1). For example, in Ireland and Spain the unemployment rate increased by about 7½ percentage points, despite the fact that output dropped by more than 8 percent in Ireland but by only half as much in Spain. Moreover, although Germany suffered an output drop of about 7 percent, its unemployment rate actually *decreased*. Such different responses suggest that, apart from the impact of output fluctuations, unemployment dynamics are also driven by institutions, policies, and shocks.

Against this backdrop, this chapter addresses the following questions:

- What explains unemployment dynamics during the Great Recession? Why have responses differed across countries with similar output declines?

- What are the near-term prospects for employment creation given current output forecasts? What policies can enhance job creation during the recovery?

To shed light on these questions, this chapter provides a systematic analysis of unemployment dynamics in a sample of advanced economies during recessions and recoveries over the past 30 years.[1]

Because these dynamics can be driven simply by output fluctuations, the chapter uses Okun's law—the relationship between changes in the unemployment rate and changes in output—as an organizing framework.

The chapter contributes to the literature by examining the role of institutions and policies in explaining changes in Okun's law across countries and over time. The chapter then goes a step further by studying how financial crises, housing busts, sectoral shifts, and uncertainty can drive the response of unemployment beyond the impact of output fluctuations. Finally, the chapter analyzes some prominent policy issues—namely, short-time work programs, job subsidies, and two-tiered labor markets (the dualism between temporary and permanent contracts).

The main findings of the chapter are as follows:

- The responsiveness of unemployment to output has increased over the past 20 years in many countries. This reflects significant institutional reform, particularly making employment protection legislation (EPL) less strict, and greater use of temporary employment contracts.

- During recessions, financial crises, large house price busts, and other sectoral shocks raise unemployment beyond the levels predicted by Okun's law. During recoveries, the impact of financial crises and house price busts continues to constrain employment creation. In addition, there is some evidence that greater macroeconomic uncertainty slows employment growth.

- During the Great Recession, the sharp increases in unemployment in Spain and the United States can be explained largely by the impact of output declines as predicted using Okun's law, by financial stress, and by the impact of house price busts. In countries that implemented large short-time work programs (Germany, Italy, Japan, Netherlands), the rise in unemployment was less than predicted by these factors. Other countries that experienced less unemployment

The main authors of this chapter are Ravi Balakrishnan, Mitali Das, and Prakash Kannan, with support from Stephanie Denis, Murad Omoev, and Andres Salazar; Tito Boeri was the external consultant.

[1]The sample includes Australia, Austria, Belgium, Canada, Denmark, Finland, France, Germany, Greece, Ireland, Italy, Japan, Netherlands, New Zealand, Norway, Portugal, Spain, Sweden, Switzerland, United Kingdom, and United States.

Figure 3.1. Change in Unemployment Rates and Output Declines during the Great Recession[1]

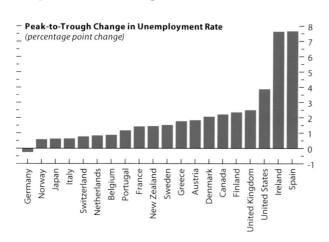

Peak-to-Trough Change in Unemployment Rate
(percentage point change)

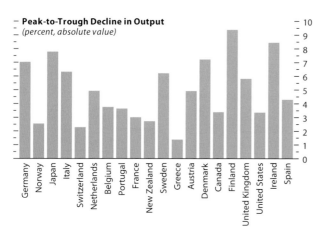

Peak-to-Trough Decline in Output
(percent, absolute value)

Source: IMF staff calculations.
[1]Because GDP in Greece and Spain has not yet reached a trough according to official data, the change in the unemployment rate and decline in output are taken from the peak to the latest data point.

than expected present more of a puzzle (Canada, United Kingdom).

- For several advanced economies, the potential for a slow recovery in output and the nature of the recent recession (financial crisis combined with a house price bust) presage persistently high near-term unemployment rates. Given the additional prospect that unemployment becomes structural, the standard macroeconomic policy levers— monetary policy and fiscal policy—remain the primary tools for boosting employment through their impact on economic activity. In countries where unemployment rates remain high and the economy is operating below potential, policy stimulus remains warranted. Financial sector repair is also essential, given that labor-intensive sectors rely heavily on bank credit.

- Several specific labor market policies could help reduce unemployment in addition to pursuit of conventional macroeconomic and financial poli-cies, encouragement of wage flexibility, and gen-eral improvements to labor market institutions. For economies with lingering macroeconomic uncertainty, but where labor productivity remains strong, targeted and temporary hiring subsidies may help advance employment creation. In coun-tries with large short-time work programs, ending these, along with carefully designed wage-loss insurance programs, could help facilitate move-ment of labor across sectors. Finally, in countries with two-tiered labor markets, transitioning to a system of open-ended labor contracts under which employment security gradually increases with tenure could help enhance human capital formation and increase unemployment benefit coverage.

To motivate the analysis in this chapter, the follow-ing section looks at broad labor market dynamics dur-ing the Great Recession, and the next section discusses the theoretical considerations behind the Okun's law framework. Then the chapter examines how institu-tions change the relationship between unemployment and output across countries and over time. It subse-quently proceeds to study unemployment dynamics during recessions and recoveries, controlling for output fluctuations and changes in Okun's law over time. Put-ting it all together, the chapter subsequently addresses the key questions: What explains cross-country variation in unemployment responses during the Great Recession? What are the prospects for recovery? What policies may help promote job creation?

Broad Labor Market Dynamics during the Great Recession

Recent labor market developments appear to have been driven largely by employment dynamics rather than by declining labor participation rates, as indicated by the fact that broad measures of unemployment (including workers marginally attached to the labor force) mirror trends in standard unemployment rates (Figure 3.2). Changes in actual participation rates during the Great Recession confirm this finding (Figure 3.3). Despite dramatic falls in employment, labor force participation rates have been fairly flat in most countries, except in Ireland.

Figure 3.4 shows labor market dynamics during the Great Recession and previous cycles in the United States, Germany, and Japan. The panels track fluctuations in labor productivity (output per hour), hours worked per employee, employment rate (share of labor force), and labor force participation (share of population), using the following identity:

$$\log\left(\frac{Y}{P}\right) = \log\left(\frac{Y}{H}\right) + \log\left(\frac{H}{E}\right) \qquad (1)$$
$$+ \log\left(\frac{E}{LF}\right) + \log\left(\frac{LF}{P}\right),$$

where Y is real GDP, P is population, H is hours, E is employment, and LF is the labor force.

The differences between the United States and Germany are striking. In the United States, there was a larger drop than in previous recessions in both the employment rate and hours worked per employee, but output per hour grew strongly despite the large output decline. In Germany, the unemployment rate actually decreased, which is even more remarkable given the much larger output drop during the Great Recession than during previous recessions. It appears that the adjustment occurred through a substantial decrease in hours worked per employee and in output per hour.

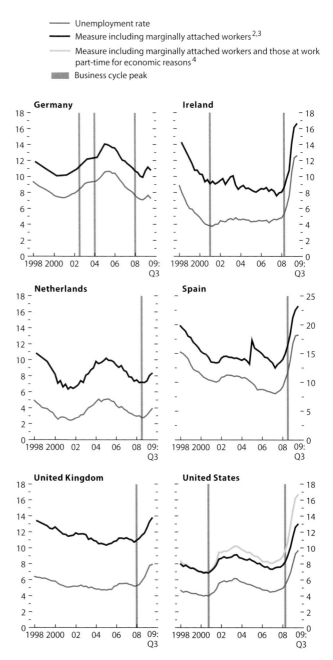

Figure 3.2. Broad Measures of Unemployment[1]
(Percent)

— Unemployment rate
— Measure including marginally attached workers[2,3]
— Measure including marginally attached workers and those at work part-time for economic reasons[4]
■ Business cycle peak

Sources: Eurostat; Haver Analytics; and IMF staff calculations.
[1]This measure of unemployment is defined as $w =$ (total unemployment + marginally attached workers)/(civilian labor force + marginally attached labor force).
[2]For European countries, the measure is defined as "inactive population; would like to work but is not seeking employment."
[3]For the United States, the measure is defined as "not in labor force: want a job now."
[4]For the United States, the measure is defined as "part-time work for economic reasons": $w =$ (total unemployment + marginally attached workers + at work part-time for economic reasons)/(civilian labor force + marginally attached labor force).

Figure 3.3. Evolution of Employment, Unemployment, and Labor Participation
(Percent of working-age population)[1]

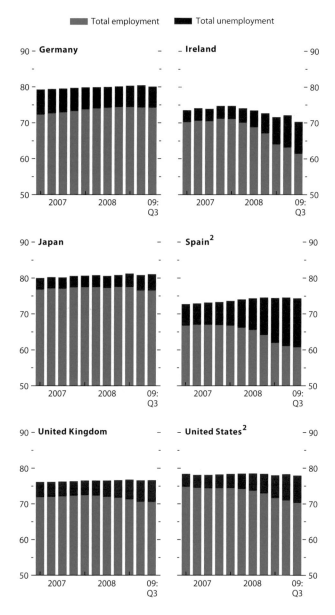

Sources: U.S. Bureau of Labor Statistics; Organization for Economic Cooperation and Development; and IMF staff calculations.
[1]Working-age population, 15–64 years.
[2]Working-age population, 16–64 years.

What underlies the different dynamics in Germany and the United States? Different labor market institutions and policies could play a role. Stricter employment protection legislation can mute the employment response during an economic downturn.[2] And according to the Organization for Economic Cooperation and Development (OECD) measure, Germany has much stricter EPL than the United States. Germany also massively expanded its short-time work program *(Kurzarbeit)* during the Great Recession, which may help explain why some of the adjustment occurred in hours worked per employee rather than in job losses.

However, the sharp difference in dynamics of output per hour in Germany and the United States—notwithstanding the larger output drop in the former—suggests other forces at work beyond institutions and labor market policies. Indeed, the nature of the shocks experienced by the two countries was markedly different: the United States experienced a housing bust combined with a systemic financial crisis, whereas Germany mainly experienced an external demand shock resulting from the open nature of its economy.

The analysis in this chapter assesses the impact of institutions, policies, and shocks (after controlling for output fluctuations) on unemployment dynamics during recessions and recoveries in advanced economies. Okun's law is the framework for the analysis, and that is outlined next.

Using Okun's Law as a Framework

Okun's law captures the relationship between unemployment and output. It is a statistical relationship that has received strong empirical support for a broad cross section of countries (see Knotek, 2007; Moosa, 1997; and Okun, 1962). As originally estimated by Okun, it has the following simple form:

Change in unemployment rate =
$$\alpha - \beta \times \text{change in real output.} \quad (2)$$

Here, α is an intercept coefficient, and β (beta) is the elasticity of the unemployment rate with respect to output, which was estimated by Okun to

[2]See Box 1.3 in the October 2009 *World Economic Outlook.*

Figure 3.4. Labor Dynamics in the United States, Germany, and Japan

(All series are in levels indexed to 100 at the business cycle peak; quarters on x-axis; peak in output at t = 0)

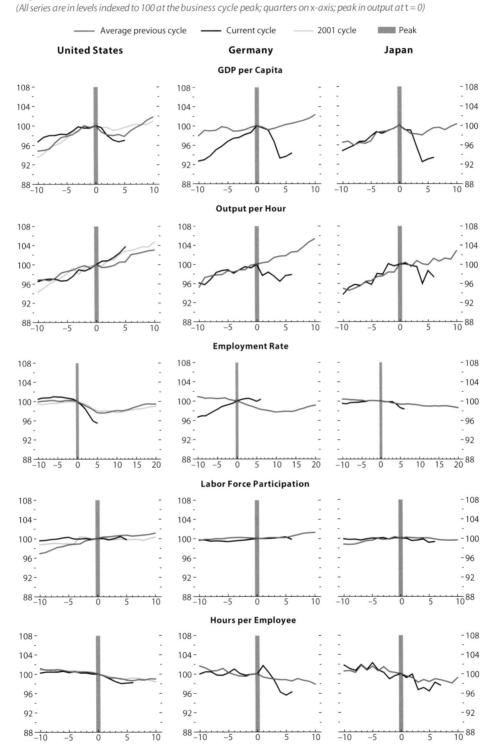

Sources: Haver Analytics; Institute for Employment Research; Organization for Economic Cooperation and Development; and IMF staff calculations.

Figure 3.5. Relationship between Unemployment and Output over Time

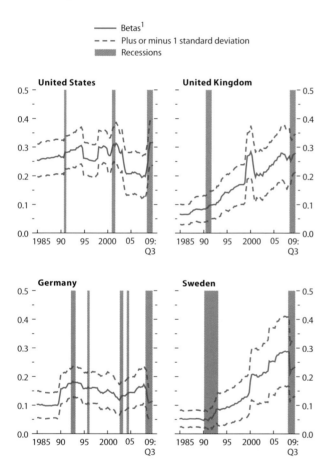

Source: IMF staff calculations.
[1]Absolute value of estimated elasticity of unemployment with respect to output from a static Okun's law relationship, which is regressed over rolling 40-quarter windows.

be about 0.3 for the United States during the early post–World War II period. The value of α/β is the minimum level of output growth needed to reduce the unemployment rate given labor force and labor productivity growth.

Figure 3.5 suggests that this relationship varies across countries and over time. For Sweden and the United Kingdom, the elasticity of the unemployment rate (beta) has trended upward for the past 20 years. For the United States, there is no discernible trend, but the beta has oscillated over time.

The variations in this relationship have important implications for unemployment dynamics during recessions and recoveries. For instance, larger betas would lead to larger predicted increases in unemployment during a recession for a given output decline. Figure 3.5 also points to gradual shifts in this relationship over time (trends) and to *episodic shifts* in the relationship (for example, the increase in the beta for the United States during the Great Recession). The analysis in this chapter differentiates between these two types of shifts by using a methodology consisting of two main steps.

Step 1: Estimate Okun's Law for Each Recession Episode

In Step 1, for each country in the sample, a dynamic version of the Okun's law equation is estimated using data on unemployment and output for the 20 years prior to the start of each recession. A country that has had more recessions will have more "episodes" over which to estimate Okun's law. Since all countries in the sample have experienced at least two recessions, the resulting set of betas varies across countries and over time.

These variations in the betas reflect the effects of several key reforms of labor market institutions (Boeri and van Ours, 2008):

- Employment protection legislation: Stricter EPL (higher hiring and firing costs) should make it more difficult to fire workers in a downturn and to hire workers during a recovery. Thus, stricter EPL should lead to a lower elasticity of unemployment with respect to changes in output.
- Unemployment benefits: In theory, the effect of unemployment benefits (as measured by the ratio of income replaced) is ambiguous. During recessions,

higher benefits limit the potential range for wage adjustments, leading to more job losses. During recoveries, higher benefits lead to higher wage expectations on the part of potential workers, thus constraining job creation.[3]

- Temporary employment contracts: Workers with temporary contracts have less employment protection relative to those with regular (open-ended) contracts. Thus, in economies with a relatively higher share of workers on temporary contracts, unemployment should be more responsive to changes in output. This issue has become more prominent since the 1980s in many countries, especially Spain (Box 3.1).

Another important factor is wage flexibility. Decentralized wage systems can facilitate downward wage flexibility, mitigating job losses. In Japan, for instance, nominal wages fell by 4.4 percent in 2009 through reductions in wage rates, paid overtime, and bonus payments. Centralized collective bargaining systems, on the other hand, can sometimes impede the adjustment of wages to deflation, which increases job losses. For example, in Spain, contractual wages increased by almost 3 percent in 2009 despite a 7 percent decline in employment. Unfortunately, the analysis in this chapter does not directly include measures of collective bargaining, which are highly imperfect and not available at the frequencies required here. Moreover, to fully capture wage flexibility requires analyzing microeconomic data, which is not the focus of this chapter. However, other institutional variables that are incorporated here capture some aspects of the variation in wage flexibility across countries.

Step 2: Compute Forecast Errors

Based on the estimated Okun's law relationships for each country, predictions about unemployment are made (1) during recessions and (2) during recoveries, using the observed changes in output for both. Actual unemployment rates are compared to the predicted rates in order to compute fore-

[3] It should be noted, however, that adequate unemployment benefits are an important automatic stabilizer and are essential for avoiding large increases in poverty following recessions.

cast errors for the behavior of unemployment in recessions and recoveries.[4] This two-step approach provides a clear and intuitive presentation of the separate effects of other episodic factors, beyond changes in output, that can affect unemployment, including

- Financial crises and stress: Historically, recessions accompanied by financial crises have been characterized by significantly larger drops and more protracted recoveries in the employment rate than normal recessions (Figure 3.6).[5] However, the output drop has also been larger during such episodes, so the conditional impact is not clear. Numerous studies, beginning with Bernanke and Gertler (1989), show how a firm's balance sheet can amplify business cycle fluctuations. For example, firms that are more highly leveraged prior to a recession may face a greater need to deleverage if the recession is associated with a credit crunch (Sharpe, 1994).[6] The conditional impact on unemployment is explored here by relating the forecast errors to the occurrence of financial crisis and the level of financial stress.

- Sectoral shocks: Examples of sectoral shocks include the negative impact of house price busts on workers in construction and real estate services, of financial crises on jobs in the financial sector, and of trade declines on employment in the tradables sector in open economies. Again, such shocks are also likely to reduce output, clouding the conditional impact on unemploy-

[4] There is a question of whether the estimation should be done in a single step using output and unemployment lags, as well as the institutional variables and shocks dummies. The empirical procedure used here treats Okun's law as the benchmark specification in the first step primarily to allow comparability with the rest of the literature. The presence of large deviations from the baseline Okun's law specification then suggests that other institutional or episodic factors could also play a role beyond the effects of output. Appendix 3.2 discusses in detail the pros and cons of a two-step approach.

[5] The definition of financial crises is based on Chapter 3 of the April 2009 *World Economic Outlook*, which in turn is based on Reinhart and Rogoff (2008).

[6] Another channel is through the larger drops in net worth typically featured in recessions associated with financial crises. This can prompt larger layoffs by firms that rely more on working capital to finance their operations during recessions accompanied by financial crises than during more normal recessions, even with similar aggregate output losses.

Box 3.1. The Dualism between Temporary and Permanent Contracts: Measures, Effects, and Policy Issues

Employment protection legislation (EPL)—the rules governing the costs to employers of dismissing workers—has been subject to frequent policy changes over the past 20 years. Only four Organization for Economic Cooperation and Development (OECD) countries out of 26 have not adjusted EPL over time. The OECD developed a widely used index to measure EPL strictness, based on an assessment of national regulations, and the changes in this index since 1990 (see first table) suggest that reforms during this period were broadly geared toward reducing dismissal costs, notably in countries that already had the strictest standards. The table lists all countries whose EPL reforms involved a change in the index exceeding 50 percent of the cross-country standard deviation in the index. Notice also the decline in the average of the overall index for OECD countries and of the cross-country standard deviation of this indicator (bottom two rows).

These reforms in most cases did not change—and may have even tightened—rules for regular, or open-ended, contracts. Instead, reforms were carried out primarily by changing rules only for new hires, introducing a wide array of flexible, fixed-term types of contracts or expanding the scope of existing temporary contracts. An inventory of reforms assembled by the Fondazione Rodolfo Debenedetti in cooperation with the Institute for the Study of Labor indicates

The author of this box is Tito Boeri.

that 92 percent of EPL regulatory changes involving a discrete change in the level of the overall index did not apply to workers with permanent contracts—in other words, there has been a dual-track (or two-tier) reform strategy. For instance, in Italy the so-called Treu Package in 1997 removed restrictions on the use of fixed-term contracts and introduced temporary agency work without modifying the rules for open-ended contracts. In Germany in 1997, the maximum duration of fixed-term contracts was extended from 9 to 12 months and the restrictions on the maximum number of contract renewals were loosened. The subsequent series of small reforms in these countries continued to increase flexibility at the margin, applying only to new hires.

As a result of these asymmetric reforms, the use of temporary workers, which had been close to zero in most countries, has steadily increased. Countries with the strictest provisions for regular, open-ended contracts experienced a large increase in the share of fixed-term (temporary) contracts in total dependent employment. Indeed, the increasing use of temporary workers has not only resulted in dual-track, two-tier labor arrangements but has also blurred the boundary between dependent employment and self-employment. The first figure displays, on the vertical axis, the share of temporary workers in 2008 and, on the horizontal axis, the EPL index for regular contracts in 1985. There is a strong positive association between the two variables (the correlation coefficient is 0.81).

OECD Employment Protection Legislation Strictness Index

	EPL, All Contracts		EPL, Regular Contracts	
	1990	2008	1990	2008
Belgium	3.15	2.18	1.68	1.73
Denmark	2.40	1.50	1.68	1.63
Germany	3.17	2.12	2.58	3.00
Greece	3.50	2.73	2.25	2.33
Italy	3.57	1.89	1.77	1.77
Netherlands	2.73	1.95	3.08	2.72
Portugal	4.10	3.15	4.83	4.17
Spain	3.82	2.98	3.88	2.46
Sweden	3.49	1.87	2.90	2.86
Mean (all OECD countries)	**2.30**	**1.93**	**2.17**	**2.05**
Standard Deviation (all OECD countries)	**1.17**	**0.85**	**0.99**	**0.85**

Source: Organization for Economic Cooperation and Development.

Note: The index ranges from 0 to 6, with higher values indicating stricter employment protection. "Regular contracts" refer to open-ended employment contracts with no fixed term, which are sometimes referred to as permanent contracts.

Share of Temporary Workers and Employment Protection Legislation Index for Regular Contracts, 1985[1]

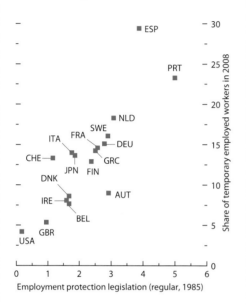

Employment protection legislation (regular, 1985)

Sources: Organization for Economic Cooperation and Development, *Employment Outlook;* and IMF staff calculations.

[1] AUT: Austria; BEL: Belgium; DNK: Denmark; FIN: Finland; FRA: France; DEU: Germany; GRC: Greece; IRE: Ireland; ITA: Italy; JPN: Japan; NLD: Netherlands; PRT: Portugal; ESP: Spain; SWE: Sweden; CHE: Switzerland; GBR: United Kingdom; USA: United States.

Temporary Workers
(Percent of dependent employment)

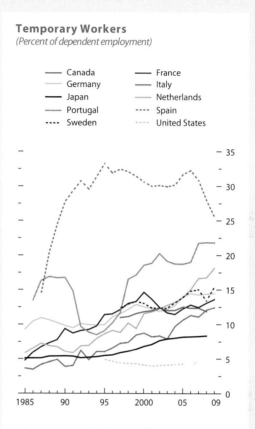

Sources: Eurostat; Organization for Economic Cooperation and Development, Labour Force Statistics; and IMF staff calculations.

As mentioned, the share of temporary contracts steadily increased before the Great Recession in countries with strict EPL (second figure). However, temporary workers experienced the majority of Great-Recession-related job losses, and so this share has fallen. For example, in Spain employment of temporary workers declined by almost 20 percent (compared with 7 percent for total employment); by almost 10 percent in Italy (compared with 1.5 percent); by 6 percent in France (compared with 0.3 percent); and by 2 percent in Germany (compared with an increase of 0.4 percent in total employment).

The two-tier nature of these labor markets is evident as well in the wage premium placed on permanent contracts. This premium reflects the stronger bargaining power of regular workers and the fact that workers with flexible contracts are not covered by EPL and have little or no access to unemployment benefits in case of job loss. The second table quantifies the premium for permanent employment. The first column shows the wage premium placed on permanent contracts with respect to fixed-term contracts. The results suggest that in countries like Italy, workers with permanent contracts are paid, other things being equal, almost one-fourth more than workers on fixed-term contracts. This price-based premium can be compared with the quantity-based measure in the second column: the share of temporary contracts in total dependent employment. The rankings differ (the Spearman's rank correlation coefficient between the two measures of dualism is 0.32), but the United Kingdom stands out as having

Box 3.1 *(continued)*

Disparity between Permanent and Temporary Employment

	Wage Premium for Permanent Contracts[1] (percent)	Share of Temporary Contracts in Total Dependent Employment	Yearly Probability of Transitioning from a Temporary to a Permanent Contract[2]
Austria	20.1	8.9	47.4
Belgium	13.9	8.8	40.4
Denmark	17.7	7.8	…
Finland	19.0	12.4	22.7
France	28.9	13.7	13.6
Germany	26.6	14.2	…
Greece	10.3	12.9	31.3
Ireland	17.8	9.0	46.3
Italy	24.1	13.4	31.2
Luxembourg	27.6	6.9	41.0
Netherlands	35.4	16.6	…
Portugal	15.8	22.2	12.1
Spain	16.9	31.9	28.3
Sweden	44.7	17.5	…
United Kingdom	6.5	5.8	45.7

Sources: European Community Household Panel and *European Union Survey of Income and Living Conditions*.

[1]Estimated as the coefficient of a dummy variable capturing permanent contracts, in a (monthly) wage regression of male dependent employment, controlling for education, tenure, and the (broad) sector of affiliation:

$$\log(w_i) = \alpha + \beta_1 EDU_i + \beta_2 EDU_i^2 + \gamma_1 TEN_i + \gamma_2 TEN_i^2 + \delta PERM_i + U,$$

where i indexes individuals, w is monthly wages of individuals, EDU is years of schooling, TEN is years of tenure, and $PERM$ is the dummy for permanent contracts.

[2]Estimated from matched records of the *European Union Survey of Income and Living Conditions* for 2004–07.

the least disparity according to both measures. The third column provides another measure of dualism: the yearly probability of transitioning from a fixed-term to a permanent contract. The larger this probability, the lower the disparity between permanent and temporary employment. Indeed, the correlation coefficient between this third measure and the other two is negative, although only the correlation between the transition and the wage premium is statistically significant.

Effects on Unemployment

The asymmetric, or two-tier, EPL reforms have increased the responsiveness of employment and unemployment to output changes. Employers can hire temporary workers during upturns and can let them go during downturns, and they do not face any dismissal costs. Fixed-term (temporary) workers are typically protected against dismissal during the duration of the contracts, and there are generally (binding) restrictions on the number of temporary contracts that a firm can issue. There is therefore some

time lag in both the growth of temporary workers during upturns and their reduction during downturns, and a long expansionary period can result in a large "buffer stock" of temporary workers, whereas a long recession could significantly reduce their share in total employment. This means that countries with more temporary workers could experience larger employment losses during a recession. Conversely, a lower share of temporary workers at the trough of the business cycle or fewer restrictions on the use of flexible contracts (which can be captured by the wage premium in the second table) imply a potential for greater employment gains during the upturn.

The effect of a two-tier labor market on employment is illustrated in the third figure, displaying labor demand as a function of wages in two extreme conditions: a recession (left-hand curve) and a boom (right-hand curve). When labor is perfectly flexible, the firm optimally hires at A when conditions are bad and at B when conditions are good. In the presence of strict EPL, the firm instead will set average employment at C to avoid paying dismissal costs.

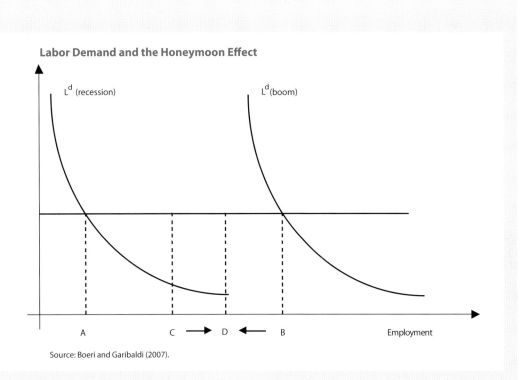

Labor Demand and the Honeymoon Effect

Source: Boeri and Garibaldi (2007).

When temporary contracts are introduced, the firm exploits any hiring flexibility when business is good by gradually building up a stock of temporary workers but has limited flexibility when business is bad because it can reduce only the number of temporary workers and not permanent workers. Thus, employment will shift during the cycle between B and C, increasing average employment compared with a fully rigid labor market.

Firms facing strict EPL will adjust employment during the course of a business cycle only to the extent allowed by natural turnover: during upturns they will replace workers who voluntarily leave the firm, and during downturns they will leave vacancies unfilled and let employment decline by attrition. The increase in average employment associated with the introduction of temporary contracts will thus be transitory, creating a sort of "honeymoon effect" (see Boeri and Garibaldi, 2007). If regulations allow, fixed-term contracts could be substituted for permanent contracts for each worker hired during the cycle, but then the honeymoon would end, because employment would shift from A to B, just as in a flexible labor market.

This simple, stylized representation suggests the following:

- Employment should be more responsive to output changes in two-tiered labor markets than in markets with strict EPL (see also Costain, Jimeno, and Thomas, forthcoming).
- The share of temporary workers should increase the elasticity of employment to output during a recession; the increase will be greater the shorter the term of temporary contracts.
- Conversely, the increase in the responsiveness of employment to output changes during a recovery should be greater the lower the initial share of temporary workers (relative to any threshold set by regulation) and the less stringent the regulations concerning the duration and renewal of temporary contracts.

Policy Issues

Temporary contracts can significantly increase employment during upturns. However, the heavy job losses associated with such contracts during the Great Recession have created strong pressure to phase out such arrangements. Firms that anticipate

Box 3.1 *(continued)*

restrictions on the use of temporary contracts may be more reluctant to hire as the recovery gains traction. In fact, discontinuing temporary contracts in the wake of a recession compounds the worst aspects of a two-tiered labor market: temporary workers suffer greater unemployment during the downturn, but then find fewer jobs created during the recovery.

To benefit from the honeymoon effect and spur job creation during the recovery, policymakers should seek to credibly retain labor market flexibility, even in the face of pressure for stricter EPL.

Another policy issue relates to the negative impact of temporary employment on human capital formation. Temporary workers receive less training than workers with open-ended contracts (fourth figure). Recoveries from financial crises are typically associated with greater use of temporary contracts because uncertainty and liquidity constraints discourage firms from making long-term commitments. Both Japan and Sweden experienced a strong rise in the share of temporary contracts in the 1990s in the wake of financial crises. This means a new generation of workers could face a lack of adequate training in the wake of the Great Recession.

One way to encourage more hiring during the recovery and to foster on-the-job training is to bridge the two tiers of the labor market by allowing for graded employment security. In particular, policymakers could promote the staged entry of workers into the permanent labor market by gradually increasing the costs faced by employers for dismissing a worker under an open-ended contract as the worker's tenure lengthens.

A staged tenure arrangement could involve open-ended contracts but with a statutory sever-

On-the-Job Training: Difference between Permanent and Temporary Employment
(Percent)

Source: European Community Household Panel.

ance payment that gradually increases with tenure (for example, five days' severance pay per quarter worked) up to the maximum under national regulations. This would reduce uncertainty for firms, lower the costs to employers of employment protection, and promote flexibility without creating a two-tiered labor market.

ment. When such shocks affect a low-productivity sector (for example, the construction sector after a housing bust), the conditional impact may be stronger.

- Uncertainty: There may be more uncertainty about future demand after major asset busts or crises than after more normal recessions. This may leave firms more reluctant to hire new work-

ers and more likely to simply adjust the hours of existing workers (Bloom, 2009).

- Policies: Finally, policies can affect the conditional impact of changes in output on unemployment dynamics. Germany's *Kurzarbeit* is perceived to have dampened the rise in unemployment during the Great Recession by giving employers financial incentives to adjust to lower demand by reducing hours worked per employee rather than by eliminating jobs.

Step 1: Okun's Law across Countries and over Time

The first step in the analysis is to estimate Okun's law equations for each of the advanced economies in the sample leading up to the start of a recession. To identify the cycles, we follow the procedure in Chapter 3 of the April 2009 *World Economic Outlook,* which uses quarterly changes in real GDP to determine cyclical peaks and troughs. The recession phase is defined as the cyclical peak to the trough; for simplicity, the recovery phase is defined as the first eight quarters after the trough.[7]

Given that there can be lags between changes in output and the unemployment response, the analysis uses a general dynamic specification of Okun's law, which also allows for betas to vary during recessions. To allow for different dynamics across countries, an optimal lag length is identified for each country and each recession.[8]

As mentioned, the window spans 20 years (80 quarterly observations), which is short enough to avoid instability in the relationship while being long enough to span at least two business cycles. Given that quarterly data is unavailable before the 1960s, the first recession episode is generally in the early 1980s. In our sample of 21 advanced economies, this results in more than 80 recession episodes.

Because the Okun's law equation allows for lagged effects, the short-term impact of a change in output on the unemployment rate can differ from the long-term impact. For example, after a demand shock, it may take time to dismiss employees, not least because employers may be initially uncertain as to whether the demand shock is temporary or more persistent. The analysis here focuses on the long-

---

[7] The level of output typically surpasses its previous peak about three quarters after the end of the recession. After eight quarters, the economy is typically well into the expansion phase.

[8] For most economies, one to two lags are chosen for each variable, confirming that the dynamics of the relationship are unlikely to be captured by a simple, static Okun's law specification. Appendix 3.2 has details about the country-specific lag lengths.

Figure 3.6. Output per Capita and Employment Rate Responses during Past Recessions[1]

(All series are in levels indexed to 100 at the peak; quarters on x-axis; peak in output at t = 0; solid line is the mean, and dashed lines are the 95 percent confidence band)

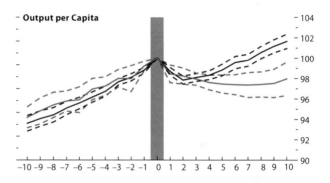

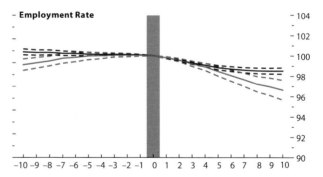

Source: IMF staff calculations.
[1] Past episodes of recessions with financial crises: Australia (1990), Germany (1980), Italy (1992), Japan (1993 and 1997), Norway (1988), Spain (1978), Sweden (1990), and United Kingdom (1973 and 1990). Current episodes with financial crises: Belgium (2008), Ireland (2008), Netherlands (2008), United Kingdom (2008), and United States (2008).

Figure 3.7. Dynamic Betas: The Long-Term Impact of Output Fluctuations on Unemployment Rate Dynamics

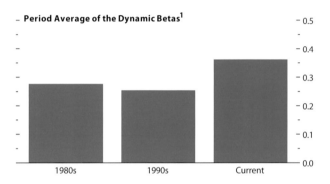

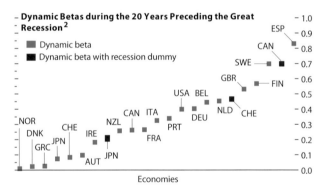

Source: IMF staff calculations.

[1]Averages taken of the dynamic betas for each recession in each economy during each decade.

[2]AUT: Austria; BEL: Belgium; CAN: Canada ; CHE: Switzerland; DEU: Germany; DNK: Denmark; ESP: Spain; FIN: Finland; FRA: France; GBR: United Kingdom; GRC: Greece; IRE: Ireland; ITA: Italy; JPN: Japan; NLD: Netherlands; NOR: Norway; NZL: New Zealand; PRT: Portugal; SWE: Sweden; USA: United States.

term impact, which is called the dynamic beta (see Appendix 3.2 for the formula and derivation).

The variation in the dynamic betas for different recession episodes should capture the differences in institutions across countries and over time.[9]

Variation in Dynamic Betas over Time and across Countries

Figure 3.7 shows the average dynamic beta across advanced economies for recession episodes in the 1980s, 1990s, and 2000s.

- Unemployment has become more responsive to changes in output. The average dynamic beta increased from about 0.25 in the 1990s to 0.36 in the 2000s. It had previously declined between the 1980s and 1990s, but this change was not significant.

- There is significant variation across countries. Over the past 20 years, Spain has had the largest average response of the unemployment rate to changes in output (about 0.8). The response has also been high in Canada, but only during recessions. The high dynamic betas of Sweden and the United Kingdom likely reflect significant labor market reform over the past 20 years. Two other Scandinavian countries, Norway and Denmark, have the lowest dynamic betas. The big continental European countries (France, Germany, Italy) along with the United States have dynamic betas somewhere in the middle of the distribution.

Impact of Institutions

Table 3.1 shows regressions of the dynamic betas using various indicators of labor market institutions.[10]

---

[9]The analysis focuses on unemployment rate specifications, the usual way that Okun's law is estimated. Similar results are obtained when using employment betas, as shown in Table 3.6.

[10]The dependent variable in the regression is the dynamic beta estimated for each recession episode. The OECD EPL strictness index is produced annually and generally goes back to the mid-1980s. It is a summary indicator based on 14 weighted components (such as dismissal procedures for regular contracts, group layoffs, use of temporary contracts). The unemployment benefits measure is a simple average of gross income replacement rates during the first and second year for a single worker without children. Temporary workers are defined as the share of workers

Table 3.1. Factors Influencing the Responsiveness of Changes in Unemployment to Changes in Output[1]

	(1)	(2)	(3)	(4)	(5)
	Okun's Law with Optimal Lag Length				
Employment Protection Legislation[2]	−0.05 [0.025]*			−0.062 [0.025]**	−0.058 [0.033]*
Unemployment Benefits		0.117 [0.103]		0.262 [0.100]**	0.233 [0.097]**
Share of Temporary Workers			0.014 [0.005]**		0.015 [0.006]**
Constant	0.415 [0.062]***	0.368 [0.063]***	0.144 [0.066]**	0.584 [0.088]***	0.383 [0.106]***
Observations	69	84	59	69	59
R^2	0.05	0.02	0.11	0.14	0.22

Source: IMF staff estimates.

Note: Standard errors in brackets. *, **, *** denote significance at the 10 percent, 5 percent, and 1 percent level, respectively.

[1]The dependent variable is the dynamic beta assoicated with the unemployment rate version of Okun's Law.

[2]For specification 5, only the subindices associated with regular contracts are used.

- Less strict EPL and a higher share of temporary workers, as expected, lead to a higher beta and are generally significant.[11]
- The unemployment benefit replacement ratio also has a positive effect, meaning that the job destruction effect outweighs the job creation effect.
- It is possible to estimate the size of the effects. Using the regression in specification 5, a 10 percentage point increase in the share of workers on temporary contracts (the approximate difference between Portugal and Spain) increases the dynamic beta by 0.15 percentage point, whereas increasing the strictness of EPL on regular contracts from the level in the United States to that in Germany reduces the dynamic beta by about 0.16 percentage point. Increasing unemployment benefits from the level in the United Kingdom to that in

Spain would increase the beta by close to 0.1 percentage point.

Step 2: Analyzing Unemployment Rate "Forecast Errors"

The analysis in the previous section shows how slow-moving variables such as institutional differences influence fluctuations in unemployment dynamics across countries and over time. This section studies how episodic factors—financial crises, sectoral shocks, uncertainty, and policies—alter the relationship between unemployment and output during recessions and recoveries.

The Okun's law estimates calculated using the 20-year prerecession quarterly samples are used to produce quarterly out-of-sample forecasts for changes in the unemployment rate. The difference between the actual change in unemployment (Δu_t) and its predicted value using the Okun's law estimates ($\Delta \hat{u}_t$) produces the unemployment forecast error:

$$\text{unemployment forecast error} \equiv \Delta u_t - \Delta \hat{u}_t. \quad (3)$$

Unemployment forecast errors are computed for both the recession and the recovery phases of each episode. The presence of forecast errors signifies that episodic factors could help explain unemployment

---

with temporary contracts (as defined by the OECD) in total dependent employment.

[11] In multivariate regressions where the share of temporary workers is included as an explanatory variable, we instead use the index of employment protection on regular contracts, because the broader index is affected by changes in legislation concerning temporary contracts.

dynamics.[12] Regression results (Tables 3.2 and 3.3) reveal the influence of these factors.[13]

Financial Crises and Stress

Financial crises have a significant impact during *recessions*, increasing unemployment by about 0.7 percentage point (Table 3.2, specification 1). A broader (and continuous) measure of financial stress is also associated with larger unemployment forecast errors (Table 3.2, specification 2).[14] The impact of financial stress during recessions is amplified by the extent of corporate leverage in the economy, as predicted by the literature (Table 3.2, specification 3).[15]

During the *recovery* phase, whether the preceding recession is associated with a financial crisis makes a significant difference, increasing the unemployment rate by about 0.3 percentage point (Table 3.3, specification 1). A 1 standard deviation increase in the measure of financial stress is also associated with higher unemployment of about 0.2 percentage point (Table 3.3, specification 2).

House Price Busts

House price busts, as opposed to financial stress, most likely affect the unemployment forecast errors through a sectoral shock, namely to employment in the construction sector. To capture the effect, we utilize a dummy for house price busts with the share of employment in the construction sector.[16] Specification 4 in Table 3.2 shows that this variable is positively associated with unemployment forecast errors during *recessions*.[17] While many of the large house price busts are associated with financial crises, this variable continues to have an independent impact even after controlling for the level of financial stress (Table 3.2, specifications 7 and 8).

Recoveries from house price busts are not significantly associated with higher unemployment forecast errors (Table 3.3, specification 4). They are, however, significantly associated with lower employment forecast errors (Table 3.8). A possible interpretation is that house price busts are associated with declines in labor participation rates, for example migrants involved in construction returning to their home countries.

Sectoral Shocks

Sectoral shocks can also be present in the absence of housing busts. To test this channel, we use the degree of dispersion in stock market returns as a measure of sectoral shocks.[18] A larger degree of dispersion indicates that the expected profitability of particular sectors, as measured by their stock returns, diverges from the average across all sectors—an indication of a sector-specific shock. Specification 5 in Table 3.2 shows that the impact of dispersion during *recessions* is positive and statistically significant, with a 1 standard deviation increase in the measure of stock market dispersion associated with about 0.2 percentage point higher unemployment. The measure of stock market dispersion continues to have an impact even after controlling for the level of financial stress and the

---

[12] The discussion that follows focuses on forecast errors based on the unemployment rate. A similar analysis—both in terms of estimating Okun's law equations and computing the forecast errors—can also be done for employment growth. Figure 3.3 shows that changes in labor participation rates have not played a significant role during the current cycle. This suggests that either the employment or unemployment rate specification should deliver similar results. Indeed, the results for the employment growth forecast errors are broadly similar and are discussed in Appendix 3.4.

[13] The regressions use forecast errors based on the dynamic specification of Okun's law with optimally chosen lag lengths. Appendix 3.4 discusses the results for the forecast errors based on a simple, static Okun's law specification.

[14] The Financial Stress Index developed in Chapter 4 of the October 2008 *World Economic Outlook* gauges stress in the markets for money, equities, and foreign exchange and elsewhere in the banking sector.

[15] The degree of leverage is captured by the aggregate debt-to-asset ratio of the corporate sector for each country in the sample. The sample average is about 24 percent. The negative impact of financial stress does not materialize until the debt-to-asset ratio is greater than 18 percent.

[16] The house price bust indicator is based on Kannan, Scott, and Rabanal (forthcoming).

[17] The incidence of a house price bust in a country whose construction sector is about 8 percent of employment (the sample average) reduces the unemployment forecast errors by about 0.7 percentage point.

[18] This measure was originally developed in Loungani, Rush, and Tave (1990). A four-quarter trailing moving average of this measure was used in the regression to capture lagged effects. See Appendix 3.1 for details.

Table 3.2. Unemployment Forecast Errors during Recessions

	(1)	(2)	(3)	(4)	(5)	(6)	(7)	(8)
Financial Crisis	0.702 [0.185]***							
Financial Stress Index (FSI—four-quarter moving average)		0.209 [0.106]**	−0.605 [0.250]**				0.266 [0.112]**	0.181 [0.114]
FSI × Corporate Leverage (at peak)			0.034 [0.011]***					
House Price Bust[1]				0.085 [0.022]***			0.08 [0.024]***	0.066 [0.024]***
Stock Market Dispersion (four-quarter moving average)					0.627 [0.301]**			1.32 [0.420]***
Dispersion of GDP Forecasts (four-quarter moving average)						−0.037 [0.106]		
Constant	0.228 [0.100]**	0.129 [0.123]	0.057 [0.115]	0.079 [0.132]	0.269 [0.108]**	−0.069 [0.112]	−0.148 [0.143]	−0.271 [0.147]*
Observations	341	257	154	303	329	136	233	232
R^2	0.04	0.02	0.06	0.05	0.01	0.00	0.09	0.12

Source: IMF staff estimates.
Note: Standard errors in brackets. *, **, *** denote significance at the 10 percent, 5 percent, and 1 percent level, respectively.
[1]Impact of house price bust takes into account the share of the construction sector in total employment.

Table 3.3. Unemployment Forecast Errors during Recoveries

	(1)	(2)	(3)	(4)	(5)	(6)	(7)	(8)
Recovery from a Financial Crisis	0.256 [0.124]**							
Financial Stress Index (FSI—four-quarter moving average)		0.215 [0.071]***	−0.110 [0.279]				0.211 [0.075]***	0.230 [0.085]***
FSI × Corporate Leverage (at recession trough)			0.011 [0.010]					
Recovery from House Price Bust[1]				−0.007 [0.013]			−0.016 [0.013]	−0.015 [0.013]
Stock Market Dispersion (four-quarter moving average)					0.013 [0.119]			−0.153 [0.232]
Dispersion of GDP forecasts (four-quarter moving average)						0.06 [0.050]		
Constant	−0.181 [0.055]***	−0.075 [0.052]	−0.061 [0.063]	−0.123 [0.070]*	−0.143 [0.057]**	−0.097 [0.056]*	−0.029 [0.073]	−0.004 [0.089]
Observations	504	377	271	446	455	160	365	357
R^2	0.01	0.02	0.02	0.00	0.00	0.01	0.02	0.02

Source: IMF staff estimates.
Note: Standard errors in brackets. *, **, *** denote significance at the 10 percent, 5 percent, and 1 percent level, respectively.
[1]Impact of house price bust takes into account the share of the construction sector in total employment.

incidence of a house price bust (Table 3.2, specification 8).

During *recoveries*, the broader stock market dispersion measure becomes insignificant (Table 3.3, specification 5).

Uncertainty

Good measures of uncertainty at the country level are scarce. Some measures (such as the VIX) are useful as proxies for the degree of global risk aversion, but they do not capture any cross-country variation.[19] To some degree, country-specific uncertainty will be captured by some components of the Financial Stress Index. In addition, this chapter uses the dispersion of GDP found in *Consensus Forecasts* as a measure of uncertainty.[20] This measure, however, is available for only about half the countries included in our sample and generally only after the early to mid-1990s. In any event, this uncertainty channel does not have a significant impact on either *recession* or *recovery* forecast errors (Table 3.2, specification 6). However, it does have a significant and negative impact on recovery forecast errors for employment growth (Table 3.8, specification 6).

The Key Issues: Drivers of Great Recession Dynamics and Recovery Prospects

This section uses the previous analysis to explain the unemployment response during the Great Recession and unemployment prospects during the recovery.

The Great Recession was a global financial crisis that also featured large house price corrections in several countries. As shown, unemployment rate changes and output declines varied tremendously across advanced economies (see Figure 3.1). How much of the recent unemployment rate dynamics can we explain? In particular, what importance can we ascribe to output declines, institutional differ-

ences (as captured by the dynamic betas), and the episodic factors we have studied?

The Effects of Output Declines, Institutional Reform, and Episodic Factors during the Great Recession

As a first step in addressing these questions, Figure 3.8 examines the predicted change in the unemployment rate using the dynamic beta estimates and actual output declines. For many countries, a significant part of the total change in unemployment during the Great Recession can be accounted for by the predicted value based on Okun's law.

- *Spain* suffered the largest rise in unemployment among the advanced economies in the sample, but much of this can be explained. This is because Spain has the highest dynamic beta among the advanced economies (that is, a very elastic response of unemployment to output), which reflects the prevalence of temporary contracts. Spain also suffered a sizable output drop.[21]
- For *Canada* and the *United Kingdom,* the predicted values are even greater than the actual unemployment increases. For the United Kingdom, this is the product of a significant increase in its dynamic beta over the past two decades and a substantial output loss (about 6 percent). For Canada, it is explained by a relatively larger dynamic beta during recessions and a sizable though smaller drop in output than for the United Kingdom.
- *Ireland* suffered the second largest rise in unemployment among countries in the sample. Although it experienced the second biggest output decline (more than 8 percent)—surpassed only by Finland—its dynamic beta is one of the lowest (less than 0.2), and so the predicted unemployment increase is less than half the actual increase.

---

[19] The VIX is a measure of the implied volatility of options on the S&P 500 index. The index is computed by the Chicago Board Options Exchange.

[20] See Appendix 3.1 for further details. Several papers, including Kannan and Köhler-Geib (2009) and Prati and Sbracia (2002), show that this particular measure has explanatory power in predicting crises in emerging markets.

[21] The centralization of collective wage bargaining in the presence of a significant "buffer stock" of fixed-term contract workers also played a role through its impact in reducing wage flexibility. Contractual wages increased by almost 3 percent in 2009. Significantly, real wages increased most in industries that initially had a larger share of fixed-term contracts. For example, in construction employment declined by 23 percent, wages increased by 4 percent, and temporary contracts accounted for more than 50 percent of total employment in 2008.

- For the *United States*, the predicted change using Okun's law can explain a significant part of the nearly 4 percent increase in the unemployment rate during the Great Recession. This results from a dynamic beta and output drop that were both moderate compared with other advanced economies.

The next step in addressing these questions is to add the role of episodic factors to the predicted changes in the unemployment rates derived from Okun's law. Figure 3.9 shows the breakdown of the cumulative change in unemployment in terms of the predicted component from Okun's law, the impact of financial stress and house price busts, and the residual unexplained component for the largest economies and those with particularly interesting dynamics.

For several countries such as Canada, the Netherlands, the United Kingdom, and the United States, the high degree of financial stress can help explain an additional 0.4–0.6 percentage point of the increase in the unemployment rate.[22] House price busts are also significant contributors to the unemployment rate increase, especially in countries such as Ireland and Spain where the share of employment in the construction sector was particularly high.

The Importance of Short-Time Work Programs and Remaining Puzzles during the Great Recession

The predicted impact of output drops using Okun's law estimates, financial stress, and house price busts explains more than the cumulative increase in unemployment for several countries, as shown by negative unexplained components in Figure 3.9. Can the lower-than-predicted response of unemployment be explained by the unprecedented expansion of short-time work programs, which encourage adjustment to demand shocks by reducing hours worked rather than by job destruction?[23]

---

[22] The impact is measured using the coefficients from Table 3.2, specification 7.

[23] The reduction in hours is met by a reduction in wages, although this reduction is typically less than proportional. Employers are subsidized for the increase in hourly wages through contributions from employers and employees or general government revenues.

Figure 3.8. Decomposition of the Actual Change in the Unemployment Rate during the Great Recession
(Peak-to-trough percentage point change)

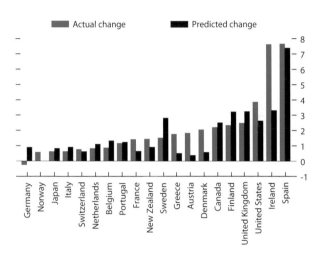

Dynamic Betas and Peak-to-Trough Declines in Output

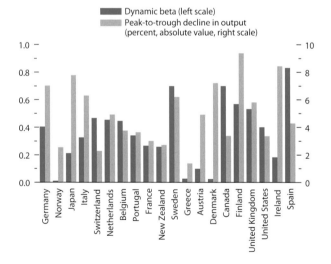

Source: IMF staff calculations.

Figure 3.9. Decomposition of the Cumulative Change in the Unemployment Rate during the Great Recession

(Peak-to-trough percentage point change, selected economies)

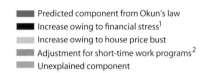

- Predicted component from Okun's law
- Increase owing to financial stress[1]
- Increase owing to house price bust
- Adjustment for short-time work programs[2]
- Unexplained component

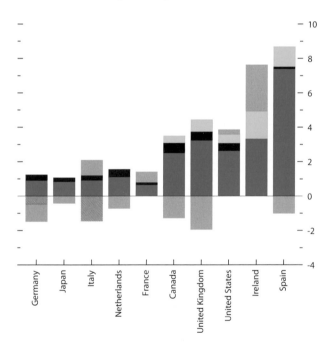

Source: IMF staff calculations.
[1]The Financial Stress Index is not available for Ireland.
[2]Detailed data on short-time work programs that allowed for the computation of full-time-equivalent employees were obtainable only for Germany and Italy.

Detailed data are available for Germany and Italy, and for these two countries the increase in participation in these programs during the Great Recession was about 0.5 and 1.5 percent of the labor force, respectively.[24] Figure 3.9 includes the contribution of the short-time work programs for these two countries, assuming that the full-time-equivalent number of workers under these programs would have otherwise been laid off. For Germany, the resulting increase in unemployment would explain about one-third of the unexplained component. For Italy, on the other hand, accounting for the short-time work programs produces a positive unexplained component.

Ideally, this exercise should be extended to all countries that employ such programs. Unfortunately, detailed data on the participation rates in other countries are unavailable. It should be noted, however, that the other two countries with large short-time work programs, Japan and the Netherlands, also have negative unexplained components, although for Japan falling nominal wages also contributed. The key design features of the larger short-time work programs are discussed in Box 3.2. The benefits of these programs include stabilizing employment; eliminating unnecessary firing, hiring, and retraining costs; and countering wage deflation pressures that can occur in severe recessions.[25] There are also costs, however, including slowing movement of labor across sectors. For example, in Italy, the sectoral decomposition of short-time

[24] It should be noted that Germany experienced a large increase in participation in its short-time work program in the second quarter of 2009, amounting to an additional 0.5 percent of the labor force. This increase is not included in the analysis, as Germany's output level is assessed to have reached a trough in the first quarter of 2009.

[25] More generally, even in mild recessions or in response to temporary demand shocks, well-designed short-time work programs could facilitate adjusting hours worked per employee in countries where tax and benefit systems incentivize employment adjustment instead. For example, in the United States, some argue that the unemployment insurance system favors temporary layoffs as opposed to short-time work programs (Feldstein, 1978; Burdett and Wright, 1989). This tendency may have been exacerbated by increasing employer contributions to employee health care insurance programs, which are largely fixed regardless of hours worked. The case for using short-time work programs outside of recessions, however, requires further study of how they interact with other labor market institutions over the longer term.

Box 3.2. Short-Time Work Programs

During the recent downturn, several advanced economies—including France, Germany, Italy, Japan, the Netherlands, Sweden, and the United States—increased their use of short-time work programs as a tool to stabilize employment in the face of large output declines. The table presents a snapshot of these programs for some major economies. Emerging economies such as Chile also introduced short-time work programs. Recognizing its importance, the International Labor Organization cites work sharing as a specific crisis management tool in its 2009 *Global Jobs Pact.*

Theoretical Pros and Cons

The defining feature of short-time work programs is an adjustment for a decline in labor demand by a reduction in hours, leaving employment essentially unchanged. Thus, unlike layoffs, where the burden is borne only by terminated workers, short-time work involves greater burden sharing. The reduction in hours worked is met by a reduction in gross wages, although the per hour wage of the worker typically rises in many short-time work programs. Employers are subsidized for the increase in hourly wages, either through unemployment insurance (UI) or other government funds.

These programs involve both costs and benefits. An oft-cited benefit of short-time work programs is that they counter potential wage deflation pressures

The author of this box is Mitali Das.

during a severe recession. By stabilizing employment and smoothing income through a downturn, such programs also mitigate large adjustments in domestic demand. In addition, there may be societal gains from reduced training and hiring costs and, potentially, productivity gains from retaining workers and thus maintaining employee morale (Vroman and Brusentsev, 2009).

The use of short-time work may also be associated with large costs. Since participation in such programs is contingent on maintaining ties with an existing employer, job lock could increase during a recession. Lower sectoral reallocation may perpetuate sectoral imbalances, leaving workers to languish in shrinking industries with skills ill suited for sectors that are growing. In the course of the recovery, as these workers search for jobs in expanding industries, unemployment could remain persistently high (Phelps, 2008).

Short-Time Work Programs during the Great Recession and Their Impact on Unemployment

Historically, short-time work has followed a strong countercyclical pattern. Accordingly, the synchronized output declines in the recent downturn were met by a similar pattern of growth in short-time work. Following low use through mid-2008, there was an abrupt increase in the use of these programs as global demand contracted at the end of 2008 (first figure). In the last quarter of 2008, this increase was sharpest in Germany, where the number of employees shifting to short-time work

Overview of Short-Time Work Programs (September 2008–September 2009)

	Maximum Usage, Peak[1]	Peak Usage	Change in Unemployment Rate	Eligibility	Duration	Experience Rating	Funding
Germany (*Kurzarbeit*)	3.5	April 2009	0.5	Yes	Yes	No	Payroll
Italy (*Cassa Integrazione*)[2]	4	September 2009	1.2	Yes	Yes	Yes	General fiscal, Payroll
Japan (Employment Adjustment Subsidy)	3.8	July 2009	1.42	Yes	Yes	No	General fiscal
United States (Workshare)	0.5	May 2009	3.506	No	No	Yes	State, Payroll

Sources: U.S. Bureau of Labor Statistics; U.S. Department of Labor; Haver Analytics; International Monetary Fund; national authorities; and IMF staff calculations.

[1]Percent of labor force.

[2]Maximum enrollment is based on total hours, not on number of individuals participating.

Box 3.2 *(continued)*

more than doubled in a single month, increasing by more than a quarter million enrollees. Growth was even more pronounced in Japan, where the number of employees targeted by job-subsidy programs grew by more than half a million enrollees in April, following an expansion of the program. Participation in Italy and the United States rose less, although given the differences in the size of their labor forces, the increase was more significant in Italy. Use of short-time work programs declined later in 2009, with the gradual bottoming out of the global recession.

Although short-time work programs share broad features across countries, there are nevertheless significant differences in design, coverage, participation, and funding. In part reflecting such differences, these programs have had mixed success in maintaining employment across countries during the downturn. To highlight these differences, the rest of the discussion will focus on the evolution of short-time work programs during the crisis in four cases: Germany, Italy, Japan, and the United States.

In Japan short-time work subsidies in May 2009 alone exceeded the annual subsidy in any year during 2003–07; the May 2009 outlay, in turn, was less than one-tenth of subsidies paid out in October. Another striking example is Germany, which experienced the largest increase in short-time work enrollment since reunification, with more than 1.5 million participants, or 3.4 percent of the labor force, at the peak. Italy's increase was also large: participation increased from less than 0.5 percent of the labor force on the eve of the crisis to more than 4 percent at the height of the downturn. The United States also experienced a very large increase in participation relative to previous downturns, although short-time work was a far smaller component of employers' response to the downturn than in the other three countries.

Despite this expansion, the effects of short-time work programs on unemployment were somewhat uneven. One way of quantifying the effects on unemployment is by calculating the full-time equivalent of participants in a program. The second figure shows that this adjustment would imply a large effect on unemployment rates in Germany and Italy. However, there are some cave-

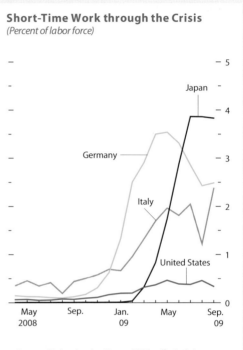

Short-Time Work through the Crisis
(Percent of labor force)

Sources: National authorities; and IMF staff calculations.

ats. First, the estimates assume that in the absence of a short-time program workers would have been unemployed; second, the size of the labor force is assumed not to have changed (for instance, no discouraged workers ceasing to look for work or dropping out of the labor force). A third caveat in the case of Japan is sizable nominal wage income reductions (4 percent in 2009) through cuts in wage rates, paid overtime, and bonus payments, which may have helped dampen the rise in unemployment. Nevertheless, it is still likely that the sheer scale of short-time work programs in the current recession contributed to the smaller changes in unemployment rates relative to other countries.

Sectoral Reallocation

Given the beneficial effects of short-time work programs during a downturn, it is also useful to consider their costs in some detail. One such cost, as previously noted, is the risk that continuing such programs after recovery can have adverse consequences for job reallocation. One way to quantify this risk is by analyzing the sectoral usage of short-time work programs before and during a recession. The premise is that if these programs are used as a temporary measure against a demand shock, usage must be different before the recession than during the recession.

The third figure shows the evolution of the relative incidence of short-time work programs in Standard International Trade Classification three-digit industries in Germany and Italy. The histograms denote the ratio of each sector's share of total short-time work program hours to the sector's share of total employment. A ratio larger than 1 indicates overrepresentation in the allocation of short-time work program funds. The figure reveals different dynamics in the use of short-time work programs in Germany and Italy. In Italy, two sectors—mechanical and textile industries—respectively received approximately 9 and 5 times more short-time work hours than their share in employment in 2005. Although the relative incidence of short-time work programs in specific sectors generally declined during the recession as other sectors increased their participation, we found that in 2008 these two sectors retained their advantage, receiving 8 and 6.5 times more short-time work hours than all sectors on average. The persistently high use of short-time work programs in specific sectors suggests that these programs may have been used to address structural layoffs rather than temporary demand shocks associated with the downturn. In Germany, on the other hand, consistent with expectations, short-time work usage in the most overrepresented sectors does decline over time.

Country-Specific Differences in Design

Given the sizable benefits both to firms and workers, it is useful to consider why participation in short-time work programs has been so uneven across countries during the recent downturn. Consider, for instance, the significant increase in the German program, *Kurzarbeit*, the Italian program, *Cassa Integrazione,* and Japan's Employment Adjustment Subsidy (EAS) program compared with participation in the U.S. Workshare program, whose participation peaked at only 0.5 percent of the labor force. What explains these discrepancies? The

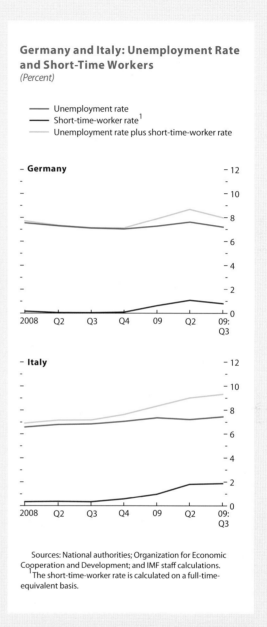

Germany and Italy: Unemployment Rate and Short-Time Workers
(Percent)

— Unemployment rate
— Short-time-worker rate[1]
— Unemployment rate plus short-time-worker rate

Sources: National authorities; Organization for Economic Cooperation and Development; and IMF staff calculations.
[1] The short-time-worker rate is calculated on a full-time-equivalent basis.

reasons are varied and include both design features and recession-specific modifications.

One of the key design features of *Kurzarbeit* is that weeks spent in the program do not affect an employee's eligibility for regular UI benefits if the worker is subsequently laid off. This differs significantly from the U.S. Workshare program, whose participants risk a decline in aggregate payments within a benefit cycle: UI entitlements drop on

Box 3.2 *(continued)*

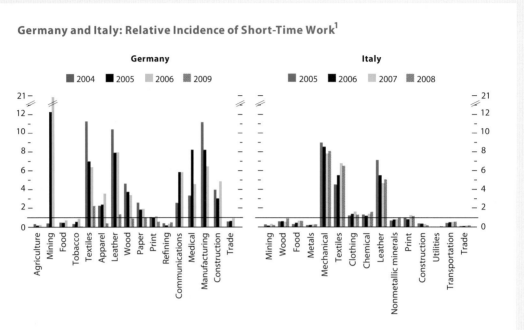

Germany and Italy: Relative Incidence of Short-Time Work[1]

Sources: National authorities; Organization for Economic Cooperation and Development; and IMF staff calculations.
[1](Short-time workers in each sector as a share of total short-time workers) divided by (employment in each sector as a share of total employment).

a dollar-for-dollar basis for (full-time-equivalent) short-time work payments. Moreover, German and Japanese employers, unlike their U.S. and Italian counterparts, are not subject to experience rating, the practice of using an employer's past claims to calculate future contribution rates (employers who make more claims face higher contribution rates). The absence of experience rating increases employers' motivation to use short-time work programs to smooth fluctuations in labor demand.

These programs' financing also differs across countries. *Kurzarbeit,* for instance, is financed through payroll taxes paid by workers and employers. EAS in Japan is funded by employer contributions to a reserve, which is managed as part of the Employment Insurance System. In Italy, funding is largely through general government revenues. Large government cofinancing increases the incentive for employers to implement short-time work programs.

Expansion of short-time work programs is an additional reason for the difference in participa-

tion rates and effects on unemployment. During the recession, expansion occurred primarily in two areas in the countries we are considering. First, there was eligibility expansion, which included the duration of participation and the extension to nonregular workers. Second, the programs received increased funding. For example, *Kurzarbeit* was initially developed with a maximum duration of 12 months, but was extended to 18 and then 24 months during the recent downturn. In Italy the *Cassa Integrazione in deroga*, which is funded out of general government revenues rather than social security contributions, was expanded significantly during the downturn to prolong the duration of the program in some firms and make new firms eligible. In addition, its usage was not subject to experience rating. EAS authorized large increases in the subsidy component, from 67 percent to 75 percent for large corporations and from 80 percent to 90 percent for small and medium-size enterprises, which include additional payments for avoiding dismissals. Furthermore, given the severity of the recession, eligibility for short-time programs in Germany, Italy, and Japan was expanded to include some nonregular, temporary contract workers. In contrast, there was no recession-induced expansion in the U.S. Workshare program.

Efficacy of Short-Time Work Programs

During a downturn, short-time work may provide exactly the sort of employment and wage stabilization needed to prevent large adjustments in the labor market. One of the key aspects of short-time work programs that has emerged during this recession, however, is that design features are critical to their effectiveness. These design features include ease of implementation, such as administrative convenience, adequate advertisement, and complementarity with (rather than punitive effects on) eligibility for regular UI benefits. Indeed, weakness in this regard may have limited the program's usage in the United States (Vroman and Brusentsev, 2009).

Although many advanced economies' experience with short-time work programs has been largely successful, these programs may not be a universal substitute for traditional stabilizers, because they require strict oversight to prevent abuse. The experiences of advanced economies show that successful implementation of short-time work must limit the subsidy component and perhaps make it countercyclical, ensure that actual work sharing takes place, and eliminate subsidies when no hours are worked.

Careful design of short-time work programs can promote job retention during a downturn, but unwinding their use as recovery begins is equally important, for example, to prevent adverse effects on job reallocation. One possibility is making experience rating contingent on the state of the business cycle. Specifically, because experience rating may discourage employers from using short-time work programs, it could be tied to statewide or economy-wide triggers, such as a particular unemployment rate.

work hours indicates that about 55 percent of the subsidized hours are concentrated in two declining manufacturing sectors (textiles and mechanical industries), which account for less than 10 percent of employment. This issue is revisited in a later section on appropriate policies for the recovery.

Unemployment dynamics in Canada and the United Kingdom remain difficult to explain: these countries have sizable negative unexplained components but did not implement large short-time work programs. For the United Kingdom, pay moderation may help explain part of this puzzle.[26] Another factor may be that output declines were concentrated in high-productivity sectors, moderating the associated rise in unemployment. For Ireland, the large positive unexplained component may be partly explained by the lack of data required to construct

the Financial Stress Index and hence its associated contribution to unemployment dynamics.

Near-Term Prospects for Employment Creation

Along with the potential for a slow recovery in output, the nature of the recent recession in several advanced economies (financial crises combined with house price busts), the high level of financial stress, and the high degree of uncertainty all weigh against a speedy recovery in job creation. This section reviews the near-term employment prospects and what policies could help.

How long does it typically take for employment to recover once the recession ends? As shown in Figure 3.10, across all recessions, it typically takes three quarters after output has started to recover for employment to start registering positive growth and an additional two quarters for the unemployment rate to peak. These lags are longer if the preceding

[26] See *Bank of England Inflation Report* (February 2010).

Figure 3.10. How Long before Employment Recovers?

(Median number of quarters before employment (unemployment) reaches its trough (peak) after the end of the recession)

■ All recessions
■ Recessions associated with financial crises
■ Recessions associated with house price busts

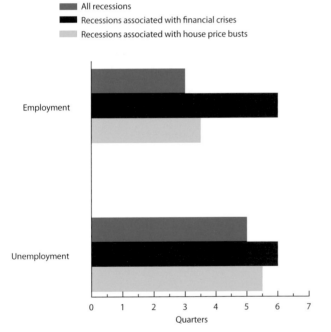

Source: IMF staff calculations.

recession is associated with a financial crisis or a house price bust.

What is the unemployment rate forecast for this recovery, assuming that there are no further financial crises or house price busts through the end of 2011? To address this question, the Okun's law estimates and *World Economic Outlook* (WEO) output forecasts are combined. To this is added the impact of financial stress, which is significant during recoveries.[27] A similar approach is used to forecast the level of employment.

The employment, unemployment rate, and GDP growth forecasts for the advanced economies as a group are shown in Figure 3.11. The unemployment rate remains high—about 9 percent—through the end of 2011. Moreover, the unemployment rate is still rising even as employment starts to grow, given the continuous expansion of the labor force. The forecasts based on Okun's law are broadly similar to the WEO unemployment projections discussed in Chapter 1, although the latter start to decline earlier.[28]

A number of other considerations that cannot be incorporated into the forecasting exercise support the conclusion that there will be persistently high unemployment rates in OECD economies over the near term. In the United States, the share of permanent versus temporary layoffs was relatively higher during the Great Recession than in previous downturns. Furthermore, in a number of countries, an increasing share of part-time workers and short-time work programs may allow firms to initially raise output by means of increased productivity and longer work hours, rather than by hiring new workers.

Policies to Jump-Start Job Creation

The prospect of persistently high unemployment increases the need for policies to jump-start job creation above and beyond generally encouraging wage flexibility and improving labor market institutions.

[27]Financial stress is assumed to revert to the mean by the end of 2010 for all economies.

[28]As an alternative approach, a vector autoregression is used to produce forecasts of the unemployment rate, employment, and GDP (see Appendix 3.5). This approach yields similar forecasts.

Although an analysis of the full spectrum of potential labor market policies is beyond the scope of this chapter (see OECD, 2009, for a recent review), this section considers a few policies that may be particularly relevant. First, in countries where labor productivity is strong but macroeconomic uncertainty remains high, temporary hiring subsidies may help advance job creation. Second, to facilitate the movement of labor across sectors, there should be a quick exit from short-time work programs, and wage loss insurance could be considered. Finally, some steps should be taken to address the negative effects of two-tiered labor markets (dualism).

Hiring Subsidies in an Uncertain Environment

The level of macroeconomic uncertainty remains higher than average although it has decreased in recent months (Figure 3.12). Such uncertainty does not appear to have a significant impact on the unemployment rate, but it does significantly reduce employment growth, conditioning on the pickup in output during recoveries (see Table 3.8). In this environment, a temporary subsidy may stimulate job creation on the margin by encouraging firms to hire new workers, rather than to "wait and see" and simply increase the hours of existing workers. Such subsidies, which have been implemented by advanced economies in the past and during this recession, reduce per worker hiring costs to employers, usually through credits for new hiring or lower payroll tax liabilities.

Such policies do raise concerns about cost and effectiveness, however. The evaluation of previous job subsidy programs has focused on two specific costs: the possibility that workers hired into subsidized jobs would have found jobs anyway *(deadweight losses)* and the replacement of an intended hire with one from a targeted group *(substitution effects)*. Deadweight losses should always be minimized, but substitution effects are not necessarily bad. An example of a positive substitution effect would be to subsidize the hiring of someone who has been unemployed for an extended time and is unlikely to be hired without assistance, even if that prevents the hiring of a worker unemployed for a short time. Overall, the evidence from a wide range of countries and time periods points to large

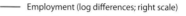

Figure 3.11. Forecasts of Employment, Unemployment Rate, and GDP for Advanced Economies, Based on Okun's Law[1,2]

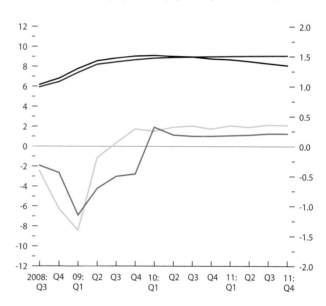

Sources: Haver Analytics; Organization for Economic Cooperation and Development; and IMF staff calculations.
[1]Okun's-law-based forecasts use a mean-reverting Financial Stress Index.
[2]Purchasing-power-parity-weighted average of Austria, Canada, Finland, France, Germany, Greece, Ireland, Italy, Japan, Netherlands, Portugal, Spain, United Kingdom, and United States. Excluded are Australia because it did not experience a recession in 2008–09 and Switzerland for lack of data. Quarterly WEO unemployment projections are not available for Belgium, Denmark, New Zealand, Norway, and Sweden.

deadweight losses, relatively small substitution costs, and a negative correlation between the size of the subsidy and deadweight losses.[29]

What characterizes an effective hiring subsidy? A larger per worker subsidy will likely increase overall job creation and reduce deadweight losses (by raising firms' incentives to create employment beyond their existing hiring targets), but will increase the cost of the program. To further reduce deadweight losses, the subsidy should be targeted and temporary. Target groups could include those with poor job prospects, such as the long-term unemployed or younger workers who represent a long-term investment in human capital formation. Furthermore, to minimize incentives for firms to simply rotate workers, the subsidy should be awarded on the basis of net job creation only. Deadweight losses and substitution costs that cannot easily be circumvented by policy design may simply need to be accepted as a price worth paying to increase job creation. No subsidy, however, should be allowed to become a tool for industrial policy (to target particular sectors or industries), and all subsidies should be designed in a manner that prevents fiscal costs from becoming permanent.

Exiting Short-Time Work Programs and Using Wage Insurance to Facilitate Mobility

The challenge is to prevent short-time work programs from becoming permanent wage subsidies to declining industries and from obstructing the movement of jobs and workers across sectors. In addition to the strain on public finances, continued state financing of such programs reduces the incentive for employers to scale them down as the recovery gains momentum. In the absence of well-defined rules to the contrary, policymakers may also have substantial discretion in deciding which firms are eligible and which are not, transforming short-time work programs into a subsidy to particular sectors.

In order to encourage an orderly unwinding of short-time work programs during the recovery

Figure 3.12. Dispersion of GDP *Consensus Forecasts*
(Purchasing-power-parity-weighted average of one-year-ahead growth forecasts for G7 economies)[1]

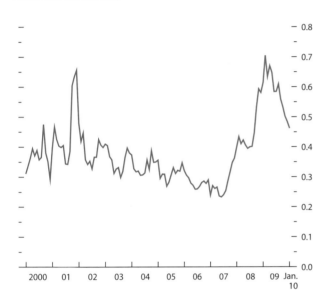

Sources: *Consensus Forecasts;* and IMF staff calculations.
[1]G7 comprises Canada, France, Germany, Italy, Japan, United Kingdom, and United States.

[29]Examples of job subsidy evaluations are in Atkinson and Meager (1994), Calmfors and Lang (1995), Byrne and Buchanan (1994), Cippolone and Guelfi (2006), and Marx (2005).

(and their scaling up during recessions), employer and employee contributions could be made contingent on the state of the business cycle. In the same way, employers could be charged rising contribution rates as they increase their use of the programs, and these experience ratings could be adjusted over the cycle.

Exit from these programs could also be encouraged by providing workers with wage loss insurance that not only insures workers against a decline in income, but smooths their movement from declining sectors to growing ones (see Kling, 2006). In recent years, wage loss insurance policies have been considered in Canada and the United States to counter long-term unemployment by cushioning the impact of a job loss through subsidies for retraining, extended unemployment insurance, or payment of up to 50 percent of the wage differential between new and old jobs.

As with other types of insurance, there is potential for abuse. Employers subsidized by new employees' insurance would have incentives to pay low wages to these workers. Such abuse could be discouraged by requirements that wage insurance recipients not be paid less by their employer than other workers. Kling (2006) also suggests additional mechanisms to limit abuse, including making such programs temporary, linking workers' benefit eligibility to tenure in their previous job, and capping total benefits.

Addressing the Negative Effects of Two-Tiered Labor Markets (Dualism)

Increasing use of temporary employment contracts over the past two decades has raised the response of unemployment to output fluctuations (increased the beta). Although having a higher beta is not by itself a problem—it increases job destruction during downturns but also raises job creation during upturns—there are negative effects from the increasingly two-tiered nature of the labor markets in many advanced economies. For example, as noted in Box 3.1, workers with temporary contracts generally receive less on-the-job training than those with open-ended contracts. Moreover, workers with temporary contracts can suffer greater social disloca-

tion after losing a job because they are usually not eligible for unemployment benefits.[30]

Yet in periods of high macroeconomic uncertainty, employers may seek to offer temporary contracts to new hires, as happened in Japan and Sweden after the financial crises of the 1990s. These and other considerations have resulted in growing political pressure to phase out fixed-term or temporary employment contracts. From a policy standpoint, however, prohibiting temporary contracts during the recovery may produce the worst of all outcomes: a strong decline in employment during the recession without compensating employment growth during the upturn.

One politically feasible way to address the negative effects of dualism in the labor market, while maintaining incentives to hire, is to allow for graded employment security in new contracts—namely, to increase the use of open-ended (permanent) contracts but gradually and smoothly increase the dismissal costs to employers over the course of a worker's tenure. This would reduce the uncertainty for firms regarding potential dismissal costs, which is an issue in countries such as France, Germany, Italy, and Spain. This could also give employers flexibility to dismiss or lay off workers, while maintaining some measure of protection for employees and encouraging on-the-job training of new hires. The adoption of such measures in conjunction with higher contributions to the unemployment insurance program for employers who use temporary contracts could help bridge the two tiers in many labor markets without reducing job creation.

Encouraging greater use of open-ended contracts would also help reverse the decline in unemployment benefit coverage that has accompanied the spread of temporary contracts and in the process reduced the effectiveness of automatic stabilizers in cushioning the impact of downturns. Of course, the transition to the use of contracts

---

[30] Blanchard and Tirole (2008) argue that one way to reduce excessive layoffs and provide an adequate safety net is a combination of a layoff tax to force employers to internalize the cost of providing unemployment insurance to laid-off workers and individual unemployment accounts to encourage the unemployed to search harder for work (they would effectively be paying for their own insurance).

with graded employment security provisions would not be without challenges, and further study is needed.

Conclusions and Implications for the Recovery

This chapter has looked at unemployment fluctuations during recessions and recoveries across a broad spectrum of advanced economies. The goal has been to provide a deeper understanding of the key factors that determine the unemployment rate in order to ultimately identify the sources of the increase in unemployment during the current recession, the prospects for recovery, and the role that policies have played—and can play—in tempering the employment cycle.

The key driver of the unemployment rate is the change in the level of economic activity. Indeed, this chapter has shown that the responsiveness of the unemployment rate to changes in output has increased over time for several advanced economies, due to less strict employment protection and greater use of temporary employment contracts. Although this increased responsiveness can exacerbate the response of unemployment during the recession phase of the business cycle, it can also amplify the bounce-back once a recovery gets under way.

Recessions associated with financial crises or housing busts lead to higher unemployment for a given decline in output. Disruptions in the supply of working capital to firms, which typically occur during periods of high financial stress, heighten job destruction, especially in economies where the corporate sector is highly leveraged. House price busts, on the other hand, generate significant shocks to particular sectors of the economy, namely construction and real estate. The evidence suggests that such shocks can also lead to higher unemployment for a given decline in output.

Overall, the analysis in this chapter presages sluggish employment growth during the recovery. Beyond the potentially slow recovery in output, the nature of the recent recession—financial crises

combined with house price busts—in several advanced economies weighs against unemployment moderating anytime soon. Indeed, based on the current path of policies, the forecasts presented in this chapter suggest that although employment growth will turn positive in many advanced economies in 2010, the unemployment rate will remain high through 2011.

Therefore, one legacy of the Great Recession will likely be persistently high unemployment rates in several advanced economies. Because high unemployment can quickly become a structural problem, this could lead to serious political and social challenges. What can policymakers do? The standard macroeconomic policy levers—monetary policy and fiscal policy—remain the primary tools for boosting employment through their impact on economic activity. In countries where unemployment rates remain high and the economy is operating below potential, policy stimulus remains warranted. Measures to restore the health of balance sheets of financial institutions are also important to ensure that the flow of credit to firms resumes.

This chapter discusses some labor market policy measures that go beyond generally encouraging wage flexibility and improving labor market institutions. In recessions, short-time work programs, such as those implemented in Germany, can be beneficial in stabilizing employment and thus help employers avoid unnecessary firing, hiring, and retraining costs. These programs can also counter wage deflation pressures in a severe recession.

The challenge during the recovery period is to exit from such programs. Indeed, short-time work programs must have well-defined rules to prevent them from becoming permanent wage subsidies to declining industries and thereby impeding the movement of labor across sectors. Wage insurance programs can help encourage exit from such programs by providing workers with access to carefully designed benefits to smooth their transition from jobs in declining sectors to employment in those that are expanding.

For the immediate recovery, given the lingering high degree of macroeconomic uncertainty in some countries, there is a potential role for temporary hiring subsidies, which could help alter the "wait-and-see" behavior that is typical during such times. Such measures have been used before in advanced economies, and the evidence suggests that their success depends on how well they are targeted, designed, and enforced.

In countries with two-tier labor markets, political pressure is building to ban the use of temporary employment contracts. This could produce the worst of all outcomes: a strong decline in employment during the recession without compensating employment growth in the upturn. However, the use of temporary contracts has been associated with lower on-the-job training and limited unemployment benefit coverage. Open-ended contracts with graded employment security provisions may maintain incentives to hire while encouraging training and employment protection for workers, although transitioning to the use of such contracts would not be without challenges, and further study is needed.

In sum, the depth and duration of the Great Recession in several advanced economies has created a need for some structural adjustments to their labor markets. The task for policymakers is to ensure that this adjustment occurs as smoothly as possible and to minimize the long-term economic and social consequences of persistent high unemployment.

Appendix 3.1. Data Sources and Construction

The author of this appendix is Prakash Kannan.

This appendix provides details on the sources of data used in this chapter and the construction of the stock market dispersion and uncertainty measures.

Table 3.4. Data Sources

Descriptor	Source
Employment	OECD,[1] *Labour Force Statistics*
Labor Force	OECD, *Labour Force Statistics*
Unemployment Rate	OECD, *Labour Force Statistics;* Haver Analytics
Real GDP	GDS (raw data from Haver Analytics)
Employment Protection Legislation	OECD
Unemployment Benefits (average replacement ratio for first two years)	IMF Structural Reform Database
Share of Temporary Workers	Eurostat, OECD
Marginally Attached and Underemployed Workers[2]	BLS,[3] Haver Analytics, Eurostat, OECD
Long-Term Unemployment (six months or more)	Eurostat, Haver Analytics, OECD
Hours per Employee	Haver Analytics, National Sources
Average Forecast GDP One Year Ahead	*Consensus Forecasts*
Sectoral Stock Market Returns	Datastream

[1]OECD = Organization for Economic Cooperation and Development.

[2]For European countries, "marginally attached" is defined as "would like to work but is not seeking employment." For the United States, marginally attached is defined as "not in labor force, want a job," and underemployment is defined as "part-time work for economic reasons."

[3]BLS = U.S. Bureau of Labor Statistics.

Dating Business Cycle Peaks and Troughs

This chapter employs a "classical" approach to dating business cycles by focusing on turning points in the level of output rather than deviations from a trend. The procedure—based on Harding and Pagan (2002)—uses a set of statistical criteria to determine the window over which an observation is classified as a local peak or trough and to determine the minimum duration of a complete cycle and the minimum duration of a phase of a business cycle. In this chapter, the observation window is set at two quarters, the minimum duration at five quarters, and the minimum phase at two quarters. Although the criteria for the minimum duration of a cycle and a phase are occasionally binding, the procedure generally dates the start of a recession as the quarter during which output is higher than the two quarters preceding and following it. This implies that a period of two quarters of negative growth is a sufficient, but not necessary, condition for a recession. Likewise, the end of a recession is generally marked as the quarter during which output is lower than the two quarters before and after it. With these criteria in place, local peaks and troughs are identified, which define recessionary and expansionary phases of the business cycle.

Measure of Stock Market Dispersion

The measure of dispersion in stock market returns follows Loungani, Rush, and Tave (1990). Stock market returns at the sectoral level for each country are obtained from Datastream. The data generally begin in the early to mid-1970s. For each country i, the time series of the stock market dispersion measure (SD_t) is computed as follows:

$$SD_{it} = \left[\sum_{N=1}^{N} \omega_{nt} (R_{nt} - \bar{R}_t)^2 \right]^{1/2},$$

where ω_{nt} is the share of total market capitalization of sector n in quarter t, R_{nt} is the quarterly return on the sector n index, and $\bar{R}_t$ is the total market quarterly return. To minimize large fluctuations in sectoral weights, the average share of market capitalization over the previous 10 years was used.

Measure of Uncertainty

The measure of uncertainty is based on Kannan and Köhler-Geib (2009). For each country, the dispersion of GDP forecasts as reported in the monthly *Consensus Forecasts* is used. In each issue of *Consensus Forecasts,* GDP projections are made for the current year and the following year. In order to construct forecasts of one-year-ahead GDP, the forecasts are weighted such that the current-year forecast has a weight of 1 in January, 11/12 in February, and so on until December. Likewise the next-year forecast gets a weight of zero in January, 1/12 in February, and so on.

Appendix 3.2. Methodological Details

The author of this appendix is Prakash Kannan.

This appendix goes through the details of the procedures used to estimate the Okun's law equation for each episode (Step 1) and the construction of the forecast errors (Step 2). The details related to the construction of the dynamic betas are also presented.

Estimating Okun's Law (Step 1)

For each recession episode in a particular country, a dynamic version of Okun's law is estimated for the 20-year period leading up to the peak in output just before the start of the recession.

The general form of the equation that is estimated is as follows:

$$\Delta u_t = \alpha + \sum_{i=0}^{p1} \beta_i \Delta y_{t-i} + \sum_{i=1}^{q} \gamma_i \Delta u_{t-i}$$

$$+ \sum_{i=0}^{p2} \delta_i \times D^R \Delta y_{t-i} + \varepsilon_t,$$

where Δu and Δy refer, respectively, to the change in the unemployment rate and the level of output growth. D^R is a dummy variable that takes on a value of 1 if the economy is in a state of recession. The use of the dummy variable allows the coefficients related to the responsiveness of changes in the unemployment rate to output growth to take on different magnitudes depending on the state of the business cycle.

To allow for different dynamics across countries, the lag lengths ($p1$, $p2$, and q in the specification above) are chosen using a Bayesian information criterion for each country and each episode. For most countries and episodes, the criterion suggests the use of fewer than two lags. Table 3.5 lists the choice of lag lengths for the most recent set of episodes.

The procedure used to estimate the Okun's law equation for changes in employment is carried out in a similar manner, with the change in log employment as the dependent variable.

Generating Forecast Errors (Step 2)

Based on the estimated Okun's law equation for each episode, forecast errors are constructed for both the recession and the recovery phases. The forecast errors are computed as the difference between the predicted changes in the unemployment rate (or the predicted changes in the logarithm of employment) based on the estimated Okun's law and the actual changes in the unemployment rate (or the changes in the logarithm of actual employment).

As an example for a particular episode, consider the recession in the United Kingdom in the early 1990s. The level of output peaked in the second quarter of 1990 and reached a trough in the third quarter of 1991. The window over which Okun's law is estimated for this episode ranged from the third quarter of 1970 to the second quarter of 1990. Based on the estimated coefficients, forecasts for the unemployment rate are generated for the recession period; that is, from the third quarter of 1990 to the third quarter of 1991. The forecast errors during the recession are then computed as the difference between the actual outturn of the unemployment rate and these forecast values. The forecast errors for the recovery period, which spanned the fourth quarter of 1991 to the third quarter of 1993, are computed based on the same Okun's law coefficients that were estimated up to the peak in output before the start of the recession.

There is some question regarding whether our estimation should be done in a single step using output and unemployment lags as well as the institutional variables and shock dummies. A two-step method is used because our underlying null hypothesis is that

Okun's law is the correct specification. That is, in the null model changes in unemployment vary systematically only as a result of changes in output (or, in the dynamic case, lags of output and unemployment). We take the presence of significant forecast errors to indicate a discrepancy with the null model and as evidence that, conditional on output, institutional features and macroeconomic shocks could be significant in explaining unemployment dynamics.

In constructing forecast errors, we exclude estimated betas that are statistically indistinguishable from zero. We do this because in some cases the estimated betas are large in magnitude, are statistically indistinguishable from zero, and overstate the size of forecast errors. We nevertheless exclude such estimates conservatively by increasing the test's ability to minimize the likelihood of excluding estimates resulting from statistical noise (Type 2 errors), with the significance level held at 0.15. Note that under the assumption that the model is correctly specified, the second-step regression does not require a standard-error correction, since there are no generated covariates in the second step.

A complementary way of thinking about the multistep approach relaxes this assumption on the null model. Suppose first-step errors have two components: a systematic component that depends on institutional variables and/or shocks and a random component. This is a generalization of Okun's law that permits the unemployment gap to vary based on factors beyond the output gap. In this case, the key assumption underlying the two-step approach is that the systematic component of the errors is statistically independent of the change in output, lag on output, and unemployment. The natural interpretation of the second-step regression is the decomposition of forecast errors into a predictable element based on the systematic component and a residual based on the random component.

Dynamic Betas

This section derives the equation for the dynamic beta multiplier, DB, which is used in the chapter. The dynamic multiplier captures the long-term impact of changes in output on changes in the unemployment rate.

We will derive the equation for the case in which there is one lag on output and one lag on unemployment. For this particular case, the Okun's law equation is as follows:

$$\Delta u_t = \alpha + \beta_0 \Delta y_t + \beta_1 \Delta y_{t-1} + \gamma_1 \Delta u_{t-1} + \varepsilon_t.$$

The dynamic beta (DB) measures the long-term impact of a one-unit change in Δy on Δu, or $\sum_{s=0}^{\infty} \Delta u_{t+s}$.[31] Using the specification above, we can write the dynamic beta for this particular case as follows:

$$DB = \sum_{s=0}^{\infty} \Delta u_{t+s}$$
$$= \sum_{s=0}^{\infty} [\beta_0 \Delta y_{t+s} + \beta_1 \Delta y_{t+s-1} + \gamma_1 \Delta u_{t+s-1}].$$

[31] We assume that the absolute value of γ is less than 1 to avoid an explosive process for Δu.

When there is a one-unit change to growth, $\Delta y = 1$, during period t and zero everywhere else, we can rewrite the equation above as

$$DB = \beta_0 + \beta_1 + \gamma_1 \sum_{s=0}^{\infty} \Delta u_{t+s-1}.$$

We can write the summation in the last term as

$$\sum_{s=0}^{\infty} \Delta u_{t+s-1} = \Delta u_{t-1} + \sum_{s=0}^{\infty} \Delta u_{t+s}.$$

We assume that the "initial condition"; that is, Δu_{t-1}, is equal to zero. In this case, we have

$$DB = \beta_0 + \beta_1 + \gamma_1 DB,$$

which leads to the equation for the dynamic beta:

$$DB = \frac{\beta_0 + \beta_1}{1 - \gamma_1}.$$

Table 3.5. Okun's Law Lag Lengths (Great Recession)

	Unemployment			Log Employment		
	Output	Unemployment	Recession Dummy	Log Output	Log Employment	Recession Dummy
Austria	1	1	no	0	0	no
Belgium	1	2	no	1	2	no
Canada	1	0	yes	0	1	no
Denmark	0	1	no	0	0	no
Finland	1	2	no	2	2	no
France	0	1	no	1	0	no
Germany	1	1	no	2	1	no
Greece	0	1	no	0	1	yes
Ireland	1	1	no	0	1	no
Italy	1	2	no	0	1	no
Japan	1	2	yes	1	1	no
Netherlands	2	2	no	2	2	no
New Zealand	1	2	no	0	1	no
Norway	0	0	no	1	2	yes
Portugal	4	5	no	0	0	no
Spain	2	1	no	1	1	no
Sweden	2	1	no	1	2	no
Switzerland	0	1	yes	...	...	...
United Kingdom	2	2	no	1	2	no
United States	1	1	no	1	0	no

Source: IMF staff estimates.

The derivation for the more general case follows the steps above in an analogous manner. The resulting specification is as follows:

$$DB = \frac{\sum_{i=0}^{p1} \beta_i + \sum_{j=0}^{p2} \delta_j}{1 - \sum_{k=1}^{q} \gamma_k}.$$

Appendix 3.3. Analysis on Dynamic Betas Derived from the Employment Version of Okun's Law

The author of this appendix is Prakash Kannan.

This appendix presents the regression results from use of the dynamic betas derived from the employment version of the Okun's law equation (Table 3.6).

Table 3.6. Factors Influencing the Responsiveness of Changes in Employment to Changes in Output[1]

	(1)	(2)	(3)	(4)	(5)
	Okun's Law with Optimal Lag Length				
Employment Protection Legislation[2]	−0.031 [0.044]			−0.058 [0.043]	−0.109 [0.062]*
Unemployment Benefits		0.332 [0.186]*		0.475 [0.165]***	0.467 [0.162]***
Share of Temporary Workers			0.020 [0.009]**		0.021 [0.011]*
Constant	0.491 [0.114]***	0.607 [0.116]***	0.215 [0.111]*	0.817 [0.156]***	0.692 [0.182]***
Observations	62	77	53	62	53
R^2	0.01	0.04	0.08	0.13	0.24

Source: IMF staff estimates.

Note: Standard errors in brackets. *, **, *** denote significance at the 10 percent, 5 percent, and 1 percent level, respectively.

[1]The dependent variable is the dynamic beta assoicated with the employment version of Okun's law.

[2]For specification 5, only the subindices associated with regular contracts are used.

The explanatory variables are the same as those used in Table 3.1 and thus have the same definitions.

Appendix 3.4. Regression Results Using Employment Forecast Errors and a Static Okun's Law Specification

The author of this appendix is Prakash Kannan.

The first part of this appendix presents regression results using employment forecast errors during recessions and during recoveries as the dependent variables. The definitions and sources of the explanatory variables are the same as in the baseline unemployment forecast errors. The regression results using forecast errors derived from a static Okun's law specification are also briefly discussed below.

Recessions associated with financial crises or house price busts (which take into account the share of the construction sector in total employment) are associated with employment forecast errors that are lower by about 1½–2 percent (Table 3.7). Sectoral shocks continue to matter: a 1 standard deviation increase in the measure of stock market dispersion is associated with lower employment forecast errors during recessions of about 2/3 percentage point. The effect of financial stress interacted with corporate leverage is positive and significant.

During recoveries, financial crises and financial stress still have a significant impact on the employment forecast errors. Unlike the results for the unemployment forecast errors, however, house price busts are significant and have a negative impact (Table 3.8, specification 4). This relation-

Table 3.7. Employment Forecast Errors during Recessions

	(1)	(2)	(3)	(4)	(5)	(6)	(7)	(8)
Financial Crisis	−1.941 [0.395]***							
Financial Stress Index (FSI—four-quarter moving average)		−0.59 [0.194]***	0.591 [0.516]				−0.628 [0.215]***	−0.478 [0.225]**
FSI × Corporate Leverage (at peak)			−0.041 [0.023]*					
House Price Bust[1]				−0.174 [0.046]***			−0.18 [0.045]***	−0.161 [0.046]***
Stock Market Dispersion (four-quarter moving average)					−1.979 [0.570]***			−1.962 [0.791]**
Dispersion of GDP Forecasts from *Consensus Forecasts*						−0.052 [0.205]		
Constant	−0.335 [0.220]	−0.393 [0.228]*	−0.134 [0.238]	−0.18 [0.287]	−0.585 [0.212]***	−0.178 [0.223]	0.264 [0.279]	0.454 [0.291]
Observations	322	238	137	288	308	125	218	215
R^2	0.07	0.04	0.03	0.05	0.04	0.00	0.12	0.15

Source: IMF staff estimates.

Note: Standard errors in brackets. *, **, *** denote significance at the 10 percent, 5 percent, and 1 percent level, respectively.

[1]Impact of house price bust takes into account the share of the construction sector in total employment.

Table 3.8. Employment Forecast Errors during Recoveries

	(1)	(2)	(3)	(4)	(5)	(6)	(7)	(8)
Recovery from a Financial Crisis	−0.843 [0.216]***							
Financial Stress Index (FSI—four-quarter moving average)		−0.344 [0.136]**	0.68 [0.504]				−0.288 [0.147]*	−0.398 [0.165]**
FSI × Corporate Leverage (at recession trough)			−0.036 [0.018]**					
Recovery from House Price Bust[1]				−0.048 [0.023]**			−0.053 [0.025]**	−0.05 [0.025]**
Stock Market Dispersion (four-quarter moving average)					−0.008 [0.213]			0.594 [0.427]
Dispersion of GDP Forecasts (four-quarter moving average)						−0.495 [0.104]***		
Constant	0.041 [0.098]	−0.139 [0.099]	−0.047 [0.119]	0.045 [0.125]	−0.139 [0.106]	−0.167 [0.121]	0.053 [0.141]	−0.104 [0.170]
Observations	467	349	234	410	419	141	329	321
R^2	0.03	0.02	0.03	0.01	0.00	0.14	0.03	0.04

Source: IMF staff estimates.

Note: Standard errors in brackets. *, **, *** denote significance at the 10 percent, 5 percent, and 1 percent level, respectively.

[1]Impact of house price bust takes into account the share of the construction sector in total employment.

ship remains significant even after controlling for the level of financial stress. Heightened uncertainty also has a significant impact: a 1 standard deviation increase in the dispersion of GDP forecasts from *Consensus Forecasts* reduces employment growth by about 0.5 percent (Table 3.8, specification 6).

Table 3.9 presents the results from regressions of employment and unemployment forecast errors both during recessions and during recoveries, based on the static Okun's law specification shown above. In general, the results show that allowing for lags in the Okun's law specification

Table 3.9. Regressions Using Forecast Errors Based on the Static Version of Okun's Law

	(1)	(2)	(3)	(4)
	Recessions		Recoveries	
	Employment	Unemployment	Employment	Unemployment
Financial Stress Index (FSI—four-quarter moving average)	0.18 [0.601]	0.511 [0.132]***	0.003 [0.762]	0.536 [0.096]***
House Price Bust[1]	−0.077 [0.126]	0.175 [0.028]***	0.215 [0.117]*	−0.008 [0.015]
Stock Market Dispersion (four-quarter moving average)	−4.159 [2.122]*	0.807 [0.488]*	−2.859 [1.974]	−0.392 [0.258]
Constant	−1.185 [0.783]	−0.312 [0.170]*	−1.89 [0.784]**	0.132 [0.099]
Observations	209	232	321	356
R^2	0.02	0.27	0.02	0.09

Source: IMF staff estimates.

Note: Standard errors in brackets. *, **, *** denote significance at the 10 percent, 5 percent, and 1 percent level, respectively.

[1]Impact of house price bust takes into account the share of the construction sector in total employment. For recovery forecast errors, house price bust refers to the preceding recession.

makes a difference. The unemployment forecast errors during recessions can be explained by fluctuations in financial stress and house price collapses, but most of the other variables in the other specifications do not explain the forecast errors as they do in the regressions based on the dynamic Okun's law. Furthermore, the coefficient on the house price bust variable in the regression of employment forecast errors during recoveries is of the opposite sign than expected and from what we obtained using the dynamic Okun's law specification.

Appendix 3.5. Vector Autoregression Forecasting Methodology

The author of this appendix is Ravi Balakrishnan.

As an alternative to the baseline forecasting approach, a four-variable vector autoregression (VAR) is used, consisting of the changes in log output, changes in log employment, the unemployment rate, and the level of financial stress (Figure 3.13). The specification allows for two lags of each variable and includes two exogenous variables: dummies for financial crises and house price busts.

Each equation of the VAR allows for country-specific constants and slope coefficients and is estimated over the period 1981:Q2–2009:Q2, with Financial Stress Index data availability determining the start and end points. The coefficients on the financial crises and house price bust variables are constrained to be the same across all countries. In order to generate the forecasts, it is assumed that there are no further financial crises or house price busts until the fourth quarter of 2011, which is the end of the forecast horizon. A dynamic forecasting procedure is used, starting in the third quarter of 2009, to produce projections of output, employment, the unemployment rate, and the level of financial stress. As the figure shows, the results are similar to the baseline forecast.

Figure 3.13. Forecasts of Employment, Unemployment Rate, and GDP for Advanced Economies, Based on Vector Autoregression[1]

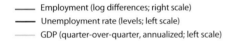

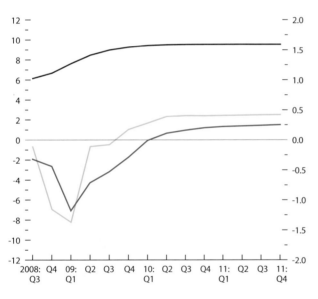

Sources: Haver Analytics; Organization for Economic Cooperation and Development; and IMF staff calculations.

[1]Advanced economies comprise Austria, Belgium, Canada, Denmark, Finland, France, Germany, Greece, Ireland, Italy, Japan, Netherlands, Norway, New Zealand, Portugal, Spain, Sweden, United Kingdom, and United States. Excluded are Australia because it did not experience a recession in 2008–09 and Switzerland for lack of data.

References

Atkinson, John, and Nigel Meager, 1994, "Evaluation of Workstart Pilots," IES Report No. 279 (Brighton, United Kingdom: Institute of Employment Studies).

Bernanke, Ben, and Mark Gertler, 1989, "Agency Costs, Net Worth and Business Fluctuations," *American Economic Review*, Vol. 79 (March), pp. 14–31.

Blanchard, Olivier, and Jean Tirole, 2008, "The Joint Design of Unemployment Insurance and Employment Protection: A First Pass," *Journal of the European Economic Association*, Vol. 6, No. 1, pp. 45–77.

Bloom, Nicholas, 2009, "The Impact of Uncertainty Shocks," *Econometrica*, Vol. 77, No. 3, pp. 623–85.

Boeri, Tito, and Pietro Garibaldi, 2007, "Two Tier Reforms of Employment Protection: A Honeymoon Effect?" *Economic Journal*, Vol. 117, No. 521, pp. 357–85.

Boeri, Tito, and Jan van Ours, 2008, *The Economics of Imperfect Labor Markets* (Princeton, New Jersey: Princeton University Press).

Burdett, Kenneth, and Randall Wright, 1989, "Unemployment Insurance and Short-Time Compensation: The Effects on Layoffs, Hours per Worker, and Wages," *Journal of Political Economy*, Vol. 97, No. 6, pp. 1479–96.

Byrne, Anne, and Karen Buchanan, 1994, *Survey of Jobstart Employers* (Canberra: Department of Employment, Education and Training).

Calmfors, Lars, and Anders Forslund, 1991, "Real-Wage Determination and Labour Market Policies: The Swedish Experience," *Economic Journal*, Vol. 101, No. 408, pp. 1130–48.

Calmfors, Lars and Harald Lang, 1995. "Macroeconomic Effects of Active Labour Market Programmes in a Union Wage-Setting Model," *Economic Journal*, Royal Economic Society, Vol. 105 (May), pp. 601–19.

Cipollone, Piero, and Anita Guelfi, 2006, "Financial Support to Permanent Jobs: The Italian Case," *Politica Economica*, No. 1, pp. 51–75.

Costain, James, Juan Francisco Jimeno, and Carlos Thomas, forthcoming, "Employment Fluctuations in a Dual Labor Market," (Madrid: Bank of Spain).

Feldstein, Martin, 1978, "The Effect of Unemployment Insurance on Temporary Layoff Unemployment," *American Economic Review*, Vol. 68, No. 5, pp. 834–46.

Harding, Don, and Adrian Pagan, 2002, "Dissecting the Cycle: A Methodological Investigation," *Journal of Monetary Economics*, Vol. 49, No. 2, pp. 365–81.

Kannan, Prakash, and Fritzi Köhler-Geib, 2009, "The Uncertainty Channel of Contagion" IMF Working Paper 09/219 (Washington: International Monetary Fund).

Kannan, Prakash, Alasdair Scott, and Pau Rabanal, forthcoming, "Recurring Patterns in the Run-Up to House Price Busts," *Applied Economics Letters*.

Kling, Jeffrey R., 2006, "Fundamental Restructuring of Unemployment Insurance: Wage-Loss Insurance and Temporary Earnings Replacement Accounts," Hamilton Project Discussion Paper No. 2006–05 (Washington: Brookings Institution).

Knotek, Edward S., 2007, "How Useful Is Okun's law?" *Federal Reserve Bank of Kansas City Economic Review* (Fourth Quarter), pp. 73–103.

Loungani, Prakash, Mark Rush, and William Tave, 1990, "Stock Market Dispersion and Unemployment," *Journal of Monetary Economics*, Vol. 25, No. 3, pp. 367–88.

Marx, Ive, 2005, "Job Subsidies and Cuts in Employers' Social Security Contributions: The Verdict of Empirical Evaluation Studies," Herman Deleeck Centre for Social Policy (Antwerp: University of Antwerp).

Moosa, Imad A., 1997, "A Cross-Country Comparison of Okun's Coefficient," *Journal of Comparative Economics*, Vol. 24, No. 3, pp. 335–56.

Okun, Arthur M., 1962, "Potential GNP: Its Measurement and Significance," American Statistical Association, proceedings of the Business and Economics Statistics Section (Alexandria, Virginia: American Statistical Association). Reprint available at http://cowles.econ.yale.edu/P/cp/p01b/p0190.pdf.

Organization for Economic Cooperation and Development (OECD), 2009, *OECD Employment Outlook* (Paris, September).

Phelps, Edmund S., 2008, "U.S. Monetary Policy and the Prospective Structural Slump," speech delivered to the 7th annual Bank for International Settlements conference on monetary policy, Lucerne, Switzerland, June 26.

Prati, Alessandro, and Massimo Sbracia, 2002, "Currency Crises and Uncertainty About Fundamentals," IMF Working Paper 02/3 (Washington: International Monetary Fund).

Reinhart, Carmen, and Kenneth Rogoff, 2008, "Is the 2007 U.S. Sub-Prime Crisis So Different? An International Historical Comparison," NBER Working Paper No. 13761 (Cambridge, Massachusetts: National Bureau of Economic Research).

Sharpe, Steven A., 1994, "Financial Market Imperfections, Firm Leverage, and the Cyclicality of Employment," *American Economic Review*, Vol. 84, No. 4, pp. 1060–74.

Vroman, Wayne, and Vera Brusentsev, 2009, "Short-Time Compensation as a Policy to Stabilize Employment," Urban Institute research paper (Washington: Urban Institute).

CHAPTER 4

GETTING THE BALANCE RIGHT: TRANSITIONING OUT OF SUSTAINED CURRENT ACCOUNT SURPLUSES

Global imbalances narrowed during the crisis, but a strong and balanced recovery requires that this narrowing be made more durable. Before the crisis, a number of economies experienced large and persistent current account imbalances (Figure 4.1). These imbalances shrank sharply in 2009, reflecting both cyclical and more lasting developments. In economies with large external deficits before the crisis, most notably the United States, private demand is likely to remain below the precrisis trend as households repair their balance sheets, and a strong recovery will require an increase in net exports. For surplus economies facing weaker demand from deficit economies, the challenge is to rebalance growth from external sources to domestic sources and to run smaller surpluses in the future. Together, these two adjustments could promote a strong and balanced global recovery.

Economies with large external surpluses may hesitate to adopt policies that help rebalance demand because of concerns that this could slow their economic growth. In particular, they may be concerned about declining competitiveness, shrinking output in the tradables sector, and a slowdown in productivity and output growth. But while there is a substantial literature that examines deficit reversals,[1] very little is known about the nature of past current account surplus reversals, including their implications for growth, especially when these reversals were policy driven.

This chapter examines the experiences of economies that ended large, sustained current account surpluses

The main authors of this chapter are Abdul Abiad, Daniel Leigh, and Marco E. Terrones, with support from Gavin Asdorian, Min Kyu Song, and Jessie Yang.

[1] The literature on deficit reversals includes Milesi-Ferretti and Razin (1998), Edwards (2004), Meissner and Taylor (2006), Adalet and Eichengreen (2007), Freund and Warnock (2007), and the September 2002 and April 2007 issues of the *World Economic Outlook* (WEO). Many of these studies were motivated by the recent U.S. experience with large and sustained current account deficits. A common lesson is that deficit reversals are typically associated with real exchange rate depreciation and a slowdown in output growth. As discussed in Chapter 1, global demand rebalancing also requires that economies with excessive deficits rebalance growth from domestic to external sources.

through policy actions such as exchange rate appreciation or macroeconomic stimulus. It subjects these historical episodes to statistical analysis and provides a narrative account of five specific transitions, examining economic performance and identifying key factors that explain various growth outcomes. To guide the analysis, the chapter focuses on the following questions:

- What were the main pretransition features of economies that undertook reversals from large and sustained current account surpluses? What policy frameworks were in place?
- What policies were implemented during surplus reversals? What role did macroeconomic, exchange rate, and structural policies play?
- What were the implications of reversals for economic performance? In particular, was there a significant change in output growth?[2] Did a reversal typically feature an acceleration of domestic demand? What happened to employment and capital growth? What were the sectoral changes?
- What lessons can be drawn for economies considering a transition away from large current account surpluses in today's environment?

The following findings stand out. First, the current account surplus narrowed significantly in response to policy changes. Although exchange rate appreciation often played a role, other policies also facilitated the reversals, including macroeconomic policies that stimulated domestic demand and, in some cases, structural reforms. Second, policy-induced current account surplus reversals were not typically associated with lower growth. Real appreciation seems to have slowed growth, but other factors tended to offset this adverse effect. Specifically, demand frequently shifted from external to domestic sources, and rising

[2] This chapter focuses on the growth implications of reductions in the current account surplus; a separate literature focuses on the relationship between trade openness and growth (see, for instance, Acemoglu, 2009; Frankel and Romer, 1999; Feyrer, 2009; and the Commission on Growth and Development, 2008). Note that the narrowing of a current account surplus does not necessarily entail a reduction in trade openness.

consumption and investment offset the fall in net exports. At the same time, supply rebalanced, with resources shifting from the tradables to the nontradables sector. In some cases, real appreciation was followed by a shift in export composition toward higher-value-added goods—that is, by a move up the export quality ladder.[3] Third, total employment rose slightly during reversals, as gains in nontradables employment more than offset employment losses in the tradables sector. Finally, there were some policy mistakes made during the rebalancing phase. Specifically, in some cases macroeconomic policy stimulus undertaken to offset the contractionary impact of appreciation was excessive, resulting in overheating and asset price booms.

The chapter is structured as follows. The first section defines and identifies policy-induced surplus reversals based on data covering a broad range of economies over the past 50 years. The second section presents a statistical analysis of these episodes, with emphasis on the behavior of key variables, including savings, investment, and growth. In particular, this section uses regression analysis to identify the domestic and external factors that account for the wide variety of growth outcomes associated with surplus reversals. Given the difficulty of quantifying some important policy variables, such as structural reforms and discretionary fiscal and monetary policy responses, the third section applies a narrative approach to five selected case studies considered relevant to what is happening in surplus economies today, which complements the statistical analysis.

Surplus Reversals: Definition and Anatomy

This section defines a policy-induced surplus reversal. It also reports how the current account typically adjusts during these episodes and how much the exchange rate tends to change.

Identifying Policy-Induced Surplus Reversals

To identify episodes that might offer lessons for economies considering a surplus reversal in

Figure 4.1. Global Imbalances[1]
(Current account balance in percent of world GDP)

Global imbalances narrowed sharply in 2009 owing to both cyclical and more lasting developments. Imbalances are projected to widen once again as the global recovery takes hold.

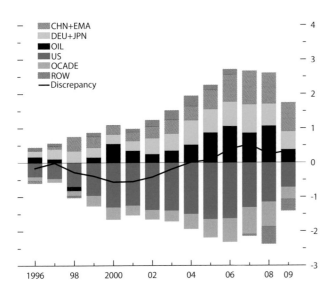

Source: IMF staff calculations.
[1]CHN+EMA: China, Hong Kong SAR, Indonesia, Korea, Malaysia, Philippines, Singapore, Taiwan Province of China, Thailand; DEU+JPN: Germany and Japan; OIL: Oil exporters; US: United States; OCADE: other current-account-deficit economies; ROW: rest of the world.

---

[3]Although an upgrade in quality could strengthen an economy's export competitiveness following real appreciation, it would not prevent imports from increasing and the trade surplus from falling.

today's environment, the chapter follows a two-step approach. First, it uses statistical criteria to identify large and persistent reductions in the current account surplus during the past 50 years.[4] Second, based on this initial list of large reversals, it selects those that were policy driven, that is, those associated with a large and deliberate exchange rate appreciation or with macroeconomic stimulus.

A surplus reversal is defined as a sustained and significant decline in the current account balance from a period of large and persistent surpluses. Figure 4.2 illustrates the basis for this definition using the example of Korea's 1989 reversal. To make the definition operational, the chapter utilizes a methodology that mirrors those used to examine deficit reversals by Milesi-Ferretti and Razin (1998) and Freund and Warnock (2007). In particular, a surplus reversal has to satisfy three key requirements:

- A period of large and persistent current account surpluses preceding the reversal: In the three years before the reversal, the current account surplus must average at least 2 percent of GDP.[5] To ensure that this average is not influenced by outliers, the surplus must exceed 2 percent of GDP in at least two of the three years preceding the reversal.
- A substantial narrowing in the surpluses following reversals: The average current account surplus in the three years starting with the reversal year must be at least 2 percentage points of GDP less than the average in the three years before the reversal.
- A sustained narrowing in the surpluses: To ensure that the reversal is sustained and not a sharp but temporary change in the current account, the maximum surplus in the three years following the reversal must be smaller than the minimum

Figure 4.2. Methodology Example (Korea 1989)
(Year of surplus reversal at t = 0; years on x-axis)

A surplus reversal is a sustained and significant decline (2 percentage points of GDP or more) in the current account balance from a period of large and persistent surpluses.

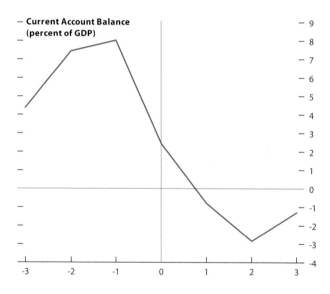

Source: IMF staff calculations.

[4] The economies and data sources utilized in the analysis are listed in Appendix 4.1.

[5] Note that 2 percent is the median of all current account surpluses, for both advanced and emerging market economies.

surplus recorded in the three years preceding the reversal.[6]

Although these requirements allow reversals to occur in consecutive years, such multiple episodes are unlikely to be independent events. To eliminate such episodes, reversals occurring within 10 years of each other are excluded from the sample.

When is a surplus reversal policy driven? In principle, many policies could induce a surplus reversal, including exchange rate policy, fiscal and monetary policies, and structural policies. Deliberate changes in structural policies are difficult to measure, and so the statistical analysis in this chapter focuses on policy-induced exchange rate appreciation and macroeconomic policy stimulus, although structural policies are analyzed in relatively greater depth in the case studies. A policy-induced exchange rate appreciation is defined here as an appreciation of at least 10 percent (trough to peak) in nominal effective terms within three years of the surplus reversal.[7] For economies with a pegged or heavily managed exchange rate, it is assumed that such large appreciations reflect a policy choice. For economies with floating exchange rates, it was verified that the appreciation was policy induced by consulting the narrative record in IMF staff reports. For macroeconomic policies, the analysis focuses on cases in which fiscal or monetary stimulus is explicitly discussed in IMF staff reports within three years of the reversal.

The application of this two-step approach to a broad sample of advanced and emerging market economies during the past 50 years yields 28 policy-induced surplus reversals.[8] Such surplus reversals were infrequent, with less than one per economy on average. In contrast, using a similar statistical approach identified twice as many deficit reversals during the same period. This may be because deficit reversals are often unavoidable, reflecting large macroeconomic and financial imbalances, whereas surplus reversals can take place from a position of strength following a policy decision.[9] (See Table 4.8 for a full list of surplus reversals.)

Anatomy of Policy-Driven Surplus Reversals

This section decomposes the current account adjustment and examines the behavior of the real exchange rate during policy-driven surplus reversals. All variable changes are measured over three years, starting with the year of the reversal, and compared with the three years before the reversal. The analysis of these 28 episodes yields the following stylized facts:

- The current account narrowed sharply during a policy-driven reversal. On average, the surplus narrowed by 5.1 percentage points of GDP, well above the minimum required adjustment of 2 percentage points (Table 4.1). After the reversal, the current account balance was relatively small (0.4 percent of GDP on average) and not statistically different from zero.
- The process of current account adjustment was typically accompanied by both a significant reduction in savings and a sharp increase in investment. On average, domestic savings fell by 2.1 percentage points of GDP. The drop in private savings during the reversal was even larger (3.3 percentage points of GDP).[10] Investment

[6] Several robustness checks were performed. First, the calculations were repeated with the prereversal period starting six years before the event, rather than three years. Second, a more stringent requirement was applied to the postreversal current account balance, with the postreversal period extended six years, rather than three years. In both cases, the results were broadly consistent with those reported here.

[7] The trough-to-peak appreciation calculation is based on monthly data for the nominal effective exchange rate.

[8] In particular, the sample is restricted to 46 advanced and emerging market economies during 1960–2008. Small economies, defined here as those with populations below 1 million, are excluded from the sample. The sample also excludes the transition economies of central and eastern Europe and the former Soviet Union because their external positions were influenced by

the output collapse associated with the transition from central planning to a market economy. The analysis initially included surplus reversals in the fuel and nonfuel commodity-exporting economies, as defined in the standard WEO classification, and found that reversals in these economies were more often brought about by terms-of-trade shocks than by domestic policies. For this reason, these episodes were excluded from the analysis.

[9] Edwards (2004) reports that there are many more deficit economies than surplus ones. Moreover, he also finds that the probability of a deficit reversal is higher for economies with large deficits, high external debt, and rapid credit growth.

[10] The timing of the macroeconomic stimulus that drove a reversal differs from the one used to measure the changes in savings. In particular, the macroeconomic stimulus often started before the reversal.

Table 4.1. Decomposition of Current Account Surplus Reversals

Current Account/GDP	
Initial Current Account (level)	5.5***
Change in Current Account	−5.1***
New Current Account (level)	0.4
Savings and Investment	
Fall in Savings/GDP (percent of episodes)	74.1***
Change in Savings/GDP	−2.1***
Fall in Private Savings/GDP (percent of episodes)	91.7***
Change in Private Savings/GDP	−3.3***
Rise in Investment/GDP (percent of episodes)	77.8***
Change in Investment/GDP	3.0***
Imports and Exports	
Rise in Imports/GDP (percent of episodes)	77.8***
Change in Imports/GDP	4.2***
Fall in Exports/GDP (percent of episodes)	51.9***
Change in Exports/GDP	0.1

Source: IMF staff calculations.

Note: Table reports changes in variables measured as three-year average starting with year of current account surplus reversal minus three-year average growth before reversal. *, **, and *** denote statistical significance at the 1, 5, and 10 percent level, respectively.

Table 4.2. Exchange Rate Developments during Current Account Surplus Reversals

Variable	Surplus Reversals	Control Group
Reduced Model-Based Undervaluation (percent of episodes)	90.5***	29.6
Reduced Statistical Undervaluation (percent of episodes)	53.6	43.6
NEER Appreciation (percent of episodes)	60.7***	29.1
NEER Appreciation (change if positive)	9.2***	2.0
NEER Appreciation (change)	2.0***	−4.7
REER Appreciation (percent of episodes)	53.6	49.4
REER Appreciation (change if positive)	10.5***	3.3
REER Appreciation (change)	3.1***	−0.4
REER Overshooting (percent of episodes)	35.7	33.2
Real Appreciation against U.S. Dollar (percent of episodes)	59.3	54.3
Real Appreciation against U.S. Dollar (change if positive)	16.0***	6.0
Real Appreciation against U.S. Dollar (change)	4.3**	1.2
Increased Exchange Rate Regime Flexibility (percent of episodes)	7.7	12.6

Source: IMF staff calculations.

Note: Model-based measure of undervaluation is described in Lee and others (2008). Statistical measure of undervaluation is based on the deviation of the real exchange rate from its Hodrick-Prescott-filtered trend. NEER = nominal effective exchange rate. REER = real effective exchange rate. Exchange rate regime flexibility is based on Reinhart and Rogoff (2004) classification. Table reports changes in variables measured as three-year average starting with year of current account surplus reversal minus three-year average growth before reversal. *, **, and *** indicate that the difference relative to the control group is statistically significant at the 1, 5, and 10 percent level, respectively. The control group comprises all observations at least two years away from a reversal.

rose during the vast majority of reversals, with an average increase of 3 percentage points of GDP.

- On average, imports increased and exports remained virtually unchanged. Imports rose in the vast majority of events by 4.2 percentage points of GDP on average, while exports as a percentage of GDP remained virtually unchanged.

- Surplus reversals were often associated with exchange rate appreciations. In most cases, the exchange rate initially appeared undervalued, according to a number of different measures,[11] and the extent of this undervaluation was reduced (Table 4.2). Moreover, in more than half the reversals, there was appreciation of both the nominal and the real effective exchange rates. In these cases, the nominal and real effective exchange rates appreciated by an average of 9.2 percent and 10.5 percent, respectively.[12] Notably,

the appreciation tended to be larger the greater the estimated undervaluation prior to the transition. The small magnitude of the real appreciation relative to the observed current account adjustment suggests that factors or policies other than the exchange rate played a role in narrowing the current account; subsequent analysis will distinguish between episodes that featured real effective appreciation and those that did not. Finally, there was not much evidence of a significant shift toward more flexible exchange rate regimes.

---

[11] Two measures of undervaluation are used here: a model-based measure following Lee and others (2008) and the deviation of the real effective exchange rate from a Hodrick-Prescott-filtered trend. The control group of nonreversals consists of all observations in the sample that are at least two years removed from the start of a surplus reversal.

[12] The average change in the exchange rate—including cases of currency depreciation—was 2 percent in nominal effective terms and 3.1 percent in real effective terms. Note that the

analysis focuses on the average change in the exchange rate over three years after the start of the reversal relative to the previous three years. This measures more persistent shifts in exchange rates than the trough-to-peak appreciation used for the purposes of identifying policy-induced appreciations. According to the trough-to-peak measure, the appreciation of both the real and the nominal exchange rates averaged about 20 percent. In addition, the timing of the trough-to-peak exchange rate appreciation need not coincide exactly with the identified reversal year.

• Policymakers may be concerned that a current account surplus reversal might lead the exchange rate to overshoot, but there is no evidence that overshooting was more likely following reversals.[13] Overshooting occurred in about one-third of the cases in both the sample of reversals and the control group, and the overshooting was mild when it did occur. The fact that overshooting is less common during surplus reversals than during deficit reversals is likely because surplus economies can control the pace of appreciation by varying the rate of reserve purchases. In contrast, deficit economies frequently lack reserves to defend the currency during deficit reversals, which makes it more difficult to control the extent of depreciation.

Are Policy-Driven Surplus Reversals Detrimental to Growth?

Having documented key stylized facts about surplus reversals, this section examines the growth implications of policy-driven surplus reversals, first by discussing growth performance and then by identifying which components drive the changes in economic growth. In addition, this section examines the extent of sectoral reallocation in these economies following a policy-driven reversal. Finally, it uses multivariate regression analysis to explore the factors that explain the variation in postreversal growth outcomes.

Whether growth will rise or fall following a surplus reversal depends on the underlying causes of the original surplus and the subsequent reversal as well as on the policy response. The following three scenarios illustrate how the source of the surplus reversal can influence the outcome for growth.

• A surplus reversal driven by a real exchange rate appreciation that eliminates or reduces undervaluation: A real exchange rate appreciation could reduce an economy's exports, increase its imports,

and slow the production of tradable goods.[14] Other things being equal, this would imply a slowdown in output growth. Some argue that these effects on growth could last longer if an undervalued currency had helped alleviate the negative growth effects of domestic distortions, such as weak institutions (Rodrik, 2008).[15]

• A surplus reversal driven by macroeconomic stimulus: Expansive fiscal and monetary policy could increase domestic demand, increase imports, narrow the current account, and boost output growth. The extent of these effects is likely, however, to depend on the composition of the policies as well as the initial conditions. For instance, an increase in government expenditure is likely to appreciate the real exchange rate and help the nontradables sector more than the tradables sector.

• A surplus reversal driven by the removal of distortions that result in high precautionary savings, low investment, and a large current account surplus: High precautionary savings could be the result of underdeveloped financial markets (including mortgage markets), inadequate public retirement systems, a limited social safety net (Blanchard and Giavazzi, 2006), and a lack of international mechanisms to mitigate sudden-stop risks.[16] In addition, poor corporate gov-

---

[13]Following Cavallo and others (2004), exchange rate overshooting is measured using monthly data for the real effective exchange rate and the following definition: overshooting occurs if the exchange rate appreciates over a 24-month period in a hump-shaped manner, with the level of the exchange rate exceeding the final value for at least half that time.

[14]Montiel (2000) and Montiel and Servén (2008) argue that an undervalued currency that is expected to reverse at some point in the future leads to changes in intertemporal relative prices that discourage consumption in favor of saving and also make investment in the tradables sector relatively more attractive than investment in the nontradables sector. Therefore, a real exchange rate appreciation that eliminates this undervaluation would lead to higher consumption and to higher investment in nontradables.

[15]Rodrik (2008) argues that the distortions in these economies hamper the tradables sector, which might be subject to dynamic learning-by-doing externalities. At the same time, he finds that the growth benefits of undervaluation are smaller in more advanced economies where institutions are likely to be stronger. In related work, Korinek and Servén (2010) show that currency undervaluation in economies with learning-by-investing externalities could lead to an improvement in welfare.

[16]Following the Asian crisis, emerging market economies substantially increased their foreign exchange reserves while exchange rates stayed undervalued. Blanchard and Milesi-Ferretti (2009) argue that this could either reflect an export-led growth strategy based on an undervalued exchange rate or the lack of international insurance mechanisms. Durdu, Mendoza, and Terrones (2009)

ernance and noncompetitive market structures could lead to excessive corporate savings. Reduction or elimination of these distortions could increase private consumption, reduce private savings, narrow the current account, and strengthen growth. Similarly, low investment might reflect the lack of a bank lending culture as well as restrictions on foreign capital inflows. Reduction or elimination of these distortions would increase investment, narrow the current account, and strengthen growth.

Beyond these factors, the effect on growth from a surplus reversal depends on specific policy actions as well as on global economic conditions. For example, if the current account surplus reversal is driven by the appreciation of an undervalued exchange rate, the effects of slower export growth could be offset by an increase in domestic demand for tradable goods or by structural reforms that foster production of nontradables. If the surplus reversal is driven by an increase in domestic demand associated with the removal of savings and investment distortions, growth may not rise if the economy is already operating at potential, if policymakers tighten macroeconomic policies, or if global growth slumps.

What do the data show? The following findings emerge from the analysis of the 28 policy-induced surplus reversals:

- There is no evidence that transitioning out of a large external surplus was associated with lower growth. The average change in growth in the three years following the start of the reversal compared with the three preceding years was an increase of 0.4 percentage point, which is not statistically different from zero (Figure 4.3). Over the medium term, the change in output growth is also statistically insignificant, at –0.3 percentage point. An alternative measure of economic performance, the change in output growth relative to the world, accounts for the effects of global economic conditions and therefore increases the likelihood of picking up effects related only to domestic policy changes. Using this adjusted measure, the change

show that the recent surge in foreign reserves in emerging market economies could reflect self-insurance behavior against sudden-stop risks and the removal of barriers to asset trading given the underdevelopment of financial markets in these economies.

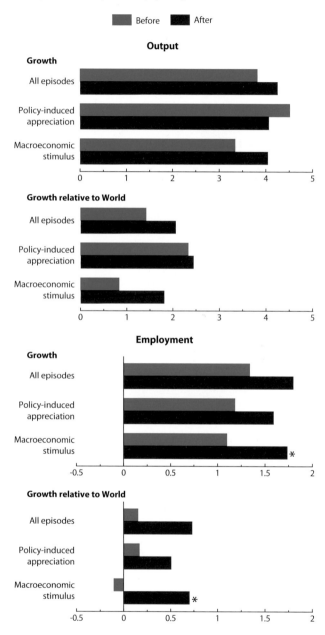

Figure 4.3. Output and Employment Growth during Surplus Reversals
(Percent)

There is no evidence that a policy-induced surplus reversal is associated with significantly lower output or employment growth. When measured relative to world growth, both output and employment growth increase.

Source: IMF staff calculations.
  Note: Figure reports average growth of real GDP per capita and employment in the three years before the reversal and the three years starting with a reversal. An asterisk (*) indicates that change in growth is statistically significant at the 10 percent level. "Policy-induced appreciation" denotes cases in which there was a policy-induced appreciation of at least 10 percent as described in the text. "Macroeconomic stimulus" denotes cases in which there was fiscal or monetary stimulus as described in the text.

Figure 4.4. Change in Growth after Surplus Reversals

(Difference from prereversal growth rate; percentage points)

The growth outcomes after a reversal are varied and somewhat skewed to the right.

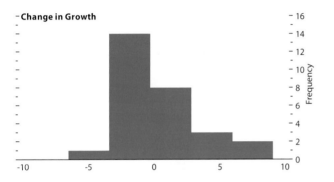

Change in Growth

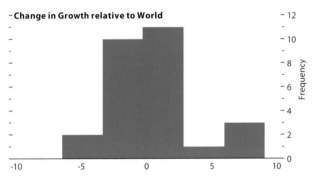

Change in Growth relative to World

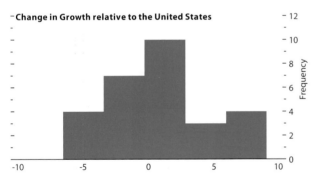

Change in Growth relative to the United States

Source: IMF staff calculations.
Note: Change in growth is measured as the three-year average starting with the reversal year minus the three-year average before reversal.

in growth was also small and statistically insignificant (see Figure 4.3). In addition, growth relative to the United States increased, suggesting that the pace of income convergence was at least as fast as before the reversal.

- The insignificant change in growth was not driven by outliers. In particular, it holds whether the sample is based on the full sample of 28 policy-induced reversal episodes, restricted to the subsample of 11 episodes associated with policy-induced appreciation, or restricted to the 23 episodes associated with macroeconomic stimulus. At the same time, as expected, reversal episodes with policy-induced appreciation experienced a small slowdown in growth, and those with macroeconomic stimulus experienced an increase in growth. However, in none of these cases was the change in growth statistically significant.

- The variation in growth outcomes was substantial. Although the average change in growth is small and insignificant, there is a wide range of growth outcomes, from –5.1 percentage points to 9.4 percentage points (Figure 4.4). The largest changes in growth occurred when there was abnormally high or low growth in the run-up to the reversal that was not the result of policies implemented during the reversal. (Disentangling the effects of initial conditions and various shocks from the role of domestic policies is addressed later using regression analysis.)

The Sources of Growth after Surplus Reversals

To better understand these results, the change in per capita real GDP growth is decomposed into underlying components. On the demand side, the change in output growth is divided into contributions from net exports and from domestic demand. Similarly, on the supply side, the change in growth is decomposed into contributions from employment per capita, capital per capita, and total factor productivity.[17]

---

[17] Note that, due to limited data availability, the sample shrinks from 28 reversal episodes to 26 observations for the demand-side decomposition and 20 observations for the factor-input decomposition, respectively. The factor-input decomposition is based on a Cobb-Douglas production function of the

The main results for the two growth decompositions are presented in Figure 4.5. The following findings emerge:

- The typical surplus reversal featured a full rebalancing of demand from net exports to domestic demand. In particular, whereas the contribution to growth from net exports declined by 1.6 percentage points, private consumption growth and investment growth rose by 1 and 0.7 percentage point, respectively, leaving output growth higher by 0.1 percentage point (see Figure 4.5). Both the increase in consumption growth and the decline in net exports growth were statistically significant, but the change in output and investment growth was not.

- The typical surplus reversal was accompanied by gains in employment and capital, although total factor productivity growth fell slightly. Again, although none of the changes were statistically significant, there was a modest increase in the growth rates of employment and capital per capita during the first three years following the reversal (see Figure 4.5). In addition, the average growth rate of employment was positive both before and after surplus episodes, implying that the level of employment increased (see Figure 4.3).

Reversals tended to be followed by an increase in the size of the nontradables sector as a share of GDP (Table 4.3).[18] The growth rates of output and employment tended to rise in the nontradables sector and decline in the tradables sector. Moreover, although the level of employment in the tradables sector declined, this change was more than offset by

---

form $Y = AE^{\alpha}K^{1-\alpha}$, where A denotes total factor productivity, E denotes employment, and K denotes the capital stock. The employment share α is assumed to be 0.65. Given the assumption of constant returns to scale, the production function can be expressed in per capita terms by dividing by population, P, yielding: $\frac{Y}{P} = A\left(\frac{E}{P}\right)^{\alpha}\left(\frac{K}{P}\right)^{1-\alpha}$. Finally, taking logs and first differences yields the decomposition used in the analysis: $\Delta g^{Y/P} = \alpha\Delta g^{E/P} + (1 - \alpha)\Delta g^{K/P} + \Delta g^{A}$, where $\Delta g^{Y/P}$ is the change in the growth rate of output per capita; $\Delta g^{E/P}$ is the change in the growth rate of employment per capita, $\Delta g^{K/P}$ is the change in the growth rate of capital per capita, and Δg^{A} is the change in total factor productivity growth.

[18] The nontradables sector is defined here as services and nonmanufacturing industries, and the tradables sector comprises agriculture and manufacturing industries.

Figure 4.5. Contributions to Growth
(Percentage points; before and after reversal)

Policy-induced surplus reversals are accompanied by demand rebalancing—from net exports to consumption and investment. At the same time, employment and capital contributions increase, while total factor productivity falls slightly, although these changes were not statistically significant.

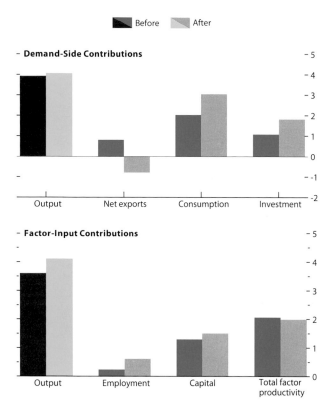

Source: IMF staff calculations.
Note: Because of limited data availability, the size of the sample is 26 observations for the demand-side decomposition and 20 observations for the factor-input decomposition.

Table 4.3. Structural Reallocation during Current Account Surplus Reversals

Variable	Surplus Reversals	Control
Increase in Nontradables/GDP (percent of episodes)	70.8	68.6
Change in Nontradables/GDP	1.3	1.2
Nontradables Output Growth (change)	0.9***	0.2
Tradables Output Growth (change)	−0.4*	0.1
Nontradables Employment Growth (change)	1.3***	−0.2
Tradables Employment Growth (change)	−1.2***	0.0
Growth of High-Tech Sector (percent of episodes)	70.8	62.8
Increase in Export Quality (percent of episodes)	66.7	54.9

Source: IMF staff calculations.

Note: Table reports changes in variables measured as three-year average starting with year of current account surplus reversal minus three-year average growth before reversal. *, **, *** indicate that the difference relative to the control group is statistically significant at the 1, 5, and 10 percent level, respectively. The control group comprises all observations at least two years away from a reversal.

an increase in nontradables sector employment, leaving the overall level of employment higher. Finally, regarding the tradables sector, data on the structure of exports reveal that the share of high-tech products and the quality of exported goods rose following the majority of reversals (see Table 4.3).[19]

What Factors Explain the Great Diversity of Growth Outcomes?

To explain the substantial variation in outcomes following surplus reversals, this section explores how the change in growth is related to various initial conditions, policies, and structural variables. Due to limited data availability, the analysis is based on a reduced sample of economies, with the number of observations ranging from 20 to 27, depending on the regression specification.[20] This section examines the importance of the following variables:

[19] Following the trade literature, export quality is measured using the unit value ratio, the relative unit value of an economy's exports to a given market with respect to the unit value of all exports to that market. See, for example, Igan, Fabrizio, and Mody (2007).

[20] Given the small sample size, a number of statistical tests were performed to ensure that outliers do not drive the regressions results. Based on these tests, one observation with a particularly large residual—Japan (1988)—was excluded from the regression sample.

- Initial growth: It is quite plausible that unusually high growth before a surplus reversal would be followed by a subsequent moderation in growth and that a recession prior to the reversal would likely be followed by an upswing. To separate the effects of such initial cyclical factors, all estimation results control for the average growth rate in the three years before the reversal. The estimation results indicate that a 1 percentage point increase in prereversal growth above the sample average is associated with a subsequent decline in growth of about 0.55–0.75 percentage point (Table 4.4, row 1). At the same time, growth that is "unusually high" in some regions may be normal in fast-growing regions such as emerging Asia. To account for that possibility, we include an emerging Asia dummy variable in the estimated equation and find it to have a positive and significant coefficient, as expected (Table 4.4, row 2).[21]
- External conditions: A favorable external environment would be expected to enhance postreversal growth, especially because many of the economies in the core subsample display a high degree of trade openness. To separate the influence of external shocks from the effects of policies implemented as part of the surplus reversal, all estimation results control for the change in the terms of trade and the change in world growth during the reversal (Table 4.4, rows 3–4). As expected, the regression results indicate that an improvement in the terms of trade is followed by an increase in postreversal growth. A 10 percent deterioration in the terms of trade is associated with a decline in growth of about 0.7–1.5 percentage points. Similarly, an increase in real world output growth is correlated with faster domestic growth: a 1 percentage point increase in world growth is associated with an increase in domestic growth of about 0.1–0.8 percentage point.
- Initial current account surplus, savings, and investment: A particularly large initial current account surplus could indicate the presence of

[21] The inclusion of the emerging Asia dummy can also be motivated by the fact that the means of other right-hand variables, such as the initial current account balance, the saving rate, or the investment rate, are likely to be substantially different in that region compared with other regions.

Table 4.4. Estimation Results: Change in Growth after Current Account Surplus Reversals

		(1)	(2)	(3)	(4)	(5)	(6)	(7)	(8)	(9)
(1)	Initial Growth	−0.752***	−0.553***	−0.694***	−0.613***	−0.660***	−0.624***	−0.587***	−0.593***	−0.663***
		[−5.184]	[−5.651]	[−5.335]	[−4.899]	[−4.923]	[−5.227]	[−4.100]	[−4.185]	[−4.549]
(2)	Emerging Asia	0.024***	0.027***	0.023***	0.021***	0.019***	0.015*	0.021**	0.020**	0.023***
		[2.854]	[4.265]	[3.446]	[3.577]	[3.091]	[2.085]	[2.855]	[2.475]	[4.181]
(3)	Change in Log Terms of Trade	0.157**	0.136**	0.147***	0.098***	0.094***	0.073**	0.086***	0.099***	0.078**
		[2.812]	[2.775]	[2.885]	[3.443]	[3.049]	[2.771]	[4.330]	[3.344]	[2.727]
(4)	Change in World Growth	0.440	0.109	0.428	0.267	0.431*	0.420*	0.676*	0.770**	0.503*
		[1.136]	[0.295]	[1.302]	[1.148]	[2.092]	[1.782]	[1.889]	[2.823]	[1.899]
(5)	Initial Current Account/GDP	−0.168*		−0.157	−0.120	−0.143**	−0.053	−0.158**	−0.219***	−0.204***
		[−1.911]		[−1.547]	[−1.417]	[−2.310]	[−0.945]	[−2.771]	[−3.442]	[−4.516]
(6)	Initial Savings/GDP		−0.177**							
			[−2.710]							
(7)	Initial Investment/GDP		0.015							
			[0.203]							
(8)	Real Appreciation			−0.067**						
				[−2.146]						
(9)	Real Appreciation (first lag)				−0.074***					
					[−2.877]					
(10)	Real Appreciation (second lag)					−0.090***	−0.146***	−0.131***	−0.125***	−0.078*
						[−3.163]	[−4.648]	[−3.896]	[−5.115]	[−2.115]
(11)	Real Appreciation × per Capita Income (second lag)						0.223**			
							[2.444]			
(12)	Per Capita Income (second lag)						−0.011			
							[−1.251]			
(13)	Real Appreciation × Export Quality (second lag)							0.152*	0.225**	
								[1.850]	[2.504]	
(14)	Export Quality (second lag)							0.003	0.009	
								[0.250]	[0.919]	
(15)	Real Appreciation × Change in Export Quality (second lag)								0.428**	
									[2.425]	
(16)	Change in Export Quality (second lag)								−0.009	
									[−0.891]	
(17)	Change in Trade Liberalization Index									0.087**
										[2.852]
(18)	Constant Term	0.037***	0.057**	0.036***	0.026***	0.028***	0.027***	0.025***	0.032***	0.026***
		[3.467]	[2.886]	[3.314]	[3.511]	[3.679]	[3.554]	[3.701]	[3.324]	[3.929]
	Observations	27	23	27	26	26	26	20	20	24
	R^2	0.678	0.749	0.719	0.771	0.785	0.841	0.820	0.866	0.793

Source: IMF staff calculations.

Note: Dependent variable is three-year average growth starting with year of current account surplus reversal minus three-year average growth before reversal. Estimation results are based on ordinary least squares with robust t-statistics in square brackets. ***, **, and * denote significance at the 1, 5, and 10 percent level, respectively.

some of the distortions discussed previously.[22] These results suggest that economies with a larger initial current account surplus tended to experience sharper declines in growth following the reversal (Table 4.4, row 5). In addition, there is evidence that high initial savings, rather than low initial investment, are behind this result (Table 4.4, rows 6–7). These results could reflect the withdrawal of policies, such as undervaluation, that resulted in both high savings and rapid growth before the reversal.

- Exchange rate appreciation:[23] A growing literature investigates the links between real appreciation and growth. For the economies in the sample, there is evidence of a significant negative association between real appreciation and growth, and this strengthens over time (Table 4.4, rows 8–10). At the two-year-lag horizon, a 10 percent appreciation of the real effective exchange rate is associated with a fall in growth of about 1 percentage point. However, there is also evidence that the relationship between the change in output growth and the real exchange rate is nonlinear. In particular, as per capita income or export quality rises, the link weakens between real appreciation and growth in both magnitude and statistical significance (Table 4.4, rows 11, 13, and 15). These results are consistent with those reported by Rodrik (2008), suggesting that real appreciation is likely to affect developing economies more than advanced economies. The results are also consistent with the notion that climbing the export quality ladder can mitigate the negative impact on growth of a real appreciation.

- Structural policies: There is evidence that trade liberalization is associated with a significant increase in growth following surplus reversals (Table 4.4, row 17). An increase in trade liberalization by 1 standard deviation corresponds to

an estimated increase in growth of 0.7 percentage point.

How should these empirical findings be interpreted? Overall, the results underscore that growth following a surplus reversal is a function of a variety of factors, only one of which is the exchange rate: other things being equal, a real exchange rate appreciation is associated with lower growth. But stronger global growth can offset the effect of the appreciation and so can a cyclical rebound. Moreover, the negative growth effects of an appreciation are less pronounced for more advanced economies and for those that undertake structural reforms and climb the export quality ladder.

Surplus Reversals: Case Studies

To complement the statistical analysis, this section focuses on five episodes whose prereversal conditions closely resemble those of today's large current account surplus economies. The five case studies ranked highest among all the episodes in the sample in terms of the similarity of their prereversal conditions with those of today's large surplus economies. As reported in Table 4.5, the ranking was based on 10 characteristics, including strong output and export growth, large and persistent surpluses, a high saving rate, and an undervalued exchange rate (Appendix 4.2 provides details on the scoring methodology). Using this approach, the top five cases included economies with globally important surpluses that were pressured into revaluing their currencies (Japan and Germany in the early 1970s and Japan in the mid-1980s) and economies that allowed their currencies to appreciate against the U.S. dollar to facilitate rebalancing (Korea and Taiwan Province of China in the late 1980s).[24] Overall, although the circumstances of these case studies were not identical to those prevailing in surplus economies today, the hope is that there are sufficient similarities to facilitate drawing some lessons.

[22] Ideally, the analysis would be based on direct measures of domestic distortions that affect savings and investment. Due to limited data availability for such direct measures, we use data on the current account surplus as an indirect proxy for underlying distortions, on the assumption that more severe distortions result in greater surpluses.

[23] Since the sample covers policy-induced reversals, featuring the exchange rate as a right-hand-side variable should not raise major concerns.

[24] One potential case study, Hong Kong in 1990, is excluded because Hong Kong SAR's status as a financial center makes it difficult to draw lessons that can be generalized to other economies.

Table 4.5. Historical Current Account Surplus Reversal Episodes: Relevance for Today's Current Account Surplus Economies

		(1) Strong Growth	(2) Strong Exports	(3) Large Current Account	(4) Globally Important Surplus	(5) Persistent Surplus	(6) High Savings	(7) High Investment	(8) Low Consumption	(9) Pegged or Heavily Managed Exchange Rate	(10) Under-valuation	(11) Total Score
Japan	1973	✓	✓		✓	✓	✓	✓	✓	✓	✓	9
Germany	1970	✓	✓		✓	✓		✓		✓	✓	7
Japan	1988	✓			✓	✓	✓	✓	✓	✓		7
Korea	1989	✓	✓	✓			✓	✓	✓	✓	✓	8
Taiwan Province of China	1988	✓	✓	✓		✓	✓		✓	✓	✓	8
Hong Kong SAR	1990	✓	✓	✓		✓	✓	✓	✓		✓	8
China	1993	✓	✓			✓	✓	✓	✓	✓		7
Korea	2001		✓	✓	✓		✓	✓	✓			6
Malaysia	1990	✓	✓	✓				✓	✓		✓	6
Norway	1986	✓		✓		✓	✓	✓	✓			6
Ireland	1998	✓	✓			✓			✓		✓	5
Malaysia	1980	✓						✓	✓		✓	4
Singapore	2000			✓		✓	✓	✓	✓			5
South Africa	1981						✓	✓	✓	✓		4
Thailand	2001		✓	✓			✓		✓	✓		5
Vietnam	2002	✓	✓				✓	✓			✓	5
Belgium	1966	✓				✓			✓		✓	4
Egypt	1994	✓		✓						✓	✓	4
Finland	2003		✓		✓					✓	✓	4
Netherlands	1998		✓	✓	✓						✓	4
Belgium	2000		✓		✓						✓	3
Jordan	1977						✓	✓			✓	3
Panama	1991		✓		✓						✓	3
Indonesia	2003		✓							✓		2
Italy	1998				✓						✓	2
Netherlands	1977					✓					✓	2
South Africa	1964	✓									✓	2
Switzerland	1978				✓							1

Source: IMF staff calculations.

Note: Table reports measures of variables in the three years prior to the current account surplus reversal (columns 1–10), with scores based on whether the variable is above or below the sample median. For Globally Important Surplus, the score is based on whether the current account surplus comprises more than 10 percent of the world's combined surpluses. For Pegged or Heavily Managed Exchange Rate, the score is based on whether the economy has a score of 1 or 2 according to Reinhart and Rogoff (2004) classification. Total Score indicates the sum of the scores for the various criteria, with each criterion receiving a weight of 1.

Figure 4.6. Case Studies: Pretransition Initial Conditions[1]

Strong, export-led growth led to large, persistent, and globally important current account surpluses...

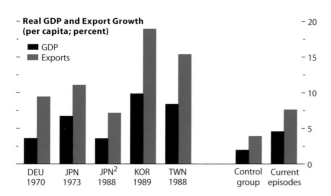

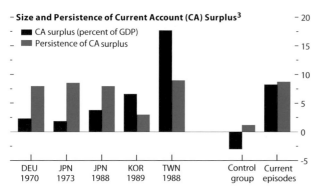

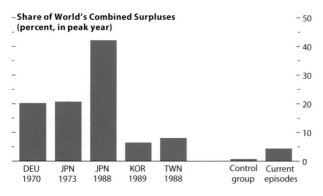

Source: IMF staff calculations.
[1]DEU: Germany; JPN: Japan; KOR: Korea; TWN: Taiwan Province of China. The control group of nonreversals consists of all observations in the sample that are at least three years removed from a surplus reversal. The sample of current surplus episodes includes all economies with large and persistent current account surpluses, averaging at least 2 percent of GDP in the three years leading up to 2008.
[2]Pretransition export growth for Japan 1988 is the average from 1980–85; exports contracted during 1986–87 following the sharp appreciation after the signing of the Plaza Accord.
[3]Persistence of CA surplus is the number of years in the decade prior to the transition during which the economy had a CA surplus.

What Were the Key Pretransition Characteristics of a Reversal?

By design, the five case studies share many pretransition characteristics with economies that have large current account surpluses today. Figure 4.6 presents some of these key characteristics for the case studies, for large current surplus economies, and for the nonreversal control observations in the sample.[25] The following characteristics stand out:

- The surplus economies had strong output growth, driven largely by exports. These were the result of long periods of macroeconomic stability and active export promotion policies—starting in the 1950s in Japan and Germany and in the late 1950s and early 1960s in Korea and Taiwan Province of China. In the latter, for example, export promotion began in 1958 with a package of policies that included a 25 percent devaluation, unified exchange rate, incentives for exports (preferential credit access, often at concessional rates), establishment of export-processing zones to attract foreign direct investment, and the easing of quantitative import restrictions.[26] All five case studies—even Germany and Japan, which were already advanced economies—had output and export growth rates that exceeded the average in the control group.

- The surplus economies had large, persistent, and in some cases "globally important" current account surpluses that created tensions with their trading partners. Average pretransition surpluses ranged from 2 percent of GDP in Japan (1970–72) to an extraordinarily high 18 percent of GDP in Taiwan Province of China (1985–87). The surpluses of Germany and Japan, though small in relation to their own GDP, were globally important in that they accounted for a substantial portion of the world's combined surpluses at their respective peaks: in 1967, Germany accounted for 20 percent of the world's combined surpluses; Japan accounted for 20 percent in 1971 and 42

[25] As in the statistical analysis, the control group of nonreversals consists of all observations in the sample that are at least two years removed from a surplus reversal.

[26] For details on the various industrial and export promotion policies pursued in these economies, see World Bank (1993), Noland and Pack (2005), and Kuchiki (2007).

percent in 1986.[27] These large surpluses created tension with these economies' trading partners—particularly the United States—that was intense enough to spur measures to address the imbalances, either unilaterally (such as the "Nixon shock"[28] of 1971) or bilaterally (such as the Plaza Accord[29] of 1985). Although the surpluses of Korea and Taiwan Province of China in the late 1980s were not globally important, their bilateral surpluses with the United States were large enough that both were cited in the U.S. Omnibus Trade and Competitiveness Act of 1988 as "manipulating their currencies" for unfair trade gain (Lindner, 1992).

- The surplus economies had high levels of investment but even higher levels of savings.[30] Prereversal levels of investment averaged 28 percent of GDP in the case studies, above the 21 percent of GDP average for the control group. But prereversal levels of savings were even higher, averaging 34 percent of GDP in the case studies compared with 19 percent in the control group. The high savings levels were associated with particularly low levels of private consumption, which averaged 52 percent of GDP in the case studies, compared with 66 percent of GDP in the control group. The low consumption levels in these economies were in part the result of structural distortions, described in greater detail below.

- Most of the case studies had a pegged or a heavily managed exchange rate. Germany and Japan in the late 1960s and early 1970s were part of the Bretton Woods system of fixed exchange rates and were pegged to the U.S. dollar (which

---

[27] For comparison, China's current account surplus accounted for 21 percent of the world's combined surpluses in 2008.

[28] On August 15, 1971, President Richard M. Nixon imposed a 10 percent tax on all imports to the United States until its trading partners agreed to revalue against the dollar. The Nixon shock led to a revaluation of the yen within two weeks and eventually to the floating of the yen in early 1973.

[29] On September 22, 1985, the major advanced economies announced their intention to coordinate foreign exchange intervention policies in order to bring about a depreciation of the U.S. dollar against the Japanese yen and Deutsche Mark.

[30] To encourage saving, Japan, Korea, and Taiwan Province of China implemented effective bank prudential supervision and regulation of entry. In addition, all three had postal savings or similar savings institutions.

Figure 4.6 *(concluded)*[1]

...driven in part by undervaluation. The resulting surpluses were characterized by high investment, even higher savings, and low consumption.

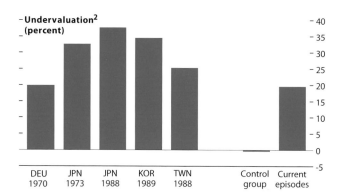

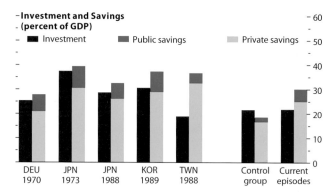

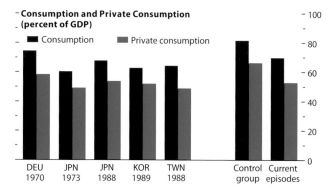

Source: IMF staff calculations.
[1]DEU: Germany; JPN: Japan; KOR: Korea; TWN: Taiwan Province of China. The control group of nonreversals consists of all observations in the sample that are at least three years removed from a surplus reversal. The sample of current surplus episodes includes all economies with large and persistent current account surpluses, averaging at least 2 percent of GDP in the three years leading up to 2008.
[2]Undervaluation estimates are based on an application of the IMF Consultative Group on Exchange Rate Issues (CGER) macroeconomic balance methodology to historical data. For Germany 1970 and Taiwan Province of China 1988, lack of data precludes the use of this methodology, and the CGER's external sustainability approach is used instead; for details see Lee and others (2008). For current surplus episodes, the value is the average of available data for Argentina, China, Israel, Japan, Malaysia, Sweden, and Switzerland.

in turn was pegged to gold). Korea and Taiwan Province of China in the mid- to late 1980s both had heavily managed exchange rates that were kept relatively stable against the U.S. dollar; these quasi pegs against the U.S. dollar stayed in place as the dollar depreciated against the yen and the Deutsche Mark in 1986 following the Plaza Accord, contributing to both economies' surpluses. Among the case studies, only Japan in the mid-1980s had a freely floating exchange rate.

- Exchange rates appeared undervalued in all of the case study economies prior to the reversals, distorting an important price signal. First, there is evidence of significant undervaluation in all five case studies. The application of a number of standard measures produces estimates of undervaluation ranging from just under 20 percent in Germany in the late 1960s to close to 40 percent in Japan in the mid-1980s.[31] These estimates are consistent with the literature, which also finds evidence of significant undervaluation using alternative methods.[32] Beyond model-based assessments of exchange rate misalignment, the strong and persistent appreciations that occurred when these currencies were allowed to float is perhaps the most convincing de facto evidence that they were undervalued prior to the transition. As discussed, by distorting relative prices, undervaluation discourages consumption and makes investment in the tradables sector relatively more attractive than investment in the nontradables sector.

- Some of these economies had other policies that resulted in additional distortions and helped support the surpluses. In Japan, Korea, and Taiwan Province of China, preferential credit was directed toward the export sector, sometimes at subsidized rates. There were also trade restrictions, particularly on imports of manufactured goods, in both Korea and Taiwan Province of China. Third, there were tax incentives to pro-

mote research and development and to support strategic industries in Korea and Taiwan Province of China. Finally, substantial capital controls were in place in Japan in the early 1970s and in Korea in the late 1980s, which allowed for some degree of sterilization.[33]

- Many of these economies had strong macroeconomic frameworks and policy room, which affected how they responded to and managed the reversal. In these economies, inflation was relatively low, averaging less than 3 percent in the prereversal period compared with close to 7 percent in the control group. Fiscal balances were also close to zero, and most of them (with the exception of Japan in the mid-1980s) had low levels of government debt.

What Policies Were Used during the Transition Period?

The current account surpluses became a policy concern for both external and domestic reasons (Table 4.6). As noted, the large surpluses created tensions with these economies' trading partners that in some cases led to unilateral or multilateral measures. Domestically, the current account surpluses led to significant balance of payments surpluses, which in the context of pegged or heavily managed exchange rates led to money supply growth that was more rapid than desired. For Germany and Taiwan Province of China, which had relatively open capital accounts, speculative capital inflows (driven by expectations of revaluation) exacerbated the problem, and in both cases the authorities decided to float the currency rather than to let money growth get out of hand (Berger, 1997; and Xu, 2008).

In all the case studies, appreciation was the main policy lever for reversing the current account surplus. The appreciation was both in nominal terms—all economies let their currencies appreciate against the U.S. dollar—and in real effective terms. And it was substantial in all cases. The extent of nominal appreciation against the dollar ranged

[31] The analysis measures undervaluation using the IMF's Consultative Group on Exchange Rate Issues (CGER) methodologies for exchange rate assessment (Lee and others, 2008).

[32] See, for example, Eichengreen (2007), Fujino (1988), and Kosai (1989) for Japan; and World Bank (1993) for Korea and Taiwan Province of China.

[33] Ostry and others (2010) argue that capital controls might be appropriate under certain circumstances, including when standard macroeconomic prescriptions are not appropriate (for example, to reduce domestic interest rates when inflation is creeping in) and when there are financial fragility concerns.

Table 4.6. Case Studies: Policies Used during Current Account Surplus Reversals

	Germany 1970	Japan 1973	Japan 1988	Korea 1989	Taiwan Province of China 1988
Were Surpluses a Policy Issue?	Yes, because of trade tensions, speculative inflows, and rapid money growth	Yes, because of trade tensions	Yes, because of trade tensions	Yes, because of trade tensions and rapid money growth	Yes, because of trade tensions, speculative inflows, and rapid money growth
What Caused Surpluses to Decline?	Appreciation	Appreciation	Appreciation	Appreciation	Appreciation
Appreciation against U.S. dollar (percent)[1]	25	34	54	25	57
Real Effective Appreciation (percent)[1]	12	27	40	32	21
Exchange Rate Policy	Revaluation in 1969; exit from peg in 1971	Revaluation in 1971; exit from peg in 1973	Coordinated attempt to appreciate yen after 1985 Plaza Accord	Appreciation against U.S. dollar after mid-1987	Exit from quasi peg in mid-1986
Fiscal Policy	Neutral in 1968–69; shift to tightening in 1971–72 as excess demand pressures continued	Expansionary in 1971–72 in expectation of weakening external demand	Stimulative after 1986 as economy began to slow following appreciation	Tight fiscal policy in 1987 to counter overheating	Fiscal consolidation
Monetary Policy	Neutral in 1968–69; shift to tightening in 1971–72 as excess demand pressures continued	Expansionary in 1971–72 in expectation of weakening external demand; shift to tightening in 1973 as inflation accelerated; sterilization of capital inflows	Easing beginning in 1986 as economy began to slow following appreciation; sterilization of capital inflows	Tight monetary policy in 1987 to counter overheating; easing in 1989 after slowdown and stock market collapse; tightening after growth rebounded in 1990–91; sterilization of capital inflows	Neutral monetary policy, without regard for surpluses and/or appreciation
Structural Policies	. . .	. . .	Interest rate controls phased out between 1985 and 1994	Removal of import restrictions and reductions in tariffs to help lower surplus; liberalization of domestic financial sector; capital account liberalization, particularly foreign direct investment	Removal of import restrictions and reductions in tariffs; liberalization of domestic financial sector; capital account liberalization, particularly foreign direct investment; establishment of standard labor laws

[1]Specific dates used to measure appreciation are as follows: September 1969–March 1969 for Germany, August 1971–March 1973 for Japan, August 1985–August 1986 for Japan post–Plaza Accord, April 1987–December 1989 for Korea, and September 1985–September 1989 for Taiwan Province of China.

from 25 percent for the Deutsche Mark and Korean won to 54 percent for the yen following the Plaza Accord. These translated to real effective appreciations between 12 and 40 percent.

The fiscal and monetary policy responses accompanying the appreciations differed across the case studies. In the German and Japanese episodes, macroeconomic policies were kept looser than would have been the case in the absence of an appreciation. In all three of these episodes, the authorities anticipated a substantial weakening in external demand and output growth following the appreciation; relatively loose policies were meant to support domestic demand. In contrast, the Korean government pursued both fiscal and monetary tightening as the won appreciated, because its main concern was to reduce overheating and excess demand pressures (IMF, 1988).[34] Finally, in Taiwan Province of China both fiscal and monetary policy were neutral—the authorities did not see a need either to support or to slow down domestic demand.

In Germany and Japan, authorities had to reverse course and tighten monetary policy when demand turned out to be stronger than expected. The "preemptive" easing pursued in these economies following the appreciation of their currencies had to be subsequently reversed. The economies experienced sharp but short-lived slowdowns, partly because of oil price increases, and subsequent domestic demand growth proved stronger than expected. In Germany and Japan in the early 1970s, this domestic demand growth, combined with oil price increases, resulted in rising inflation; Germany began tightening monetary policy in 1971–72, and Japan in 1973, and this slowed down the economy in both cases. In Japan following the Plaza Accord, there were few signs of consumer price pressures, but lower interest rates and the appreciation-induced improvement in the terms of trade led to domestic demand growth of 8 percent in 1988 and to sharp rises in equity and property markets. The Bank of Japan tightened monetary policy rapidly in 1989 (Box 4.1).

[34] The Korean authorities eased monetary policy subsequently in 1989 in response to a collapse in the equity market (IMF, 1990, p. 7).

A number of structural policies were pursued to aid the transition or to mitigate its potential effects on growth and employment. In both Korea and Taiwan Province of China, further trade liberalization—specifically, removing restrictions on manufactured imports and lowering import tariffs on many goods—was an integral part of the adjustment process (IMF, 1990; World Bank, 1993). Both also liberalized the capital account, removing exchange restrictions and barriers to foreign direct investment inflows and outflows. And both (and to a lesser extent Japan in the mid-1980s) undertook substantial steps to liberalize their domestic financial sectors around the time of the transition, by deregulating interest rates and reducing the extent of directed and/or subsidized credit (World Bank, 1993), although these were not pursued for the purposes of lowering the large external surpluses.

What Were the Consequences of a Reversal?

An analysis of posttransition macroeconomic outcomes in the case studies (Figure 4.7; Table 4.7) confirms many of the findings of the statistical analysis.

- There was no uniform trend toward either lower or higher output growth after the reversals. In principle, a surplus reversal induced by an exchange rate appreciation would lower aggregate demand and thus reduce output and inflation.[35] In fact, inflation did not fall in any case study, suggesting that insufficient aggregate demand was not a problem: disinflationary effects were typically more than offset by macroeconomic stimulus or oil price shocks. GDP growth increased in one case, declined in two, and remained broadly unchanged in another two.[36] When compared with world growth or U.S. growth, the change in output growth is positive in two cases, negative in two, and unchanged in one. The biggest growth decline occurred in Japan, where the 1974 oil price shock played a large role (Figure

[35] An appreciation also affects inflation through the price of imports.
[36] As in the statistical analysis, the average change in output growth across the case studies was not significantly different from zero.

Box 4.1. Japan after the Plaza Accord

This box provides a narrative account of Japan's surplus reversal after the Plaza Accord. There are two important lessons from this episode: the importance of exiting in a timely manner from supportive macroeconomic policies and the need to implement complementary structural reforms.

The Plaza Accord of 1985 was a response to the widening of Japan's current account surplus on the back of strengthening global demand and an undervalued currency (Cargill, Hutchison, and Ito, 1997). The surplus reached 3.7 percent of GDP in 1985, from 0.6 percent of GDP in 1982 (first figure). Calls intensified from the United States for protectionist measures, and in its annual consultation with the IMF in 1984, the Japanese authorities said they "would like to see a substantial strengthening of the yen, to help moderate the current account surplus" (IMF, 1985, p. 18). On September 22, 1985, the G5 announced their intention to coordinate foreign exchange intervention policies in order to bring about a depreciation of the U.S. dollar vis-à-vis the Japanese yen and the Deutsche Mark.[1]

The appreciation of the yen that followed the Plaza Accord was very rapid, resulting in slower growth and complicating policymaking. By the end of 1986, the yen had appreciated 46 percent against the dollar and 30 percent in real effective terms. The effects of this sharp appreciation on the manufacturing sector were swift—export volumes contracted 6 percent in 1986, business investment growth decelerated to 6 percent (from 12 percent in 1985), and GDP growth slowed to 2.5 percent in 1986 from 5 percent the previous year. In response, the government quickly shifted to a stimulative monetary and fiscal policy stance and signed the Louvre Accord in February 1987 to help stabilize the yen.

Japan's experience highlights how hard it is to time the withdrawal of macroeconomic stimulus intended to offset the effects of currency appreciation. By the late 1980s, Japan's economy was once again booming and asset price bubbles were beginning to form, but tighter monetary policy was not implemented. Estimates from Jinushi, Kuroki, and Miyao (2000);

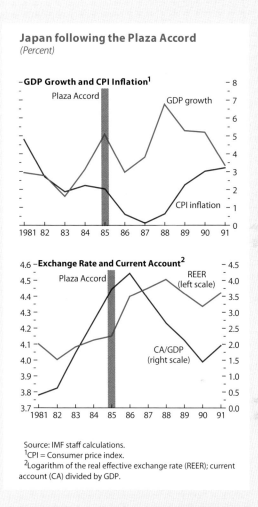

Japan following the Plaza Accord
(Percent)

Source: IMF staff calculations.
[1]CPI = Consumer price index.
[2]Logarithm of the real effective exchange rate (REER); current account (CA) divided by GDP.

Leigh (2009); and others suggest that the Bank of Japan's policy rate was about 4 percentage points too low relative to an implicit Taylor rule during 1987–89 (second figure). Tighter policy could have restrained rapid domestic demand growth, helped reduce the still-sizable external surplus via further appreciation of the yen, and headed off incipient asset price bubbles. However, the authorities felt that "further appreciation would adversely affect business confidence" (IMF, 1988, p. 13), and both the authorities and the IMF staff expressed little concern about the potential adverse effects of new bubbles.[2]

---

[1] The G5 comprises France, Germany, Japan, United Kingdom, and United States.

[2] Additional reasons for the delay in tightening monetary policy may have been market instability following the U.S. stock market crash of October 1987.

Box 4.1 *(continued)*

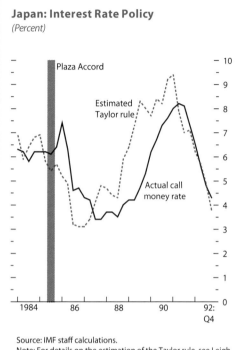

Japan: Interest Rate Policy
(Percent)

Source: IMF staff calculations.
Note: For details on the estimation of the Taylor rule, see Leigh (2009).

Furthermore, structural reforms—which would have acted as a "third leg" to aid rebalancing along with appreciation and expansionary macroeconomic policies—were not implemented in many areas. Japan's post-Plaza appreciation was large by historical standards and support for expansionary fiscal and monetary policies was sizable, yet the current account surplus did not fall as much as intended,

remaining above 2 percent of GDP. The structural reforms recommended in the "Maekawa Report" endorsed by Prime Minister Yasuhiro Nakasone could have reinforced the rebalancing effects of appreciation.[3] The reforms included expanding food imports by reducing trade protection for Japan's agricultural sector; eliminating distortions that encouraged saving, such as the tax exemption for postal savings; and reducing restrictions on land use that limited supply and exacerbated property price pressures. But following the large appreciation of the yen, and given the political difficulty of pursuing them, many of these reforms were set aside.

The period culminated in Japan's asset market bust of the early 1990s and was followed by years of disappointing economic performance—Japan's "Lost Decade." However, it would be incorrect to conclude that Japan's surplus reversal in the late 1980s caused the Lost Decade. The accepted wisdom is that Japan's slump dragged on so long because of delays in cleaning up the banking system; the zero lower bound on nominal interest rates, which limited the Bank of Japan's ability to stimulate demand; and external shocks such as the 1991 U.S. recession and the 1997 Asian financial crisis (Mikitani and Posen, 2000).

---

[3] Prime Minister Nakasone established the "Maekawa Commission" and tasked it with identifying ways to reduce Japan's current account surplus. He presented the commission's recommendations—the "Maekawa Report"—to President Ronald Reagan during his visit to the United States in April 1986. As Taylor (2008) emphasizes, "the suggested policies made sense whether or not the current account was a problem."

4.8).[37] Taiwan Province of China also experienced a moderation in growth, but postreversal growth remained relatively high at 6 percent, and the rebalancing was very large. In the remaining

cases, growth remained unchanged or increased slightly.

• As for output, employment growth in the case studies exhibited no clear trend. Employment growth increased in two cases, but declined in three; the average change in employment growth was not statistically different from zero. As explored below, however, this ambiguity in economy-wide employment dynamics in the case

---

[37] Based on the estimates reported in Table 4.4, only about one-third of the 5 percentage point fall in Japan's growth was due to the exchange rate appreciation. This result is obtained based on the estimated coefficient on real appreciation reported in Table 4.4 (column 3, row 8), along with the real appreciation observed in Japan during the 1973 episode.

studies masks more distinct patterns of employment reallocation across sectors.

- Output responded much better than the effects of exchange rate changes alone would suggest. In the absence of offsetting factors, output growth in the five case studies should have fallen by 2 to 4 percentage points, according to the coefficient estimates from the regressions in the statistical analysis and the size of the appreciations. The fact that growth in most of them did better than predicted is due to the presence of offsetting factors, including complementary policies (supporting fiscal, monetary, and structural policies) and in some cases strong external demand.

- Private consumption growth is an alternative measure of postreversal performance, and this increased in four of the five case studies. The exception is Japan in 1973, where consumption was adversely affected by monetary tightening and the oil-price-induced recession. In the other cases, private consumption growth ranged from 5 to 11 percent following the reversal, reflecting an increase of between 1 and 3 percentage points relative to prereversal growth rates. In addition, in all cases, the process of income convergence continued—that is, relative per capita incomes in purchasing power parity terms continued to rise toward U.S. levels after the transition.

- In most case studies, the appreciation led to rebalancing—a declining contribution of net exports to growth, which was partially or fully offset by an increase in the contribution of domestic demand. Again, the exception is Japan in 1973, where domestic demand growth fell sharply and external demand remained unchanged. In the other cases, the contribution of net exports remained unchanged or fell substantially following the reversal, by as much as 7 percentage points in the case of Taiwan Province of China, but the contribution of domestic demand rose by between 1 and 5 percentage points.

- The sharp falls in the current account surpluses in the case studies reflected both lower (private) savings rates and higher investment rates, as indicated by the statistical analysis. Investment rose in all cases, except Japan in 1973, by between 3 and 7 percent of GDP relative to prereversal

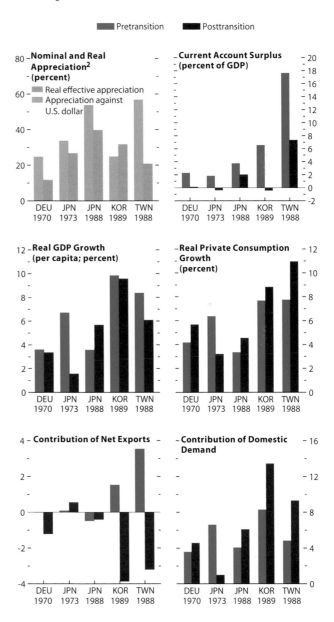

Figure 4.7. Case Studies: Posttransition Implications[1]

Strong nominal and real appreciation led to a decline in surpluses, with varying effects on output growth and private consumption growth. There was a rebalancing from external demand to domestic demand.

Source: IMF staff calculations.
[1]See Figure 4.6 for abbreviations.
[2]Specific dates used to measure appreciation are as follows: September 1969–March 1972 for Germany; August 1971–March 1973 for Japan; August 1985–August 1986 for Japan following the Plaza Accord; April 1987–December 1989 for Korea; September 1985–September 1989 for Taiwan Province of China.

Table 4.7. Case Studies: Key Indicators after Current Account Surplus Reversals

	Germany 1970	Japan 1973	Japan 1988	Korea 1989	Taiwan Province of China 1988	Average	Median
Output and Consumption							
Real GDP per Capita Growth	3.4	1.6	5.7	9.6	6.1	5.3	5.7
Real GDP per Capita Growth (change)	−0.2	−5.1	2.1	−0.3	−2.3	−1.2	−0.3
Real GDP per Capita Growth relative to World (change)	...	−3.8	2.1	0.9	−2.3	−0.8	−0.7
Real GDP per Capita Growth relative to United States (change)	0.1	−3.5	2.7	1.9	−1.7	−0.1	0.1
Real Private Consumption Growth	5.7	3.2	4.6	8.9	11.0	6.7	5.7
Real Private Consumption Growth (change)	1.5	−3.2	1.2	1.2	3.2	0.8	1.2
Convergence to United States (change in income gap)	5.0	2.3	6.0	8.0	5.7	5.4	5.7
Changes in Output Components							
Contribution of Net Exports	−1.2	0.6	−0.4	−3.9	−3.2	−1.6	−1.2
Contribution of Net Exports (change)	−1.2	0.5	0.1	−5.4	−6.8	−2.6	−1.2
Contribution of Domestic Demand	4.6	1.0	6.1	3.5	9.3	6.9	6.1
Contribution of Domestic Demand (change)	1.0	−5.6	2.0	5.2	4.5	1.4	2.0
Labor Productivity Growth	3.9	2.5	4.1	6.8	6.0	4.7	4.1
Labor Productivity Growth (change)	0.6	−4.6	0.8	0.5	−0.1	−0.6	0.5
Employment Growth	0.0	−1.0	1.5	2.3	−0.1	0.6	0.0
Employment Growth (change)	1.0	−0.4	1.2	−0.7	−2.0	−0.2	−0.4
Change in Current Account, Savings, and Investment							
Current Account Surplus (percent of GDP, change)	−2.1	−2.2	−1.7	−7.0	−10.3	−4.7	−2.2
Savings (percent of GDP, change)	0.7	−3.1	1.8	−0.3	−6.0	−1.4	−0.3
Private Savings (percent of GDP, change)	−0.1	−1.4	−1.5	−1.0	−6.7	−2.1	−1.4
Investment (percent of GDP, change)	2.9	−0.9	3.5	6.8	4.3	3.3	3.5
Sectoral Reallocation							
Share of Nontradables (change)[1]	...	1.6	0.5	4.3	6.6	3.2	3.0
Share of High- and Medium-Tech (change)	...	...	1.1	1.8	9.8	4.2	1.8
Tradables Employment Growth	...	−3.6	0.2	−1.6	−4.1	−2.3	−2.6
Nontradables Employment Growth	...	0.7	2.7	5.5	3.6	3.1	3.1
Overheating Indicators							
Consumer Price Index Inflation	4.6	14.3	2.0	7.6	3.2	6.3	4.6
Consumer Price Index Inflation (change)	2.9	8.2	1.1	3.3	2.9	3.7	2.9
Output Gap	0.6	0.9	1.7	0.2	0.7	0.8	0.7
Output Gap (change)	0.7	1.3	4.2	1.5	1.2	1.8	1.3

Source: IMF staff calculations.

[1]Numbers for Japan are derived from data from the Organization for Economic Cooperation and Development STAN database. Numbers for Taiwan Province of China are calculated from two data points (1985, 1990) as published in Xu (2008, Table 2).

levels. Savings, and particularly private savings, either remained unchanged or fell, substantially in the case of Taiwan Province of China.

- There was a clear sectoral reallocation of resources, from the tradables to the nontradables sector. The share of the nontradables sector in the economy rose in all cases, most substantially in Korea and Taiwan Province of China, where there was more scope for reallocation given the relatively smaller size of the nontradables sector prior to the reversal. Employment in the tradables sector was either stagnant or declined; in Taiwan Province of China the loss of manufacturing jobs was particularly large as Taiwanese firms moved their production offshore to lower-cost economies in southeast Asia and later to mainland China. But these losses were either partially or fully offset by gains in the nontradables sector; employment growth in this sector was positive in all cases and was substantial in the case of Japan, Korea, and Taiwan Province of China in the mid- to late 1980s.

- There is evidence that these economies climbed the export quality ladder, with the share of high- and medium-tech exports rising. This was more pronounced where there was more room to improve—most notably in Taiwan Province of China (Box 4.2)—than in economies such as Japan, where high-tech manufactures already accounted for a large share of exports. In Taiwan Province of China, the reallocation of production toward higher-value-added industries was also supported by structural policies such as tax incentives that encouraged investment in research and development.

In sum, exchange rate appreciation was only one among several important factors in the process of reversing the current account surpluses in the case study economies. The analysis indicates that differences in macroeconomic management and in the external environment are central to economic performance following surplus reversals. In terms of fiscal and monetary policy, the lesson that emerges is not that domestic demand might be too weak following an appreciation, but rather that it has tended to be stronger than expected, creating problems when preemptive stimulus policies were pursued. Structural policies can play an important role in helping sustain the rebalancing from exports

Figure 4.8. Japan at the End of Bretton Woods
(Percent)

Japan's economy featured stagflation, largely reflecting an unfavorable oil price shock in 1974.

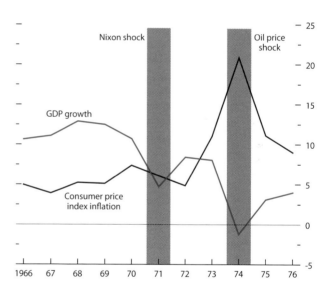

Source: IMF staff calculations.

Box 4.2. Taiwan Province of China in the Late 1980s

This box illustrates the role of sectoral rebalancing during a current account reversal in an emerging market economy, including climbing the export quality ladder and outsourcing.[1]

Taiwan Province of China's current account surplus exceeded 20 percent of GDP in the mid-1980s after years of strong export-oriented growth and a stable currency. But following the Plaza Accord, speculative inflows based on market expectations that the Taiwan dollar would appreciate against the U.S. dollar forced the central bank to abandon the currency's quasi peg and let the currency appreciate.[2] In the four years following the Plaza Accord, September 1985–September 1989, the Taiwan dollar appreciated 57 percent against the U.S. dollar and 21 percent in real effective terms. At the same time, the current account surplus dropped sharply, from its peak of 21 percent of GDP in 1986 to 7½ percent of GDP by 1989 and to less than 4 percent of GDP for much of the 1990s (first figure).

Exports slowed in response to the appreciation, but consumption and investment strengthened. Consumption growth, which averaged close to 6 percent a year in the first half of the 1980s, accelerated to 9½ percent a year in the second half of the decade, cushioning the effect of the slowdown in exports. The consumption-to-GDP ratio increased from 63 percent in 1986 to 73 percent in 1995 and has remained high and stable ever since. Investment growth was also buoyant in the late 1980s, averaging 12 percent a year, as the Taiwanese government implemented various tax incentives to encourage private investment in research and development (Wang and Mai, 2001). Overall, despite the Taiwan dollar's sharp appreciation, average GDP growth during 1987–91 remained at

Taiwan Province of China in the Late 1980s

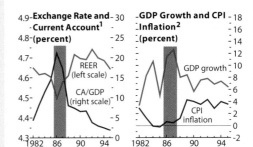

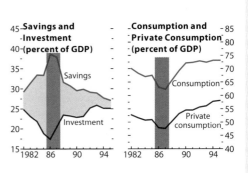

Source: IMF staff calculations.
[1]Logarithm of the real effective exchange rate (REER); current account (CA) divided by GDP.
[2]CPI = Consumer price index.

8.5 percent, close to the 8 percent average GDP growth during 1982–86.[3]

Firms in the tradables sector took a hit as a result of the appreciation but adjusted by climbing the export quality ladder and by outsourcing. The initial loss in competitiveness was severe: export growth slowed from an average 14 percent during

---

[1] This case study draws on Xu (2008).

[2] As the U.S. dollar began its post–Plaza Accord fall against the yen and Deutsche Mark in late 1985, speculation in the markets increased that the Taiwan dollar would appreciate as well. The central bank initially resisted the pressure to appreciate, but as reserves doubled and growth accelerated in the M1 money supply (money readily available for spending), the central bank decided to let the currency float freely with minimal intervention.

[3] Note that, in contrast to some of the other case studies, Taiwanese authorities made no attempt to preemptively ease monetary (or fiscal) policy in anticipation of the weakening external demand that an appreciation would engender. In the end, such an easing was not needed, because Taiwanese exporters moved to high-value-added exports—aided by structural policies to support private sector research and development—which mitigated the loss in competitiveness.

1982–86 to less than 9 percent on average during 1987–91.[4] One response of the manufacturing sector was to climb faster up the export quality ladder. Production of capital-intensive, higher-value-added products such as computers and electronics started rising, accounting for 32 percent of manufactures in 1985 and 43 percent by 1996 (second figure). The share of labor-intensive, low-value-added products such as textiles fell from 36 percent to 22 percent over the same period. The other response of the manufacturing sector was to shift production overseas, to economies with lower costs. Initially most of Taiwan's outward foreign direct investment benefited southeast Asian economies, such as Malaysia, but in the 1990s more of this investment was directed toward mainland China.

Finally, losses in the tradables sector were offset by gains in the nontradables sector. The share of services in GDP, which had been stable at about 47 percent in the first half of the 1980s, began to increase, from 48 percent in the mid-1980s to 60 percent by the mid-1990s (see second figure). Labor resources also shifted, with the share of employment in services increasing from 41 percent to 51 percent over the same period (Wang and Mai, 2001). Overall, economy-wide employment continued to grow on average by 2 percent a year.

[4] Growth of real value added in manufacturing fell from 11 percent to 4½ percent over the same period. In addition to the appreciation, another factor that adversely affected exports and manufacturing was the downturn in the U.S. economy during 1990–91 related to the Gulf War and the spike in oil prices.

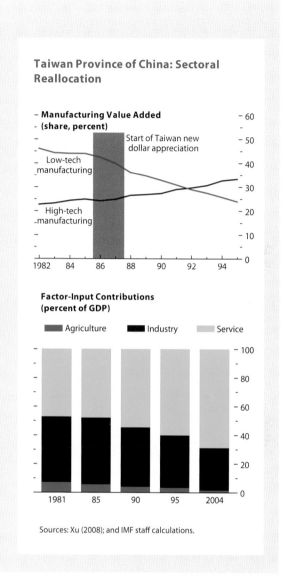

Taiwan Province of China: Sectoral Reallocation

Manufacturing Value Added (share, percent)

Start of Taiwan new dollar appreciation

Low-tech manufacturing

High-tech manufacturing

Factor-Input Contributions (percent of GDP)

Agriculture   Industry   Service

Sources: Xu (2008); and IMF staff calculations.

toward domestic demand, as evidenced in Korea and Taiwan Province of China.

Lessons for Economies Considering a Transition out of External Surpluses

This section outlines key lessons for economies considering a transition away from current account surpluses in today's environment, drawing from the analysis here of historical surplus reversals and from related research.

First, reducing a current account surplus does not necessarily entail lowering output growth. In principle, there are many reasons for growth to either increase or decrease following surplus reversals. The empirical evidence suggests that output growth on average did not decline during policy-induced surplus reversals during the past 50 years. Moreover, growth after these reversals was more balanced across domestic and external sources, and, despite some employment losses in the tradables sector, economy-wide employment growth tended to increase. Although current account reversals were associated with a wide range of growth outcomes, when large swings in growth occurred, they resulted primarily from shocks unrelated to policies aimed at reversing the current account surpluses.

Second, although real exchange rate appreciation itself seems to have slowed growth, other factors tended to offset this adverse effect. In particular, in many cases macroeconomic policy stimulus boosted domestic demand and offset the contractionary effects of appreciation. In addition, in some cases firms in the tradables sector responded to appreciation by improving the quality of their products. Finally, an improving external environment supported growth in a number of episodes.

Third, although expansionary macroeconomic policies can support the rebalancing of demand from exports toward domestic demand, there is a risk that such policies can stoke inflation and asset price booms. Encouragingly, surplus economies typically had accumulated ample policy room, enabling them to implement fiscal and monetary stimulus when exchange rates were allowed to appreciate. At the same time, however, it is possible to overestimate how much exchange rate appreciation will likely constrain growth and to react with excessive stimulus to aggregate demand, potentially leading to overheating and asset price booms.

Fourth, trade liberalization can help reduce large current account surpluses while supporting growth. The same holds for a broad range of structural reforms that foster growth of the nontradables sector. Moreover, economies that implement policies to facilitate upgrades in the quality of their exports and that have more room for such reallocation and upgrading experienced a smaller decline in growth following real exchange rate appreciation.

Appendix 4.1. Sample for Analysis and Data Sources

This appendix specifies the economies covered by the analysis and provides data sources.

Table 4.8. Sample for Analysis and Current Surplus Episodes
(Surplus reversal years listed in parentheses)

Sample for Analysis	Current Surplus Episodes
Argentina	Argentina
Australia	Austria
Austria	China
Belgium (1966[2], 2000[2])	Denmark
Brazil	Finland
Canada	Germany
China (1993[2])	Hong Kong SAR
Colombia	Israel
Denmark	Japan
Dominican Republic	Malaysia
Egypt (1994[1])	Netherlands
Finland (2003[2])	Norway
France	Philippines
Germany (1970[1,2])	Singapore
Greece	Sweden
Hong Kong SAR (1990[2])	Switzerland
India	Taiwan Province of China
Indonesia (2003[2])	
Ireland (1998[2])	
Israel	
Italy (1998[2])	
Japan (1973[1,2], 1988[1,2])	
Jordan (1977[2])	
Korea (1989[1], 2001[2])	
Malaysia (1980[1,2], 1990[1])	
Mexico	
Morocco	
Netherlands (1977[1], 1998[2])	
New Zealand	
Norway (1986[2])	
Pakistan	
Panama (1991[2])	
Peru	
Philippines	
Portugal	
Singapore (2000[2])	
South Africa (1964[2], 1981[1,2])	
Spain	
Sweden	
Switzerland (1978[1,2])	
Taiwan Province of China (1988[1])	
Thailand (2001[2])	
Turkey	
United Kingdom	
United States	
Vietnam (2002[2])	

[1]Denotes reversals associated with policy-induced appreciation, as described in the text.
[2]Denotes reversals associated with macroeconomic stimulus, as described in the text.

Table 4.9. Data Sources

Variable	Source
Real GDP	World Bank World Development Indicators (WDI) Database, World Economic Outlook (WEO) Database
Population	WDI Database, WEO Database
Real Consumption	WDI Database, WEO Database
Real Private Consumption	WDI Database, WEO Database
Real Government Consumption	WDI Database, WEO Database
Real Exports	WDI Database, WEO Database
Real Imports	WDI Database, WEO Database
Real Investment	WDI Database, WEO Database
Current Account Balance	WDI Database, WEO Database
Consumer Price Index	International Financial Statistics (IFS) Database, WEO Database
Employment	WDI Database, WEO Database
Trade Liberalization Index	IMF
Domestic Finance Liberalization Index	IMF
Capital Account Liberalization Index	IMF
Exchange Rate	Penn World Tables, IFS Database
Nominal Effective Exchange Rate	IMF
Real Effective Exchange Rate	IMF
Real Capital Stock	Penn World Tables
Terms of Trade	WDI Database, WEO Database
Total Savings	WEO Database
Private Savings	WEO Database
Public Savings	WEO Database
Interest Rates	IFS Database
Policy Rates	Bloomberg Financial Markets, National Authorities, Thomson Datastream
Undervaluation	IMF
UVR[1]	IMF
Sector-Specific Output Data	WDI Database, Organization for Economic Cooperation and Development Structural Analysis (STAN) Database

[1]UVR is the unit value of an economy's exports divided by the unit value of world exports.

Appendix 4.2. Scoring Method Used to Group Economies

Each episode was scored on the following criteria, which measure similarity with current account surplus episodes:

- High output growth: Per capita GDP growth that is above the sample median
- High export growth: Per capita export growth that is above the sample median
- Relatively large current account: A current account surplus in percent of GDP that is above the sample median
- Globally important surplus: A current account surplus that accounts for at least 10 percent of the world's combined surpluses
- Persistent surplus: A fraction of the past decade spent in surplus that is above the sample median
- High savings: Savings as a percent of GDP that is above the sample median
- High investment: Investment as a percent of GDP that is above the sample median
- Low consumption: Consumption as a percent of GDP that is below the sample median
- Relatively inflexible exchange rate: An exchange rate regime that is either a peg or a heavily managed float, as classified by Reinhart and Rogoff (2004)
- Undervaluation: An estimated undervaluation, using an application of the IMF Consultative Group on Exchange Rate Issues—CGER—macroeconomic balance approach, that is above the sample median

Each criterion was given equal weight. The relevance score for each surplus reversal is the sum of the scores for the various criteria. As a result, the relevance score ranges from 0 to 10.

References

Acemoglu, Daron, 2009, *Introduction to Modern Economic Growth* (Princeton, New Jersey: Princeton University Press).

Adalet, Muge, and Barry Eichengreen, 2007, "Current Account Reversals: Always a Problem?" in *G7 Current Account Imbalances: Sustainability and Adjustment,* ed. by Richard H. Clarida (Chicago: University of Chicago Press).

Berger, Helge, 1997, "The Bundesbank's Path to Independence: Evidence from the 1950s," *Public Choice,* Vol. 93, No. 3–4, pp. 427–53.

Blanchard, Olivier, and Francesco Giavazzi, 2006, "Rebalancing Growth in China: A Three-Handed Approach," *China and the World Economy,* Vol. 14, No. 4, pp. 1–20.

Blanchard, Olivier, and Gian Maria Milesi-Ferretti, 2009, "Global Imbalances: In Midstream?" IMF Staff Position Note 09/29 (Washington: International Monetary Fund).

Cargill, Thomas F., Michael M. Hutchison, and Takatoshi Ito, 1997, *The Political Economy of Japanese Monetary Policy* (Cambridge, Massachusetts: MIT Press).

Cavallo, Michele, Kate Kisselev, Fabrizio Perry, and Nouriel Roubini, 2004, "Exchange Rate Overshooting and the Costs of Floating" (unpublished).

Commission on Growth and Development, 2008, *The Growth Report: Strategies for Sustained Growth and Inclusive Development* (Washington: International Bank for Reconstruction and Development and World Bank).

Durdu, Ceyhun Bora, Enrique Mendoza, and Marco E. Terrones, 2009, "Precautionary Demand for Foreign Assets in Sudden Stop Economies: An Assessment of the New Mercantilism," *Journal of Development Economics,* Vol. 89, No. 2, pp. 194–209.

Edwards, Sebastian, 2004, "Thirty Years of Current Account Imbalances, Current Account Reversals and Sudden Stops," NBER Working Paper No. 10276 (Cambridge, Massachussetts: National Bureau of Economic Research).

Edwards, Sebastian, 2007, "On Current Account Surpluses and the Correction of Global Imbalances," NBER Working Paper No. 12904 (Cambridge, Massachusetts: National Bureau of Economic Research).

Eichengreen, Barry, 2007, *Global Imbalances and the Lessons of Bretton Woods* (Cambridge, Massachusetts: MIT Press).

———, and Mariko Hatase, 2005, "Can a Rapidly-Growing Export-Oriented Economy Smoothly Exit an Exchange Rate Peg? Lessons for China from Japan's High-Growth Era," NBER Working Paper No. 11625 (Cambridge, Massachusetts: National Bureau of Economic Research).

Feyrer, James, 2009, "Trade and Income—Exploiting Time Series in Geography," NBER Working Paper No. 14910 (Cambridge, Massachusetts: National Bureau of Economic Research).

Frankel, Jeffrey A., and David Romer, 1999, "Does Trade Cause Growth?" *American Economic Review*, Vol. 89, No. 3, pp. 379–99.

Freund, Caroline, and Frank Warnock, 2007, "Current Account Deficits in Industrial Countries: The Bigger They Are, The Harder They Fall?" in *G7 Current Account Imbalances: Sustainability and Adjustment,* ed. by Richard H. Clarida (Chicago: University of Chicago Press).

Fujino, Shozaburo, 1988, "The Balance of Payments of Postwar Japan," *Keizai Kenkyu (Economic Review)*, Vol. 39, pp. 97–108.

Igan, Deniz, Stefania Fabrizio, and Ashoka Mody, 2007, "The Dynamics of Product Quality and International Competitiveness," IMF Working Paper 07/97 (Washington: International Monetary Fund).

International Monetary Fund (IMF), *Federal Republic of Germany—Article VIII Consultations*, 1969, 1971, 1972 (Washington: International Monetary Fund).

———, *Japan—Article IV Consultations*, 1985, 1987, 1988, 1991, 1992 (Washington: International Monetary Fund).

———, *Korea—Article IV Consultations*, 1986, 1988, 1989, 1990 (Washington: International Monetary Fund).

Jinushi, Toshiki, Yoshihiro Kuroki, and Ryuzo Miyao, 2000, "Monetary Policy in Japan since the Late 1980s: Delayed Policy Actions and Some Explanations," in *Japan's Financial Crisis and Its Parallels to U.S. Experience,* ed. by Ryoichi Mikitani and Adam S. Posen (Washington: Institute for International Economics).

Korinek, Anton, and Luis Servén, 2010, "Real Exchange Rate Undervaluation: Static Losses, Dynamic Gains" (unpublished).

Kosai, Yutaka, 1989, "Economic Policy during the Era of High Growth," in *Economic History of Japan*, Vol. 8, ed. by Yasukichi Yasuba and Takenori Inoki (Tokyo: Iwanami Shoten).

Kuchiki, Akifumi, 2007, "Industrial Policy in Asia," IDE Discussion Paper No. 128 (Chiba, Japan: Institute of Developing Economies).

Kuroda, Haruhiko, 2004, "The 'Nixon Shock' and the 'Plaza Agreement': Lessons from Two Seemingly Failed Cases of Japan's Exchange Rate Policy," *China and the World Economy,* Vol. 12, No. 1, pp. 3–10.

Kuttner, Kenneth N., and Adam S. Posen, 2002, "Fiscal Policy Effectiveness in Japan," *Journal of the Japanese and International Economies*, Vol. 16, No. 4, pp. 536–58.

Lee, Jaewoo, Gian Maria Milesi-Ferretti, Jonathan Ostry, Alessandro Prati, and Luca Antonio Ricci, 2008, *Exchange Rate Assessments: CGER Methodologies,* IMF Occasional Paper No. 261 (Washington: International Monetary Fund).

Leigh, Daniel, 2009, "Monetary Policy and the Lost Decade: Lessons from Japan," IMF Working Paper 09/232 (Washington: International Monetary Fund).

Lindner, Deborah J., 1992, "The Political Economy of the Won: U.S.–Korean Bilateral Negotiations on Exchange Rates," International Finance Discussion Paper No. 434 (Washington: Federal Reserve Board).

Meissner, Christopher M., and Alan M. Taylor, 2006, "Losing Our Marbles in the New Century? The Great Rebalancing in Historical Perspective," paper presented at the June 2006 Federal Reserve Bank of Boston conference on global imbalances.

Mikitani, Ryoichi, and Adam S. Posen, eds., 2000, *Japan's Financial Crisis and Its Parallels to U.S. Experience* (Washington: Institute for International Economics).

Milesi-Ferretti, Gian Maria, and Assaf Razin, 1998, "Current Account Reversals and Currency Crises: Empirical Regularities," NBER Working Paper No. 6620 (Cambridge, Massachusetts: National Bureau of Economic Research).

Montiel, Peter, 2000, "What Drives Consumption Booms?" *The World Bank Economic Review,* Vol. 14, No. 3, pp. 457–80.

———, and Luis Servén, 2008, "Real Exchange Rates, Saving, and Growth: Is There a Link?" Policy Research Working Paper No. 4636 (Washington: World Bank).

Noland, Marcus, and Howard Pack, 2005, "The East Asian Industrial Policy Experience: Implications for the Middle East," IIE Working Paper No. 05-14 (Washington: Institute for International Economics).

Ostry, Jonathan, Atish Ghosh, Karl Habermeier, Marcos Chamon, Mahvash Qureshi, and Dennis Reinhardt, 2010, "Capital Inflows: The Role of Controls," IMF Staff Position Note 10/04 (Washington: International Monetary Fund).

Reinhart, Carmen, and Kenneth Rogoff, 2004, "The Modern History of Exchange Rate Arrangements: A Reinterpretation," *Quarterly Journal of Economics,* Vol. 119 (February), pp. 1–48.

Rodrik, Dani, 2008, "The Real Exchange Rate and Economic Growth," *Brookings Papers on Economic Activity* (Fall), pp. 365–412.

———, 2009, "Making Room for China in the World Economy" (unpublished; Cambridge, Massachusetts: Harvard University John F. Kennedy School of Government).

Taylor, John B., 2008, "The Mayekawa Lecture: The Way Back to Stability and Growth in the Global Economy," presented at the 2008 International Conference "Frontiers in Monetary Policy and Theory," Institute for Monetary and Economic Studies, Bank of Japan, Tokyo, May 28–29.

Wang, Jiann-Chyuan, and Chao-Cheng Mai, 2001, "Industrial Development Strategy and Structural Transformation," in *Taiwan's Economic Success Since 1980,* ed. by Chao-Cheng Mai and Chien-Sheng Shih (Cheltenham, United Kingdom, and Northampton, Massachusetts: Edward Elgar).

Woodford, Michael, 2009, "Is an Undervalued Currency the Key to Economic Growth?" Department of Economics Discussion Paper No. 0809-13 (New York: Columbia University).

World Bank, 1993, *The East Asian Miracle: Economic Growth and Public Policy* (New York: Oxford University Press).

Xu, Yingfeng, 2008, "Lessons from Taiwan's Experience of Currency Appreciation," *China Economic Review*, Vol. 19, No. 1, pp. 53–65.

IMF EXECUTIVE BOARD DISCUSSION OF THE OUTLOOK, APRIL 2010

The following remarks by the Acting Chair were made at the conclusion of the Executive Board's discussion of the World Economic Outlook on April 7, 2010.

Executive Directors noted that the global recovery has been better than expected, driven by highly accommodative macroeconomic policies in response to the deep downturn. However, activity has been picking up unevenly across countries and regions. The recovery under way in major advanced economies is expected to be sluggish compared with recoveries in emerging and developing economies and with recoveries after previous recessions. Among emerging and developing economies, Asia is leading the recovery, whereas a number of eastern European and Commonwealth of Independent States economies are lagging behind.

Directors observed that although a variety of risks have receded, the growth outlook remains unusually uncertain, and near-term risks are generally to the downside. First, as public debt is growing in many advanced economies, room for policy maneuvers has either been largely exhausted or is much more limited, leaving the fragile recoveries exposed to new shocks. Second, heightened concerns about sovereign risks, though unlikely to be widespread across major advanced economies, are dampening investor confidence and threatening financial stability. Third, bank exposures to real estate and household indebtedness continue to pose downside risks, mainly in the United States and parts of Europe.

Directors stressed that the key policy task ahead is to ensure a smooth transition of demand from government to the private sector and from economies with excessive external deficits to those with excessive surpluses. For most advanced economies, it will be important to fully implement the planned fiscal stimulus and maintain supportive monetary policies for this year, while repairing the financial sector and reforming prudential policies and frameworks. Given relatively weak growth prospects in advanced economies, the challenge for some emerging economies is to absorb rising capital inflows and nurture domestic demand without triggering a new boom-bust cycle. Continued strengthening of prudential policies is also in order. While the timing of exit depends on individual country circumstances, international policy coordination is critical to minimizing negative spillovers and to sustaining strong, balanced growth.

Directors underscored that addressing fiscal fragilities is a top priority. In many advanced and some emerging and developing economies where the economic slowdown and stimulus measures have pushed debts and deficits to very high levels, there is a pressing need to design and communicate credible medium-term fiscal consolidation strategies. Such strategies should include clear timelines to bring down gross debt-to-GDP ratios to more prudent levels, as well as concrete measures to raise potential output over the medium term. If macroeconomic developments proceed as expected, most advanced economies should embark on fiscal consolidation in 2011. For economies facing large increases in risk premiums, consolidation needs to begin now. Entitlement reforms that do not detract from demand in the short term should be implemented without delay, contributing to long-term fiscal sustainability.

Directors considered that the key challenges facing monetary policymakers are when and how to unwind accommodative conditions. Still-low levels of capital utilization and well-anchored inflation expectations are expected to keep inflation in check in most economies. In major advanced economies, monetary policy can remain accommodative as fiscal consolidation progresses, provided inflation pressure remains subdued. This can be achieved even as central banks begin to withdraw the emergency support provided to financial sectors. Major emerging and some advanced economies will likely continue to lead the tightening cycle, as they are expected to experience faster recoveries and renewed capital flows.

Directors noted that in emerging economies with excessive surpluses, monetary tightening should be supported with nominal effective exchange rate appreciation as excess demand pressures build. In cases where monetary tightening risks attracting more capital inflows, leading to exchange rate appreciation and undermining competitiveness, specific macroprudential measures should be considered. Other measures that can be taken include fiscal tightening to ease pressure on interest rates, some buildup of reserves, or easing of controls on capital outflows. Temporary controls on capital inflows—carefully designed to avoid creating new distortions and minimize implementation costs—could play a complementary role, and, in the view of some Directors, should be used only in exceptional circumstances.

Directors observed that the response of unemployment to the sharp declines in output during the crisis has been markedly different across the advanced economies, depending in part on factors such as the magnitude of the output decline, financial stress, and house price busts. Given the

expected sluggish recovery in output and the lingering effects of financial stress, unemployment rates are likely to remain high through 2011 in many advanced economies. Preventing temporary joblessness from turning into long-term unemployment requires, first, appropriately supportive macroeconomic policies; second, sound restructuring of the banking system that would help restore credit for employment-intensive sectors; and, third, appropriate labor market policies, notably adequate unemployment benefits and education and training.

Directors highlighted the urgency of rebalancing global demand, supported by appropriately sequenced financial sector and structural reforms. Economies with excessive external deficits before the crisis need to consolidate their public finances in ways that limit damage to growth and demand and encourage private savings. Economies with excessive current account surpluses need to increase domestic demand further as excessive-deficit economies scale back their imports in response to lower expectations about future income. In this context, Directors took note of the IMF staff's findings that reversing current account surpluses does not necessarily entail lower output growth and that appropriate macroeconomic and structural policies—particularly those aimed at promoting resource reallocation and higher-value-added industries—could help offset the contractionary effects of a real exchange rate appreciation.

STATISTICAL APPENDIX

The Statistical Appendix presents historical data, as well as projections. It comprises five sections: Assumptions, What's New, Data and Conventions, Classification of Countries, and Statistical Tables.

The assumptions underlying the estimates and projections for 2010–11 and the medium-term scenario for 2012–15 are summarized in the first section. The second section presents a brief description of changes to the database and statistical tables. The third section provides a general description of the data and of the conventions used for calculating country group composites. The classification of countries in the various groups presented in the *World Economic Outlook* is summarized in the fourth section.

The last, and main, section comprises the statistical tables. Data in these tables have been compiled on the basis of information available through mid-April 2010. The figures for 2010 and beyond are shown with the same degree of precision as the historical figures solely for convenience; because they are projections, the same degree of accuracy is not to be inferred.

Assumptions

Real effective *exchange rates* for the advanced economies are assumed to remain constant at their average levels during the period February 23–March 23, 2010. For 2010 and 2011, these assumptions imply average U.S. dollar/SDR conversion rates of 1.534 and 1.529, U.S. dollar/euro conversion rates of 1.364 and 1.350, and yen/U.S. dollar conversion rates of 90.1 and 89.0, respectively.

It is assumed that the *price of oil* will average $80.00 a barrel in 2010 and $83.00 a barrel in 2011.

Established *policies* of national authorities are assumed to be maintained. The more specific policy assumptions underlying the projections for selected economies are described in Box A1.

With regard to *interest rates*, it is assumed that the London interbank offered rate (LIBOR) on six-month U.S. dollar deposits will average 0.5 percent in 2010 and 1.7 percent in 2011, that three-month euro deposits will average 0.9 percent in 2010 and 1.6 percent in 2011, and that six-month yen deposits will average 0.6 percent in 2010 and 0.7 percent in 2011.

With respect to *introduction of the euro*, on December 31, 1998, the Council of the European Union decided that, effective January 1, 1999, the irrevocably fixed conversion rates between the euro and currencies of the member states adopting the euro are as follows.

1 euro	=	13.7603	Austrian schillings
	=	40.3399	Belgian francs
	=	0.585274	Cyprus pound[1]
	=	1.95583	Deutsche mark
	=	5.94573	Finnish markkaa
	=	6.55957	French francs
	=	340.750	Greek drachma[2]
	=	0.787564	Irish pound
	=	1,936.27	Italian lire
	=	40.3399	Luxembourg francs
	=	0.42930	Maltese lira[3]
	=	2.20371	Netherlands guilders
	=	200.482	Portuguese escudos
	=	30.1260	Slovak koruna[4]
	=	239.640	Slovenian tolars[5]
	=	166.386	Spanish pesetas

---

[1]Established on January 1, 2008.
[2]Established on January 1, 2001.
[3]Established on January 1, 2008.
[4]Established on January 1, 2009.
[5]Established on January 1, 2007.

See Box 5.4 of the October 1998 *World Economic Outlook* for details on how the conversion rates were established.

What's New

- Starting with the April 2010 *World Economic Outlook*, Algeria, Djibouti, Mauritania, Morocco, Sudan, and Tunisia, previously classified as mem-

Box A1. Economic Policy Assumptions Underlying the Projections for Selected Economies

Fiscal Policy Assumptions

The short-term fiscal policy assumptions used in the *World Economic Outlook* (WEO) are based on officially announced budgets, adjusted for differences between the national authorities and the IMF staff regarding macroeconomic assumptions and projected fiscal out-turns. The medium-term fiscal projections incorporate policy measures that are judged likely to be implemented. In cases where the IMF staff has insufficient information to assess the authorities' budget intentions and prospects for policy implementation, an unchanged structural primary balance is assumed, unless indicated otherwise. Specific assumptions used in some of the advanced economies follow (see also Tables B5, B6, B7, and B9 in the Statistical Appendix for data on fiscal net lending/borrowing and structural balances).[1]

Argentina: The 2010 forecasts are based on the 2009 outturn and IMF staff assumptions. For the outer years, the IMF staff assumes unchanged policies.

Australia: The fiscal projections are based on the Mid-Year Economic and Fiscal Outlook (2009–10) and IMF staff projections.

Austria: The fiscal projections for 2010 are based on the authorities' budget, adjusted for differences in the IMF staff's macro framework. The projections for 2011 onward assume unchanged policies.

Belgium: Projections for 2010 are IMF staff estimates based on the 2010 budgets approved by the federal, regional, and community parliaments and

---

[1] The output gap is actual less potential output, as a percent of potential output. Structural balances are expressed as a percent of potential output. The structural budget balance is the budgetary position that would be observed if the level of actual output coincided with potential output. Changes in the structural budget balance consequently include effects of temporary fiscal measures, the impact of fluctuations in interest rates and debt-service costs, and other noncyclical fluctuations in the budget balance. The computations of structural budget balances are based on IMF staff estimates of potential GDP and revenue and expenditure elasticities (see the October 1993 *World Economic Outlook*, Annex I). Net debt is defined as gross debt less financial assets of the general government, which include assets held by the social security insurance system. Estimates of the output gap and of the structural balance are subject to significant margins of uncertainty.

further strengthened by the Intergovernmental Agreement 2009–10. Projections for the outer years are IMF staff estimates, assuming unchanged policies.

Brazil: The 2010 forecasts are based on the budget law and IMF staff assumptions. For the outer years, the IMF staff assumes unchanged policies, with a further increase in public investment in line with the authorities' intentions.

Canada: Projections use the baseline forecasts in the latest Budget 2010—Leading the Way on Jobs and Growth. The IMF staff makes some adjustments to this forecast for differences in macroeconomic projections. The IMF staff forecast also incorporates the most recent data releases from Statistics Canada, including provincial and territorial budgetary outturns through the end of 2009.

China: For 2010–11, the government is assumed to continue and complete the stimulus program it announced in late 2008, although the lack of details published on this package complicates IMF staff analysis. Specifically, the IMF staff assumes the stimulus is not withdrawn in 2010, and so there is no significant fiscal impulse. Stimulus is withdrawn in 2011, resulting in a negative fiscal impulse of about 1 percent of GDP (reflecting both higher revenue and lower spending).

Denmark: Projections for 2010–11 are aligned with the latest official budget estimates and the underlying economic projections, adjusted where appropriate for the IMF staff's macroeconomic assumptions. For 2012–15, the projections incorporate key features of the medium-term fiscal plan as embodied in the authorities' 2009 Convergence Program submitted to the European Union.

France: Projections for 2010 are based on the 2010 budget and the latest Stability Program and are adjusted for differences in macroeconomic assumptions. Projections for the outer years incorporate the IMF staff's assessment of current policies and implementation of announced adjustment measures.

Germany: Projections for 2010 are based on the 2010 budget, adjusted for differences in the IMF staff's macro framework. The IMF staff's projections for the medium-term outlook incorporate the withdrawal of fiscal stimulus, planned income tax cuts envisaged for 2011, and the IMF staff's assessment of feasible adjustment policies already announced.

Greece: Projections for 2010 are based on the 2010 Stability Program and other forecasts and data provided by the authorities, but with the IMF staff's more subdued growth outlook. Fiscal projections for 2011–15 are the IMF staff's baseline projections— that is, they reflect the impact of measures already announced and in place from 2010 onward but do not assume further adjustments at this time. Therefore, the medium-term fiscal path deviates from the objectives of the Stability Program, which assume that further measures will be implemented in due course. In addition, the projections for 2011–15 are based on the assumptions underlying the IMF staff's medium-term macroeconomic scenario, which continues to be more subdued than the medium-term growth recovery assumed by the authorities. The IMF staff will include further measures in its fiscal projections for 2011–15 as these are defined and implemented.

Hong Kong SAR: Projections are based on the authorities' medium-term fiscal projection.

Hungary: The 2010 forecast is based on the implementation of the budget and the macro framework agreed to during the Fifth Review of the Stand-By Arrangement. The IMF staff assumes additional measures to those of the authorities for 2011–15: in 2011, 1¼ percent of GDP, to achieve the authorities' announced objectives and in the medium term to ensure fiscal sustainability. Additional information is available in the IMF staff report.

India: Historical data are based on budgetary execution data. Projections are based on available information on the authorities' fiscal plans, with some adjustments for the IMF staff's assumptions. Projections are based on the budget itself as well as the semiannual budget review. Subnational data are incorporated with a lag of up to two years; general government data are thus finalized only long after central government data. IMF presentation differs from Indian national accounts data, particularly regarding subsidies and certain loans.

Indonesia: The 2009 preliminary outturn for the overall fiscal deficit was 1.6 percent of estimated GDP. The outturn was lower than the revised budget deficit, largely as a result of lower interest payments and underspending on personnel, material goods, and other spending. About 85 percent of the announced 2009 stimulus measures were implemented (1.1 percent of GDP), with revenue measures comprising nearly three-quarters of the total package. The 2010 expected fiscal stimulus is 0.6 percent of GDP, comprised entirely of revenue measures. The 2010 revised budget draft envisages a budget deficit of 2.1 percent of GDP, higher than the previous target of 1.6 percent of GDP. However, with a built-in cushion arising from very high spending allocations in some categories and a track record of underexecution, the 2010 deficit is likely to be below the announced deficit target. The IMF staff's overall deficit projection is about 1.8 percent of GDP.

Ireland: Fiscal projections for 2010 are based on the 2010 budget, adjusted for differences in macroeconomic assumptions. The government announced comprehensive financial sector support on March 30, 2010, including the use of promissory notes to provide capital to banks. The use of promissory notes is likely to raise the gross debt of the general government in 2010, and possibly its deficit and net debt, to the extent that the returns on the capital are low. However, given that the statistical impact of these transactions is still being worked out, the fiscal projections do not incorporate the promissory notes, awaiting a final assessment. For 2011–12, the IMF staff projections incorporate most of the adjustment efforts announced by the authorities in their Stability Program Update, although two-thirds of these measures have still not been specified or agreed by the government. For the remainder of the projection period and in the absence of specifically identified budgetary measures, the projections do not incorporate further budgetary adjustments. The authorities have announced their intention to take further steps to lower the deficit below 3 percent of GDP by 2014 and have identified broad areas where savings will be found, but have yet to specify and put in place the measures to bring this about.

Italy: The fiscal projections incorporate the impact of the 2010 Budget Law and the authorities' latest revisions to the unchanged legislation scenario, which

Box A1 *(concluded)*

was presented in the January 2010 "Nota di aggior-namento 2010–2012." In the absence of specific measures and details underlying their policy scenario, the authorities' estimates for an unchanged legislation scenario are used as a basis for the WEO projections, adjusted mainly for differences in the macroeconomic assumptions. From 2013 onward, a constant structural primary balance (net of one-time items) is assumed.

Japan: The 2010 projections assume that fiscal stimulus will be implemented as announced by the government. The medium-term projections typically assume that expenditure and revenue of the general government are adjusted in line with current underly-ing trends (excluding fiscal stimulus).

Korea: The fiscal projections assume that fiscal policies will be implemented in 2010 as announced by the government. The 2010 budget targets a scaling back of stimulus measures relative to 2009, implying a negative fiscal impulse estimated at 2 percent of GDP. Expenditure numbers for 2010 correspond to the expenditure numbers presented in the govern-ment's budget proposal. Revenue projections reflect the IMF staff's macroeconomic assumptions, adjusted for the estimated costs of tax measures included in the multiyear stimulus package introduced last year and discretionary revenue-raising measures included in the 2010 budget proposal. The medium-term projections assume that the government will resume its consolida-tion plans and balance the budget (excluding social security funds) in 2014.

Mexico: Fiscal projections are based on (1) the IMF staff's macroeconomic projections, (2) the modified balanced budget rule under the Fiscal Responsibil-ity Legislation, and (3) the authorities' projections of spending on pensions and health care and of wage-bill restraint. For 2010–11, projections take into account the departure from the balanced budget target under the exceptional clause of the fiscal framework, which allows for a small deficit reflecting cyclical deteriora-tion in revenues.

Netherlands: Fiscal projections for the period 2009–10 are based on the Bureau for Economic Policy Analysis budget projections, after adjusting for differences in macroeconomic assumptions. For 2011, the projection incorporates previously announced measures detailed in the authorities' January 2010

Stability Program. For the remainder of the projection period, the projection assumes unchanged policies.

New Zealand: The fiscal projections are based on the authorities' Half Year Budget December 2009 budget update and IMF staff estimates. The New Zealand fiscal accounts switched to new generally accepted accounting principles beginning in fiscal year 2006/07, with no comparable historical data.

Portugal: For 2010, fiscal projections are based on the 2010 budget adjusted for differences between the government's and the IMF staff's macroeconomic assumptions. For 2011 and beyond, the IMF staff largely incorporates the specific fiscal measures in the medium-term fiscal plan, adjusted for the IMF staff's macroeconomic projections.

Russia: Projections for 2010 are based on the nomi-nal expenditures in the 2010 Budget and the IMF staff's revenue projections. Projections for 2011–12 are based on the non-oil deficit in percent of GDP implied by the medium-term budget and on the IMF staff's revenue projections. The IMF staff assumes an unchanged non-oil federal government balance in percent of GDP during 2012–15.

Saudi Arabia: The authorities systematically under-estimate revenues and expenditures in the budget relative to actual outturns. IMF staff projections of oil revenues are based on the WEO baseline oil prices discounted by 5 percent, reflecting the higher sulfur content in Saudi crude oil. Regarding non-oil revenues, customs receipts are assumed to grow in line with imports, investment income in line with the London interbank offered rate (LIBOR), and fees and charges as a function of non-oil GDP. On the expenditure side, wages are assumed to rise above the natural rate of increase, reflecting a salary increase of 15 percent distributed over 2008–10, and goods and services are projected to grow in line with inflation over the medium term. In 2010 and 2013, 13th-month pay is awarded based on the lunar calendar. Interest payments are projected to decline in line with the authorities' policy of repaying public debt. Capital spending in 2010 is projected to be higher than in the budget by about 16 percent and in line with the authorities' announcements of $400 billion in spend-ing over the medium term. The pace of spending is projected to slow over the medium term, leading to a tightening of the fiscal stance.

Singapore: For fiscal year 2010/11, projections are based on budget numbers. Medium-term projections assume that capital gains on fiscal reserves will be included in investment income.

South Africa: Fiscal projections are based on the authorities' 2010 budget and policy intentions stated in the budget review, published February 17, 2010.

Spain: For 2010, fiscal projections are based on the 2010 budget adjusted for differences between the government's and the IMF staff's macroeconomic assumptions. For 2011 and beyond, the IMF staff largely incorporates the specific fiscal measures in the medium-term fiscal plan, adjusted for the IMF staff's macroeconomic projections.

Sweden: Fiscal projections for 2010 are in line with authorities' projections. The impact of cyclical developments on the fiscal accounts is calculated using the Organization for Economic Cooperation and Development's latest semi-elasticity.

Switzerland: Projections for 2008–15 are based on IMF staff calculations, which incorporate measures to restore balance in the federal accounts and strengthen social security finances.

Turkey: Fiscal projections reflect the IMF staff's assessment of the known policy measures underpinning the authorities' medium-term plans.

United Kingdom: The estimates for 2009 incorporate a fiscal stimulus of about 1.5 percent of GDP (1.1 percent revenue measures, 0.4 percent expenditure measures). The fiscal projections from 2010 onward are based on the authorities' Pre-Budget Report, announced in December 2009. The pro-

jections are adjusted for differences in forecasts of macroeconomic and financial variables.

United States: The fiscal projections are based on the administration's budget for fiscal year 2010 and the U.S. Congressional Budget Office's baseline budget outlook for 2010–19. These projections include the $787 billion stimulus package under the American Recovery and Reinvestment Act of 2009. The projections are adjusted for differences in forecasts of (1) macroeconomic and financial variables, (2) the timing of stimulus disbursements, (3) additional costs to support financial institutions and government-sponsored enterprises, and (4) the effect of financial sector support on government-owned financial assets.

Monetary Policy Assumptions

Monetary policy assumptions are based on the established policy framework in each country. In most cases, this implies a nonaccommodative stance over the business cycle: official interest rates will increase when economic indicators suggest that inflation will rise above its acceptable rate or range, and they will decrease when indicators suggest that prospective inflation will not exceed the acceptable rate or range, that prospective output growth is below its potential rate, and that the margin of slack in the economy is significant. On this basis, the LIBOR on six-month U.S. dollar deposits is assumed to average 0.5 percent in 2010 and 1.7 percent in 2011 (see Table 1.1). The rate on three-month euro deposits is assumed to average 0.9 percent in 2010 and 1.6 percent in 2011. The interest rate on six-month Japanese yen deposits is assumed to average 0.6 percent in 2010 and 0.7 percent in 2011.

---

bers of the Africa region, have been added to the former Middle East region to create the Middle East and North Africa (MENA) region. Accordingly, the former Africa region is replaced by sub-Saharan Africa (SSA).
- Following the IMF's *Government Finance Statistics Manual 2001*, the government balance is now called net lending(+)/borrowing(–), which is calculated as revenue minus expenditure. Not all countries have adopted the new presentation; for those, net lending/borrowing is the previous

calculation of total revenue and grants minus total expenditure and net lending.
- The country composition of the fuel-exporting group and analytical composition of the net external position group have been revised to reflect the periodic update of the classification criteria.
- Country weights calculated as nominal GDP valued at purchasing-power-parity (PPP) exchange rates as a share of total world GDP are updated to reflect revisions to countries' historical GDP data and projections.

- Data for Kosovo are now included in the appendix tables for real GDP, consumer prices, and payments balances on current account, but are omitted from the emerging and developing economies group composites because of data limitations.

Data and Conventions

Data and projections for 183 economies form the statistical basis for the *World Economic Outlook* (the WEO database). The data are maintained jointly by the IMF's Research Department and regional departments, with the latter regularly updating country projections based on consistent global assumptions.

Although national statistical agencies are the ultimate providers of historical data and definitions, international organizations are also involved in statistical issues, with the objective of harmonizing methodologies for the compilation of national statistics, including analytical frameworks, concepts, definitions, classifications, and valuation procedures used in the production of economic statistics. The WEO database reflects information from both national source agencies and international organizations.

The comprehensive revision of the standardized *System of National Accounts 1993,* the IMF's *Balance of Payments Manual, Fifth Edition,* the *Monetary and Financial Statistics Manual* (MFSM), and the *Government Finance Statistics Manual 2001* represented significant improvements in the standards of economic statistics and analysis.[1] The IMF was actively involved in all these projects, particularly the *Balance of Payments, Monetary and Financial Statistics,* and *Government Finance Statistics* manuals, which reflect the IMF's special interest in countries' external positions, financial sector stability, and public sector fiscal positions. The process of adapt-

ing country data to the new definitions began in earnest when the manuals were released. However, full concordance with the manuals is ultimately dependent on the provision by national statistical compilers of revised country data; hence, the *World Economic Outlook* estimates are still only partially adapted to these manuals.

Several countries have phased out their traditional *fixed-base-year* method of calculating real macroeconomic variable levels and growth by switching to a *chain-weighted* method of computing aggregate growth, in line with recent improvements in standards for reporting economic statistics. Switching to the chain-weighted method of computing aggregate growth, which uses current price information, allows countries to measure GDP growth more accurately by eliminating upward biases in new data.[2] Currently, real macroeconomic data for Albania, Algeria, Australia, Austria, Azerbaijan, Belarus, Belgium, Bulgaria, Canada, Cyprus, the Czech Republic, Denmark, Estonia, the euro area, Finland, France, Georgia, Germany, Greece, Guatemala, Hong Kong SAR, Hungary, Iceland, Ireland, Israel, Italy, Japan, Kazakhstan, Korea, Lithuania, Luxembourg, Malta, Mauritania, the Netherlands, New Zealand, Norway, Poland, Portugal, Romania, Russia, Singapore, Slovenia, Spain, Sweden, Switzerland, Ukraine, the United Kingdom, and the United States are based on chain-weighted methodology. However, data before 1994 (Azerbaijan, Kazakhstan), 1995 (Belgium, Cyprus, Estonia, euro area, Ireland, Luxembourg, Poland, Russia, Slovenia, Spain), 1996 (Albania, Georgia), 2000 (Greece, Korea, Malta, Singapore), and 2001 (Bulgaria) are based on unrevised national accounts and subject to revision in the future.

Composite data for country groups in the *World Economic Outlook* are either sums or weighted averages of data for individual countries. Unless indicated otherwise, multiyear averages of growth rates are expressed as compound annual rates of change.[3] Arithmetically weighted averages are used for all data except inflation and money growth for

---

[1] Commission of the European Communities, International Monetary Fund, Organization for Economic Cooperation and Development, United Nations, and World Bank, *System of National Accounts 1993* (Brussels/Luxembourg, New York, Paris, and Washington, 1993); International Monetary Fund, *Balance of Payments Manual, Fifth Edition* (Washington, 1993); International Monetary Fund, *Monetary and Financial Statistics Manual* (Washington, 2000); and International Monetary Fund, *Government Finance Statistics Manual* (Washington, 2001).

[2] Charles Steindel, 1995, "Chain-Weighting: The New Approach to Measuring GDP," *Current Issues in Economics and Finance* (Federal Reserve Bank of New York), Vol. 1 (December).

[3] Averages for real GDP and its components, employment, per capita GDP, inflation, factor productivity, trade, and commodity prices are calculated based on the compound annual rate of

the emerging and developing economies group, for which geometric averages are used. The following conventions apply.

- Country group composites for exchange rates, interest rates, and growth rates of monetary aggregates are weighted by GDP converted to U.S. dollars at market exchange rates (averaged over the preceding three years) as a share of group GDP.
- Composites for other data relating to the domestic economy, whether growth rates or ratios, are weighted by GDP valued at purchasing power parity (PPP) as a share of total world or group GDP.[4]
- Composites for data relating to the domestic economy for the euro area (16 member countries throughout the entire period unless noted otherwise) are aggregates of national source data using GDP weights. Annual data are not adjusted for calendar day effects. For data prior to 1999, data aggregations apply 1995 European currency unit exchange rates.
- Composite unemployment rates and employment growth are weighted by labor force as a share of group labor force.
- Composites relating to the external economy are sums of individual country data after conversion to U.S. dollars at the average market exchange rates in the years indicated for balance of payments data and at end-of-year market exchange rates for debt denominated in currencies other than U.S. dollars. Composites of changes in foreign trade volumes and prices, however, are arithmetic averages of percent changes for individual countries weighted by the U.S. dollar value of exports or imports as a share of total world or group exports or imports (in the preceding year).

All data refer to calendar years, except for the following countries, which refer to fiscal years: Afghani-

stan, Islamic Republic of Iran, and Myanmar (April/March); Egypt, Mauritius, Nepal, Pakistan, and Samoa (July/June); and Haiti (October/September).

Classification of Countries

Summary of the Country Classification

The country classification in the *World Economic Outlook* divides the world into two major groups: advanced economies, and emerging and developing economies.[5] This classification is not based on strict criteria, economic or otherwise, and it has evolved over time. The objective is to facilitate analysis by providing a reasonably meaningful method for organizing data. Table A provides an overview of the country classification, showing the number of countries in each group by region and summarizing some key indicators of their relative size (GDP valued by purchasing power parity, total exports of goods and services, and population).

Some countries remain outside the country classification and therefore are not included in the analysis. Cuba and the Democratic People's Republic of Korea are not IMF members, and their economies therefore are not monitored by the IMF. San Marino is omitted from the group of advanced economies for lack of a fully developed database. Likewise, the Marshall Islands, the Federated States of Micronesia, Palau, and Somalia are omitted from the emerging and developing economies group composites because of data limitations.

General Features and Composition of Groups in the *World Economic Outlook* Classification

Advanced Economies

The 33 advanced economies are listed in Table B. The seven largest in terms of GDP—the United States, Japan, Germany, France, Italy, the United Kingdom, and Canada—constitute the subgroup of *major advanced economies,* often referred to as the Group of

---

change, except for the unemployment rate, which is based on the simple arithmetic average.

[4] See Box A2 of the April 2004 *World Economic Outlook* for a summary of the revised PPP-based weights and Annex IV of the May 1993 *World Economic Outlook*. See also Anne-Marie Gulde and Marianne Schulze-Ghattas, "Purchasing Power Parity Based Weights for the *World Economic Outlook,*" in *Staff Studies for the World Economic Outlook* (International Monetary Fund, December 1993), pp. 106–23.

[5] As used here, the terms "country" and "economy" do not in all cases refer to a territorial entity that is a state as understood by international law and practice. It also covers some territorial entities that are not states but for which statistical data are maintained on a separate and independent basis.

Table A. Classification by *World Economic Outlook* Groups and Their Shares in Aggregate GDP, Exports of Goods and Services, and Population, 2009[1]

(Percent of total for group or world)

	Number of Countries	GDP		Exports of Goods and Services		Population	
		Advanced Economies	World	Advanced Economies	World	Advanced Economies	World
Advanced Economies	**33**	**100.0**	**53.9**	**100.0**	**65.9**	**100.0**	**15.0**
United States		38.0	20.5	15.0	9.9	30.4	4.6
Euro Area	16	28.2	15.2	43.7	28.8	32.3	4.8
Germany		7.5	4.0	13.0	8.6	8.1	1.2
France		5.6	3.0	6.0	4.0	6.2	0.9
Italy		4.7	2.5	4.9	3.2	5.9	0.9
Spain		3.6	2.0	3.4	2.2	4.5	0.7
Japan		11.1	6.0	6.5	4.3	12.6	1.9
United Kingdom		5.8	3.1	5.9	3.9	6.1	0.9
Canada		3.4	1.8	3.7	2.4	3.3	0.5
Other Advanced Economies	13	13.5	7.3	25.3	16.7	15.3	2.3
Memorandum							
Major Advanced Economies	7	76.1	41.0	55.0	36.3	72.6	10.9
Newly Industrialized Asian Economies	4	6.9	3.7	13.8	9.1	8.3	1.2

	Number of Countries	Emerging and Developing Economies	World	Emerging and Developing Economies	World	Emerging and Developing Economies	World
Emerging and Developing Economies	**149**	**100.0**	**46.1**	**100.0**	**34.1**	**100.0**	**85.0**
Regional Groups							
Central and Eastern Europe	14	7.5	3.5	10.8	3.7	3.1	2.6
Commonwealth of Independent States[2]	13	9.3	4.3	9.9	3.4	4.9	4.2
Russia		6.6	3.0	6.4	2.2	2.5	2.1
Developing Asia	26	48.9	22.5	42.4	14.4	61.8	52.5
China		27.2	12.5	24.8	8.5	23.3	19.8
India		11.0	5.1	4.6	1.6	21.0	17.8
Excluding China and India	24	10.7	5.0	13.0	4.4	17.5	14.9
Middle East and North Africa	20	10.7	5.0	16.9	5.8	7.0	6.0
Sub-Saharan Africa	44	5.1	2.4	5.1	1.8	13.4	11.4
Excluding Nigeria and South Africa	42	2.6	1.2	2.8	1.0	9.9	8.4
Western Hemisphere	32	18.4	8.5	14.9	5.1	9.8	8.3
Brazil		6.2	2.9	3.4	1.2	3.3	2.8
Mexico		4.5	2.1	4.6	1.6	1.9	1.6
Analytical Groups							
By Source of Export Earnings							
Fuel	27	18.6	8.6	25.9	8.8	11.4	9.7
Nonfuel	122	81.4	37.5	74.1	25.3	88.6	75.3
Of Which, Primary Products	20	2.3	1.1	2.5	0.9	4.6	3.9
By External Financing Source							
Net Debtor Countries	121	51.2	23.6	44.7	15.2	62.0	52.7
Of Which, Official Financing	36	3.1	1.4	2.1	0.7	11.6	9.9
Net Debtor Countries by Debt-Servicing Experience							
Countries with Arrears and/or Rescheduling during 2004–08	43	5.0	2.3	4.5	1.5	9.3	7.9
Other Net Debtor Countries	78	46.2	21.3	40.2	13.7	52.7	44.8
Other Groups							
Heavily Indebted Poor Countries	35	2.1	1.0	1.7	0.6	9.6	8.2

[1]The GDP shares are based on the purchasing-power-parity valuation of countries' GDP. The number of countries comprising each group reflects those for which data are included in the group aggregates.

[2]Georgia and Mongolia, which are not members of the Commonwealth of Independent States, are included in this group for reasons of geography and similarities in economic structure.

Table B. Advanced Economies by Subgroup

Major Currency Areas	Other Subgroups					
	Euro Area		Newly Industrialized Asian Economies	Major Advanced Economies	Other Advanced Economies	
United States	Austria	Italy	Hong Kong SAR[1]	Canada	Australia	New Zealand
Euro Area	Belgium	Luxembourg	Korea	France	Czech Republic	Norway
Japan	Cyprus	Malta	Singapore	Germany	Denmark	Singapore
	Finland	Netherlands	Taiwan Province of China	Italy	Hong Kong SAR[1]	Sweden
	France	Portugal		Japan	Iceland	Switzerland
	Germany	Slovak Republic		United Kingdom	Israel	Taiwan Province of China
	Greece	Slovenia		United States	Korea	
	Ireland	Spain				

[1]On July 1, 1997, Hong Kong was returned to the People's Republic of China and became a Special Administrative Region of China.

Seven (G7). The 16 members of the *euro area* and the four *newly industrialized Asian economies* are also distinguished as subgroups. Composite data shown in the tables for the euro area cover the current members for all years, even though the membership has increased over time.

Table C lists the member countries of the European Union, not all of which are classified as advanced economies in the *World Economic Outlook*.

Emerging and Developing Economies

The group of emerging and developing economies (149 countries) includes all countries that are not classified as advanced economies.

The *regional breakdowns* of emerging and developing economies are *central and eastern Europe (CEE), Commonwealth of Independent States (CIS),* *developing Asia, Middle East and North Africa (MENA), sub-Saharan Africa (SSA),* and *Western Hemisphere.*

Emerging and developing economies are also classified according to *analytical criteria.* The analytical criteria reflect countries' composition of export earnings and other income from abroad; a distinction between net creditor and net debtor countries; and, for the net debtor countries, financial criteria based on external financing sources and experience with external debt servicing. The detailed composition of emerging and developing economies in the regional and analytical groups is shown in Tables D and E.

The analytical criterion, by *source of export earnings,* distinguishes between categories: *fuel* (Standard International Trade Classification—SITC 3) and *nonfuel* and then focuses on *nonfuel primary products* (SITCs 0, 1, 2, 4, and 68).

Table C. European Union

Austria	Finland	Latvia	Romania
Belgium	France	Lithuania	Slovak Republic
Bulgaria	Germany	Luxembourg	Slovenia
Cyprus	Greece	Malta	Spain
Czech Republic	Hungary	Netherlands	Sweden
Denmark	Ireland	Poland	United Kingdom
Estonia	Italy	Portugal	

Table D. Emerging and Developing Economies by Region and Main Source of Export Earnings

	Fuel	Nonfuel Primary Products
Commonwealth of Independent States	Azerbaijan	Mongolia
	Kazakhstan	Uzbekistan
	Russia	
	Turkmenistan	
Developing Asia	Brunei Darussalam	Papua New Guinea
	Timor-Leste	Solomon Islands
Middle East and North Africa	Algeria	Mauritania
	Bahrain	
	Iran, Islamic Republic of	
	Iraq	
	Kuwait	
	Libya	
	Oman	
	Qatar	
	Saudi Arabia	
	Sudan	
	United Arab Emirates	
	Yemen, Republic of	
Sub-Saharan Africa	Angola	Burkina Faso
	Chad	Burundi
	Congo, Republic of	Congo, Democratic Republic of
	Equatorial Guinea	Guinea
	Gabon	Guinea-Bissau
	Nigeria	Malawi
		Mali
		Mozambique
		Sierra Leone
		Zambia
		Zimbabwe
Western Hemisphere	Ecuador	Chile
	Trinidad and Tobago	Guyana
	Venezuela	Peru
		Suriname

Note: Mongolia, which is not a member of the Commonwealth of Independent States, is included in this group for reasons of geography and similarities in economic structure.

The financial criteria focus on *net creditor countries, net debtor countries,* and *heavily indebted poor countries* (HIPCs). Net debtor countries are further differentiated on the basis of two additional financial criteria: by *official external financing* and by *experience with debt servicing.*[6] The HIPC group comprises the countries considered by the IMF and the World Bank for their debt initiative, known as the HIPC Initiative, with the aim of reducing the external debt burdens of all the eligible HIPCs to a "sustainable" level in a reasonably short period of time.[7]

[6] During 2004–08, 43 countries incurred external payments arrears or entered into official or commercial bank debt-rescheduling agreements. This group of countries is referred to as *countries with arrears and/or rescheduling during 2004–08.*

[7] See David Andrews, Anthony R. Boote, Syed S. Rizavi, and Sukwinder Singh, *Debt Relief for Low-Income Countries: The Enhanced HIPC Initiative*, IMF Pamphlet Series, No. 51 (Washington: International Monetary Fund, November 1999).

Table E. Emerging and Developing Economies by Region, Net External Position, and Status as Heavily Indebted Poor Countries

	Net External Position		Heavily Indebted Poor Countries		Net External Position		Heavily Indebted Poor Countries
	Net Creditor	Net Debtor[1]			Net Creditor	Net Debtor[1]	
Central and Eastern Europe				Indonesia	*		
Albania		*		Kiribati	*		
Bosnia and Herzegovina		*		Lao People's Democratic Republic		*	
Bulgaria		*		Malaysia	*		
Croatia		*		Maldives		*	
Estonia		*		Myanmar		*	
Hungary		*		Nepal		•	
Latvia		*		Pakistan		*	
Lithuania		*		Papua New Guinea	*		
Macedonia, Former Yugoslav Republic of		*		Philippines		*	
Montenegro		*		Samoa		•	
Poland		*		Solomon Islands		•	
Romania		*		Sri Lanka		•	
Serbia		*		Thailand		*	
Turkey		*		Timor-Leste	*		
Commonwealth of Independent States[2]				Tonga		•	
Armenia		*		Vanuatu		*	
Azerbaijan	*			Vietnam		*	
Belarus		*		**Middle East and North Africa**			
Georgia		*		Algeria	*		
Kazakhstan		*		Bahrain	*		
Kyrgyz Republic		•		Djibouti		*	
Moldova		*		Egypt		*	
Mongolia		•		Iran, Islamic Republic of	*		
Russia	*			Iraq	*		
Tajikistan		*		Jordan		*	
Turkmenistan	*			Kuwait	*		
Ukraine		*		Lebanon		*	
Uzbekistan	*			Libya	*		
Developing Asia				Mauritania		*	*
Afghanistan, Islamic Republic of		•	*	Morocco		*	
Bangladesh		•		Oman	*		
Bhutan		•		Qatar	*		
Brunei Darussalam	*			Saudi Arabia	*		
Cambodia		*		Sudan		*	
China	*			Syrian Arab Republic		•	
Fiji		*		Tunisia		*	
India		*		United Arab Emirates	*		
				Yemen, Republic of		*	

Table E (concluded)

	Net External Position		Heavily Indebted Poor Countries
	Net Creditor	Net Debtor[1]	
Sub-Saharan Africa			
Angola	*		
Benin		*	*
Botswana	*		
Burkina Faso		•	*
Burundi		•	*
Cameroon		*	*
Cape Verde		*	
Central African Republic		•	*
Chad		*	*
Comoros		•	
Congo, Democratic Republic of		•	*
Congo, Republic of		•	*
Côte d'Ivoire		*	*
Equatorial Guinea		*	
Eritrea		•	
Ethiopia		•	*
Gabon	*		
Gambia, The		•	*
Ghana		•	*
Guinea		*	*
Guinea-Bissau		*	*
Kenya		•	
Lesotho		*	
Liberia		*	*
Madagascar		*	*
Malawi		•	*
Mali		•	*
Mauritius		*	
Mozambique		•	*
Namibia	*		
Niger		*	*
Nigeria	*		
Rwanda		•	*
São Tomé and Príncipe		*	*
Senegal		*	*
Seychelles		*	
Sierra Leone		•	*
South Africa		*	

	Net External Position		Heavily Indebted Poor Countries
	Net Creditor	Net Debtor[1]	
Swaziland		*	
Tanzania		•	*
Togo		•	*
Uganda		*	*
Zambia		*	*
Zimbabwe		•	
Western Hemisphere			
Antigua and Barbuda		*	
Argentina		*	
Bahamas, The		*	
Barbados		*	
Belize		*	
Bolivia		•	*
Brazil		*	
Chile		*	
Colombia		*	
Costa Rica		*	
Dominica		*	
Dominican Republic		*	
Ecuador		*	
El Salvador		*	
Grenada		*	
Guatemala		*	
Guyana		•	*
Haiti		•	*
Honduras		*	*
Jamaica		•	
Mexico		*	
Nicaragua		*	*
Panama		*	
Paraguay		*	
Peru		*	
St. Kitts and Nevis		*	
St. Lucia		*	
St. Vincent and the Grenadines		•	
Suriname		•	
Trinidad and Tobago	*		
Uruguay		*	
Venezuela	*		

[1]Dot instead of star indicates that the net debtor's main external finance source is official financing.

[2]Georgia and Mongolia, which are not members of the Commonwealth of Independent States, are included in this group for reasons of geography and similarities in economic structure.

List of Tables

Table A1. Summary of World Output[1]

(Annual percent change)

	Average 1992–2001	2002	2003	2004	2005	2006	2007	2008	2009	Projections 2010	2011	2015
World	**3.2**	**2.9**	**3.6**	**4.9**	**4.5**	**5.1**	**5.2**	**3.0**	**−0.6**	**4.2**	**4.3**	**4.6**
Advanced Economies	**2.8**	**1.7**	**1.9**	**3.2**	**2.7**	**3.0**	**2.8**	**0.5**	**−3.2**	**2.3**	**2.4**	**2.3**
United States	3.5	1.8	2.5	3.6	3.1	2.7	2.1	0.4	−2.4	3.1	2.6	2.4
Euro Area	2.1	0.9	0.8	2.2	1.7	3.0	2.8	0.6	−4.1	1.0	1.5	1.7
Japan	0.9	0.3	1.4	2.7	1.9	2.0	2.4	−1.2	−5.2	1.9	2.0	1.7
Other Advanced Economies[2]	3.7	3.3	2.5	4.0	3.5	3.9	3.9	1.2	−2.3	3.0	3.4	3.1
Emerging and Developing Economies	**3.8**	**4.8**	**6.2**	**7.5**	**7.1**	**7.9**	**8.3**	**6.1**	**2.4**	**6.3**	**6.5**	**6.7**
Regional Groups												
Central and Eastern Europe	2.6	4.4	4.8	7.3	5.9	6.5	5.5	3.0	−3.7	2.8	3.4	4.0
Commonwealth of Independent States[3]	...	5.2	7.7	8.2	6.7	8.5	8.6	5.5	−6.6	4.0	3.6	5.0
Developing Asia	7.3	6.9	8.2	8.6	9.0	9.8	10.6	7.9	6.6	8.7	8.7	8.5
Middle East and North Africa	3.4	3.8	6.9	5.8	5.3	5.7	5.6	5.1	2.4	4.5	4.8	4.8
Sub-Saharan Africa	2.8	7.4	5.0	7.1	6.3	6.5	6.9	5.5	2.1	4.7	5.9	5.4
Western Hemisphere	3.0	0.5	2.2	6.0	4.7	5.6	5.8	4.3	−1.8	4.0	4.0	4.0
Memorandum												
European Union	2.3	1.4	1.5	2.7	2.2	3.4	3.1	0.9	−4.1	1.0	1.8	2.1
Analytical Groups												
By Source of Export Earnings												
Fuel	0.3	4.8	7.0	7.9	6.7	7.2	7.2	5.3	−1.8	4.0	4.1	4.6
Nonfuel	4.8	4.8	6.0	7.4	7.2	8.1	8.6	6.3	3.3	6.9	7.0	7.1
of Which, Primary Products	3.7	3.8	4.3	5.6	6.2	6.2	6.6	6.7	1.5	5.8	6.1	5.6
By External Financing Source												
Net Debtor Economies	3.3	3.2	4.6	6.6	6.0	6.7	6.7	4.8	0.5	5.1	5.3	5.5
of Which, Official Financing	3.5	3.9	3.9	5.8	6.3	6.4	6.2	5.7	5.0	5.1	6.5	6.1
Net Debtor Economies by Debt-Servicing Experience												
Economies with Arrears and/or Rescheduling during 2004–08	2.8	−0.6	6.4	7.9	8.0	7.8	7.8	6.2	2.0	3.8	4.2	4.6
Memorandum												
Median Growth Rate												
Advanced Economies	3.1	1.9	1.9	3.9	3.2	3.6	3.6	1.2	−3.0	1.3	2.0	2.4
Emerging and Developing Economies	3.6	3.9	4.8	5.5	5.6	6.1	6.2	5.0	1.5	3.7	4.2	4.7
Output per Capita												
Advanced Economies	2.1	1.1	1.3	2.5	1.9	2.3	2.0	−0.2	−3.7	1.7	1.8	1.7
Emerging and Developing Economies	2.4	3.6	5.0	6.3	6.0	6.8	7.2	5.0	1.3	5.3	5.4	5.8
World Growth Based on Market Exchange Rates	**2.6**	**2.0**	**2.7**	**4.0**	**3.4**	**3.9**	**3.9**	**1.8**	**−2.0**	**3.2**	**3.4**	**3.7**
Value of World Output in Billions of U.S. Dollars												
At Market Exchange Rates	29,136	33,210	37,332	41,998	45,431	49,155	55,392	61,221	57,937	61,781	65,003	81,790
At Purchasing Power Parities	35,317	45,993	48,640	52,495	56,505	61,251	66,190	69,569	69,809	73,200	77,436	99,395

[1]Real GDP.

[2]In this table, Other Advanced Economies means advanced economies excluding the United States, Euro Area countries, and Japan.

[3]Georgia and Mongolia, which are not members of the Commonwealth of Independent States, are included in this group for reasons of geography and similarities in economic structure.

Table A2. Advanced Economies: Real GDP and Total Domestic Demand[1]

(Annual percent change)

	Average 1992–2001	2002	2003	2004	2005	2006	2007	2008	2009	Projections 2010	2011	2015	2009:Q4[2]	Projections 2010:Q4[2]	2011:Q4[2]
Real GDP															
Advanced Economies	**2.8**	**1.7**	**1.9**	**3.2**	**2.7**	**3.0**	**2.8**	**0.5**	**−3.2**	**2.3**	**2.4**	**2.3**	**−0.5**	**2.2**	**2.5**
United States	3.5	1.8	2.5	3.6	3.1	2.7	2.1	0.4	−2.4	3.1	2.6	2.4	0.1	2.8	2.4
Euro Area	2.1	0.9	0.8	2.2	1.7	3.0	2.8	0.6	−4.1	1.0	1.5	1.7	−2.2	1.2	1.8
Germany	1.7	0.0	−0.2	1.2	0.7	3.2	2.5	1.2	−5.0	1.2	1.7	1.2	−2.4	1.2	2.1
France	2.1	1.1	1.1	2.3	1.9	2.4	2.3	0.3	−2.2	1.5	1.8	2.2	−0.3	1.5	1.9
Italy	1.6	0.5	0.0	1.5	0.7	2.0	1.5	−1.3	−5.0	0.8	1.2	1.3	−3.0	1.4	1.3
Spain	3.0	2.7	3.1	3.3	3.6	4.0	3.6	0.9	−3.6	−0.4	0.9	1.7	−3.1	−0.1	1.8
Netherlands	3.0	0.1	0.3	2.2	2.0	3.4	3.6	2.0	−4.0	1.3	1.3	1.8	−2.6	1.7	1.2
Belgium	2.3	1.4	0.8	3.1	2.0	2.8	2.8	0.8	−3.0	1.2	1.3	1.9	−0.6	0.7	1.8
Greece	2.5	3.4	5.9	4.6	2.2	4.5	4.5	2.0	−2.0	−2.0	−1.1	1.4	−2.5	−1.5	−0.4
Austria	2.2	1.6	0.8	2.5	2.5	3.5	3.5	2.0	−3.6	1.3	1.7	2.2	−1.8	1.8	1.4
Portugal	2.9	0.8	−0.8	1.5	0.9	1.4	1.9	0.0	−2.7	0.3	0.7	1.4	−1.0	−0.4	0.3
Finland	2.9	1.8	2.0	4.1	2.9	4.4	4.9	1.2	−7.8	1.2	2.2	2.1	−5.1	0.9	4.2
Ireland	7.5	6.5	4.4	4.6	6.2	5.4	6.0	−3.0	−7.1	−1.5	1.9	2.5	−5.0	0.5	2.8
Slovak Republic	...	4.6	4.8	5.0	6.7	8.5	10.6	6.2	−4.7	4.1	4.5	4.2	−2.7	3.0	5.4
Slovenia	...	4.0	2.8	4.3	4.5	5.8	6.8	3.5	−7.3	1.1	2.0	3.8	−3.0	2.8	1.7
Luxembourg	4.4	4.1	1.5	4.4	5.4	5.6	6.5	0.0	−4.2	2.1	2.4	2.5	−0.5	3.4	2.6
Cyprus	4.8	2.1	1.9	4.2	3.9	4.1	5.1	3.6	−1.7	−0.7	1.9	3.3	−2.8	0.7	2.3
Malta	...	2.6	−0.3	0.7	3.9	3.6	3.8	2.1	−1.9	0.5	1.5	2.7	0.5	0.8	1.0
Japan	0.9	0.3	1.4	2.7	1.9	2.0	2.4	−1.2	−5.2	1.9	2.0	1.7	−1.4	1.6	2.3
United Kingdom	2.9	2.1	2.8	3.0	2.2	2.9	2.6	0.5	−4.9	1.3	2.5	2.5	−3.1	2.3	2.6
Canada	3.3	2.9	1.9	3.1	3.0	2.9	2.5	0.4	−2.6	3.1	3.2	2.1	−1.2	3.4	3.3
Korea	6.0	7.2	2.8	4.6	4.0	5.2	5.1	2.3	0.2	4.5	5.0	4.0	6.1	3.4	6.2
Australia	3.8	3.9	3.2	3.6	3.2	2.6	4.7	2.4	1.3	3.0	3.5	3.2	2.7	2.9	4.0
Taiwan Province of China	5.3	5.3	3.7	6.2	4.7	5.4	6.0	0.7	−1.9	6.5	4.8	5.0	8.5	2.1	6.3
Sweden	2.2	2.4	1.9	4.1	3.3	4.2	2.6	−0.2	−4.4	1.2	2.5	2.3	−0.1	1.7	2.4
Switzerland	1.3	0.4	−0.2	2.5	2.6	3.6	3.6	1.8	−1.5	1.5	1.8	2.0	0.0	1.3	2.1
Hong Kong SAR	3.4	1.8	3.0	8.5	7.1	7.0	6.4	2.1	−2.7	5.0	4.4	4.2	2.4	5.1	3.5
Czech Republic	...	1.9	3.6	4.5	6.3	6.8	6.1	2.5	−4.3	1.7	2.6	3.5	−4.1	2.3	3.5
Norway	3.6	1.5	1.0	3.9	2.7	2.3	2.7	1.8	−1.5	1.1	1.8	2.0	−1.2	1.8	1.7
Singapore	6.6	4.2	3.8	9.2	7.6	8.7	8.2	1.4	−2.0	5.7	5.3	4.5	4.0	5.6	6.1
Denmark	2.5	0.5	0.4	2.3	2.4	3.4	1.7	−0.9	−5.1	1.2	1.6	2.3	−3.3	0.7	−1.2
Israel	5.3	−0.7	1.5	5.0	5.1	5.3	5.2	4.0	0.7	3.2	3.5	3.7	1.7	2.8	4.0
New Zealand	3.3	4.9	4.1	4.4	3.2	1.0	2.8	−0.1	−1.6	2.9	3.2	2.4	0.4	3.8	2.9
Iceland	3.0	0.1	2.4	7.7	7.5	4.6	6.0	1.0	−6.5	−3.0	2.3	3.4	−9.1	−1.2	3.4
Memorandum															
Major Advanced Economies	2.6	1.3	1.8	2.9	2.4	2.6	2.2	0.2	−3.4	2.4	2.3	2.1	−0.9	2.3	2.3
Newly Industrialized Asian Economies	5.5	5.8	3.2	5.9	4.8	5.8	5.8	1.8	−0.9	5.2	4.9	4.3	6.1	3.4	5.9
Real Total Domestic Demand															
Advanced Economies	**2.9**	**1.8**	**2.2**	**3.2**	**2.7**	**2.8**	**2.3**	**0.1**	**−3.4**	**2.1**	**2.3**	**2.3**	**−1.3**	**2.2**	**2.4**
United States	3.9	2.4	2.8	4.0	3.2	2.6	1.4	−0.7	−3.4	3.3	2.8	2.5	−0.8	3.3	2.6
Euro Area	1.9	0.4	1.4	1.9	1.9	2.9	2.4	0.7	−3.4	0.1	1.1	1.5	−2.7	0.7	1.3
Germany	1.5	−2.0	0.6	−0.1	0.0	2.2	1.0	1.7	−1.8	−0.6	1.3	1.0	−3.0	1.2	1.4
France	1.9	1.1	1.8	3.0	2.8	2.7	3.2	0.7	−2.0	1.4	1.5	2.0	−0.5	0.9	1.8
Italy	1.3	1.3	0.8	1.3	0.9	2.0	1.3	−1.5	−3.8	1.0	1.2	1.2	−2.1	1.3	1.6
Spain	2.9	3.2	3.8	4.8	5.1	5.2	4.2	−0.5	−6.0	−1.0	0.6	1.7	−5.0	−0.5	1.6
Japan	1.0	−0.4	0.8	1.9	1.7	1.2	1.3	−1.3	−4.0	1.0	1.5	1.5	−3.3	1.7	1.4
United Kingdom	3.1	3.2	2.9	3.5	2.1	2.4	3.0	0.1	−5.3	0.6	1.9	2.5	−2.7	0.9	2.2
Canada	2.7	3.2	4.6	4.2	4.9	4.2	4.2	2.4	−2.5	3.7	3.1	1.9	−0.1	3.1	3.4
Other Advanced Economies	3.8	4.0	1.9	4.5	3.4	4.0	4.5	1.9	−2.4	4.1	3.6	3.7	2.9	2.4	5.0
Memorandum															
Major Advanced Economies	2.7	1.4	2.2	3.0	2.5	2.4	1.7	−0.3	−3.3	2.1	2.2	2.1	−1.6	2.4	2.2
Newly Industrialized Asian Economies	4.8	5.0	0.8	4.7	2.9	4.2	4.3	1.9	−3.0	5.1	4.3	4.4	4.2	2.1	6.5

[1]When economies are not listed alphabetically, they are ordered on the basis of economic size.
[2]From the fourth quarter of the preceding year.

Table A3. Advanced Economies: Components of Real GDP
(Annual percent change)

	Averages		2002	2003	2004	2005	2006	2007	2008	2009	Projections	
	1992–2001	2002–11									2010	2011
Private Consumer Expenditure												
Advanced Economies	**3.0**	**1.8**	**2.3**	**2.0**	**2.7**	**2.7**	**2.6**	**2.5**	**0.3**	**−0.8**	**1.6**	**1.9**
United States	3.9	2.1	2.7	2.8	3.5	3.4	2.9	2.7	−0.2	−0.6	2.4	2.1
Euro Area	1.5	1.0	0.9	1.2	1.6	1.8	2.0	1.6	0.4	−1.1	0.1	1.0
Germany	1.9	0.1	−0.8	0.1	0.1	0.3	1.3	−0.3	0.4	0.2	−1.1	0.7
France	1.9	1.8	2.3	2.1	2.3	2.5	2.6	2.4	1.0	0.9	1.0	1.2
Italy	1.5	0.5	0.2	1.0	0.7	1.1	1.2	1.1	−0.8	−1.8	0.9	1.2
Spain	2.7	1.7	2.8	2.9	4.2	4.2	3.8	3.6	−0.6	−4.9	0.2	1.2
Japan	1.4	0.8	1.1	0.4	1.6	1.3	1.5	1.6	−0.7	−1.0	1.3	0.8
United Kingdom	3.3	1.5	3.5	3.0	3.1	2.2	1.5	2.1	0.9	−3.2	0.2	1.4
Canada	2.8	3.1	3.6	3.0	3.3	3.7	4.1	4.6	3.0	0.2	3.0	3.0
Other Advanced Economies[1]	4.2	2.9	4.2	1.7	3.5	3.6	3.6	4.5	1.4	0.4	2.8	3.7
Memorandum												
Major Advanced Economies	2.9	1.6	2.0	2.0	2.5	2.5	2.3	2.1	0.0	−0.7	1.5	1.7
Newly Industrialized Asian Economies	5.7	3.2	5.9	0.5	2.9	3.9	3.9	4.7	1.0	0.4	3.8	4.7
Public Consumption												
Advanced Economies	**1.8**	**1.8**	**3.4**	**2.2**	**1.7**	**1.3**	**1.6**	**2.0**	**2.5**	**2.3**	**1.3**	**−0.6**
United States	1.3	1.5	4.5	2.2	1.4	0.6	1.0	1.4	3.0	1.8	1.7	−1.9
Euro Area	1.0	1.7	2.4	1.7	1.6	1.6	2.1	2.3	2.1	2.2	0.8	0.4
Germany	1.7	1.1	1.5	0.4	−0.7	0.4	1.0	1.7	2.0	3.0	0.9	0.9
France	1.4	1.5	1.9	2.0	2.2	1.2	1.3	1.5	1.1	1.6	1.5	0.7
Italy	0.3	1.1	2.4	1.9	2.2	1.9	0.5	0.9	0.8	0.6	0.2	0.0
Spain	3.0	4.1	4.5	4.8	6.3	5.5	4.6	5.5	5.4	3.8	0.4	0.0
Japan	2.9	1.4	2.4	2.3	1.9	1.6	0.4	1.5	0.3	1.6	2.7	−0.2
United Kingdom	1.3	2.0	3.5	3.4	3.0	2.0	1.6	1.2	2.6	2.2	1.3	−1.0
Canada	0.9	2.7	2.5	3.1	2.0	1.4	3.0	3.3	3.7	3.0	4.2	0.6
Other Advanced Economies	2.8	2.3	3.3	2.3	1.8	2.1	3.2	2.9	2.9	3.6	0.0	1.0
Memorandum												
Major Advanced Economies	1.6	1.5	3.3	2.1	1.5	1.0	1.0	1.5	2.2	1.9	1.7	−0.9
Newly Industrialized Asian Economies	4.0	2.6	3.8	2.3	2.3	2.5	3.8	3.7	3.6	4.6	−1.6	0.9
Gross Fixed Capital Formation												
Advanced Economies	**3.7**	**0.7**	**−1.2**	**2.1**	**4.5**	**4.3**	**3.9**	**2.2**	**−1.9**	**−12.0**	**0.9**	**5.4**
United States	6.4	0.4	−2.7	3.1	6.2	5.3	2.5	−1.2	−3.6	−14.5	1.8	9.3
Euro Area	1.7	0.5	−1.5	1.3	2.3	3.2	5.4	4.8	−0.4	−11.1	−0.4	1.9
Germany	1.2	0.6	−6.1	−0.3	−0.3	0.9	7.8	5.0	3.1	−8.9	2.9	3.2
France	2.0	1.4	−1.7	2.2	3.3	4.4	4.4	6.5	0.6	−6.9	−0.8	2.4
Italy	1.4	−0.3	3.7	−1.2	2.3	0.8	2.9	1.7	−4.0	−12.1	1.7	2.4
Spain	3.6	0.5	3.4	5.9	5.1	7.0	7.2	4.6	−4.4	−15.3	−5.1	−0.7
Japan	−1.0	−1.8	−4.9	−0.5	1.4	3.1	0.5	−1.2	−2.6	−14.3	−2.5	4.4
United Kingdom	4.0	0.8	3.6	1.1	5.1	2.4	6.5	7.8	−3.5	−14.9	−2.6	4.7
Canada	3.7	3.0	1.6	6.2	7.8	9.3	6.9	3.7	0.9	−10.1	3.8	1.6
Other Advanced Economies	4.1	3.3	3.8	2.7	6.2	4.7	5.5	6.6	0.2	−5.2	4.9	4.4
Memorandum												
Major Advanced Economies	3.7	0.3	−2.2	1.8	4.4	4.2	3.4	1.1	−2.3	−13.1	0.8	6.4
Newly Industrialized Asian Economies	4.4	2.6	2.6	2.0	6.1	2.2	3.8	4.5	−2.7	−3.8	6.7	4.6

Table A3 (concluded)

	Averages		2002	2003	2004	2005	2006	2007	2008	2009	Projections	
	1992–2001	2002–11									2010	2011
Final Domestic Demand												
Advanced Economies	**2.9**	**1.6**	**1.7**	**2.0**	**2.9**	**2.8**	**2.7**	**2.4**	**0.2**	**−2.5**	**1.5**	**2.0**
United States	4.0	1.7	1.9	2.8	3.6	3.3	2.5	1.7	−0.4	−2.7	2.2	2.5
Euro Area	1.4	1.0	0.7	1.3	1.8	2.1	2.8	2.4	0.6	−2.6	0.1	1.0
Germany	1.7	0.4	−1.4	0.1	−0.1	0.5	2.5	1.2	1.4	−1.2	0.2	1.3
France	1.8	1.7	1.4	2.1	2.5	2.6	2.7	3.0	0.9	−0.6	0.8	1.3
Italy	1.2	0.5	1.3	0.7	1.4	1.2	1.4	1.2	−1.2	−3.5	0.9	1.2
Spain	3.0	1.9	3.2	4.0	4.8	5.2	4.9	4.2	−0.6	−6.1	−1.0	0.5
Japan	1.0	0.3	−0.2	0.5	1.6	1.9	1.1	1.0	−0.9	−3.7	0.9	1.3
United Kingdom	3.0	1.5	3.5	2.8	3.4	2.2	2.3	2.9	0.5	−4.1	0.0	1.4
Canada	2.6	3.0	3.0	3.7	3.9	4.4	4.5	4.1	2.6	−1.6	3.4	2.2
Other Advanced Economies	3.9	3.0	3.9	1.9	3.9	3.6	3.9	4.7	1.4	−0.3	3.2	3.5
Memorandum												
Major Advanced Economies	2.7	1.3	1.3	2.0	2.7	2.6	2.3	1.8	0.0	−2.6	1.5	2.0
Newly Industrialized Asian Economies	5.0	2.9	4.6	1.2	3.6	3.2	3.9	4.6	0.5	0.1	3.7	4.1
Stock Building[2]												
Advanced Economies	**0.0**	**0.0**	**0.1**	**0.1**	**0.3**	**−0.1**	**0.1**	**−0.1**	**−0.2**	**−0.9**	**0.7**	**0.2**
United States	0.0	0.1	0.5	0.1	0.4	−0.1	0.1	−0.3	−0.4	−0.9	1.1	0.3
Euro Area	0.4	−0.1	−0.3	0.1	0.2	−0.2	0.1	0.0	0.1	−0.7	0.0	0.1
Germany	−0.2	−0.2	−0.6	0.5	0.0	−0.4	−0.2	−0.1	0.1	−0.5	−0.8	0.0
France	0.1	−0.1	−0.3	−0.3	0.5	0.2	0.0	0.2	−0.3	−1.4	0.6	0.2
Italy	0.0	0.0	0.0	0.1	−0.1	−0.3	0.5	0.1	−0.3	−0.3	0.6	0.0
Spain	−0.1	0.0	0.0	−0.1	0.0	−0.1	0.3	−0.1	0.1	0.0	0.0	0.1
Japan	0.0	0.0	−0.3	0.2	0.3	−0.1	0.2	0.3	−0.4	−0.3	0.1	0.1
United Kingdom	0.1	0.0	−0.3	0.2	0.1	0.0	0.0	0.1	−0.4	−1.2	0.7	0.5
Canada	0.1	0.2	0.2	0.8	0.1	0.3	−0.1	0.2	−0.1	−0.8	0.3	1.0
Other Advanced Economies	−0.1	0.0	0.1	−0.1	0.6	0.0	0.0	−0.3	0.4	−2.0	1.3	0.2
Memorandum												
Major Advanced Economies	0.0	0.0	0.1	0.1	0.3	−0.1	0.1	−0.1	−0.3	−0.8	0.6	0.3
Newly Industrialized Asian Economies	−0.3	0.0	0.3	−0.3	0.9	−0.1	0.3	−0.4	1.2	−3.4	1.5	0.3
Foreign Balance[2]												
Advanced Economies	**−0.1**	**0.1**	**−0.1**	**−0.3**	**−0.2**	**−0.1**	**0.2**	**0.5**	**0.4**	**0.4**	**0.3**	**0.1**
United States	−0.5	0.0	−0.7	−0.5	−0.7	−0.3	−0.1	0.6	1.2	1.2	−0.3	−0.4
Euro Area	0.5	0.1	0.6	−0.6	0.3	−0.2	0.1	0.4	0.0	−0.7	0.8	0.4
Germany	0.2	0.4	2.0	−0.8	1.4	0.7	1.1	1.5	−0.3	−3.3	1.8	0.5
France	0.2	−0.4	0.0	−0.7	−0.7	−0.9	−0.4	−0.9	−0.4	−0.2	0.1	0.2
Italy	0.3	−0.3	−0.8	−0.8	0.2	−0.3	0.0	0.2	0.1	−1.3	−0.1	−0.1
Spain	−0.1	−0.2	−0.6	−0.8	−1.7	−1.7	−1.4	−0.9	1.4	2.8	0.6	0.3
Japan	0.0	0.5	0.7	0.7	0.8	0.3	0.8	1.1	0.1	−1.2	1.4	0.5
United Kingdom	−0.2	0.0	−1.1	−0.1	−0.7	0.0	0.4	−0.6	0.5	0.7	0.5	0.6
Canada	0.7	−1.1	−0.1	−2.5	−0.9	−1.7	−1.3	−1.6	−1.9	−0.4	−0.6	0.0
Other Advanced Economies	0.4	0.5	−0.1	0.5	0.3	0.7	0.9	0.9	0.0	1.6	0.0	0.6
Memorandum												
Major Advanced Economies	−0.1	0.0	−0.1	−0.4	−0.2	−0.2	0.1	0.5	0.5	0.1	0.3	0.0
Newly Industrialized Asian Economies	0.4	1.4	0.7	1.9	1.1	1.7	1.8	2.3	0.4	2.1	0.9	1.1

[1]In this table, Other Advanced Economies means advanced economies excluding the G7 and Euro Area countries.

[2]Changes expressed as percent of GDP in the preceding period.

Table A4. Emerging and Developing Economies: Real GDP[1]

(Annual percent change)

	Average 1992–2001	2002	2003	2004	2005	2006	2007	2008	2009	Projections		
										2010	2011	2015
Central and Eastern Europe[2]	**2.6**	**4.4**	**4.8**	**7.3**	**5.9**	**6.5**	**5.5**	**3.0**	**−3.7**	**2.8**	**3.4**	**4.0**
Albania	5.5	4.2	5.8	5.7	5.8	5.4	6.0	7.8	2.8	2.3	3.2	5.0
Bosnia and Herzegovina	...	5.0	3.5	6.3	4.3	6.2	6.5	5.4	−3.4	0.5	4.0	4.5
Bulgaria	−2.5	4.5	5.0	6.6	6.2	6.3	6.2	6.0	−5.0	0.2	2.0	5.0
Croatia	...	5.4	5.0	4.2	4.2	4.7	5.5	2.4	−5.8	0.2	2.5	3.0
Estonia	...	7.9	7.6	7.2	9.4	10.0	7.2	−3.6	−14.1	0.8	3.6	3.3
Hungary	2.5	4.4	4.3	4.9	3.5	4.0	1.0	0.6	−6.3	−0.2	3.2	3.0
Kosovo	...	−0.7	5.4	2.6	3.8	3.8	4.0	5.4	4.0	4.8	6.3	5.3
Latvia	...	6.5	7.2	8.7	10.6	12.2	10.0	−4.6	−18.0	−4.0	2.7	4.0
Lithuania	...	6.9	10.2	7.4	7.8	7.8	9.8	2.8	−15.0	−1.6	3.2	2.9
Macedonia, Former Yugoslav Republic of	−0.8	0.9	2.8	4.1	4.1	3.9	5.9	4.8	−0.7	2.0	3.0	4.0
Montenegro	...	1.9	2.5	4.4	4.2	8.6	10.7	6.9	−7.0	−1.7	4.6	4.0
Poland	4.6	1.4	3.9	5.3	3.6	6.2	6.8	5.0	1.7	2.7	3.2	4.0
Romania	0.3	5.0	5.3	8.5	4.1	7.9	6.3	7.3	−7.1	0.8	5.1	4.1
Serbia	...	3.9	2.4	8.3	5.6	5.2	6.9	5.5	−2.9	2.0	3.0	5.0
Turkey	3.0	6.2	5.3	9.4	8.4	6.9	4.7	0.7	−4.7	5.2	3.4	4.0
Commonwealth of Independent States[2],[3]	...	**5.2**	**7.7**	**8.2**	**6.7**	**8.5**	**8.6**	**5.5**	**−6.6**	**4.0**	**3.6**	**5.0**
Russia	...	4.7	7.3	7.2	6.4	7.7	8.1	5.6	−7.9	4.0	3.3	5.0
Excluding Russia	...	6.6	9.1	10.8	7.6	10.5	10.0	5.3	−3.5	3.9	4.5	5.1
Armenia	...	13.2	14.0	10.5	13.9	13.2	13.7	6.8	−14.4	1.8	3.0	4.5
Azerbaijan	...	8.1	10.5	10.2	26.4	34.5	25.0	10.8	9.3	2.7	0.6	0.7
Belarus	...	5.0	7.0	11.4	9.4	10.0	8.6	10.0	0.2	2.4	4.6	6.6
Georgia	...	5.5	11.1	5.9	9.6	9.4	12.3	2.3	−4.0	2.0	4.0	5.0
Kazakhstan	...	9.8	9.3	9.6	9.7	10.7	8.9	3.2	1.2	2.4	4.2	6.5
Kyrgyz Republic	...	0.0	7.0	7.0	−0.2	3.1	8.5	8.4	2.3	4.6	5.3	3.4
Moldova	...	7.8	6.6	7.4	7.5	4.8	3.0	7.8	−6.5	2.5	3.6	4.0
Mongolia	1.2	4.7	7.0	10.6	7.3	8.6	10.2	8.9	−1.6	7.2	7.1	12.8
Tajikistan	...	9.1	10.2	10.6	6.7	7.0	7.8	7.9	3.4	4.0	5.0	5.0
Turkmenistan	...	15.8	17.1	14.7	13.0	11.4	11.6	10.5	4.1	12.0	12.2	6.9
Ukraine	...	5.2	9.6	12.1	2.7	7.3	7.9	2.1	−15.1	3.7	4.1	4.0
Uzbekistan	...	4.0	4.2	7.7	7.0	7.3	9.5	9.0	8.1	8.0	7.0	6.0

Table A4 *(continued)*

	Average 1992–2001	2002	2003	2004	2005	2006	2007	2008	2009	Projections 2010	2011	2015
Developing Asia	**7.3**	**6.9**	**8.2**	**8.6**	**9.0**	**9.8**	**10.6**	**7.9**	**6.6**	**8.7**	**8.7**	**8.5**
Afghanistan, Islamic Republic of	...	...	15.1	8.8	16.1	8.2	14.2	3.4	22.5	8.6	7.0	7.1
Bangladesh	5.0	4.8	5.8	6.1	6.3	6.5	6.3	6.0	5.4	5.4	5.9	6.2
Bhutan	5.6	10.8	4.0	8.0	7.0	6.4	19.7	5.0	6.3	6.8	6.6	4.7
Brunei Darussalam	2.2	3.9	2.9	0.5	0.4	4.4	0.2	−1.9	−0.5	0.5	1.0	1.6
Cambodia	7.0	6.6	8.5	10.3	13.3	10.8	10.2	6.7	−2.5	4.8	6.8	6.8
China	10.3	9.1	10.0	10.1	10.4	11.6	13.0	9.6	8.7	10.0	9.9	9.5
Fiji	3.1	3.2	1.0	5.5	0.6	1.9	−0.5	−0.1	−2.5	2.1	2.4	2.6
India	5.7	4.6	6.9	7.9	9.2	9.8	9.4	7.3	5.7	8.8	8.4	8.1
Indonesia	3.6	4.5	4.8	5.0	5.7	5.5	6.3	6.0	4.5	6.0	6.2	7.0
Kiribati	4.0	6.1	2.3	2.2	3.9	1.9	0.4	−1.1	−0.7	1.5	1.2	1.2
Lao People's Democratic Republic	6.1	6.9	6.2	7.0	6.8	8.6	7.8	7.8	7.6	7.2	7.4	9.2
Malaysia	6.2	5.4	5.8	6.8	5.3	5.8	6.2	4.6	−1.7	4.7	5.0	5.0
Maldives	7.1	6.5	8.5	9.5	−4.6	18.0	7.2	6.3	−3.0	3.4	3.7	4.5
Myanmar	8.3	12.0	13.8	13.6	13.6	13.1	11.9	3.6	4.8	5.3	5.0	5.0
Nepal	4.9	0.1	3.9	4.7	3.5	3.4	3.3	5.3	4.7	3.0	4.0	4.8
Pakistan	3.6	3.2	4.9	7.4	7.7	6.1	5.6	2.0	2.0	3.0	4.0	6.0
Papua New Guinea	3.6	2.0	4.4	0.6	3.9	2.3	7.2	6.7	4.5	8.0	5.5	5.0
Philippines	3.3	4.4	4.9	6.4	5.0	5.3	7.1	3.8	0.9	3.6	4.0	4.0
Samoa	4.0	6.2	3.8	4.2	7.0	2.2	2.3	5.0	−4.9	−2.8	3.0	3.0
Solomon Islands	1.1	−2.8	6.5	4.9	5.4	6.9	10.7	7.3	−2.2	3.4	5.2	10.5
Sri Lanka	4.6	4.0	5.9	5.4	6.2	7.7	6.8	6.0	3.5	5.5	6.5	6.5
Thailand	3.8	5.3	7.1	6.3	4.6	5.1	4.9	2.5	−2.3	5.5	5.5	5.0
Timor-Leste	...	2.4	0.1	4.2	6.2	−5.8	8.4	12.8	7.4	7.5	7.4	5.8
Tonga	1.2	3.1	1.8	0.0	−0.2	−0.3	0.4	0.8	−0.5	0.6	1.7	1.8
Vanuatu	2.7	−4.2	3.7	4.4	5.1	7.2	6.7	6.3	3.3	3.8	4.2	4.5
Vietnam	7.7	7.1	7.3	7.8	8.4	8.2	8.5	6.2	5.3	6.0	6.5	7.5
Middle East and North Africa	**3.4**	**3.8**	**6.9**	**5.8**	**5.3**	**5.7**	**5.6**	**5.1**	**2.4**	**4.5**	**4.8**	**4.8**
Algeria	2.0	4.7	6.9	5.2	5.1	2.0	3.0	2.4	2.0	4.6	4.1	4.2
Bahrain	4.9	5.2	7.2	5.6	7.9	6.7	8.1	6.1	2.9	3.5	4.0	5.3
Djibouti	−1.1	2.6	3.2	3.0	3.2	4.8	5.1	5.8	5.0	4.5	5.4	7.0
Egypt	4.5	3.2	3.2	4.1	4.5	6.8	7.1	7.2	4.7	5.0	5.5	6.5
Iran, Islamic Republic of	2.9	7.5	7.2	5.1	4.7	5.8	7.8	2.3	1.8	3.0	3.2	3.2
Iraq	...	...	...	...	−0.7	6.2	1.5	9.5	4.2	7.3	7.9	6.6
Jordan	5.1	5.8	4.2	8.6	8.1	8.0	8.9	7.8	2.8	4.1	4.5	5.5
Kuwait	9.3	3.0	17.3	10.2	10.6	5.1	2.5	6.4	−2.7	3.1	4.8	4.9
Lebanon	4.2	3.3	4.1	7.5	2.5	0.6	7.5	9.0	9.0	6.0	4.5	4.0
Libya	−1.7	−1.3	13.0	4.4	10.3	6.7	7.5	3.4	1.8	5.2	6.1	6.8
Mauritania	2.9	1.1	5.6	5.2	5.4	11.4	1.0	3.7	−1.1	4.6	5.2	4.7
Morocco	2.4	3.3	6.3	4.8	3.0	7.8	2.7	5.6	5.2	3.2	4.5	5.0
Oman	4.4	2.1	0.3	3.4	4.9	6.0	7.7	12.3	3.4	4.7	4.7	4.5
Qatar	7.9	3.2	6.3	17.7	9.2	15.0	13.7	15.8	9.0	18.5	14.3	4.9
Saudi Arabia	1.9	0.1	7.7	5.3	5.6	3.2	2.0	4.3	0.1	3.7	4.0	4.6
Sudan	4.5	5.4	7.1	5.1	6.3	11.3	10.2	6.8	4.5	5.5	6.0	5.0
Syrian Arab Republic	4.1	5.9	−2.1	6.7	4.5	5.1	4.3	5.2	4.0	5.0	5.5	5.6
Tunisia	4.9	1.7	5.6	6.0	4.1	5.3	6.3	4.6	3.0	4.0	5.0	5.4
United Arab Emirates	4.3	2.6	11.9	9.7	8.2	8.7	6.1	5.1	−0.7	1.3	3.1	4.8
Yemen, Republic of	5.4	3.9	3.7	4.0	5.6	3.2	3.3	3.6	3.9	7.8	3.8	4.6

Table A4 *(continued)*

	Average 1992–2001	2002	2003	2004	2005	2006	2007	2008	2009	Projections 2010	2011	2015
Sub-Saharan Africa	**2.8**	**7.4**	**5.0**	**7.1**	**6.3**	**6.5**	**6.9**	**5.5**	**2.1**	**4.7**	**5.9**	**5.4**
Angola	1.5	14.5	3.3	11.2	20.6	18.6	20.3	13.2	−0.4	7.1	8.3	4.5
Benin	4.7	4.4	4.0	3.0	2.9	3.8	4.6	5.0	2.7	3.2	4.4	6.0
Botswana	5.4	9.0	6.3	6.0	1.6	5.1	4.8	3.1	−6.0	6.3	5.1	6.6
Burkina Faso	5.1	4.4	7.8	4.5	8.7	5.5	3.6	5.2	3.2	4.4	4.7	6.5
Burundi	−2.1	4.4	−1.2	4.8	0.9	5.1	3.6	4.5	3.5	3.9	4.5	4.9
Cameroon[4]	2.2	4.0	4.0	3.7	2.3	3.2	3.3	2.9	2.0	2.6	2.9	3.5
Cape Verde	7.3	5.3	4.7	4.3	6.5	10.8	7.8	5.9	4.1	5.0	5.5	6.2
Central African Republic	1.3	−0.6	−7.1	1.0	2.4	3.8	3.7	2.0	1.7	3.3	4.0	5.5
Chad	2.9	8.5	14.7	33.6	7.9	0.2	0.2	−0.4	−1.6	4.4	3.9	2.7
Comoros	2.0	4.1	2.5	−0.2	4.2	1.2	0.5	1.0	1.1	1.5	2.5	4.0
Congo, Democratic Republic of	−5.0	3.5	5.8	6.6	7.9	5.6	6.3	6.1	2.8	5.4	7.0	7.0
Congo, Republic of	1.6	4.6	0.8	3.5	7.8	6.2	−1.6	5.6	7.6	12.1	6.6	1.9
Côte d'Ivoire	3.3	−1.6	−1.7	1.6	1.9	0.7	1.6	2.3	3.8	3.0	4.0	6.0
Equatorial Guinea	38.3	19.5	14.0	38.0	9.7	1.3	21.4	10.7	5.3	0.9	2.1	0.7
Eritrea	...	3.0	−2.7	1.5	2.6	−1.0	1.4	−9.8	3.6	1.8	2.8	3.7
Ethiopia	4.4	1.2	−3.5	9.8	12.6	11.5	11.8	11.2	9.9	7.0	7.7	7.7
Gabon	1.3	−0.3	2.4	1.1	3.0	1.2	5.3	2.7	−1.4	5.4	4.9	2.0
Gambia, The	4.6	−3.2	6.9	7.0	5.1	6.5	6.3	6.1	4.6	4.8	5.0	5.1
Ghana	4.3	4.5	5.2	5.6	5.9	6.4	5.7	7.3	3.5	4.5	20.1	4.8
Guinea	4.3	4.2	1.2	2.3	3.0	2.5	1.8	4.9	−0.3	3.0	3.6	3.9
Guinea-Bissau	0.8	1.8	−3.5	3.1	5.0	2.2	0.3	3.5	3.0	3.5	4.3	4.7
Kenya	2.1	0.3	2.8	4.6	5.9	6.4	7.0	1.5	2.1	4.1	5.8	6.5
Lesotho	4.2	1.1	4.3	2.3	1.1	6.5	2.4	4.5	1.4	3.0	2.8	12.6
Liberia	...	3.8	−31.3	2.6	5.3	7.8	9.4	7.1	4.6	5.9	9.0	5.7
Madagascar	3.0	−12.4	9.8	5.3	4.6	5.0	6.2	7.1	−5.0	−1.0	3.7	5.1
Malawi	2.1	1.7	5.7	5.4	3.3	13.6	1.2	9.4	8.0	6.0	6.3	7.1
Mali	3.9	4.3	7.2	1.2	6.1	6.1	4.2	4.9	4.5	5.1	6.3	4.4
Mauritius	5.6	1.9	4.3	5.5	1.5	3.9	5.4	4.2	1.5	4.1	4.7	5.2
Mozambique	7.1	9.2	6.5	8.8	8.7	6.3	7.3	6.7	6.3	6.5	7.5	7.8
Namibia	3.5	4.8	4.3	12.3	2.5	7.1	5.5	3.3	−0.7	1.7	2.2	3.0
Niger	1.5	5.3	7.1	−0.8	8.4	5.8	3.4	9.3	−0.9	4.4	3.8	4.0
Nigeria	2.7	21.2	10.3	10.6	5.4	6.2	7.0	6.0	5.6	7.0	7.3	6.0
Rwanda	1.7	13.5	1.4	7.0	9.0	8.6	5.5	11.2	4.1	5.4	5.9	7.1
São Tomé and Príncipe	1.7	11.6	5.4	6.6	5.7	6.7	6.0	5.8	4.0	4.5	5.5	6.0
Senegal	3.3	0.7	6.7	5.9	5.6	2.4	4.8	2.3	1.5	3.4	4.1	5.0
Seychelles	4.0	1.2	−5.9	−2.9	5.8	8.3	11.5	−0.9	−7.6	4.0	5.0	5.0
Sierra Leone	−5.3	27.4	9.5	7.4	7.2	7.3	6.4	5.5	4.0	4.8	5.5	6.5
South Africa	2.2	3.7	2.9	4.6	5.3	5.6	5.5	3.7	−1.8	2.6	3.6	4.5
Swaziland	2.9	1.8	3.9	2.5	2.2	2.9	3.5	2.4	0.4	1.1	2.5	2.4
Tanzania	3.3	7.2	6.9	7.8	7.4	6.7	7.1	7.4	5.5	6.2	6.7	7.0
Togo	0.6	−0.3	5.2	2.4	1.2	3.9	1.9	1.8	2.5	2.6	3.3	4.3
Uganda	6.6	8.7	6.5	6.8	6.3	10.8	8.4	8.7	7.1	5.6	6.4	7.5
Zambia	0.3	3.3	5.1	5.4	5.3	6.2	6.2	5.7	6.3	5.8	6.0	6.5
Zimbabwe[5]	...	...	...	...	...	−3.8	−3.6	−14.5	4.0	2.2	0.0	2.0

Table A4 (concluded)

	Average 1992–2001	2002	2003	2004	2005	2006	2007	2008	2009	Projections 2010	2011	2015
Western Hemisphere	**3.0**	**0.5**	**2.2**	**6.0**	**4.7**	**5.6**	**5.8**	**4.3**	**−1.8**	**4.0**	**4.0**	**4.0**
Antigua and Barbuda	3.3	2.0	4.3	5.4	5.0	12.9	6.5	1.8	−6.7	−2.0	0.8	4.4
Argentina[6]	2.7	−10.9	8.8	9.0	9.2	8.5	8.7	6.8	0.9	3.5	3.0	3.0
Bahamas, The	2.7	2.6	−0.9	−0.8	5.7	4.3	0.7	−1.7	−5.0	−0.5	2.0	2.5
Barbados	1.1	0.7	2.0	4.8	3.9	3.2	3.4	0.2	−5.3	−0.5	3.0	2.5
Belize	5.4	5.1	9.3	4.6	3.0	4.7	1.2	3.8	−1.1	1.0	2.0	2.5
Bolivia	3.4	2.5	2.7	4.2	4.4	4.8	4.6	6.1	3.3	4.0	4.0	4.0
Brazil	2.6	2.7	1.1	5.7	3.2	4.0	6.1	5.1	−0.2	5.5	4.1	4.1
Chile	6.0	2.2	4.0	6.0	5.6	4.6	4.6	3.7	−1.5	4.7	6.0	4.5
Colombia	2.7	2.5	4.6	4.7	5.7	6.9	7.5	2.4	0.1	2.2	4.0	4.5
Costa Rica	5.1	2.9	6.4	4.3	5.9	8.8	7.9	2.8	−1.1	3.5	4.2	4.4
Dominica	1.5	−5.1	0.1	3.0	3.3	4.8	2.5	3.2	−0.3	1.4	2.5	3.0
Dominican Republic	6.2	5.8	−0.3	1.3	9.3	10.7	8.5	5.3	3.5	3.5	6.0	8.0
Ecuador	2.3	3.4	3.3	8.8	5.7	4.7	2.0	7.2	0.4	2.5	2.3	2.0
El Salvador	4.4	2.3	2.3	1.9	3.3	4.2	4.3	2.4	−3.5	1.0	2.5	4.0
Grenada	3.8	1.6	7.1	−5.7	11.0	−2.3	4.9	2.2	−7.7	0.8	2.0	4.0
Guatemala	3.6	3.9	2.5	3.2	3.3	5.4	6.3	3.3	0.6	2.5	3.5	3.5
Guyana	4.5	1.1	−0.7	1.6	−1.9	5.1	7.0	2.0	3.3	4.4	4.9	3.3
Haiti	0.1	−0.3	0.4	−3.5	1.8	2.2	3.3	0.8	2.9	−8.5	7.0	4.5
Honduras	3.2	3.8	4.5	6.2	6.1	6.6	6.2	4.0	−1.9	2.0	2.0	3.0
Jamaica	0.5	1.0	3.5	1.4	1.0	2.7	1.5	−0.9	−2.8	−0.3	1.5	2.1
Mexico	3.0	0.8	1.7	4.0	3.2	4.9	3.3	1.5	−6.5	4.2	4.5	4.0
Nicaragua	3.9	0.8	2.5	5.3	4.3	4.2	3.1	2.8	−1.5	1.8	2.5	4.0
Panama	4.6	2.2	4.2	7.5	7.2	8.5	12.1	10.7	2.4	5.0	6.3	6.5
Paraguay	1.7	0.0	3.8	4.1	2.9	4.3	6.8	5.8	−4.5	5.3	5.0	4.5
Peru	3.8	5.0	4.0	5.0	6.8	7.7	8.9	9.8	0.9	6.3	6.0	5.8
St. Kitts and Nevis	4.3	1.0	0.5	7.6	5.6	5.5	2.0	4.6	−5.5	−1.0	0.5	2.0
St. Lucia	1.7	0.6	3.5	3.8	4.4	4.8	1.5	0.7	−5.2	1.1	2.3	3.8
St. Vincent and the Grenadines	2.9	3.2	2.8	6.8	2.6	7.6	8.0	−0.6	−2.5	0.5	1.5	4.5
Suriname	0.8	2.8	6.3	8.5	4.4	3.8	5.2	6.0	2.5	4.0	4.7	6.0
Trinidad and Tobago	4.6	7.9	14.4	7.9	6.2	13.5	4.6	2.3	−3.5	2.1	2.3	2.8
Uruguay	2.2	−7.1	2.3	4.6	6.8	4.3	7.5	8.5	2.9	5.7	3.9	3.9
Venezuela	1.5	−8.9	−7.8	18.3	10.3	9.9	8.2	4.8	−3.3	−2.6	0.4	2.3

[1]For many countries, figures for recent years are IMF staff estimates. Data for some countries are for fiscal years.

[2]Data for some countries refer to real net material product (NMP) or are estimates based on NMP. For many countries, figures for recent years are IMF staff estimates. The figures should be interpreted only as indicative of broad orders of magnitude because reliable, comparable data are not generally available. In particular, the growth of output of new private enterprises of the informal economy is not fully reflected in the recent figures.

[3]Georgia and Mongolia, which are not members of the Commonwealth of Independent States, are included in this group for reasons of geography and similarities in economic structure.

[4]The percent changes in 2002 are calculated over a period of 18 months, reflecting a change in the fiscal year cycle (from July–June to January–December).

[5]The Zimbabwe dollar ceased circulating in early 2009. Data are based on IMF staff estimates of price and exchange rate developments in U.S. dollars. IMF staff estimates of U.S. dollar values may differ from authorities' estimates. Real GDP is in constant 2009 prices.

[6]Private analysts are of the view that real GDP growth has been lower than the official reports since the last quarter of 2008.

Table A5. Summary of Inflation
(Percent)

	Average 1992–2001	2002	2003	2004	2005	2006	2007	2008	2009	Projections 2010	2011	2015
GDP Deflators												
Advanced Economies	**2.0**	**1.6**	**1.8**	**2.0**	**2.1**	**2.2**	**2.3**	**2.0**	**0.9**	**0.8**	**1.1**	**1.8**
United States	1.9	1.6	2.2	2.8	3.3	3.3	2.9	2.1	1.2	0.7	1.5	1.9
Euro Area	2.1	2.6	2.2	1.9	2.0	2.0	2.4	2.3	1.1	0.6	1.1	1.8
Japan	−0.3	−1.5	−1.6	−1.1	−1.2	−0.9	−0.7	−0.8	−1.0	−1.7	−1.2	0.6
Other Advanced Economies[1]	2.8	1.9	2.2	2.4	1.9	2.1	2.7	3.1	1.0	2.2	1.8	2.4
Consumer Prices												
Advanced Economies	**2.4**	**1.6**	**1.8**	**2.0**	**2.3**	**2.4**	**2.2**	**3.4**	**0.1**	**1.5**	**1.4**	**2.0**
United States	2.7	1.6	2.3	2.7	3.4	3.2	2.9	3.8	−0.3	2.1	1.7	2.2
Euro Area[2]	2.3	2.3	2.1	2.2	2.2	2.2	2.1	3.3	0.3	1.1	1.3	1.9
Japan	0.4	−0.9	−0.3	0.0	−0.3	0.3	0.0	1.4	−1.4	−1.4	−0.5	1.0
Other Advanced Economies[1]	2.7	1.7	1.8	1.8	2.1	2.1	2.1	3.8	1.5	2.3	2.0	2.2
Emerging and Developing Economies	**39.0**	**6.9**	**6.7**	**5.9**	**5.9**	**5.6**	**6.5**	**9.2**	**5.2**	**6.2**	**4.7**	**3.8**
Regional Groups												
Central and Eastern Europe	52.9	18.6	11.1	6.6	5.9	5.9	6.0	8.1	4.7	5.2	3.6	3.2
Commonwealth of Independent States[3]	...	14.0	12.3	10.4	12.1	9.5	9.7	15.6	11.2	7.2	6.1	5.1
Developing Asia	7.4	2.1	2.6	4.1	3.8	4.2	5.4	7.4	3.1	5.9	3.7	2.8
Middle East and North Africa	10.1	4.9	5.5	6.5	6.4	7.5	10.0	13.5	6.6	6.5	6.4	5.3
Sub-Saharan Africa	26.3	11.3	10.9	7.6	8.9	7.3	7.1	11.6	10.6	8.0	6.9	5.5
Western Hemisphere	51.9	8.5	10.4	6.6	6.3	5.3	5.4	7.9	6.0	6.2	5.9	5.1
Memorandum												
European Union	6.3	2.5	2.2	2.3	2.3	2.3	2.4	3.7	0.9	1.5	1.5	2.0
Analytical Groups												
By Source of Export Earnings												
Fuel	72.1	11.9	11.5	9.8	10.0	9.0	10.1	15.0	9.4	8.0	7.5	6.2
Nonfuel	30.5	5.7	5.6	5.0	4.9	4.8	5.6	7.9	4.3	5.8	4.1	3.3
of Which, Primary Products	35.9	5.6	5.0	3.8	5.2	5.2	5.1	9.1	5.2	4.2	4.1	3.6
By External Financing Source												
Net Debtor Countries	39.8	7.9	7.4	5.5	5.9	5.8	6.1	9.0	7.1	7.5	5.1	4.1
of Which, Official Financing	19.0	4.3	8.2	7.3	8.4	8.7	9.3	14.1	9.1	7.3	6.6	5.0
Net Debtor Countries by Debt-Servicing Experience												
Countries with Arrears and/or Rescheduling during 2004–08	30.6	16.3	11.9	7.8	8.1	9.0	8.4	11.3	6.7	7.9	6.9	6.4
Memorandum												
Median Inflation Rate												
Advanced Economies	2.5	2.3	2.1	2.0	2.1	2.2	2.1	3.8	0.8	1.6	1.7	2.0
Emerging and Developing Economies	8.5	3.6	4.4	4.5	6.0	6.1	6.5	10.3	3.9	4.9	4.6	4.0

[1]In this table, Other Advanced Economies means advanced economies excluding the United States, Euro Area countries, and Japan.

[2]Based on Eurostat's harmonized index of consumer prices.

[3]Georgia and Mongolia, which are not members of the Commonwealth of Independent States, are included in this group for reasons of geography and similarities in economic structure.

Table A6. Advanced Economies: Consumer Prices
(Annual percent change)

	Average 1992–2001	2002	2003	2004	2005	2006	2007	2008	2009	Projections 2010	2011	2015	End of Period 2009	Projections 2010	2011
Consumer Prices															
Advanced Economies	**2.4**	**1.6**	**1.8**	**2.0**	**2.3**	**2.4**	**2.2**	**3.4**	**0.1**	**1.5**	**1.4**	**2.0**	**1.0**	**1.3**	**1.5**
United States	2.7	1.6	2.3	2.7	3.4	3.2	2.9	3.8	−0.3	2.1	1.7	2.2	2.0	1.7	1.9
Euro Area[1]	2.3	2.3	2.1	2.2	2.2	2.2	2.1	3.3	0.3	1.1	1.3	1.9	0.9	1.2	1.5
Germany	2.1	1.4	1.0	1.8	1.9	1.8	2.3	2.8	0.1	0.9	1.0	2.0	0.8	0.9	1.0
France	1.6	1.9	2.2	2.3	1.9	1.9	1.6	3.2	0.1	1.2	1.5	1.8	0.1	1.2	1.5
Italy	3.3	2.6	2.8	2.3	2.2	2.2	2.0	3.5	0.8	1.4	1.7	2.0	1.0	1.5	1.7
Spain	3.7	3.6	3.1	3.1	3.4	3.6	2.8	4.1	−0.3	1.2	1.0	1.8	0.9	1.1	1.0
Netherlands	2.5	3.8	2.2	1.4	1.5	1.7	1.6	2.2	1.0	1.1	1.3	1.5	1.0	1.1	1.3
Belgium	1.9	1.6	1.5	1.9	2.5	2.3	1.8	4.5	−0.2	1.6	1.5	1.7	0.1	1.2	1.3
Greece	7.6	3.9	3.4	3.0	3.5	3.3	3.0	4.2	1.4	1.9	1.0	1.7	2.0	0.9	1.1
Austria	1.9	1.7	1.3	2.0	2.1	1.7	2.2	3.2	0.4	1.3	1.5	2.0	1.1	1.3	1.5
Portugal	4.0	3.7	3.3	2.5	2.1	3.0	2.4	2.7	−0.9	0.8	1.1	1.8	−0.9	0.8	1.1
Finland	1.8	2.0	1.3	0.1	0.8	1.3	1.6	3.9	1.6	1.1	1.4	1.7	1.8	1.1	1.4
Ireland	2.7	4.7	4.0	2.3	2.2	2.7	2.9	3.1	−1.7	−2.0	−0.6	2.0	−2.6	−1.1	0.1
Slovak Republic	...	3.5	8.4	7.5	2.8	4.3	1.9	3.9	0.9	0.8	2.0	3.0	0.0	1.4	2.4
Slovenia	...	7.5	5.6	3.6	2.5	2.5	3.6	5.7	0.8	1.5	2.3	2.9	1.6	2.1	2.4
Luxembourg	2.1	2.1	2.0	2.2	2.5	2.7	2.3	3.4	0.8	1.0	1.3	1.9	2.5	0.7	1.2
Cyprus	3.5	2.8	4.0	1.9	2.0	2.2	2.2	4.4	0.2	2.7	2.3	2.4	1.6	2.1	2.5
Malta	3.1	2.6	1.9	2.7	2.5	2.6	0.7	4.7	1.8	2.0	2.1	2.4	−0.4	4.2	1.5
Japan	0.4	−0.9	−0.3	0.0	−0.3	0.3	0.0	1.4	−1.4	−1.4	−0.5	1.0	−1.7	−1.1	−0.2
United Kingdom[1]	2.1	1.3	1.4	1.3	2.0	2.3	2.3	3.6	2.2	2.7	1.6	2.0	2.1	2.0	1.7
Canada	1.7	2.3	2.7	1.8	2.2	2.0	2.1	2.4	0.3	1.8	2.0	2.0	0.8	1.8	2.0
Korea	4.6	2.8	3.5	3.6	2.8	2.2	2.5	4.7	2.8	2.9	3.0	3.0	2.8	3.0	3.0
Australia	2.3	3.0	2.8	2.3	2.7	3.5	2.3	4.4	1.8	2.4	2.4	2.5	2.1	2.3	2.3
Taiwan Province of China	2.2	−0.2	−0.3	1.6	2.3	0.6	1.8	3.5	−0.9	1.5	1.5	2.0	−6.4	1.5	1.5
Sweden	2.0	1.9	2.3	1.0	0.8	1.5	1.7	3.3	2.2	2.4	2.1	2.0	3.1	2.2	2.0
Switzerland	1.5	0.6	0.6	0.8	1.2	1.1	0.7	2.4	−0.4	0.7	1.0	1.0	−0.4	0.7	1.0
Hong Kong SAR	4.1	−3.0	−2.6	−0.4	0.9	2.0	2.0	4.3	0.5	2.0	1.7	2.6	−2.6	2.0	1.7
Czech Republic	...	1.9	0.1	2.8	1.8	2.5	2.9	6.3	1.0	1.6	2.0	2.0	1.0	2.3	2.2
Norway	2.3	1.3	2.5	0.5	1.5	2.3	0.7	3.8	2.2	2.5	1.8	2.5	2.0	2.3	2.2
Singapore	1.5	−0.4	0.5	1.7	0.5	1.0	2.1	6.5	0.2	2.1	1.9	2.4	−0.3	2.3	1.3
Denmark	2.1	2.4	2.1	1.2	1.8	1.9	1.7	3.4	1.3	2.0	2.0	2.0	1.2	2.6	2.0
Israel	7.8	5.7	0.7	−0.4	1.4	2.1	0.5	4.6	3.3	2.3	2.6	2.5	4.0	2.6	2.6
New Zealand	1.8	2.6	1.7	2.3	3.0	3.4	2.4	4.0	2.1	2.1	2.5	2.0	2.0	2.3	0.5
Iceland	3.2	4.8	2.1	3.2	4.0	6.8	5.0	12.4	12.0	6.2	3.8	2.5	7.5	4.2	3.4
Memorandum															
Major Advanced Economies	2.1	1.3	1.7	2.0	2.3	2.4	2.2	3.2	−0.1	1.4	1.3	1.9	1.1	1.2	1.4
Newly Industrialized Asian Economies	3.6	1.0	1.5	2.4	2.2	1.6	2.2	4.5	1.3	2.3	2.3	2.6	−0.6	2.4	2.3

[1]Based on Eurostat's harmonized index of consumer prices.

Table A7. Emerging and Developing Economies: Consumer Prices[1]

(Annual percent change)

	Average 1992–2001	2002	2003	2004	2005	2006	2007	2008	2009	Projections 2010	2011	2015	End of Period 2009	Projections 2010	2011
Central and Eastern Europe[2]	**52.9**	**18.6**	**11.1**	**6.6**	**5.9**	**5.9**	**6.0**	**8.1**	**4.7**	**5.2**	**3.6**	**3.2**	**4.6**	**4.7**	**3.8**
Albania	31.1	5.2	2.3	2.9	2.4	2.4	2.9	3.4	2.2	3.5	2.9	3.0	3.5	2.9	2.9
Bosnia and Herzegovina	...	0.3	0.5	0.3	3.6	6.1	1.5	7.4	−0.4	1.6	1.9	2.5	0.0	1.6	1.9
Bulgaria	80.8	5.8	2.3	6.1	6.0	7.4	7.6	12.0	2.5	2.2	2.9	3.0	1.6	2.7	3.0
Croatia	...	1.7	1.8	2.0	3.3	3.2	2.9	6.1	2.4	2.3	2.8	3.0	1.9	2.6	2.7
Estonia	...	3.6	1.3	3.0	4.1	4.4	6.6	10.4	−0.1	0.8	1.1	2.5	−1.7	1.0	1.2
Hungary	17.6	5.3	4.6	6.8	3.6	3.9	7.9	6.1	4.2	4.3	2.5	3.0	5.6	3.0	2.4
Kosovo	...	3.6	0.3	−1.1	−1.4	0.6	4.4	9.4	−2.4	1.5	1.7	1.8	0.1	1.6	2.3
Latvia	...	2.0	2.9	6.2	6.9	6.6	10.1	15.3	3.3	−3.7	−2.5	1.0	−1.4	−3.3	−0.5
Lithuania	...	0.3	−1.1	1.2	2.7	3.8	5.8	11.1	4.2	−1.2	−1.0	1.6	1.2	−1.0	−0.3
Macedonia, Former Yugoslav Republic of	72.6	2.2	1.2	−0.4	0.5	3.2	2.3	8.3	−0.8	1.9	3.0	3.0	−1.6	2.0	3.0
Montenegro	...	19.7	7.5	3.1	3.4	2.1	3.5	9.0	3.6	−0.6	3.0	3.2	...	...	...
Poland	20.2	1.9	0.8	3.5	2.1	1.0	2.5	4.2	3.5	2.3	2.4	2.5	3.5	2.4	2.5
Romania	88.2	22.5	15.3	11.9	9.0	6.6	4.8	7.8	5.6	4.0	3.1	3.0	4.7	3.2	3.0
Serbia	...	19.5	11.7	10.1	17.3	12.7	6.5	12.4	8.1	4.8	4.8	4.0	6.6	6.0	4.5
Turkey	74.9	45.1	25.3	8.6	8.2	9.6	8.8	10.4	6.3	9.7	5.7	4.0	6.5	8.4	6.1
Commonwealth of Independent States[2,3]	...	**14.0**	**12.3**	**10.4**	**12.1**	**9.5**	**9.7**	**15.6**	**11.2**	**7.2**	**6.1**	**5.1**	**8.6**	**6.6**	**5.9**
Russia	...	15.8	13.7	10.9	12.7	9.7	9.0	14.1	11.7	7.0	5.7	5.0	8.8	6.0	5.4
Excluding Russia	...	9.2	8.7	9.1	10.7	8.9	11.5	19.5	10.2	7.7	7.2	5.2	8.1	8.0	7.0
Armenia	...	1.1	4.7	7.0	0.6	2.9	4.4	9.0	3.4	6.8	5.2	4.0	6.5	6.2	4.7
Azerbaijan	...	2.8	2.2	6.7	9.7	8.4	16.6	20.8	1.5	4.7	3.5	3.0	0.9	4.0	3.0
Belarus	...	42.6	28.4	18.1	10.3	7.0	8.4	14.8	13.0	7.3	6.2	5.5	10.1	8.0	5.5
Georgia	...	5.6	4.8	5.7	8.3	9.2	9.2	10.0	1.7	4.9	5.0	5.0	3.0	5.0	5.0
Kazakhstan	...	5.9	6.6	7.1	7.9	8.7	10.8	17.1	7.3	7.3	6.6	6.0	6.3	7.7	6.8
Kyrgyz Republic	...	2.1	3.1	4.1	4.3	5.6	10.2	24.5	6.8	8.4	7.6	8.0	0.0	13.0	6.3
Moldova	...	5.2	11.7	12.4	11.9	12.7	12.4	12.7	0.0	7.7	5.7	4.0	0.4	9.0	5.0
Mongolia	57.1	0.9	5.1	7.9	12.5	4.5	8.2	26.8	6.3	7.3	5.3	5.0	1.9	7.5	5.5
Tajikistan	...	12.2	16.4	7.2	7.3	10.0	13.2	20.4	6.5	7.0	8.3	5.0	5.1	9.0	7.5
Turkmenistan	...	8.8	5.6	5.9	10.7	8.2	6.3	14.5	−2.7	5.0	5.4	4.5	0.0	4.7	6.0
Ukraine	...	0.7	5.2	9.0	13.5	9.1	12.8	25.2	15.9	9.2	8.9	4.9	12.3	9.4	9.0
Uzbekistan	...	27.3	11.6	6.6	10.0	14.2	12.3	12.7	14.1	9.2	9.4	7.0	10.6	10.0	9.0

Table A7 *(continued)*

	Average 1992–2001	2002	2003	2004	2005	2006	2007	2008	2009	Projections 2010	Projections 2011	Projections 2015	End of Period 2009	End of Period Projections 2010	End of Period Projections 2011
Developing Asia	**7.4**	**2.1**	**2.6**	**4.1**	**3.8**	**4.2**	**5.4**	**7.4**	**3.1**	**5.9**	**3.7**	**2.8**	**4.7**	**4.9**	**3.4**
Afghanistan, Islamic Republic of	...	5.1	24.1	13.2	12.3	5.1	13.0	26.8	−12.0	2.3	4.4	4.0	−2.2	5.0	4.0
Bangladesh	4.9	3.7	5.4	6.1	7.0	7.1	9.1	7.7	6.1	7.4	7.2	4.0	6.2	8.5	6.1
Bhutan	8.3	2.5	2.1	4.6	5.3	5.0	5.2	8.4	8.7	8.0	4.5	3.9	8.3	7.0	4.5
Brunei Darussalam	1.9	−2.3	0.3	0.9	1.1	0.2	0.3	2.7	1.8	1.8	1.8	1.8	...	...	...
Cambodia	17.8	0.1	1.0	3.9	6.3	6.1	7.7	25.0	−0.7	5.2	7.7	3.0	5.3	7.5	5.2
China	6.9	−0.8	1.2	3.9	1.8	1.5	4.8	5.9	−0.7	3.1	2.4	2.0	0.7	3.1	2.4
Fiji	3.2	0.8	4.2	2.8	2.4	2.5	4.8	7.8	3.7	4.0	3.0	3.0	6.8	3.0	3.0
India	8.0	4.3	3.8	3.8	4.2	6.2	6.4	8.3	10.9	13.2	5.5	4.0	15.0	8.1	4.6
Indonesia	13.4	11.8	6.8	6.1	10.5	13.1	6.0	9.8	4.8	4.7	5.8	4.2	2.8	5.7	5.3
Kiribati	3.1	3.2	1.9	−0.9	−0.3	−1.5	4.2	11.0	8.8	2.4	2.5	2.5	0.1	2.4	2.5
Lao People's Democratic Republic	28.5	10.6	15.5	10.5	7.2	6.8	4.5	7.6	0.0	6.9	6.8	3.6	3.9	7.7	6.3
Malaysia	3.3	1.8	1.1	1.4	3.0	3.6	2.0	5.4	0.6	2.0	2.1	2.5	1.2	2.0	2.1
Maldives	5.9	0.9	−2.8	6.3	2.5	3.5	7.4	12.3	4.0	4.3	5.2	3.0	4.0	4.5	6.0
Myanmar	24.7	58.1	24.9	3.8	10.7	26.3	32.9	22.5	7.9	7.8	9.1	9.2	6.5	9.0	9.2
Nepal	8.6	2.9	4.7	4.0	4.5	8.0	6.4	7.7	13.2	11.8	8.0	5.0	11.4	12.1	6.0
Pakistan	8.3	2.5	3.1	4.6	9.3	7.9	7.8	12.0	20.8	11.5	7.5	6.0	13.1	12.0	8.0
Papua New Guinea	9.7	11.8	14.7	2.1	1.8	2.4	0.9	10.8	6.9	7.1	8.0	5.0	5.7	8.5	7.5
Philippines	7.5	3.0	3.5	6.0	7.6	6.2	2.8	9.3	3.2	5.0	4.0	4.0	4.4	4.5	4.0
Samoa	3.9	7.4	4.3	7.8	7.8	3.2	4.5	6.2	14.4	−0.2	3.0	4.0	9.8	−0.6	6.0
Solomon Islands	9.6	9.5	10.5	6.9	7.0	11.1	7.7	17.4	7.1	4.8	6.2	5.2	1.8	6.5	6.0
Sri Lanka	9.9	9.6	9.0	9.0	11.0	10.0	15.8	22.6	3.4	9.4	8.2	7.0	4.8	9.1	7.3
Thailand	4.1	0.7	1.8	2.8	4.5	4.6	2.2	5.5	−0.8	3.2	1.9	1.4	3.5	2.7	2.0
Timor-Leste	...	4.7	7.2	3.2	1.8	4.1	8.9	7.6	1.3	4.0	4.0	4.0	2.7	4.0	4.0
Tonga	4.0	10.8	11.5	10.6	8.3	6.0	7.5	7.3	3.5	3.2	4.2	6.0	2.8	4.2	4.1
Vanuatu	2.8	2.0	3.0	1.4	1.2	2.0	3.9	4.8	4.5	3.7	3.0	3.0	2.3	3.9	3.0
Vietnam	8.6	4.1	3.3	7.9	8.4	7.5	8.3	23.1	6.7	12.0	10.3	5.0	6.5	12.5	8.0
Middle East and North Africa	**10.1**	**4.9**	**5.5**	**6.5**	**6.4**	**7.5**	**10.0**	**13.5**	**6.6**	**6.5**	**6.4**	**5.3**	**5.2**	**6.7**	**6.2**
Algeria	14.1	1.4	2.6	3.6	1.6	2.3	3.6	4.9	5.7	5.5	5.2	4.5	5.8	5.3	5.1
Bahrain	−0.3	−0.5	1.7	2.2	2.6	2.0	3.3	3.5	2.8	2.4	2.0	2.0	2.8	2.0	2.0
Djibouti	3.1	0.6	2.0	3.1	3.1	3.5	5.0	12.0	1.7	3.0	4.0	3.0	2.2	3.1	3.5
Egypt	7.7	2.4	3.2	8.1	8.8	4.2	11.0	11.7	16.2	12.0	9.5	6.5	10.0	10.0	9.0
Iran, Islamic Republic of	23.0	15.7	15.6	15.3	10.4	11.9	18.4	25.4	10.3	8.5	10.0	10.0	8.0	10.0	10.0
Iraq	...	...	...	...	37.0	53.2	30.8	2.7	−2.8	5.1	5.0	4.0	−4.4	6.0	5.0
Jordan	2.9	1.8	1.6	3.4	3.5	6.3	5.4	14.9	−0.7	5.3	4.6	2.5	2.7	5.3	4.6
Kuwait	1.6	0.8	1.0	1.3	4.1	3.1	5.5	10.5	4.7	4.5	4.0	3.5	4.7	4.5	4.0
Lebanon	13.8	1.8	1.3	1.7	−0.7	5.6	4.1	10.8	1.2	5.0	3.4	2.2	3.4	4.2	2.8
Libya	3.6	−9.9	−2.1	1.0	2.9	1.4	6.2	10.4	2.7	4.5	3.5	3.0	2.7	4.5	3.5
Mauritania	5.4	5.4	5.3	10.4	12.1	6.2	7.3	7.3	2.2	4.8	4.8	5.0	5.0	4.6	5.1
Morocco	3.2	2.8	1.2	1.5	1.0	3.3	2.0	3.9	1.0	2.0	2.6	2.6	−1.6	2.0	2.6
Oman	−0.1	−0.3	0.2	0.7	1.9	3.4	5.9	12.6	3.5	3.9	2.9	1.5	3.7	3.4	2.5
Qatar	2.4	0.2	2.3	6.8	8.8	11.8	13.8	15.0	−4.9	1.0	3.0	4.0	−4.9	1.0	3.0
Saudi Arabia	0.3	0.2	0.6	0.4	0.6	2.3	4.1	9.9	5.1	5.2	5.0	3.0	4.2	5.5	4.7
Sudan	55.7	8.3	7.7	8.4	8.5	7.2	8.0	14.3	11.3	10.0	9.0	5.5	11.5	10.0	8.0
Syrian Arab Republic	5.1	−0.5	5.8	4.4	7.2	10.4	4.7	15.2	2.5	5.0	5.0	5.0	2.5	5.0	5.0
Tunisia	3.8	2.7	2.7	3.6	2.0	4.5	3.1	5.0	3.7	4.2	3.5	2.9	4.3	4.7	3.5
United Arab Emirates	3.4	2.9	3.1	5.0	6.2	9.3	11.6	11.5	1.0	2.2	3.0	3.2	1.6	2.6	3.1
Yemen, Republic of	31.2	12.2	10.8	12.5	9.9	10.8	7.9	19.0	3.7	9.3	8.4	7.0	8.8	9.7	7.1

Table A7 *(continued)*

	Average 1992–2001	2002	2003	2004	2005	2006	2007	2008	2009	Projections 2010	2011	2015	End of Period 2009	Projections 2010	2011
Sub-Saharan Africa	**26.3**	**11.3**	**10.9**	**7.6**	**8.9**	**7.3**	**7.1**	**11.6**	**10.6**	**8.0**	**6.9**	**5.5**	**8.2**	**7.7**	**6.4**
Angola	569.9	108.9	98.3	43.6	23.0	13.3	12.2	12.5	14.0	15.0	9.8	6.0	14.0	13.0	9.5
Benin	7.8	2.4	1.5	0.9	5.4	3.8	1.3	8.0	2.2	2.5	2.8	2.8	−2.9	2.8	2.8
Botswana	10.0	8.0	9.2	7.0	8.6	11.6	7.1	12.6	8.1	6.1	6.2	5.3	5.8	5.9	6.0
Burkina Faso	4.6	2.3	2.0	−0.4	6.4	2.4	−0.2	10.7	2.6	2.3	2.0	2.0	−0.3	2.0	2.0
Burundi	15.3	−1.3	10.7	8.0	13.4	2.8	8.3	24.4	11.3	8.0	7.2	5.0	8.5	7.5	7.0
Cameroon[4]	5.2	6.3	0.6	0.3	2.0	4.9	1.1	5.3	3.0	3.0	2.7	2.7	0.9	3.0	2.7
Cape Verde	5.5	1.9	1.2	−1.9	0.4	4.8	4.4	6.8	1.2	1.4	2.0	2.0	1.0	1.4	2.0
Central African	4.6	2.3	4.4	−2.2	2.9	6.7	0.9	9.3	3.5	2.1	2.9	2.5	−1.2	3.4	2.5
Chad	5.3	5.2	−1.8	−4.8	3.7	7.7	−7.4	8.3	10.1	6.0	3.0	3.0	4.7	3.0	3.0
Comoros	4.3	3.6	3.7	4.5	3.0	3.4	4.5	4.8	4.8	2.2	2.3	3.0	2.2	2.1	2.6
Congo, Democratic Republic of	818.7	25.3	12.8	4.0	21.4	13.2	16.7	18.0	46.2	26.2	13.5	8.3	52.3	15.0	12.0
Congo, Republic of	6.4	3.0	1.7	3.7	2.5	4.7	2.6	6.0	4.3	4.0	3.0	3.0	2.5	3.0	3.0
Côte d'Ivoire	6.3	3.1	3.3	1.5	3.9	2.5	1.9	6.3	1.0	1.4	2.5	2.5	−1.7	2.1	2.5
Equatorial Guinea	7.8	7.6	7.3	4.2	5.7	4.5	2.8	4.3	7.1	7.1	6.6	5.6	7.7	6.9	6.4
Eritrea	...	16.9	22.7	25.1	12.5	15.1	9.3	19.9	34.7	20.5	15.0	14.0	30.2	16.8	14.5
Ethiopia	4.6	−7.2	15.1	8.6	6.8	12.3	15.8	25.3	36.4	3.8	9.3	6.0	2.7	10.5	7.0
Gabon	5.5	0.2	2.1	0.4	1.2	−1.4	5.0	5.3	2.1	7.5	9.0	3.0	0.8	7.5	9.0
Gambia, The	3.8	8.6	17.0	14.3	5.0	2.1	5.4	4.5	4.6	3.9	5.0	5.0	2.7	5.0	5.0
Ghana	27.1	14.8	26.7	12.6	15.1	10.2	10.7	16.5	19.3	10.6	8.9	5.0	16.0	9.5	8.5
Guinea	6.0	3.0	11.0	17.5	31.4	34.7	22.9	18.4	4.7	16.6	12.3	5.0	7.9	19.4	8.0
Guinea-Bissau	27.3	3.3	−3.5	0.8	3.3	0.7	4.6	10.4	−1.7	2.5	2.5	2.5	−6.0	2.5	2.5
Kenya	14.5	2.0	9.8	11.6	10.3	14.5	9.8	13.1	11.8	8.0	5.0	5.0	11.5	7.2	5.0
Lesotho	9.5	12.5	7.3	5.0	3.4	6.1	8.0	10.7	7.7	5.9	5.7	4.7	5.1	5.8	5.6
Liberia	...	14.2	10.3	3.6	6.9	7.2	13.7	17.5	7.4	7.2	4.3	5.0	9.7	4.8	4.7
Madagascar	16.1	16.2	−1.1	14.0	18.4	10.8	10.4	9.2	9.0	9.6	8.9	5.0	8.0	9.2	8.5
Malawi	33.0	17.4	9.6	11.4	15.5	13.9	7.9	8.7	8.4	8.4	7.7	5.6	7.6	8.1	7.2
Mali	4.0	4.9	−1.2	−3.1	6.4	1.5	1.5	9.1	2.2	2.1	2.6	3.4	1.6	2.3	2.8
Mauritius	6.8	6.5	3.9	4.7	4.9	9.0	8.8	9.7	2.5	2.1	2.4	2.5	1.5	2.5	2.7
Mozambique	26.1	16.8	13.5	12.6	6.4	13.2	8.2	10.3	3.3	9.3	5.6	5.6	4.2	8.0	5.6
Namibia	9.7	11.3	7.2	4.1	2.3	5.1	6.7	10.0	9.1	6.5	5.9	4.9	7.0	6.1	5.7
Niger	5.3	2.7	−1.8	0.4	7.8	0.1	0.1	11.3	4.3	8.4	2.0	2.0	−3.1	4.2	2.0
Nigeria	29.2	12.9	14.0	15.0	17.9	8.2	5.4	11.6	12.4	11.5	9.5	8.5	11.9	10.7	8.5
Rwanda	14.6	2.0	7.4	12.0	9.1	8.8	9.1	15.4	10.4	6.4	6.5	5.0	5.7	7.0	6.0
São Tomé and Príncipe	31.9	9.2	9.6	12.8	17.2	23.1	18.5	26.0	17.0	12.3	7.4	3.0	16.1	9.0	6.0
Senegal	4.6	2.3	0.0	0.5	1.7	2.1	5.9	5.8	−1.1	1.6	2.1	2.1	−2.2	2.1	2.1
Seychelles	2.7	0.2	3.3	3.9	0.6	−1.9	5.3	37.0	31.8	3.2	2.5	3.0	−2.5	6.9	3.0
Sierra Leone	23.5	−3.7	7.5	14.2	12.0	9.5	11.6	14.8	9.2	15.5	7.8	5.7	10.8	12.5	9.5
South Africa	8.0	9.2	5.8	1.4	3.4	4.7	7.1	11.5	7.1	5.8	5.8	4.5	6.3	5.8	5.7
Swaziland	8.8	11.7	7.4	3.4	4.8	5.3	8.2	13.1	7.6	6.2	5.6	4.8	5.4	5.9	5.3
Tanzania	17.1	4.6	4.4	4.1	4.4	7.3	7.0	10.3	12.1	7.8	5.0	5.0	12.2	5.4	5.0
Togo	6.5	3.1	−0.9	0.4	6.8	2.2	1.0	8.7	2.0	2.1	2.6	2.4	−2.4	4.5	1.5
Uganda	11.0	−2.0	5.7	5.0	8.0	6.6	6.8	7.3	14.2	10.5	7.5	5.0	12.3	8.2	5.9
Zambia	52.4	22.2	21.4	18.0	18.3	9.0	10.7	12.4	13.4	8.2	7.5	5.0	9.9	8.0	7.0
Zimbabwe[5]	...	...	...	...	...	...	...	...	...	5.0	5.0	5.0	...	8.9	1.9

Table A7 *(concluded)*

	Average 1992–2001	2002	2003	2004	2005	2006	2007	2008	2009	Projections 2010	Projections 2011	Projections 2015	End of Period 2009	End of Period Projections 2010	End of Period Projections 2011
Western Hemisphere	**51.9**	**8.5**	**10.4**	**6.6**	**6.3**	**5.3**	**5.4**	**7.9**	**6.0**	**6.2**	**5.9**	**5.1**	**4.8**	**6.8**	**5.8**
Antigua and Barbuda	2.4	2.4	2.0	2.0	2.1	1.8	1.4	5.3	−0.6	3.5	1.6	2.2	2.4	1.9	2.1
Argentina[6]	4.6	25.9	13.4	4.4	9.6	10.9	8.8	8.6	6.3	10.1	9.1	9.7	7.7	9.7	9.7
Bahamas, The	2.0	2.2	3.0	1.0	2.2	1.8	2.5	4.5	2.1	1.7	1.4	2.0	1.3	1.7	1.2
Barbados	2.5	−1.2	1.6	1.4	6.1	7.3	4.0	8.1	3.5	5.3	4.7	2.2	3.2	7.3	2.2
Belize	1.6	2.2	2.6	3.1	3.7	4.2	2.3	6.4	2.0	1.5	3.0	2.5	−0.4	3.5	2.5
Bolivia	7.1	0.9	3.3	4.4	5.4	4.3	8.7	14.0	3.5	3.3	3.7	3.5	0.3	4.0	3.5
Brazil	157.1	8.4	14.8	6.6	6.9	4.2	3.6	5.7	4.9	5.1	4.6	4.5	4.3	5.3	4.8
Chile	7.6	2.5	2.8	1.1	3.1	3.4	4.4	8.7	1.7	2.0	3.0	3.0	−1.4	3.7	3.0
Colombia	17.8	6.3	7.1	5.9	5.0	4.3	5.5	7.0	4.2	3.5	3.7	3.0	2.0	3.8	3.4
Costa Rica	14.2	9.2	9.4	12.3	13.8	11.5	9.4	13.4	7.8	4.9	5.2	4.0	4.0	5.5	5.0
Dominica	1.7	0.1	1.6	2.4	1.6	2.6	3.2	6.4	0.0	2.3	1.5	1.5	3.2	1.5	1.5
Dominican Republic	7.2	5.2	27.4	51.5	4.2	7.6	6.1	10.6	1.5	6.5	4.3	4.1	5.8	6.0	4.0
Ecuador	41.4	12.6	7.9	2.7	2.1	3.3	2.3	8.4	5.1	4.0	3.5	3.0	4.3	3.7	3.2
El Salvador	7.2	1.9	2.1	4.5	4.7	4.0	4.6	7.3	0.5	0.5	2.2	2.8	−0.2	1.5	2.8
Grenada	2.1	1.1	2.2	2.3	3.5	4.2	3.9	8.0	−0.3	3.6	1.9	2.0	−2.4	4.7	2.0
Guatemala	9.0	8.1	5.6	7.6	9.1	6.6	6.8	11.4	1.9	3.3	3.4	4.0	−0.3	4.3	4.0
Guyana	8.9	5.4	6.0	4.7	6.9	6.7	12.2	8.1	2.9	3.8	4.0	4.0	3.6	4.0	4.0
Haiti	19.8	9.3	26.7	28.3	16.8	14.2	9.0	14.4	3.4	5.6	7.8	6.5	−4.7	8.5	8.0
Honduras	15.9	7.7	7.7	8.1	8.8	5.6	6.9	11.4	5.5	5.1	6.5	6.5	3.0	6.5	6.5
Jamaica	19.3	7.0	10.1	13.5	15.1	8.5	9.3	22.0	9.6	14.9	7.0	6.0	10.2	13.2	6.1
Mexico	16.7	5.0	4.5	4.7	4.0	3.6	4.0	5.1	5.3	4.6	3.7	3.0	3.6	5.3	3.0
Nicaragua	10.7	3.8	5.3	8.5	9.6	9.1	11.1	19.8	3.7	5.1	6.4	6.9	0.9	7.0	7.0
Panama	1.1	1.0	0.6	0.5	2.9	2.5	4.2	8.8	2.4	3.3	2.9	2.5	1.9	3.0	2.7
Paraguay	11.8	10.5	14.2	4.3	6.8	9.6	8.1	10.2	2.6	3.9	3.6	3.2	1.9	4.0	3.5
Peru	17.5	0.2	2.3	3.7	1.6	2.0	1.8	5.8	2.9	1.5	1.8	2.0	0.2	2.0	2.0
St. Kitts and Nevis	3.1	2.1	2.3	2.2	3.4	8.5	4.5	5.4	1.9	2.5	2.2	2.2	1.0	2.2	2.2
St. Lucia	3.1	−0.3	1.0	1.5	3.9	3.6	1.9	7.2	0.6	1.7	2.5	2.2	1.0	1.9	2.1
St. Vincent and the Grenadines	2.0	1.3	0.2	3.0	3.7	3.0	6.9	10.1	0.6	1.8	2.7	2.9	−1.5	2.4	2.9
Suriname	77.3	15.5	23.0	9.1	9.9	11.3	6.4	14.6	0.7	5.5	5.5	5.5	5.7	5.5	4.9
Trinidad and Tobago	5.3	4.2	3.8	3.7	6.9	8.3	7.9	12.1	7.0	3.2	5.0	5.0	1.3	5.0	5.0
Uruguay	26.5	14.0	19.4	9.2	4.7	6.4	8.1	7.9	7.1	6.2	6.0	5.0	5.9	6.5	5.5
Venezuela	40.8	22.4	31.1	21.7	16.0	13.7	18.7	30.4	27.1	29.7	33.1	23.9	25.1	34.3	32.0

[1]In accordance with standard practice in the *World Economic Outlook,* movements in consumer prices are indicated as annual averages rather than as December–December changes during the year, as is the practice in some countries. For many countries, figures for recent years are IMF staff estimates. Data for some countries are for fiscal years.

[2]For many countries, inflation for the earlier years is measured on the basis of a retail price index. Consumer price index (CPI) inflation data with broader and more up-to-date coverage are typically used for more recent years.

[3]Georgia and Mongolia, which are not members of the Commonwealth of Independent States, are included in this group for reasons of geography and similarities in economic structure.

[4]The percent changes in 2002 are calculated over a period of 18 months, reflecting a change in the fiscal year cycle (from July–June to January–December).

[5]The Zimbabwe dollar ceased circulating in early 2009. Data are based on IMF staff estimates of price and exchange rate developments in U.S. dollars. IMF staff estimates of U.S. dollar values may differ from authorities' estimates.

[6]Private analysts estimate that CPI inflation has been considerably higher. The authorities have established a board of academic advisors to assess these issues.

Table A8. Major Advanced Economies: General Government Fiscal Balances and Debt[1]

(Percent of GDP unless noted otherwise)

	Average 1994–2003	2004	2005	2006	2007	2008	2009	Projections 2010	2011	2015
Major Advanced Economies										
Net Lending/Borrowing	−3.6	−4.2	−3.3	−2.3	−2.1	−4.7	−10.0	−9.5	−7.6	−5.4
Output Gap[2]	−0.5	−0.2	0.1	0.8	1.2	−0.2	−4.5	−3.1	−2.1	−0.1
Structural Balance[2]	−3.2	−3.6	−3.0	−2.5	−2.4	−4.0	−6.4	−7.3	−6.2	−5.4
United States										
Net Lending/Borrowing	...	−4.4	−3.2	−2.0	−2.7	−6.6	−12.5	−11.0	−8.2	−6.5
Output Gap[2]	−0.7	0.1	1.0	1.5	1.6	0.1	−3.8	−2.0	−1.0	0.0
Structural Balance[2]	...	−3.5	−2.7	−2.5	−2.9	−5.4	−7.9	−9.2	−7.3	−6.6
Net Debt	44.4	42.2	42.6	41.9	42.3	47.2	58.3	66.2	72.0	85.5
Gross Debt	63.3	61.4	61.6	61.1	62.1	70.6	83.2	92.6	97.4	109.7
Euro Area										
Net Lending/Borrowing	−2.7	−2.9	−2.5	−1.3	−0.6	−2.0	−6.3	−6.8	−6.1	−4.0
Output Gap[2]	−0.1	−0.5	−0.5	0.8	1.9	1.1	−3.4	−3.1	−2.5	0.0
Structural Balance[2]	−2.7	−2.9	−2.7	−2.0	−1.7	−2.6	−4.3	−4.7	−4.5	−4.1
Net Debt	60.7	61.3	61.7	59.6	57.0	59.5	68.3	73.9	77.8	84.2
Gross Debt	69.1	69.1	69.7	67.9	65.7	69.1	78.3	84.1	88.1	94.9
Germany[3]										
Net Lending/Borrowing	−2.5	−3.8	−3.3	−1.6	0.2	0.0	−3.3	−5.7	−5.1	−1.7
Output Gap[2]	0.0	−1.9	−2.3	−0.4	0.9	1.0	−4.3	−3.5	−2.6	−0.1
Structural Balance[2,4]	−1.9	−2.6	−2.2	−1.4	0.0	−0.5	−1.1	−3.8	−3.7	−1.7
Net Debt	51.8	61.1	63.3	61.8	58.4	59.3	64.3	68.6	71.8	74.8
Gross Debt	58.6	65.7	68.0	67.6	65.0	65.9	72.5	76.7	79.6	81.5
France										
Net Lending/Borrowing	−3.3	−3.6	−3.0	−2.3	−2.7	−3.4	−7.9	−8.2	−7.0	−4.1
Output Gap[2]	0.0	0.4	0.3	0.8	1.0	−0.2	−3.5	−3.1	−2.8	−0.1
Structural Balance[2,4]	−3.1	−3.6	−3.4	−2.6	−3.1	−3.2	−4.9	−4.6	−4.5	−4.3
Net Debt	48.4	55.2	56.7	53.9	54.1	57.8	67.7	74.5	78.9	85.1
Gross Debt	57.6	64.9	66.3	63.7	63.8	67.5	77.4	84.2	88.6	94.8
Italy										
Net Lending/Borrowing	−4.2	−3.6	−4.4	−3.3	−1.5	−2.7	−5.3	−5.2	−4.9	−4.6
Output Gap[2]	−0.1	0.0	−0.4	0.8	1.5	−0.5	−3.7	−3.3	−2.8	0.0
Structural Balance[2,5]	−4.4	−4.8	−4.6	−3.3	−2.5	−2.6	−3.9	−3.5	−3.4	−4.6
Net Debt	110.5	102.0	103.8	104.4	101.2	103.9	113.2	116.0	117.8	122.1
Gross Debt	113.9	103.8	105.8	106.5	103.4	106.0	115.8	118.6	120.5	124.7
Japan										
Net Lending/Borrowing	−6.0	−6.2	−4.8	−4.0	−2.4	−4.2	−10.3	−9.8	−9.1	−7.3
Output Gap[2]	−0.9	−1.1	−0.8	−0.4	0.4	−1.6	−7.1	−5.7	−4.2	−0.2
Structural Balance[2]	−5.6	−5.7	−4.5	−3.9	−2.5	−3.5	−7.4	−7.5	−7.4	−7.2
Net Debt	48.3	82.7	84.3	83.8	81.5	96.9	111.6	121.7	129.8	154.0
Gross Debt	125.9	178.1	191.1	190.1	187.7	198.8	217.6	227.3	234.1	248.8
United Kingdom										
Net Lending/Borrowing	−2.1	−3.4	−3.3	−2.6	−2.7	−4.8	−10.9	−11.4	−9.4	−4.3
Output Gap[2]	−0.1	0.1	−0.3	0.0	0.4	−0.3	−5.5	−5.0	−3.9	−0.4
Structural Balance[2]	−1.9	−3.3	−3.1	−2.7	−2.9	−5.2	−7.8	−7.6	−6.2	−3.8
Net Debt	37.8	35.5	37.3	38.0	38.3	45.5	61.5	71.6	78.3	83.9
Gross Debt	43.1	40.2	42.1	43.2	44.1	52.0	68.2	78.2	84.9	90.6
Canada										
Net Lending/Borrowing	−0.9	0.9	1.5	1.6	1.6	0.1	−5.0	−5.1	−2.8	0.0
Output Gap[2]	0.4	0.4	0.6	0.7	0.7	−1.2	−5.2	−3.6	−2.2	0.0
Structural Balance[2]	−0.9	0.7	1.3	1.2	1.2	0.7	−2.0	−3.0	−1.5	0.0
Net Debt	55.4	34.7	30.4	25.9	22.8	22.6	28.2	31.8	33.0	30.4
Gross Debt	89.5	71.5	70.3	68.7	64.2	70.4	81.6	82.3	80.9	70.5

Note: The methodology and specific assumptions for each country are discussed in Box A1 in this Statistical Appendix.

[1]Debt data refer to the end of the year. Debt data are not always comparable across countries.

[2]Percent of potential GDP.

[3]Beginning in 1995, the debt and debt-service obligations of the Treuhandanstalt (and of various other agencies) were taken over by the general government. This debt is equivalent to 8 percent of GDP, and the associated debt service to ½ to 1 percent of GDP.

[4]Excludes sizable one-time receipts from the sale of assets, including licenses.

[5]Excludes one-time measures based on the authorities' data and, in the absence of the latter, receipts from the sale of assets.

Table A9. Summary of World Trade Volumes and Prices

(Annual percent change)

	Averages		2002	2003	2004	2005	2006	2007	2008	2009	Projections	
	1992–2001	2002–11									2010	2011
Trade in Goods and Services												
World Trade[1]												
Volume	6.6	4.7	3.6	5.4	10.7	7.7	8.8	7.2	2.8	−10.7	7.0	6.1
Price Deflator												
In U.S. Dollars	−1.1	4.7	1.1	10.4	9.6	5.4	5.5	8.3	11.4	−10.9	6.7	1.9
In SDRs	−0.3	2.8	−0.6	2.1	3.7	5.6	5.9	4.1	7.9	−8.7	7.3	2.2
Volume of Trade												
Exports												
Advanced Economies	6.4	3.6	2.5	3.3	9.1	6.2	8.6	6.3	1.9	−11.7	6.6	5.0
Emerging and Developing Economies	8.0	7.5	7.1	11.0	14.8	11.5	10.4	9.7	4.0	−8.2	8.3	8.4
Imports												
Advanced Economies	6.6	3.2	2.7	4.2	9.2	6.5	7.6	4.7	0.6	−12.0	5.4	4.6
Emerging and Developing Economies	6.5	8.4	6.3	10.3	15.9	11.7	10.9	12.7	8.5	−8.4	9.7	8.2
Terms of Trade												
Advanced Economies	0.0	−0.1	0.8	1.0	−0.2	−1.4	−1.1	0.2	−1.7	2.9	−1.3	−0.3
Emerging and Developing Economies	−0.3	1.2	0.3	0.8	2.3	5.0	2.7	−0.2	3.7	−5.1	3.0	−0.4
Trade in Goods												
World Trade[1]												
Volume	6.9	4.6	3.8	6.2	10.9	7.5	8.8	6.5	2.4	−11.8	8.0	6.2
Price Deflator												
In U.S. Dollars	−1.2	4.8	0.5	10.0	9.8	6.2	6.2	8.4	12.2	−12.1	7.2	2.1
In SDRs	−0.5	2.9	−1.2	1.7	3.9	6.5	6.6	4.2	8.6	−9.9	7.8	2.4
World Trade Prices in U.S. Dollars[2]												
Manufactures	−1.6	4.5	2.0	14.5	8.6	3.6	3.7	8.7	8.5	−6.9	2.7	1.1
Oil	2.3	13.1	2.5	15.8	30.7	41.3	20.5	10.7	36.4	−36.3	29.5	3.8
Nonfuel Primary Commodities	−1.3	6.3	1.9	5.9	15.2	6.1	23.2	14.1	7.5	−18.7	13.9	−0.5
Food	−2.0	5.5	3.5	6.3	14.0	−0.9	10.5	15.2	23.4	−14.7	3.1	−0.6
Beverages	−2.0	7.6	24.3	4.8	−0.9	18.1	8.4	13.8	23.3	1.6	−0.4	−10.8
Agricultural Raw Materials	0.1	1.4	−0.2	0.6	4.1	0.5	8.8	5.0	−0.8	−17.0	22.6	−5.5
Metal	−1.1	11.3	−3.5	11.8	34.6	22.4	56.2	17.4	−8.0	−28.6	30.9	3.9
World Trade Prices in SDRs[2]												
Manufactures	−0.9	2.6	0.3	5.9	2.7	3.9	4.2	4.5	5.1	−4.6	3.3	1.3
Oil	3.1	11.0	0.8	7.1	23.6	41.6	21.0	6.4	32.1	−34.8	30.3	4.0
Nonfuel Primary Commodities	−0.6	4.3	0.2	−2.1	9.0	6.3	23.8	9.6	4.1	−16.7	14.5	−0.2
Food	−1.3	3.6	1.8	−1.7	7.8	−0.7	11.0	10.7	19.5	−12.6	3.7	−0.3
Beverages	−1.3	5.7	22.2	−3.1	−6.3	18.3	8.8	9.4	19.4	4.1	0.1	−10.6
Agricultural Raw Materials	0.9	−0.5	−1.9	−7.0	−1.6	0.8	9.3	0.9	−3.9	−14.9	23.4	−5.2
Metal	−0.4	9.3	−5.1	3.3	27.3	22.7	56.9	12.8	−10.9	−26.8	31.6	4.2
World Trade Prices in Euros[2]												
Manufactures	1.7	0.3	−3.2	−4.4	−1.2	3.4	2.9	−0.4	1.0	−1.6	4.9	2.1
Oil	5.7	8.5	−2.8	−3.3	18.9	41.0	19.5	1.4	27.1	−32.7	32.2	4.9
Nonfuel Primary Commodities	2.0	2.0	−3.3	−11.6	4.8	5.9	22.3	4.5	0.1	−14.1	16.3	0.6
Food	1.3	1.3	−1.8	−11.2	3.7	−1.1	9.6	5.6	14.9	−9.8	5.3	0.5
Beverages	1.2	3.3	17.9	−12.5	−9.9	17.8	7.5	4.2	14.8	7.3	1.7	−9.9
Agricultural Raw Materials	3.4	−2.7	−5.4	−16.0	−5.3	0.3	8.0	−3.8	−7.6	−12.3	25.2	−4.5
Metal	2.2	6.8	−8.4	−6.7	22.4	22.2	55.0	7.5	−14.3	−24.6	33.6	5.0

Table A9 (concluded)

	Averages		2002	2003	2004	2005	2006	2007	2008	2009	Projections	
	1992–2001	2002–11									2010	2011
Trade in Goods												
Volume of Trade												
Exports												
Advanced Economies	6.6	3.4	2.5	3.9	9.0	5.7	8.6	5.3	1.5	−13.5	8.1	5.2
Emerging and Developing Economies	7.7	7.1	6.9	11.5	14.0	10.7	9.5	8.7	3.9	−9.1	8.5	8.2
Fuel Exporters	3.5	4.2	2.4	11.8	8.9	5.6	4.0	4.4	2.3	−8.6	6.5	5.6
Nonfuel Exporters	9.3	8.2	8.5	11.3	15.8	12.6	11.9	10.6	4.6	−9.3	9.2	9.3
Imports												
Advanced Economies	7.1	3.3	3.1	4.9	9.6	6.4	7.9	4.2	0.0	−13.0	6.7	4.8
Emerging and Developing Economies	6.9	8.4	6.3	11.5	16.7	11.8	10.4	12.4	7.9	−9.5	10.1	8.5
Fuel Exporters	1.8	9.8	9.2	9.0	15.0	16.4	11.9	21.7	14.0	−12.8	9.2	8.6
Nonfuel Exporters	8.5	8.1	5.7	12.0	17.0	10.9	10.1	10.4	6.5	−8.7	10.3	8.5
Price Deflators in SDRs												
Exports												
Advanced Economies	−1.1	2.2	−1.0	2.7	3.0	3.7	4.2	3.8	5.7	−6.7	5.4	1.9
Emerging and Developing Economies	1.8	5.2	−0.2	1.2	7.5	14.3	12.1	5.5	13.9	−14.3	12.7	3.0
Fuel Exporters	3.5	9.2	0.9	4.5	17.4	32.6	18.7	7.9	26.0	−28.0	22.1	4.0
Nonfuel Exporters	1.2	3.6	−0.5	0.1	4.0	7.5	9.3	4.4	8.8	−7.7	9.0	2.6
Imports												
Advanced Economies	−1.2	2.3	−1.9	1.5	3.3	5.5	5.7	3.5	8.0	−10.3	6.5	2.1
Emerging and Developing Economies	1.9	3.6	−0.7	0.0	4.3	7.5	8.5	5.4	10.0	−9.9	9.5	3.4
Fuel Exporters	1.7	3.8	0.5	0.8	4.8	7.8	8.9	5.4	8.7	−7.0	7.3	2.0
Nonfuel Exporters	1.7	3.6	−1.0	−0.1	4.2	7.5	8.5	5.4	10.4	−10.6	10.0	3.8
Terms of Trade												
Advanced Economies	0.1	−0.1	0.9	1.2	−0.3	−1.7	−1.4	0.3	−2.2	4.0	−1.1	−0.2
Emerging and Developing Economies	−0.1	1.5	0.6	1.2	3.1	6.3	3.3	0.1	3.5	−4.9	2.9	−0.4
Regional Groups												
Central and Eastern Europe	−0.6	−0.1	0.4	0.8	1.1	−0.1	−1.8	1.4	−2.2	3.2	−3.2	−0.7
Commonwealth of Independent States[3]	...	4.4	−1.9	8.7	12.1	14.8	9.3	2.2	15.7	−21.1	8.4	1.5
Developing Asia	−0.3	−0.5	0.7	−0.6	−2.0	−1.4	−1.1	−2.3	−2.9	6.0	0.4	−1.3
Middle East and North Africa	1.7	4.3	0.3	1.2	8.8	22.6	5.2	0.9	13.4	−18.1	12.3	1.4
Sub-Saharan Africa	−0.2	3.5	1.9	1.5	3.7	12.6	8.2	2.9	10.2	−16.4	11.3	2.0
Western Hemisphere	0.0	1.8	1.4	2.4	5.5	5.1	8.4	2.0	2.9	−5.4	−2.2	−1.7
Analytical Groups												
By Source of Export Earnings												
Fuel Exporters	1.7	5.2	0.3	3.7	12.0	23.0	9.1	2.4	15.9	−22.5	13.7	2.0
Nonfuel Exporters	−0.4	0.0	0.4	0.3	−0.2	0.0	0.7	−0.9	−1.4	3.3	−0.9	−1.1
Memorandum												
World Exports in Billions of U.S. Dollars												
Goods and Services	6,424	14,657	8,008	9,329	11,322	12,893	14,844	17,278	19,748	15,716	17,981	19,446
Goods	5,123	11,688	6,367	7,441	9,035	10,334	11,951	13,817	15,859	12,285	14,288	15,502
Average Oil Price[4]	2.3	13.1	2.5	15.8	30.7	41.3	20.5	10.7	36.4	−36.3	29.5	3.8
In U.S. Dollars a Barrel	19.22	60.22	24.95	28.89	37.76	53.35	64.27	71.13	97.03	61.78	80.00	83.00
Export Unit Value of Manufactures[5]	−1.6	4.5	2.0	14.5	8.6	3.6	3.7	8.7	8.5	−6.9	2.7	1.1

[1]Average of annual percent change for world exports and imports.

[2]As represented, respectively, by the export unit value index for manufactures of the advanced economies; the average of U.K. Brent, Dubai, and West Texas Intermediate crude oil prices; and the average of world market prices for nonfuel primary commodities weighted by their 2002–04 shares in world commodity exports.

[3]Georgia and Mongolia, which are not members of the Commonwealth of Independent States, are included in this group for reasons of geography and similarities in economic structure.

[4]Average of U.K. Brent, Dubai, and West Texas Intermediate crude oil prices.

[5]For manufactures exported by the advanced economies.

Table A10. Summary of Balances on Current Account

(Billions of U.S. dollars)

	2002	2003	2004	2005	2006	2007	2008	2009	Projections 2010	Projections 2011	Projections 2015
Advanced Economies	**−217.1**	**−219.3**	**−219.8**	**−409.8**	**−449.9**	**−347.6**	**−528.8**	**−147.3**	**−185.3**	**−220.0**	**−373.7**
United States	−459.1	−521.5	−631.1	−748.7	−803.5	−726.6	−706.1	−418.0	−487.2	−523.9	−638.2
Euro Area[1]	47.9	42.9	116.9	45.3	47.6	47.3	−106.0	−43.8	−4.7	13.1	−7.4
Japan	112.6	136.2	172.1	165.7	170.4	211.0	157.1	141.7	149.7	131.1	113.8
Other Advanced Economies[2]	81.6	123.0	122.4	128.0	135.6	120.7	126.2	172.8	156.9	159.7	158.1
Memorandum											
Newly Industrialized Asian Economies	55.8	80.8	82.9	79.4	89.7	111.7	84.8	142.5	121.3	128.2	152.8
Emerging and Developing Economies	**80.5**	**149.0**	**222.3**	**449.7**	**665.6**	**657.9**	**709.2**	**321.7**	**420.1**	**491.1**	**769.1**
Regional Groups											
Central and Eastern Europe	−19.3	−32.2	−53.2	−58.5	−87.1	−132.6	−152.1	−37.9	−63.0	−72.4	−99.3
Commonwealth of Independent States[3]	30.3	35.7	63.5	87.5	96.3	71.7	107.5	42.6	78.6	81.4	−4.0
Developing Asia	66.9	85.0	92.9	167.5	289.2	414.7	424.1	319.0	349.7	389.9	731.8
Middle East and North Africa	31.4	63.9	106.2	219.2	286.4	279.2	347.8	34.8	119.1	174.0	256.7
Sub-Saharan Africa	−12.6	−12.7	−8.5	−2.7	31.0	10.1	8.6	−18.1	−17.1	−22.0	−20.0
Western Hemisphere	−16.2	9.2	21.4	36.7	49.8	14.8	−26.7	−18.6	−47.3	−59.9	−96.2
Memorandum											
European Union	18.7	17.8	65.5	−8.3	−41.6	−69.2	−196.1	−49.8	−34.3	−21.1	−64.1
Analytical Groups											
By Source of Export Earnings											
Fuel	60.6	107.8	188.7	355.6	481.7	441.9	602.2	136.7	300.0	365.1	371.5
Nonfuel	19.9	41.1	33.5	94.1	183.9	216.0	107.0	185.0	120.1	126.0	397.6
of Which, Primary Products	−4.4	−4.4	−0.9	−1.6	9.5	6.1	−12.3	−3.0	−11.4	−17.0	−17.3
By External Financing Source											
Net Debtor Countries	−36.7	−31.7	−57.2	−94.3	−116.6	−215.1	−361.8	−160.5	−265.0	−313.5	−406.7
of Which, Official Financing	−5.6	−7.4	−6.2	−8.4	−8.9	−11.2	−22.6	−15.4	−22.1	−22.8	−22.5
Net Debtor Countries by Debt-Servicing Experience											
Countries with Arrears and/or Rescheduling during 2004–08	2.2	2.3	−6.1	−7.6	−5.5	−17.9	−32.7	−27.4	−28.9	−35.5	−37.3
World[1]	**−136.6**	**−70.3**	**2.5**	**40.0**	**215.7**	**310.3**	**180.4**	**174.4**	**234.8**	**271.1**	**395.4**
Memorandum											
In Percent of Total World Current Account Transactions	−0.8	−0.4	0.0	0.2	0.7	0.9	0.5	0.6	0.7	0.7	0.8
In Percent of World GDP	−0.4	−0.2	0.0	0.1	0.4	0.6	0.3	0.3	0.4	0.4	0.5

[1]Reflects errors, omissions, and asymmetries in balance of payments statistics on current account, as well as the exclusion of data for international organizations and a limited number of countries. Calculated as the sum of the balance of individual Euro Area countries. See "Classification of Countries" in the introduction to this Statistical Appendix.

[2]In this table, Other Advanced Economies means advanced economies excluding the United States, Euro Area countries, and Japan.

[3]Georgia and Mongolia, which are not members of the Commonwealth of Independent States, are included in this group for reasons of geography and similarities in economic structure.

Table A11. Advanced Economies: Balance on Current Account

(Percent of GDP)

| | 2002 | 2003 | 2004 | 2005 | 2006 | 2007 | 2008 | 2009 | Projections | | |
									2010	2011	2015
Advanced Economies	**−0.8**	**−0.7**	**−0.7**	**−1.2**	**−1.2**	**−0.9**	**−1.3**	**−0.4**	**−0.4**	**−0.5**	**−0.7**
United States	−4.3	−4.7	−5.3	−5.9	−6.0	−5.2	−4.9	−2.9	−3.3	−3.4	−3.5
Euro Area[1]	0.7	0.5	1.2	0.4	0.4	0.4	−0.8	−0.4	0.0	0.1	−0.1
Germany	2.0	1.9	4.7	5.1	6.5	7.6	6.7	4.8	5.5	5.6	3.6
France	1.4	0.8	0.6	−0.4	−0.5	−1.0	−2.3	−1.5	−1.9	−1.8	−0.9
Italy	−0.8	−1.3	−0.9	−1.7	−2.6	−2.4	−3.4	−3.4	−2.8	−2.7	−2.4
Spain	−3.3	−3.5	−5.3	−7.4	−9.0	−10.0	−9.6	−5.1	−5.3	−5.1	−5.0
Netherlands	2.5	5.5	7.5	7.3	9.3	8.7	4.8	5.2	5.0	5.3	5.0
Belgium	4.6	4.1	3.5	2.6	2.0	2.2	−2.5	−0.3	−0.5	−0.1	2.2
Greece	−6.5	−6.5	−5.8	−7.5	−11.3	−14.4	−14.6	−11.2	−9.7	−8.1	−7.3
Austria	2.7	1.7	2.1	2.0	2.8	3.1	3.5	1.4	1.8	1.7	1.9
Portugal	−8.1	−6.1	−7.6	−9.5	−10.0	−9.4	−12.1	−10.1	−9.0	−10.2	−8.9
Finland	8.8	5.2	6.6	3.6	4.6	4.2	3.0	1.4	2.0	1.8	1.9
Ireland	−1.0	0.0	−0.6	−3.5	−3.6	−5.3	−5.2	−2.9	0.4	−0.1	−0.7
Slovak Republic	−7.9	−5.9	−7.8	−8.5	−7.8	−5.3	−6.5	−3.2	−1.8	−1.9	−2.7
Slovenia	1.1	−0.8	−2.7	−1.7	−2.5	−4.8	−6.2	−0.3	−1.5	−1.2	1.8
Luxembourg	10.5	8.1	11.9	11.0	10.3	9.7	5.3	5.7	11.2	11.6	13.3
Cyprus	−3.7	−2.2	−5.0	−5.9	−7.0	−11.7	−17.7	−9.3	−11.4	−10.9	−11.0
Malta	2.5	−3.1	−6.0	−8.8	−9.2	−6.2	−5.4	−3.9	−5.1	−5.1	−4.5
Japan	2.9	3.2	3.7	3.6	3.9	4.8	3.2	2.8	2.8	2.4	1.8
United Kingdom	−1.7	−1.6	−2.1	−2.6	−3.3	−2.7	−1.5	−1.3	−1.7	−1.6	−1.4
Canada	1.7	1.2	2.3	1.9	1.4	1.0	0.5	−2.7	−2.6	−2.5	−1.9
Korea	0.9	1.9	3.9	1.8	0.6	0.6	−0.6	5.1	1.6	2.2	1.9
Australia	−3.6	−5.2	−6.0	−5.7	−5.2	−6.1	−4.4	−4.1	−3.5	−3.7	−5.8
Taiwan Province of China	8.8	9.8	5.8	4.8	7.0	8.4	6.2	11.2	8.5	7.7	8.0
Sweden	5.0	7.2	6.7	7.0	8.6	8.6	7.8	6.4	5.4	5.8	5.7
Switzerland	8.3	12.8	13.3	14.0	15.2	10.0	2.4	8.7	9.5	9.6	11.9
Hong Kong SAR	7.6	10.4	9.5	11.4	12.1	12.3	13.6	11.1	12.1	10.1	7.6
Czech Republic	−5.7	−6.3	−5.3	−1.3	−2.6	−3.1	−3.1	−1.0	−1.7	−2.4	−2.5
Norway	12.6	12.3	12.7	16.3	17.2	14.1	18.6	13.8	16.8	16.7	15.1
Singapore	13.2	23.4	17.5	22.0	24.9	27.6	19.2	19.1	22.0	22.4	21.3
Denmark	2.5	3.4	3.1	4.3	3.0	1.5	2.2	4.0	3.1	2.6	1.0
Israel	−1.1	0.5	1.7	3.1	5.1	2.9	0.7	3.7	3.9	3.7	3.2
New Zealand	−3.9	−4.2	−6.2	−8.3	−8.4	−8.0	−8.6	−3.0	−4.6	−5.7	−8.2
Iceland	1.6	−4.8	−9.8	−16.1	−25.6	−16.3	−15.8	3.8	5.4	1.8	4.5
Memorandum											
Major Advanced Economies	−1.4	−1.5	−1.4	−1.9	−2.0	−1.3	−1.5	−0.9	−1.1	−1.2	−1.4
Euro Area[2]	0.6	0.3	0.8	0.1	−0.1	0.1	−1.5	−0.6	−0.3	−0.2	−0.3
Newly Industrialized Asian Economies	4.9	6.7	6.2	5.3	5.4	6.1	4.9	8.9	6.6	6.6	6.0

[1]Calculated as the sum of the balances of individual Euro Area countries.
[2]Corrected for reporting discrepancies in intra-area transactions.

Table A12. Emerging and Developing Economies: Balance on Current Account
(Percent of GDP)

| | 2002 | 2003 | 2004 | 2005 | 2006 | 2007 | 2008 | 2009 | Projections | | |
									2010	2011	2015
Central and Eastern Europe	**−3.0**	**−4.0**	**−5.4**	**−5.0**	**−6.6**	**−8.0**	**−7.8**	**−2.3**	**−3.5**	**−3.9**	**−4.3**
Albania	−7.2	−5.0	−4.0	−6.1	−5.6	−10.4	−15.2	−14.0	−12.6	−11.3	−5.2
Bosnia and Herzegovina	−17.8	−19.4	−16.4	−18.0	−8.4	−12.6	−14.9	−7.5	−7.2	−6.8	−5.8
Bulgaria	−2.4	−5.5	−6.6	−12.4	−18.4	−26.9	−24.2	−9.5	−6.3	−5.8	−6.3
Croatia	−7.3	−5.4	−4.6	−5.7	−6.7	−7.6	−9.2	−5.6	−6.3	−6.8	−7.0
Estonia	−10.6	−11.3	−11.3	−10.0	−16.9	−17.8	−9.4	4.6	4.7	3.9	−4.6
Hungary	−7.0	−8.0	−8.4	−7.2	−7.5	−6.8	−7.2	0.4	−0.4	−1.0	−3.5
Kosovo	−6.7	−8.1	−8.3	−7.4	−6.7	−8.8	−16.0	−18.7	−18.3	−21.0	−13.4
Latvia	−6.6	−8.1	−12.9	−12.5	−22.5	−22.3	−13.0	9.4	7.0	6.3	4.0
Lithuania	−5.2	−6.9	−7.6	−7.1	−10.7	−14.6	−11.9	3.8	2.7	2.6	−0.8
Macedonia, Former Yugoslav Republic of	−9.4	−4.1	−8.4	−2.6	−0.9	−7.2	−13.1	−7.3	−6.0	−5.3	−4.0
Montenegro	...	−6.7	−7.2	−8.5	−24.1	−39.5	−52.4	−27.2	−17.0	−12.0	−9.0
Poland	−2.5	−2.1	−4.0	−1.2	−2.7	−4.8	−5.1	−1.6	−2.8	−3.2	−2.9
Romania	−3.3	−5.8	−8.4	−8.6	−10.4	−13.4	−12.2	−4.4	−5.5	−5.5	−5.5
Serbia	−8.3	−7.2	−12.1	−8.7	−10.1	−15.6	−17.5	−5.7	−8.2	−8.6	−7.3
Turkey	−0.3	−2.5	−3.7	−4.6	−6.0	−5.8	−5.7	−2.3	−4.0	−4.4	−4.7
Commonwealth of Independent States[1]	**6.5**	**6.2**	**8.2**	**8.7**	**7.4**	**4.2**	**4.9**	**2.6**	**4.0**	**3.6**	**−0.1**
Russia	8.4	8.2	10.1	11.0	9.5	6.0	6.2	3.9	5.1	4.6	−0.4
Excluding Russia	1.0	0.2	2.2	1.3	0.6	−1.3	1.0	−1.2	0.2	0.2	1.2
Armenia	−6.2	−6.8	−0.5	−1.0	−1.8	−6.4	−11.5	−13.8	−13.0	−12.6	−7.9
Azerbaijan	−12.3	−27.8	−29.8	1.3	17.6	27.3	35.5	23.6	25.3	24.2	23.7
Belarus	−2.3	−2.4	−5.3	1.4	−3.9	−6.7	−8.6	−12.9	−10.4	−9.2	−4.8
Georgia	−6.4	−9.6	−6.9	−11.1	−15.1	−19.7	−22.7	−12.2	−14.2	−13.8	−12.7
Kazakhstan	−4.2	−0.9	0.8	−1.8	−2.5	−7.9	4.6	−3.1	0.7	−0.2	−0.9
Kyrgyz Republic	−4.0	1.7	4.9	2.8	−3.1	−0.2	−8.1	3.5	−15.4	−12.5	−3.9
Moldova	−1.2	−6.6	−1.8	−7.6	−11.4	−15.3	−16.3	−7.9	−9.7	−9.7	−7.5
Mongolia	−8.6	−7.1	1.3	1.3	7.0	6.7	−14.0	−5.6	−6.6	−16.5	4.8
Tajikistan	−3.5	−1.3	−3.9	−2.7	−2.8	−8.6	−7.7	−7.3	−8.0	−8.3	−9.1
Turkmenistan	6.7	2.7	0.6	5.1	15.7	15.5	18.7	−9.7	−8.7	1.3	18.3
Ukraine	7.5	5.8	10.6	2.9	−1.5	−3.7	−7.1	−1.7	−2.3	−2.3	−3.3
Uzbekistan	1.2	5.8	7.2	7.7	9.1	7.3	12.5	5.1	5.1	5.0	4.9

Table A12 *(continued)*

| | 2002 | 2003 | 2004 | 2005 | 2006 | 2007 | 2008 | 2009 | Projections | | |
									2010	2011	2015
Developing Asia	**2.5**	**2.8**	**2.7**	**4.2**	**6.1**	**7.0**	**5.7**	**4.1**	**4.1**	**4.1**	**5.0**
Afghanistan, Islamic Republic of	−3.7	−17.0	−4.6	−2.5	−4.9	0.9	−1.6	0.7	−1.7	−1.3	−3.2
Bangladesh	0.3	0.3	−0.3	0.0	1.2	1.1	1.9	2.9	2.1	1.1	0.6
Bhutan	−15.1	−22.8	−17.6	−29.2	−4.3	12.2	−2.2	−9.6	−7.2	−13.8	−23.4
Brunei Darussalam	41.2	47.7	48.6	52.8	56.3	50.9	57.9	47.0	45.9	47.6	56.4
Cambodia	−2.4	−3.6	−2.2	−3.8	−0.6	−1.8	−10.2	−4.8	−9.4	−10.8	−7.8
China	2.4	2.8	3.6	7.2	9.5	11.0	9.4	5.8	6.2	6.5	8.0
Fiji	2.5	−6.4	−12.6	−9.9	−18.7	−13.6	−17.9	−9.6	−11.7	−13.9	−8.5
India	1.4	1.5	0.1	−1.3	−1.1	−1.0	−2.2	−2.1	−2.2	−2.0	−2.0
Indonesia	4.0	3.5	0.6	0.1	3.0	2.4	0.0	2.0	1.4	0.4	−1.1
Kiribati	7.6	−19.5	−11.1	−18.5	−2.9	−1.0	−0.6	−4.1	−7.1	−8.1	−10.3
Lao People's Democratic Republic	−9.8	−13.1	−17.8	−18.1	−10.8	−15.8	−17.8	−16.5	−10.1	−14.0	−16.5
Malaysia	8.0	12.0	12.1	15.0	16.4	15.7	17.5	16.7	15.4	14.7	12.2
Maldives	−5.6	−4.5	−15.8	−36.4	−33.0	−41.5	−51.4	−31.0	−24.9	−15.8	−7.4
Myanmar	0.2	−1.0	2.4	3.7	7.1	0.6	−2.5	−1.0	−1.9	−2.0	3.1
Nepal	4.1	2.4	2.7	1.6	2.1	−0.1	2.7	4.3	−2.1	0.0	−1.4
Pakistan	3.9	4.9	1.8	−1.4	−3.9	−4.8	−8.4	−5.6	−3.8	−4.1	−3.4
Papua New Guinea	−1.4	4.3	2.1	6.1	8.0	3.3	10.0	−6.8	−16.1	−18.5	5.6
Philippines	−0.4	0.4	1.9	2.0	4.5	4.9	2.2	5.3	3.5	2.3	0.4
Samoa	−8.9	−8.3	−8.4	−9.6	−11.1	−15.9	−6.2	−2.0	−20.1	−20.0	−8.5
Solomon Islands	−4.4	6.3	16.3	−7.0	−1.6	−8.2	−16.4	−21.1	−31.2	−28.0	−32.9
Sri Lanka	−1.4	−0.4	−3.1	−2.5	−5.3	−4.3	−9.4	0.3	−1.9	−1.4	−0.9
Thailand	3.7	3.4	1.7	−4.3	1.1	6.3	0.6	7.7	2.5	0.3	0.2
Timor-Leste	−15.9	−15.4	20.7	78.4	165.2	296.1	404.8	191.0	171.1	234.1	185.7
Tonga	0.6	0.7	0.4	−5.2	−8.2	−8.8	−11.6	−15.7	−18.6	−20.0	−12.1
Vanuatu	−4.6	−5.7	−6.0	−8.4	−5.3	−6.9	−5.9	−2.2	−4.4	−5.0	−6.3
Vietnam	−1.7	−4.9	−3.5	−1.1	−0.3	−9.8	−11.9	−7.8	−6.9	−6.0	−4.8
Middle East and North Africa	**4.1**	**7.3**	**10.4**	**17.2**	**19.0**	**15.7**	**15.5**	**1.8**	**5.2**	**7.0**	**7.7**
Algeria	7.7	13.0	13.0	20.5	24.7	22.8	20.2	0.3	2.5	3.4	6.0
Bahrain	−0.7	2.0	4.2	11.0	13.8	15.8	10.6	4.1	5.5	5.7	6.0
Djibouti	−1.6	3.4	−1.3	−3.2	−14.7	−24.1	−27.6	−17.3	−25.5	−32.0	−47.5
Egypt	0.7	2.4	4.3	3.2	1.6	1.9	0.5	−2.4	−2.6	−2.1	−1.5
Iran, Islamic Republic of	3.1	0.6	0.6	8.8	9.2	11.9	7.2	2.4	2.3	1.7	0.3
Iraq	...	...	...	6.1	18.9	12.7	15.1	−19.4	−21.0	−5.5	2.0
Jordan	5.7	11.5	0.1	−18.0	−11.6	−17.6	−10.3	−5.6	−8.9	−9.7	−6.4
Kuwait	11.2	19.7	30.6	42.5	49.8	44.7	40.8	25.8	31.6	32.6	42.3
Lebanon	−14.1	−13.2	−15.5	−13.4	−5.3	−6.8	−11.5	−11.1	−12.8	−12.8	−12.3
Libya	3.0	19.9	21.4	38.9	44.6	40.7	40.7	16.9	24.5	25.6	29.7
Mauritania	3.0	−13.6	−34.6	−47.2	−1.3	−18.3	−15.7	−12.8	−7.5	−9.7	−3.6
Morocco	3.7	3.2	1.7	1.8	2.2	−0.1	−5.2	−5.0	−5.0	−4.4	−2.7
Oman	6.8	2.4	4.5	16.8	15.4	6.2	9.1	0.3	2.4	3.2	1.2
Qatar	21.9	25.3	22.4	33.2	28.3	30.7	33.0	16.4	25.1	39.4	26.9
Saudi Arabia	6.3	13.1	20.8	28.5	27.8	24.3	27.9	5.5	9.1	10.8	10.2
Sudan	−10.3	−7.9	−6.5	−11.1	−15.2	−12.5	−9.0	−12.9	−8.4	−8.5	−7.8
Syrian Arab Republic	−3.6	−12.6	−1.6	−2.3	−1.8	−2.2	−3.6	−4.5	−4.0	−3.5	−4.0
Tunisia	−3.6	−2.9	−2.7	−1.0	−2.0	−2.6	−4.2	−3.4	−2.7	−3.0	−3.2
United Arab Emirates	4.9	8.5	9.0	16.9	22.1	9.4	8.5	−3.1	7.8	7.7	11.1
Yemen, Republic of	4.1	1.5	1.6	3.8	1.1	−7.0	−4.6	−10.7	−3.6	−5.6	−3.8

Table A12 (continued)

	2002	2003	2004	2005	2006	2007	2008	2009	Projections 2010	Projections 2011	Projections 2015
Sub-Saharan Africa	**−3.8**	**−2.9**	**−1.5**	**−0.4**	**4.3**	**1.2**	**0.9**	**−2.1**	**−1.7**	**−2.0**	**−1.4**
Angola	−1.3	−5.2	3.5	16.8	25.2	15.9	7.5	−3.3	3.6	3.1	2.8
Benin	−8.4	−8.3	−7.2	−5.5	−4.5	−9.4	−6.4	−7.0	−7.3	−6.6	−6.0
Botswana	3.2	5.7	3.5	15.2	17.2	15.4	4.9	−5.1	−7.6	−7.7	2.0
Burkina Faso	−10.2	−9.0	−11.0	−11.6	−9.1	−8.2	−11.7	−6.3	−7.7	−7.1	−5.1
Burundi	−3.5	−4.6	−8.4	−1.2	−14.5	−15.7	−12.2	−12.1	−10.2	−7.6	−15.0
Cameroon	−5.1	−1.8	−3.4	−3.4	1.6	1.4	−1.8	−2.7	−4.3	−4.9	−1.9
Cape Verde	−11.2	−11.2	−14.4	−3.4	−5.0	−8.7	−12.4	−19.4	−25.1	−24.3	−13.2
Central African Republic	−1.6	−2.2	−1.7	−6.5	−3.0	−6.2	−10.3	−7.7	−7.9	−8.3	−7.7
Chad	−94.7	−48.8	−17.4	2.4	−9.0	−10.6	−13.7	−32.5	−29.7	−26.3	−7.4
Comoros	−1.7	−3.2	−4.6	−7.2	−6.1	−6.7	−11.6	−5.1	−10.1	−10.5	−9.9
Congo, Democratic Republic of	−1.6	1.0	−2.4	−10.4	−2.1	−1.5	−15.9	−13.1	−20.0	−20.8	−11.9
Congo, Republic of	0.6	2.5	−7.3	2.2	1.5	−8.6	−1.2	−12.4	−0.5	2.9	2.3
Côte d'Ivoire	6.7	2.1	1.6	0.2	2.8	−0.7	2.4	7.3	4.4	3.2	−2.6
Equatorial Guinea	0.9	−33.3	−21.6	−6.2	7.1	4.2	9.9	−13.8	−5.0	−10.8	−3.6
Eritrea	6.8	9.7	−0.7	0.3	−3.6	−6.1	−5.5	−5.0	−2.2	3.2	−3.5
Ethiopia	−4.7	−1.4	−4.0	−6.3	−9.1	−4.5	−5.6	−5.0	−7.8	−9.3	−5.5
Gabon	6.8	9.5	11.2	22.9	15.8	18.2	21.3	11.6	2.1	2.3	3.9
Gambia, The	−2.8	−4.9	−10.1	−18.5	−13.4	−12.3	−16.0	−14.3	−14.4	−13.6	−10.2
Ghana	−1.1	−1.6	−4.0	−8.3	−9.9	−12.0	−18.7	−5.1	−12.8	−8.1	−5.1
Guinea	−2.5	−0.8	−2.8	−0.4	−2.2	−8.8	−11.4	−10.2	−10.0	−8.4	−8.8
Guinea-Bissau	−2.8	−3.3	4.6	−0.2	−5.5	5.8	2.8	1.6	−1.2	−0.2	0.4
Kenya	2.2	−0.2	0.1	−0.8	−2.5	−4.1	−6.9	−6.2	−6.7	−6.4	−2.5
Lesotho	−21.7	−13.5	−6.1	−7.9	4.7	14.1	9.6	−1.5	−19.9	−15.7	−11.9
Liberia	−12.7	−34.2	−33.4	−38.3	−13.7	−31.2	−57.8	−23.9	−41.6	−43.2	−19.7
Madagascar	−6.0	−6.0	−9.2	−10.6	−8.8	−12.7	−20.5	−16.8	−13.2	−5.6	−7.4
Malawi	−8.6	−11.4	−11.1	−15.4	−7.8	−1.6	−9.9	−7.9	−1.0	−1.0	−1.6
Mali	−3.1	−6.3	−8.5	−8.6	−4.2	−7.8	−7.9	−9.7	−9.4	−9.2	−9.1
Mauritius	5.2	1.7	−1.8	−5.2	−9.4	−5.6	−10.4	−8.2	−8.6	−8.3	−5.1
Mozambique	−20.7	−17.3	−10.7	−11.6	−10.7	−9.7	−11.9	−11.9	−13.6	−13.2	−14.4
Namibia	3.4	6.1	7.0	4.7	13.8	9.1	2.7	−2.2	−6.6	−5.0	−3.8
Niger	−9.7	−7.5	−7.3	−8.9	−8.6	−7.8	−13.2	−22.3	−22.6	−20.6	−6.7
Nigeria	−13.0	−6.0	5.5	6.5	26.5	18.8	20.4	11.6	12.4	12.0	11.0
Rwanda	−2.0	−2.5	1.8	1.0	−4.3	−2.2	−4.9	−7.2	−7.3	−5.8	−5.2
São Tomé and Príncipe	−17.0	−14.5	−16.8	−10.3	−28.8	−38.1	−50.1	−32.2	−38.3	−39.7	−55.4
Senegal	−5.6	−6.1	−6.1	−7.7	−9.5	−11.8	−14.3	−8.7	−8.7	−9.0	−9.4
Seychelles	−13.4	0.2	−5.9	−19.7	−13.9	−20.8	−44.7	−23.1	−32.5	−28.8	−23.8
Sierra Leone	−2.0	−4.8	−5.7	−7.0	−5.6	−5.5	−11.7	−8.4	−9.6	−9.0	−11.3
South Africa	0.8	−1.0	−3.0	−3.5	−5.3	−7.2	−7.1	−4.0	−5.0	−6.7	−7.4
Swaziland	9.1	4.4	4.4	−4.1	−7.4	0.7	−4.1	−6.3	−12.8	−12.4	−5.5
Tanzania	−6.2	−4.2	−3.6	−4.1	−7.7	−9.0	−9.8	−9.4	−8.0	−8.2	−7.2
Togo	−5.5	−4.2	−3.0	5.3	−3.0	−6.2	−7.4	−5.7	−6.9	−6.4	−4.5
Uganda	−4.6	−4.7	0.1	−1.4	−3.4	−3.9	−3.2	−4.8	−5.3	−6.1	−4.9
Zambia	−14.0	−14.9	−11.4	−8.4	1.2	−6.5	−7.1	−3.3	−3.5	−3.9	−4.7
Zimbabwe[2]	...	...	...	−13.2	−10.1	−8.2	−24.0	−30.1	−23.5	−13.7	−13.6

Table A12 *(concluded)*

	2002	2003	2004	2005	2006	2007	2008	2009	Projections 2010	2011	2015
Western Hemisphere	**−0.9**	**0.5**	**1.0**	**1.4**	**1.6**	**0.4**	**−0.6**	**−0.5**	**−1.0**	**−1.2**	**−1.6**
Antigua and Barbuda	−11.5	−12.9	−14.5	−18.8	−31.6	−32.9	−28.9	−23.1	−15.8	−16.0	−18.9
Argentina	8.5	6.3	1.7	2.6	3.2	2.3	1.5	2.8	2.8	2.0	1.4
Bahamas, The	−7.0	−5.2	−2.8	−9.6	−18.9	−17.5	−15.4	−11.4	−14.4	−13.6	−11.4
Barbados	−6.5	−6.3	−12.0	−13.1	−8.4	−5.4	−10.5	−5.1	−5.7	−5.5	−5.1
Belize	−17.7	−18.2	−14.7	−13.6	−2.1	−4.0	−10.1	−7.0	−6.2	−5.2	−8.3
Bolivia	−4.1	1.0	3.8	6.5	11.3	12.0	12.1	3.5	2.6	2.0	2.1
Brazil	−1.5	0.8	1.8	1.6	1.3	0.1	−1.7	−1.5	−2.9	−2.9	−3.2
Chile	−0.9	−1.1	2.2	1.2	4.9	4.4	−1.5	2.2	−0.8	−2.1	−2.8
Colombia	−1.5	−1.1	−0.8	−1.3	−1.8	−2.8	−2.8	−1.8	−3.1	−2.9	−1.1
Costa Rica	−5.1	−5.0	−4.3	−4.9	−4.5	−6.3	−9.2	−2.2	−4.3	−4.6	−4.9
Dominica	−18.9	−20.0	−20.4	−26.0	−15.7	−25.0	−31.8	−28.1	−29.8	−30.5	−24.9
Dominican Republic	−3.2	5.1	4.8	−1.4	−3.6	−5.3	−9.9	−5.0	−6.1	−5.5	−3.3
Ecuador	−3.9	−1.4	−1.6	1.0	3.9	3.6	2.2	−1.1	−0.6	−1.6	−3.4
El Salvador	−2.8	−4.7	−4.1	−3.5	−4.2	−6.0	−7.6	−1.8	−2.7	−2.8	−2.7
Grenada	−26.6	−25.3	−9.0	−31.3	−33.2	−43.2	−38.7	−25.7	−25.0	−26.0	−24.8
Guatemala	−6.1	−4.7	−4.9	−4.6	−5.0	−5.2	−4.5	−0.6	−3.3	−3.7	−4.4
Guyana	−7.5	−5.8	−6.7	−10.1	−13.1	−11.1	−13.2	−8.5	−10.0	−9.4	−7.0
Haiti	−0.9	−1.6	−1.6	2.6	−1.4	−0.3	−4.5	−3.2	−9.5	−6.0	−5.4
Honduras	−3.6	−6.8	−7.7	−3.0	−3.7	−9.0	−12.9	−3.2	−6.1	−6.7	−6.8
Jamaica	−11.3	−7.5	−6.4	−9.6	−9.9	−16.3	−18.1	−11.7	−9.1	−7.5	−3.2
Mexico	−2.0	−1.0	−0.7	−0.5	−0.5	−0.8	−1.5	−0.6	−1.1	−1.4	−1.5
Nicaragua	−18.3	−16.2	−14.5	−15.1	−13.4	−17.6	−23.8	−15.0	−18.1	−17.4	−11.3
Panama	−0.8	−4.5	−7.5	−4.9	−3.1	−7.2	−11.6	0.0	−8.5	−8.9	−4.4
Paraguay	1.8	2.3	2.1	0.3	1.4	1.7	−2.4	−0.2	−1.5	−1.2	−0.2
Peru	−1.9	−1.5	0.0	1.4	3.1	1.1	−3.7	0.2	−0.7	−1.8	−2.0
St. Kitts and Nevis	−39.1	−34.8	−20.1	−18.3	−20.4	−24.1	−34.3	−27.3	−27.7	−26.5	−20.3
St. Lucia	−15.0	−14.7	−10.9	−17.1	−30.2	−31.3	−30.7	−20.0	−21.2	−22.1	−23.7
St. Vincent and the Grenadines	−11.5	−20.8	−24.8	−22.3	−24.0	−34.6	−37.3	−29.6	−28.5	−27.2	−19.2
Suriname	−14.4	−18.0	−10.3	−13.0	7.5	7.5	3.9	−2.0	−5.7	−4.4	10.1
Trinidad and Tobago	0.9	8.7	12.4	22.5	39.6	25.7	33.8	14.5	24.0	23.7	17.6
Uruguay	2.9	−0.7	0.0	0.2	−2.0	−0.9	−4.8	0.8	−1.0	−0.9	0.3
Venezuela	8.2	14.1	13.8	17.7	14.7	8.8	12.3	2.5	10.5	10.8	8.2

[1]Georgia and Mongolia, which are not members of the Commonwealth of Independent States, are included in this group for reasons of geography and similarities in economic structure.

[2]The Zimbabwe dollar ceased circulating in early 2009. Data are based on IMF staff estimates of price and exchange rate developments in U.S. dollars. IMF staff estimates of U.S. dollar values may differ from authorities' estimates.

Table A13. Emerging and Developing Economies: Net Financial Flows[1]

(Billions of U.S. dollars)

	Average 1999–2001	2002	2003	2004	2005	2006	2007	2008	2009	Projections 2010	Projections 2011
Emerging and Developing Economies											
Private Financial Flows, Net	74.5	60.6	178.6	230.3	289.3	254.2	689.3	179.2	180.2	209.8	211.5
Private Direct Investment, Net	162.0	150.0	147.8	186.7	252.1	255.8	412.1	439.9	274.8	294.1	322.6
Private Portfolio Flows, Net	−23.3	−45.8	3.1	23.1	36.5	−43.4	88.6	−84.7	23.2	−27.8	−22.4
Other Private Financial Flows, Net	−64.3	−43.5	27.7	20.5	0.7	41.8	188.6	−176.0	−117.9	−56.5	−88.8
Official Financial Flows, Net[2]	−8.7	17.6	−54.4	−63.0	−105.8	−193.6	−98.4	−116.9	80.2	−2.3	−85.6
Change in Reserves[3]	−70.7	−154.6	−304.1	−422.5	−539.7	−718.1	−1,226.0	−666.6	−538.8	−632.4	−608.2
Memorandum											
Current Account[4]	41.8	80.5	149.0	222.3	449.7	665.6	657.9	709.2	321.7	420.1	491.1
Central and Eastern Europe											
Private Financial Flows, Net	24.2	16.5	39.0	52.2	102.5	118.2	186.1	153.9	23.0	57.1	82.7
Private Direct Investment, Net	16.1	13.0	15.1	31.7	40.0	64.4	77.7	67.8	31.3	41.8	46.9
Private Portfolio Flows, Net	2.6	0.5	5.6	17.0	18.3	−0.6	−3.6	−10.0	8.7	16.0	13.7
Other Private Financial Flows, Net	5.5	3.0	18.3	3.5	44.2	54.5	111.9	96.1	−16.9	−0.7	22.0
Official Financial Flows, Net[2]	0.7	15.3	4.9	9.5	3.2	4.8	−6.2	22.9	34.7	26.3	6.3
Change in Reserves[3]	−5.4	−8.0	−10.8	−12.8	−44.1	−32.7	−36.1	−5.2	−22.3	−21.1	−17.3
Commonwealth of Independent States[5]											
Private Financial Flows, Net	−8.0	0.0	22.0	6.1	29.3	52.2	129.8	−95.6	−55.6	−56.5	−34.6
Private Direct Investment, Net	4.0	5.1	5.4	13.2	11.7	21.3	28.3	53.0	18.9	19.2	29.8
Private Portfolio Flows, Net	1.0	1.0	2.0	4.7	3.9	4.9	19.5	−30.9	2.4	−9.1	−1.5
Other Private Financial Flows, Net	−13.0	−6.1	14.5	−11.8	13.7	26.0	82.0	−117.7	−77.0	−66.6	−62.8
Official Financial Flows, Net[2]	−7.7	5.0	−12.2	−10.6	−18.6	−26.4	−6.6	−25.9	14.5	18.3	−1.7
Change in Reserves[3]	−13.8	−15.1	−32.7	−54.9	−77.1	−127.8	−168.1	33.1	−14.0	−41.7	−47.2
Developing Asia											
Private Financial Flows, Net	6.9	53.0	82.3	144.1	88.1	54.2	195.9	33.8	145.5	76.0	8.5
Private Direct Investment, Net	49.0	60.1	58.6	68.0	93.7	85.2	152.6	133.5	66.8	48.1	35.8
Private Portfolio Flows, Net	−12.5	−12.1	23.9	39.0	14.4	−46.1	68.9	−4.6	20.3	−8.4	−10.4
Other Private Financial Flows, Net	−29.6	5.0	−0.2	37.0	−20.0	15.0	−25.6	−95.0	58.3	36.3	−16.9
Official Financial Flows, Net[2]	2.2	−10.7	−17.7	0.7	1.6	−2.5	−0.6	8.7	9.8	7.4	9.0
Change in Reserves[3]	−34.2	−111.9	−167.8	−259.3	−234.2	−322.0	−627.9	−440.5	−460.8	−448.1	−419.4
Middle East and North Africa											
Private Financial Flows, Net	−1.8	−19.0	11.0	−4.1	2.0	−19.9	43.9	5.4	16.8	12.9	4.7
Private Direct Investment, Net	7.9	9.8	17.7	12.5	35.9	45.0	43.2	61.2	70.0	71.7	77.8
Private Portfolio Flows, Net	−8.0	−18.3	−15.5	−23.7	−10.6	−30.2	−44.1	0.4	−44.8	−56.2	−63.3
Other Private Financial Flows, Net	−1.7	−10.4	8.9	7.1	−23.3	−34.6	44.8	−56.2	−8.4	−2.5	−9.8
Official Financial Flows, Net[2]	−14.4	−11.3	−32.9	−46.4	−41.8	−76.5	−75.5	−121.5	−28.3	−75.8	−104.6
Change in Reserves[3]	−14.7	−19.7	−57.3	−52.5	−127.9	−153.3	−231.6	−186.0	8.0	−60.0	−71.0
Sub-Saharan Africa											
Private Financial Flows, Net	4.1	2.1	5.9	19.1	21.3	15.8	26.3	24.8	18.2	40.6	51.7
Private Direct Investment, Net	10.3	10.7	12.7	11.8	16.7	9.0	22.9	32.6	22.8	25.4	30.8
Private Portfolio Flows, Net	−0.7	−1.3	−0.5	9.9	5.8	17.2	9.5	−20.6	6.9	11.6	13.4
Other Private Financial Flows, Net	−5.5	−7.3	−6.3	−2.5	−1.2	−10.3	−6.1	12.8	−11.6	3.6	7.5
Official Financial Flows, Net[2]	−0.7	3.2	−1.2	−6.4	−8.8	−43.1	−3.8	−3.3	6.2	7.9	8.1
Change in Reserves[3]	−2.8	−1.4	−1.8	−18.9	−23.2	−31.9	−29.2	−17.1	8.2	−12.8	−16.2
Western Hemisphere											
Private Financial Flows, Net	49.1	7.9	18.5	13.0	46.1	33.7	107.4	56.9	32.3	79.7	98.4
Private Direct Investment, Net	74.8	51.3	38.3	49.6	54.2	30.9	87.4	91.9	65.0	87.9	101.5
Private Portfolio Flows, Net	−5.6	−15.6	−12.4	−23.8	4.8	11.5	38.3	−19.0	29.7	18.4	25.7
Other Private Financial Flows, Net	−20.1	−27.8	−7.4	−12.8	−12.9	−8.7	−18.4	−16.0	−62.4	−26.6	−28.7
Official Financial Flows, Net[2]	11.1	16.1	4.7	−9.8	−41.4	−50.0	−5.8	2.2	43.4	13.7	−2.7
Change in Reserves[3]	0.2	1.4	−33.8	−24.1	−33.2	−50.4	−133.1	−50.9	−57.8	−48.7	−37.2
Memorandum											
Fuel Exporting Countries											
Private Financial Flows, Net	−18.5	−29.3	18.8	−8.3	7.1	−4.7	116.7	−161.3	−95.4	−85.0	−79.6
Other Countries											
Private Financial Flows, Net	93.0	90.0	159.8	238.7	282.3	258.9	572.6	340.5	275.6	294.8	291.0

[1]Net financial flows comprise net direct investment, net portfolio investment, and other net official and private financial flows, and changes in reserves.

[2]Excludes grants and includes transactions in external assets and liabilities of official agencies.

[3]A minus sign indicates an increase.

[4]The sum of the current account balance, net private financial flows, net official flows, and the change in reserves equals, with the opposite sign, the sum of the capital account and errors and omissions.

[5]Georgia and Mongolia, which are not members of the Commonwealth of Independent States, are included in this group for reasons of geography and similarities in economic structure.

Table A14. Emerging and Developing Economies: Private Financial Flows[1]

(Billions of U.S. dollars)

	Average 1999–2001	2002	2003	2004	2005	2006	2007	2008	2009	Projections 2010	Projections 2011
Emerging and Developing Economies											
Private Financial Flows, Net	74.5	60.6	178.6	230.3	289.3	254.2	689.3	179.2	180.2	209.8	211.5
Assets	−128.2	−102.3	−137.7	−237.6	−392.8	−749.4	−1,034.4	−627.5	−299.1	−450.1	−544.6
Liabilities	202.7	163.0	316.3	468.0	682.2	1,003.6	1,723.8	806.7	479.2	659.9	756.1
Central and Eastern Europe											
Private Financial Flows, Net	24.2	16.5	39.0	52.2	102.5	118.2	186.1	153.9	23.0	57.1	82.7
Assets	−9.0	−2.6	−10.4	−31.0	−17.6	−55.3	−45.6	−28.4	−5.1	−18.6	−13.7
Liabilities	33.2	19.0	49.4	83.2	120.1	173.6	231.6	182.4	28.2	75.7	96.4
Commonwealth of Independent States											
Private Financial Flows, Net	−8.0	0.0	22.0	6.1	29.3	52.2	129.8	−95.6	−55.6	−56.5	−34.6
Assets	−16.5	−24.1	−24.4	−53.1	−80.4	−100.3	−160.5	−261.5	−80.9	−128.9	−126.3
Liabilities	8.5	24.2	46.4	59.1	109.8	152.5	290.3	165.9	25.3	72.5	91.7
Developing Asia											
Private Financial Flows, Net	6.9	53.0	82.3	144.1	88.1	54.2	195.9	33.8	145.5	76.0	8.5
Assets	−52.1	−34.2	−37.6	−27.7	−141.2	−237.4	−326.5	−270.5	−119.9	−147.7	−215.7
Liabilities	59.0	87.2	119.9	171.8	229.3	291.6	522.4	304.3	265.3	223.7	224.2
Middle East and North Africa											
Private Financial Flows, Net	−1.8	−19.0	11.0	−4.1	2.0	−19.9	43.9	5.4	16.8	12.9	4.7
Assets	−7.4	−7.0	−22.5	−70.6	−91.6	−238.1	−361.9	20.0	13.8	−32.6	−59.4
Liabilities	5.6	−11.9	33.5	66.5	93.6	218.3	405.9	−14.6	3.1	45.5	64.1
Sub-Saharan Africa											
Private Financial Flows, Net	4.1	2.1	5.9	19.1	21.3	15.8	26.3	24.8	18.2	40.6	51.7
Assets	−9.4	−8.1	−10.7	−9.4	−15.4	−27.9	−28.0	−6.3	−9.0	−18.2	−18.3
Liabilities	13.6	10.3	16.6	28.6	36.6	43.8	54.4	31.2	27.2	58.8	70.1
Western Hemisphere											
Private Financial Flows, Net	49.1	7.9	18.5	13.0	46.1	33.7	107.4	56.9	32.3	79.7	98.4
Assets	−33.7	−26.3	−32.0	−45.8	−46.7	−90.2	−111.8	−80.6	−97.9	−104.0	−111.2
Liabilities	82.8	34.2	50.5	58.7	92.7	123.9	219.2	137.5	130.2	183.7	209.6

[1]Private financial flows comprise direct investment, portfolio investment, and other long- and short-term investment flows.

Table A15. Emerging and Developing Economies: Reserves[1]

	2002	2003	2004	2005	2006	2007	2008	2009	Projections 2010	2011
					Billions of U.S. Dollars					
Emerging and Developing Economies	1,032.7	1,363.7	1,815.3	2,310.6	3,080.8	4,377.3	4,961.4	5,500.2	6,132.5	6,740.7
Regional Groups										
Central and Eastern Europe	92.8	115.9	135.8	166.2	211.7	268.1	265.5	287.8	308.9	326.2
Commonwealth of Independent States[2]	58.1	92.3	148.8	214.4	356.1	548.7	504.0	518.1	559.8	606.9
Russia	44.6	73.8	121.5	176.5	296.2	467.6	413.4	424.6	446.4	478.0
Excluding Russia	13.5	18.5	27.3	37.9	59.8	81.2	90.6	93.5	113.3	129.0
Developing Asia	497.1	671.1	935.8	1,157.7	1,491.5	2,131.6	2,537.4	2,998.2	3,446.2	3,865.6
China	292.0	409.2	615.5	822.5	1,069.5	1,531.3	1,950.3	2,343.5	2,706.1	3,051.1
India	68.2	99.5	127.2	132.5	171.3	267.6	248.0	268.2	296.2	324.8
Excluding China and India	136.9	162.4	193.1	202.7	250.7	332.6	339.0	386.4	443.9	489.7
Middle East and North Africa	188.9	250.2	313.8	436.5	597.5	839.0	1,001.6	993.6	1,053.6	1,124.6
Sub-Saharan Africa	35.2	38.9	60.5	80.5	113.7	144.7	155.5	147.3	160.1	176.2
Excluding Nigeria and South Africa	21.6	25.0	30.1	33.4	48.1	63.6	71.6	72.0	81.5	93.7
Western Hemisphere	160.5	195.4	220.6	255.3	310.3	445.1	497.5	555.3	604.0	641.2
Brazil	37.5	48.9	52.5	53.3	85.2	179.5	192.9	238.4	258.1	273.3
Mexico	50.6	59.0	64.1	74.1	76.3	87.1	95.1	100.5	115.5	130.5
Analytical Groups										
By Source of Export Earnings										
Fuel	214.9	291.7	419.1	612.9	927.2	1,343.1	1,474.2	1,444.9	1,541.4	1,663.3
Nonfuel	817.8	1,071.9	1,396.2	1,697.7	2,153.6	3,034.1	3,487.2	4,055.2	4,591.1	5,077.4
of Which, Primary Products	30.1	32.0	35.6	39.0	47.3	59.0	72.1	81.8	87.6	93.6
By External Financing Source										
Net Debtor Countries	462.2	587.1	688.6	780.7	981.2	1,363.5	1,415.4	1,564.1	1,726.1	1,858.9
of Which, Official Financing	22.8	40.1	44.4	45.4	51.2	61.5	64.5	76.1	84.1	93.5
Net Debtor Countries by Debt-Servicing Experience										
Countries with Arrears and/or Rescheduling during 2004–08	30.1	36.1	47.1	61.1	74.5	103.2	107.6	123.6	139.9	148.8
Other Groups										
Heavily Indebted Poor Countries	15.4	18.0	22.3	23.1	30.4	40.9	45.1	53.0	57.5	65.2

Table A15 *(continued)*

	2002	2003	2004	2005	2006	2007	2008	2009	Projections 2010	Projections 2011
									Ratio of Reserves to Imports of Goods and Services[3]		
Emerging and Developing Economies	**54.3**	**60.4**	**63.1**	**67.0**	**75.3**	**86.7**	**80.3**	**108.8**	**102.4**	**100.9**
Regional Groups										
Central and Eastern Europe	39.5	37.9	33.9	35.6	37.4	37.4	30.7	47.3	44.9	43.9
Commonwealth of Independent States[2]	40.9	52.5	65.3	76.8	101.2	115.6	81.3	119.3	107.7	103.8
Russia	52.9	71.5	93.0	107.4	141.7	165.5	112.3	166.9	141.1	132.3
Excluding Russia	23.3	25.4	28.1	33.0	41.9	42.3	36.0	51.9	55.8	57.8
Developing Asia	67.7	74.0	79.1	81.4	89.3	106.7	106.5	144.6	135.3	132.3
China	89.0	91.1	101.5	115.5	125.4	148.0	158.2	211.6	188.9	182.5
India	90.0	107.1	97.0	72.8	75.5	95.1	73.6	88.1	87.2	82.4
Excluding China and India	41.4	44.5	43.3	38.4	42.4	48.8	41.7	58.4	57.3	57.2
Middle East and North Africa	69.3	80.2	80.3	90.7	104.1	114.1	104.6	117.1	111.6	109.5
Sub-Saharan Africa	30.6	27.2	34.5	38.3	47.9	49.0	43.1	49.4	45.6	46.2
Excluding Nigeria and South Africa	35.7	34.5	33.5	31.1	39.7	41.2	35.3	40.7	39.6	42.1
Western Hemisphere	40.2	47.2	44.4	43.4	44.8	53.8	50.0	70.2	64.3	62.9
Brazil	60.8	76.8	65.6	54.4	70.7	113.8	87.6	136.5	120.1	115.7
Mexico	27.3	31.4	29.8	30.5	27.4	28.5	28.5	39.1	35.4	36.8
Analytical Groups										
By Source of Export Earnings										
Fuel	57.3	67.1	77.0	89.7	112.7	123.7	106.0	126.7	116.1	114.1
Nonfuel	53.6	58.8	59.9	61.4	65.8	76.6	72.8	103.6	98.5	97.3
of Which, Primary Products	60.3	57.1	52.1	45.9	48.4	47.5	44.4	63.1	55.5	53.9
By External Financing Source										
Net Debtor Countries	42.9	47.1	43.9	41.6	43.9	50.1	42.7	59.8	57.5	56.3
of Which, Official Financing	35.9	54.2	50.4	43.0	41.8	41.6	35.6	45.5	44.8	45.5
Net Debtor Countries by Debt-Servicing Experience										
Countries with Arrears and/or Rescheduling during 2004–08	30.4	30.8	31.6	33.8	35.0	39.0	32.3	43.0	46.6	45.5
Other Groups										
Heavily Indebted Poor Countries	31.0	30.8	30.9	26.9	30.8	33.6	30.0	35.1	37.4	39.1

[1]In this table, official holdings of gold are valued at SDR 35 an ounce. This convention results in a marked underestimation of reserves for countries that have substantial gold holdings.

[2]Georgia and Mongolia, which are not members of the Commonwealth of Independent States, are included in this group for reasons of geography and similarities in economic structure.

[3]Reserves at year-end in percent of imports of goods and services for the year indicated.

Table A16. Summary of Sources and Uses of World Savings

(Percent of GDP)

	Averages		2004	2005	2006	2007	2008	2009	Projections		
	1988–95	1996–2003							2010	2011	2012–15
World											
Savings	22.6	21.9	22.2	22.9	24.2	24.3	23.9	21.4	22.6	23.5	24.7
Investment	23.4	22.1	22.1	22.6	23.3	23.7	23.8	21.5	22.3	23.1	24.3
Advanced Economies											
Savings	22.2	21.1	20.1	20.2	21.0	20.7	19.5	17.1	17.8	18.5	19.2
Investment	22.7	21.3	20.7	21.1	21.6	21.5	21.0	18.0	18.4	19.0	20.0
Net Lending	−0.6	−0.2	−0.6	−0.9	−0.6	−0.8	−1.5	−0.9	−0.6	−0.5	−0.8
Current Transfers	−0.4	−0.5	−0.7	−0.7	−0.7	−0.8	−0.8	−0.8	−0.8	−0.8	−0.8
Factor Income	−0.5	0.3	0.5	0.7	1.1	0.5	0.1	−0.2	0.1	0.1	−0.1
Resource Balance	0.3	0.0	−0.5	−0.9	−1.0	−0.6	−0.7	0.2	0.1	0.1	0.1
United States											
Savings	15.9	17.0	14.5	15.1	16.2	14.5	12.6	10.8	12.2	13.5	15.0
Investment	18.4	19.6	19.7	20.3	20.5	19.5	18.2	15.0	15.7	16.9	18.5
Net Lending	−2.5	−2.7	−5.2	−5.2	−4.3	−5.0	−5.6	−4.3	−3.5	−3.4	−3.6
Current Transfers	−0.4	−0.6	−0.7	−0.8	−0.7	−0.8	−0.9	−0.9	−0.8	−0.7	−0.7
Factor Income	−0.7	0.8	0.7	1.3	2.0	0.8	0.1	−0.7	0.7	0.9	0.5
Resource Balance	−1.3	−2.9	−5.1	−5.7	−5.7	−5.0	−4.8	−2.6	−3.4	−3.6	−3.3
Euro Area											
Savings	...	21.4	21.6	21.3	22.1	22.6	21.3	18.7	18.9	19.1	19.6
Investment	...	20.8	20.4	20.8	21.7	22.2	22.0	19.1	19.0	19.1	19.7
Net Lending	...	0.6	1.2	0.5	0.5	0.4	−0.8	−0.4	−0.1	0.0	−0.1
Current Transfers[1]	−0.6	−0.7	−0.8	−0.9	−0.9	−1.0	−1.1	−1.1	−1.1	−1.2	−1.3
Factor Income[1]	−0.7	−0.5	−0.1	−0.2	0.1	−0.3	−0.9	−0.8	−1.0	−1.2	−1.4
Resource Balance[1]	0.9	1.8	2.1	1.6	1.3	1.7	1.1	1.6	2.1	2.4	2.7
Germany											
Savings	23.1	20.1	21.8	22.0	24.1	26.0	25.9	21.8	21.6	22.0	21.3
Investment	23.6	20.2	17.1	16.9	17.6	18.3	19.2	17.0	16.1	16.4	17.0
Net Lending	−0.5	−0.1	4.7	5.1	6.5	7.6	6.7	4.8	5.5	5.6	4.3
Current Transfers	−1.6	−1.3	−1.3	−1.3	−1.2	−1.3	−1.4	−1.5	−1.6	−1.7	−2.1
Factor Income	−0.5	−0.5	0.9	1.1	1.9	1.8	1.2	1.0	0.3	−0.2	−1.4
Resource Balance	1.6	1.7	5.0	5.3	5.7	7.2	6.9	5.3	6.8	7.5	7.8
France											
Savings	20.2	21.0	20.1	19.9	20.6	21.2	19.9	17.7	18.4	18.9	19.9
Investment	20.3	18.9	19.5	20.3	21.1	22.2	22.2	19.2	20.3	20.7	21.2
Net Lending	−0.2	2.1	0.6	−0.4	−0.5	−1.0	−2.3	−1.5	−1.9	−1.8	−1.3
Current Transfers	−0.7	−0.9	−1.1	−1.3	−1.2	−1.2	−1.2	−1.3	−1.3	−1.3	−1.3
Factor Income	−0.6	1.0	1.1	1.4	1.6	1.5	1.3	1.4	1.4	1.4	1.4
Resource Balance	1.0	2.0	0.6	−0.5	−0.9	−1.3	−2.3	−1.6	−2.0	−1.9	−1.3
Italy											
Savings	20.4	20.9	19.9	19.0	19.0	19.4	17.7	15.5	16.1	16.2	16.9
Investment	21.0	20.2	20.8	20.7	21.6	21.9	21.1	18.9	18.9	18.9	19.3
Net Lending	−0.6	0.7	−0.9	−1.7	−2.6	−2.4	−3.4	−3.4	−2.8	−2.7	−2.5
Current Transfers	−0.5	−0.5	−0.6	−0.7	−0.9	−0.9	−1.0	−1.1	−0.8	−0.8	−0.8
Factor Income	−1.5	−1.1	−1.1	−1.0	−0.9	−1.3	−1.9	−1.9	−2.0	−2.0	−1.6
Resource Balance	1.3	2.3	0.7	0.0	−0.8	−0.3	−0.5	−0.4	0.0	0.1	−0.1
Japan											
Savings	33.1	28.1	26.8	27.2	27.7	28.4	26.8	23.0	22.7	23.0	23.4
Investment	30.7	25.6	23.0	23.6	23.8	23.7	23.6	20.3	19.8	20.6	21.5
Net lending	2.3	2.5	3.7	3.6	3.9	4.7	3.2	2.7	2.8	2.4	1.9
Current Transfers	−0.2	−0.2	−0.2	−0.2	−0.2	−0.3	−0.3	−0.2	−0.2	−0.2	−0.2
Factor Income	0.8	1.5	1.9	2.3	2.7	3.1	3.1	2.5	2.5	2.5	2.7
Resource Balance	1.7	1.3	2.0	1.5	1.4	1.9	0.4	0.5	0.5	0.1	−0.7
United Kingdom											
Savings	15.8	16.0	15.0	14.5	14.2	15.6	15.3	12.5	12.3	13.3	14.5
Investment	18.4	17.4	17.1	17.1	17.5	18.3	16.9	13.8	14.0	14.9	16.0
Net Lending	−2.6	−1.5	−2.1	−2.6	−3.3	−2.7	−1.5	−1.3	−1.7	−1.6	−1.5
Current Transfers	−0.7	−0.8	−0.9	−0.9	−0.9	−1.0	−1.0	−1.0	−1.1	−1.1	−1.1
Factor Income	−0.4	0.7	1.5	1.7	0.7	1.5	2.1	2.1	1.8	1.6	1.6
Resource Balance	−1.5	−1.3	−2.7	−3.4	−3.1	−3.2	−2.6	−2.3	−2.4	−2.2	−2.1
Canada											
Savings	16.7	20.8	23.0	24.0	24.4	24.4	23.7	18.5	18.4	19.0	20.3
Investment	19.9	19.8	20.7	22.1	23.0	23.4	23.2	21.2	21.0	21.5	22.4
Net Lending	−3.2	1.0	2.3	1.9	1.4	1.0	0.5	−2.7	−2.6	−2.5	−2.1
Current Transfers	−0.1	0.1	−0.1	−0.1	−0.1	−0.1	−0.1	−0.1	−0.2	−0.2	−0.2
Factor Income	−3.5	−2.9	−1.9	−1.7	−1.0	−0.7	−0.9	−0.8	−1.4	−1.5	−1.7
Resource Balance	0.5	3.8	4.2	3.7	2.5	1.9	1.5	−1.8	−1.0	−0.7	−0.2

Table A16 (continued)

	Averages		2004	2005	2006	2007	2008	2009	Projections		
	1988–95	1996–2003							2010	2011	2012–15
Newly Industrialized Asian Economies											
Savings	35.6	32.3	32.9	31.6	31.9	32.4	32.8	32.4	31.8	31.9	31.7
Investment	32.2	28.1	26.7	26.1	26.4	26.1	27.8	23.6	25.5	25.8	25.9
Net Lending	3.4	4.1	6.2	5.5	5.5	6.4	5.0	8.8	6.2	6.2	5.8
Current Transfers	−0.1	−0.4	−0.7	−0.7	−0.7	−0.7	−0.6	−0.6	−0.5	−0.5	−0.4
Factor Income	1.2	0.5	0.6	0.2	0.6	1.0	1.7	1.5	−0.5	−0.4	0.2
Resource Balance	2.3	4.1	6.3	5.9	5.6	6.1	3.8	7.9	7.2	7.0	6.0
Emerging and Developing Economies											
Savings	24.2	25.0	29.8	31.6	33.5	33.6	33.7	31.1	32.6	33.3	34.1
Investment	26.2	24.9	27.3	27.4	28.3	29.4	29.9	29.2	30.4	31.0	31.7
Net Lending	−1.9	0.1	2.5	4.2	5.2	4.2	3.7	1.9	2.2	2.3	2.4
Current Transfers	0.6	1.1	1.7	1.7	1.8	1.7	1.5	1.4	1.4	1.3	1.3
Factor Income	−1.6	−1.8	−1.9	−1.8	−1.6	−1.5	−1.6	−1.3	−1.5	−1.3	−0.6
Resource Balance	−0.9	0.8	2.8	4.3	5.1	4.1	3.8	1.7	2.3	2.2	1.8
Memorandum											
Acquisition of Foreign Assets	1.6	4.0	7.0	9.4	11.5	14.2	6.9	4.2	4.9	4.9	4.7
Change in Reserves	0.7	1.5	4.7	5.0	5.7	7.9	3.5	3.0	3.1	2.7	2.4
Regional Groups											
Central and Eastern Europe											
Savings	22.1	18.2	16.4	16.6	16.9	16.9	16.9	16.5	16.4	16.7	17.7
Investment	24.1	21.4	21.8	21.5	23.5	25.0	24.8	18.8	19.9	20.5	21.8
Net Lending	−1.8	−3.2	−5.4	−5.0	−6.6	−8.1	−7.8	−2.3	−3.5	−3.8	−4.1
Current Transfers	1.7	2.1	2.0	1.9	2.0	1.8	1.7	1.9	1.7	1.7	1.6
Factor Income	−2.1	−1.3	−2.5	−2.0	−2.4	−3.0	−2.7	−2.3	−2.2	−2.3	−2.2
Resource Balance	−1.4	−4.0	−4.9	−4.8	−6.2	−6.9	−6.9	−2.0	−3.1	−3.2	−3.5
Memorandum											
Acquisition of Foreign Assets	0.9	2.0	4.0	5.1	6.1	5.2	2.2	1.1	2.5	2.2	2.6
Change in Reserves	−0.1	1.2	1.3	3.7	2.5	2.2	0.3	1.4	1.2	0.9	1.0
Commonwealth of Independent States[2]											
Savings	...	25.4	30.4	30.5	30.7	31.1	30.8	22.6	26.0	26.9	26.5
Investment	...	20.8	22.1	21.7	23.4	27.0	26.0	19.9	21.8	23.3	25.2
Net Lending	...	4.6	8.4	8.8	7.3	4.0	4.8	2.8	4.1	3.7	1.3
Current Transfers	...	0.5	0.5	0.5	0.5	0.3	0.5	0.4	0.3	0.3	0.2
Factor Income	...	−2.9	−2.2	−2.7	−3.4	−3.0	−3.5	−3.6	−3.5	−2.6	−1.4
Resource Balance	...	6.9	9.9	11.0	10.3	6.8	8.0	5.8	7.2	6.0	2.6
Memorandum											
Acquisition of Foreign Assets	...	6.5	14.0	15.4	14.8	17.5	9.8	2.3	6.9	6.5	4.7
Change in Reserves	...	2.1	7.1	7.7	9.8	9.9	−1.5	0.9	2.1	2.1	1.1

Table A16 *(continued)*

	Averages		2004	2005	2006	2007	2008	2009	Projections		
	1988–95	1996–2003							2010	2011	2012–15
Developing Asia											
Savings	30.6	33.1	38.4	41.5	44.1	45.0	43.9	43.6	45.4	45.7	46.0
Investment	32.9	31.7	35.8	37.3	38.0	37.9	38.2	39.5	41.3	41.5	41.3
Net Lending	−2.3	1.4	2.6	4.2	6.1	7.1	5.7	4.1	4.1	4.1	4.6
Current Transfers	0.9	1.5	2.1	2.2	2.2	2.2	2.1	1.8	1.9	1.9	1.8
Factor Income	−1.7	−1.5	−1.0	−0.6	−0.4	−0.1	−0.1	−0.2	−0.1	0.0	0.3
Resource Balance	−1.5	1.4	1.6	2.6	4.3	5.0	3.8	2.5	2.3	2.3	2.6
Memorandum											
Acquisition of Foreign Assets	4.2	5.5	7.3	9.6	11.6	15.1	8.9	6.6	5.7	5.5	5.3
Change in Reserves	1.5	2.3	7.4	5.8	6.8	10.7	6.0	5.9	5.2	4.4	3.5
Middle East and North Africa											
Savings	20.2	27.3	35.5	41.2	42.8	41.6	42.4	29.6	32.7	34.1	34.6
Investment	24.3	23.4	25.3	23.9	24.0	26.0	26.8	27.8	27.3	27.0	26.6
Net Lending	−4.0	3.9	10.3	17.5	19.1	15.8	15.5	2.5	6.2	7.5	8.3
Current Transfers	−2.1	−1.3	−0.6	0.0	−0.4	−0.6	−0.7	−1.1	−1.1	−1.2	−1.3
Factor Income	1.0	0.7	−0.4	−0.1	1.1	1.3	0.5	0.1	−0.9	−0.1	2.3
Resource Balance	−2.9	4.5	11.3	17.6	18.6	15.2	15.8	3.0	7.4	8.3	7.1
Memorandum											
Acquisition of Foreign Assets	0.3	5.6	15.2	24.0	32.5	36.3	12.5	1.0	6.3	8.1	8.5
Change in Reserves	0.3	2.2	5.1	10.1	10.2	13.0	8.3	−0.4	2.6	2.9	3.7
Sub-Saharan Africa											
Savings	16.2	16.1	18.3	19.4	25.0	22.8	23.3	20.3	21.6	21.5	21.6
Investment	17.1	18.3	19.7	19.6	20.4	21.6	22.1	21.9	22.7	23.0	22.4
Net Lending	−0.9	−2.2	−1.4	−0.2	4.6	1.2	0.9	−1.9	−1.5	−1.8	−1.1
Current Transfers	1.9	2.2	2.6	2.5	4.5	4.5	4.4	4.8	4.0	3.8	3.4
Factor Income	−3.0	−4.1	−5.1	−5.5	−4.4	−6.0	−6.1	−4.3	−5.0	−5.2	−4.6
Resource Balance	0.2	−0.3	1.1	2.7	4.4	2.6	2.4	−2.5	−0.6	−0.4	0.0
Memorandum											
Acquisition of Foreign Assets	0.5	2.6	2.7	4.5	8.7	7.9	4.2	2.3	5.0	4.7	4.5
Change in Reserves	0.5	0.8	3.6	3.8	4.5	3.6	1.8	−0.9	1.3	1.5	2.1
Western Hemisphere											
Savings	18.2	18.3	21.9	22.0	23.2	22.5	22.8	19.2	19.9	20.4	21.2
Investment	19.1	20.6	20.8	20.5	21.6	22.2	23.4	19.5	20.8	21.7	22.7
Net Lending	−0.9	−2.3	1.1	1.5	1.6	0.3	−0.7	−0.3	−1.0	−1.3	−1.6
Current Transfers	0.8	1.2	2.1	2.0	2.1	1.8	1.5	1.5	1.3	1.4	1.4
Factor Income	−2.1	−2.8	−3.1	−2.9	−3.1	−2.8	−2.6	−2.0	−2.5	−2.5	−2.2
Resource Balance	0.3	−0.7	2.1	2.4	2.6	1.3	0.4	0.2	0.2	−0.1	−0.8
Memorandum											
Acquisition of Foreign Assets	0.4	2.0	2.6	3.0	2.9	5.8	2.0	3.6	2.9	2.7	2.1
Change in Reserves	0.7	0.3	1.1	1.3	1.6	3.6	1.2	1.5	1.1	0.8	0.7
Analytical Groups											
By Source of Export Earnings											
Fuel Exporters											
Savings	25.6	28.1	34.5	38.4	40.1	38.3	38.7	27.8	31.4	32.4	31.8
Investment	28.5	22.9	23.7	22.6	23.4	26.1	25.5	23.9	24.1	24.6	25.2
Net Lending	−2.8	5.2	10.8	15.9	16.8	12.3	13.1	4.2	7.7	7.9	6.7
Current Transfers	−2.0	−1.8	−1.1	−0.6	−0.3	−0.5	−0.6	−0.8	−0.8	−0.8	−0.9
Factor Income	−1.2	−1.2	−2.1	−2.4	−1.9	−1.9	−2.5	−2.1	−2.8	−2.0	0.1
Resource Balance	0.4	8.2	14.1	18.8	19.2	14.9	16.4	6.8	10.7	10.5	7.5
Memorandum											
Acquisition of Foreign Assets	0.6	6.6	14.7	20.9	25.2	27.2	12.2	2.0	7.4	8.3	7.4
Change in Reserves	−0.3	1.7	6.6	9.3	10.5	11.1	3.6	−0.8	2.3	2.6	2.5
Nonfuel Exporters											
Savings	23.6	24.4	28.7	29.8	31.7	32.2	32.1	31.9	32.9	33.5	34.8
Investment	25.2	25.3	28.2	28.6	29.7	30.4	31.3	30.6	32.0	32.7	33.5
Net Lending	−1.5	−1.0	0.5	1.2	2.0	1.9	0.8	1.4	0.8	0.8	1.3
Current Transfers	1.3	1.7	2.3	2.4	2.4	2.3	2.1	2.0	2.0	1.9	1.9
Factor Income	−1.7	−2.0	−1.9	−1.6	−1.5	−1.4	−1.3	−1.0	−1.2	−1.1	−0.8
Resource Balance	−1.2	−0.7	0.0	0.4	1.1	1.0	−0.1	0.4	0.0	−0.1	0.2
Memorandum											
Acquisition of Foreign Assets	1.8	3.5	5.1	6.4	7.6	10.4	5.3	4.7	4.3	4.0	3.9
Change in Reserves	0.9	1.4	4.2	3.9	4.3	7.0	3.5	4.0	3.4	2.8	2.4

Table A16 *(concluded)*

	Averages		2004	2005	2006	2007	2008	2009	Projections		
	1988–95	1996–2003							2010	2011	2012–15
By External Financing Source											
Net Debtor Countries											
Savings	20.0	19.0	21.6	21.7	22.8	23.1	22.5	21.4	21.8	22.3	23.7
Investment	21.7	21.2	22.7	23.2	24.3	25.6	26.2	23.1	24.4	25.2	26.5
Net Lending	−1.5	−2.2	−1.1	−1.4	−1.5	−2.5	−3.7	−1.7	−2.6	−2.9	−2.9
Current Transfers	1.6	2.3	3.0	3.0	3.1	2.9	2.8	2.9	2.6	2.6	2.6
Factor Income	−1.5	−2.1	−2.5	−2.4	−2.5	−2.5	−2.4	−2.1	−2.3	−2.3	−2.2
Resource Balance	−1.7	−2.4	−1.6	−2.0	−2.1	−2.9	−4.1	−2.5	−2.9	−3.2	−3.3
Memorandum											
Acquisition of Foreign Assets	0.5	2.0	3.3	3.3	4.4	6.3	1.6	2.4	2.6	2.3	2.2
Change in Reserves	0.7	0.8	1.7	2.0	2.5	4.2	1.0	1.7	1.6	1.2	1.2
Official Financing											
Savings	16.7	17.7	20.7	21.0	21.6	22.4	21.4	22.1	22.2	23.0	24.1
Investment	20.0	20.7	23.0	23.8	23.9	24.4	24.4	23.5	24.6	25.1	25.2
Net Lending	−3.3	−3.0	−2.3	−2.8	−2.3	−2.0	−3.6	−2.0	−3.0	−2.8	−1.6
Current Transfers	5.3	6.5	9.5	10.2	10.3	10.7	10.4	10.5	10.1	9.8	9.3
Factor Income	−2.2	−2.0	−2.3	−2.2	−1.8	−0.7	−0.6	−0.6	−0.6	−0.6	−0.1
Resource Balance	−6.5	−7.4	−9.5	−10.9	−10.9	−12.0	−13.5	−12.0	−12.7	−11.9	−10.8
Memorandum											
Acquisition of Foreign Assets	1.0	0.5	1.4	0.8	0.4	2.4	−0.1	1.2	1.2	1.1	1.5
Change in Reserves	1.3	1.3	0.9	0.8	1.7	2.7	0.9	2.6	1.7	1.8	1.9
Net Debtor Countries by Debt-Servicing Experience											
Countries with Arrears and/or Rescheduling during 2004–08											
Savings	15.7	15.0	19.6	21.3	23.0	21.8	21.2	19.7	20.1	20.3	20.1
Investment	18.6	17.9	20.1	21.4	22.5	23.6	24.2	21.7	21.9	23.3	22.7
Net Lending	−2.2	−2.8	−0.4	−0.1	0.5	−1.8	−3.3	−2.3	−2.1	−3.3	−2.9
Current Transfers	1.6	2.9	5.3	5.2	5.0	4.6	3.9	4.5	4.0	3.9	3.7
Factor Income	−2.2	−3.8	−4.7	−3.4	−2.9	−3.5	−3.5	−1.4	−3.1	−3.8	−3.2
Resource Balance	−1.6	−2.0	−1.2	−2.0	−1.7	−2.9	−3.8	−5.7	−3.1	−3.5	−3.4
Memorandum											
Acquisition of Foreign Assets	1.8	3.0	2.9	2.2	3.1	4.9	0.8	1.4	2.2	1.4	1.8
Change in Reserves	0.3	0.3	3.0	3.3	2.2	3.7	0.5	1.9	1.8	0.9	1.5

Note: The estimates in this table are based on individual countries' national accounts and balance of payments statistics. Country group composites are calculated as the sum of the U.S. dollar values for the relevant individual countries. This differs from the calculations in the April 2005 and earlier issues of the *World Economic Outlook,* where the composites were weighted by GDP valued at purchasing power parities as a share of total world GDP. For many countries, the estimates of national savings are built up from national accounts data on gross domestic investment and from balance-of-payments-based data on net foreign investment. The latter, which is equivalent to the current account balance, comprises three components: current transfers, net factor income, and the resource balance. The mixing of data source, which is dictated by availability, implies that the estimates for national savings that are derived incorporate the statistical discrepancies. Furthermore, errors, omissions, and asymmetries in balance of payments statistics affect the estimates for net lending; at the global level, net lending, which in theory would be zero, equals the world current account discrepancy. Despite these statistical shortcomings, flow of funds estimates, such as those presented in these tables, provide a useful framework for analyzing developments in savings and investment, both over time and across regions and countries.

[1]Calculated from the data of individual Euro Area countries.

[2]Georgia and Mongolia, which are not members of the Commonwealth of Independent States, are included in this group for reasons of geography and similarities in economic structure.

Table A17. Summary of World Medium-Term Baseline Scenario

	Averages				Projections			
	1992–99	2000–07	2008	2009	2010	2011	2008–11	2012–15
	Annual Percent Change unless Noted Otherwise							
World Real GDP	**3.1**	**4.2**	**3.0**	**−0.6**	**4.2**	**4.3**	**2.7**	**4.5**
Advanced Economies	2.8	2.6	0.5	−3.2	2.3	2.4	0.5	2.4
Emerging and Developing Economies	3.5	6.4	6.1	2.4	6.3	6.5	5.3	6.7
Memorandum								
Potential Output								
Major Advanced Economies	2.6	2.1	1.5	0.9	0.9	1.2	1.1	1.7
World Trade, Volume[1]	**6.9**	**7.0**	**2.8**	**−10.7**	**7.0**	**6.1**	**1.1**	**6.8**
Imports								
Advanced Economies	6.9	5.7	0.6	−12.0	5.4	4.6	−0.6	5.4
Emerging and Developing Economies	6.2	10.4	8.5	−8.4	9.7	8.2	4.2	9.2
Exports								
Advanced Economies	6.6	5.9	1.9	−11.7	6.6	5.0	0.2	5.4
Emerging and Developing Economies	7.9	10.1	4.0	−8.2	8.3	8.4	2.9	8.9
Terms of Trade								
Advanced Economies	0.2	−0.3	−1.7	2.9	−1.3	−0.3	−0.1	0.0
Emerging and Developing Economies	−0.7	1.6	3.7	−5.1	3.0	−0.4	0.2	−0.2
World Prices in U.S. Dollars								
Manufactures	−0.9	3.9	8.5	−6.9	2.7	1.1	1.2	1.5
Oil	−0.9	18.8	36.4	−36.3	29.5	3.8	3.9	1.2
Nonfuel Primary Commodities	−1.5	7.9	7.5	−18.7	13.9	−0.5	−0.3	−1.4
Consumer Prices								
Advanced Economies	2.5	2.1	3.4	0.1	1.5	1.4	1.6	1.9
Emerging and Developing Economies	48.0	6.7	9.2	5.2	6.2	4.7	6.3	3.9
Interest Rates (in percent)								
Real Six-Month LIBOR[2]	3.2	1.1	0.9	−0.1	−0.2	0.3	0.2	2.7
World Real Long-Term Interest Rate[3]	3.8	2.1	0.4	3.2	2.2	3.1	2.2	3.5
	Percent of GDP							
Balances on Current Account								
Advanced Economies	0.0	−0.9	−1.3	−0.4	−0.4	−0.5	−0.6	−0.7
Emerging and Developing Economies	−1.5	2.7	3.7	1.8	2.1	2.2	2.5	2.4
Total External Debt								
Emerging and Developing Economies	37.5	32.7	24.2	26.9	25.0	24.3	25.1	22.5
Debt Service								
Emerging and Developing Economies	6.8	8.6	7.5	7.8	6.8	6.5	7.1	6.2

[1]Data refer to trade in goods and services.
[2]London interbank offered rate on U.S. dollar deposits minus percent change in U.S. GDP deflator.
[3]GDP-weighted average of 10-year (or nearest maturity) government bond rates for Canada, France, Germany, Italy, Japan, the United Kingdom, and the United States.

WORLD ECONOMIC OUTLOOK
SELECTED TOPICS

World Economic Outlook Archives

I. Methodology—Aggregation, Modeling, and Forecasting

II. Historical Surveys

III. Economic Growth—Sources and Patterns

IV. Inflation and Deflation, and Commodity Markets

V. Fiscal Policy

VI. Monetary Policy, Financial Markets, and Flow of Funds

VII. Labor Markets, Poverty, and Inequality

VIII. Exchange Rate Issues

IX. External Payments, Trade, Capital Movements, and Foreign Debt

X. Regional Issues

XI. Country-Specific Analyses

XII. Special Topics

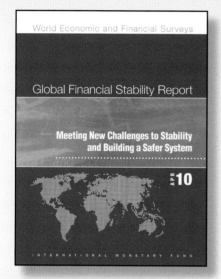